AN INTRODUCTION TO W. R. BION'S 'A MEMOIR OF THE FUTURE'

VOLUME TWO

Facts of Matter or a Matter of Fact?

P. C. Sandler

Routledge
Taylor & Francis Group
LONDON AND NEW YORK

First published 2015 by
Karnac Books Ltd.

Published 2018 by Routledge
2 Park Square, Milton Park, Abingdon, Oxon OX14 4RN
711 Third Avenue, New York, NY 10017, USA

Routledge is an imprint of the Taylor & Francis Group, an informa business

British Library Cataloguing in Publication Data

A C.I.P. for this book is available from the British Library

ISBN-13: 9781782201144 (pbk)

Typeset by V Publishing Solutions Pvt Ltd., Chennai, India

AN INTRODUCTION TO W. R. BION'S 'A MEMOIR OF THE FUTURE'

VOLUME TWO

To Ester, Daniela, Carolina, Luiz, Antoine, Clara and Beatriz

To the memory of my parents
Dr Jayme Sandler and Mrs Bertha Lerner Sandler
and of Mrs Francesca Bion

CONTENTS

ACKNOWLEDGEMENTS

Even if this book deals with a timeless work, I feel obliged, out of sorrow, to introduce it under the sign of our times. In hindsight, I must recognise that I am guilty of having abused time. I am not talking about the decades which had to be spent to publish this work in the English language (one may see its history in Volume I). I am rather sharing with the eventual reader a too human experience. Five years ago, Francesca Bion, with her characteristic and sophisticated good humour, always intrinsically linked to her incomparable love for truth and consideration for reality as it is, gave me a mixture of invitation and warning. "Paulo, the last time you came here to visit me was in 2005! Please come back, because I will not be around much longer now." As ever, she was right. Fortunately, she was able to see, via her dedicated daughter, Nicola, one of the first copies of Volume I, swiftly sent by Oliver Rathbone.

So the second volume of what is my best way to thank her for her continuing stimulus and real friendship sees the light of the day in a dark hour. She is not here any more, but my deep gratitude to her lingers on.

I was able to see James Grotstein again in October 2014, when the first volume was released. He was very pleased to receive a copy from the same first batch. In his own low-profile way, seated in a wheelchair, he told me, "I knew that your attempt to spread the word about *A Memoir* would succeed". It was part of our emotional, passionate farewell. Both of us knew it.

Francesca and James had encouraged me more than anyone else to pursue the publication of this book in English. Now they have passed away, but their work has not, due to their kindness and equanimity; they were the most loving, unprejudiced people I had ever met in the psychoanalytic movement, reminding me strongly of my own wife and father. Many psychoanalysts to whom I owe a debt of gratitude are listed in the first volume. To them I must add Dr Avedis Panajian, a brother-in-soul who agreed to write the preface for this second volume.

I must aknowledge three kinds of helpers, different in their functions, but similar in their passionate care and attention. First, the physicians who have kept me alive: Dr Eduardo Berger, Dr Valdemar Ortiz, Dr Luiz Paulo Kowalsky, Dr Marcelo Ferraz Sampaio, Dr Gisela Tinoni, Dr Mauricio Ibrahim Scanavacca, Dr José Eduardo de Souza, Dr Paulo Sakai and Dr Orlando Bordin—gifted surgeons and specialists who seem to me to be endowed with the same intuition we psychoanalysts strive to obtain, but put it into effect by other means. Second, the editorial and administrative staff of Karnac Books: Mr Oliver Rathbone, Mr Alex Massey, Mrs Anna Nilsen, Ms Constance Govindin and Ms Cecily Blench. Finally, my patients, who remain anonymous for ethical reasons. I suppose that they contributed more than anyone to my continuous realisation of what a memoir of the future is all about.

ABOUT THE AUTHOR

Paulo Cesar Sandler, MD, MSc, MhFAB, is a Training Analyst at the Sociedade Brasileira de Psicanálise de São Paulo, Psychiatrist at the Institute of Physical Medicine and Rehabilitation (IMREA) at the Hospital das Clinicas, Faculdade de Medicina da Universidade de São Paulo, and author of several books in Portuguese, including the eight-volume series *A Apreensão da Realidade Psíquica* (The Apprehension of Psychic Reality), published by Imago. He has written many papers and book chapters, some of which have been published in English and French. He has translated most of Bion's books and papers into Portuguese, including the first foreign version of Bion's *A Memoir of the Future*, and has organised several international meetings on the work of Bion. Dr Sandler teaches at the Institute of Psychoanalysis of the SBPSP, giving courses about the work of Freud, Klein and Bion; he is a former professor of a postgraduate course at the University of São Paulo. He has worked in private psychoanalytic practice since 1974, having previously worked with psychotics in a traditional in-patient clinic as well as in group-oriented community psychiatry, including epidemiology of mental disorders, in the local Public Health School.

PREFACE

Avedis Panajian, PhD*

Paulo Sandler's impressive and exhaustive volume springs from his own reverie and dreaming stimulated by Bion's Trilogy. In a way, it is a set of comprehensive associations on Bion's model of the mind. Furthermore, it is a study of the complex field that develops between the patient and the analyst. The present writer is going to surrender to his own reverie and dreaming while reading Sandler's work.

Plato did not mind making up his own myths to spread his ideas. In his myth of Er, Plato writes that Er came from Anatolia, "every man's land." Er was killed in a battle, but during the funeral he was found to be alive and told his story. He said the souls of those who had died were directed either up to heaven or down into the earth. The souls were judged for the good or evil that they had done. The souls had the choice of a new life. They had to pick what they wanted. They made their own choice, and could not blame any god for the outcome. Each soul had a destiny to choose. In the myth, even though the roots of the soul are in heaven, the challenge of life is to grow down in this world. The soul

*Avedis Panajian, PhD, ABPP-Clinical, is a faculty member at the Pacifica Graduate Institute and a training analyst at the Psychoanalytic Center of California.

has a guide, a companion, a voice (or voices) to help him or her through life. To listen, recognise and honour one's calling takes devotion and years of disciplined practice. It takes a passionate commitment to one's soul guide and an unquenchable thirst to continue such a commitment. Bion's soul guide seems to me to have helped him to stay open to any field of study that deepened, nourished and stretched the limits of his imagination. He remained open to study and question our origins. Bion and Sandler listen to their heart's calling and challenge us with their ideas.

Bion knew that imaginative conjectures needed memory as a partner to help each other. Only by working as partners can some coherence be achieved. In imagination we extend our body and soul in the direction of imagination. In the partnership of imagination and remembering, the soul and the spirit are brought together. Commonly, imagination is thought of as an upward movement: from body to soul, and from soul to spirit. This way of looking at imagination is seen as having a unifying force in human experience. Linking body with soul has a major place in psychoanalytic work and understanding. Linking soul with spirit has an increasing role in building metaphysical and philosophical structures. The attempt to understand people in this way avoids understanding people as having distinctly separate parts. Bion's model focused on indefinite modes of human existence.

Casey (2004) discusses the upward movement of imagination which cannot be separated from its downwardly synthesising movement. The downward movement occurs from spirit to soul, and from soul to body. In upward movement, memory provides imagination, personal history and tradition. Remembering takes us back down to the origin of events and provides us the fuel to contemplate our origins. Our personal experiences and meanings become our personal sources that provide the energy for imagination. Memories bring spirit down to feelings and to the body. The soul seeks its own bodily basis. The soul that does not find a bodily basis is a homeless and soulless spirit. These are our patients who feel so dead, and we struggle to find out where and how they live without a soul. It is very difficult for the analyst to find the language and the imagination to try and reach them. Imagining and remembering harmonise their movements upward or downward. Upward, forward and not yet on the one hand; downward, past and remembering on the other hand. For Kant, memory was "reproductive imagination." In imagining, we make time for the soul. We take time to pay attention to the diseases of the soul. We also create time in the soul.

For Bion, taking time to pay attention, to listen carefully to the various voices in him, to engage them in passionate dialogue, and not to be concerned with outcomes or conclusions, is a remarkable achievement. Bion's aesthetic appreciation and intuitions are revealed in his manner of presenting and expressing his inner voices. In doing so, introspection does not become the dominant mental preoccupation. He finds himself in a luminous space where he is able to illuminate his voices and narrate them very clearly. These narrations are not from a self-enclosed space of human subjectivity. The Trilogy shows Bion's capacity to synchronise various aspects of his existence. We can see Bion at work in the way he synthesises sensations with reasons following the Kantian "form of intuitions", synthesising body and soul as in his expression of passions. He has the capacity for sensitive identifications as he attunes one soul with another soul.

The imaginal is never taken away from the surroundings in which it is set. Bion is capable of creating a syncretic movement in returning the soul to the world; he moves beyond personal consciousness and subjectivity. He is able to take psychology and psychoanalysis beyond sensation and feelings. A central message in *A Memoir of the Future* is "catastrophic change". The various characters or voices as a group must find some ways of expanding in order to contain the catastrophic anxiety triggered by "messianic ideas". At the same time, it is essential that the group should not destroy or denude the messianic idea or destroy the mystic. The group also must avoid being fragmented or exploded by the messianic idea.

Bion stressed that aspects of personality link together if we are able to tolerate catastrophic change and catastrophic anxiety. In the *Memoir*, Bion dramatised a "critical situation" triggered by a "messianic idea". Bion's voices, characters, his internal group is filled with explosions, and transitions from one state to another. Birth, war, dinosaur, human mind: all are represented as unintegrated. The *Memoir* attempts to show the fights between forces that tend to give in to the sense of catastrophe and forces that attempt to fight catastrophic anxiety in order to achieve integration and curiosity. It is a war between expanding the mind and exploding the mind. A war between disciplined thinking and action. A war between "messianic idea" and the nuclear bomb.

> P.A. I am familiar with reports of terrifying experiences described in terms of varying inadequacy—as you have just been doing. We are both aware of the awe-ful experience. Many are not; they fear

> "going mad", some indescribable disaster, "break-down"; they may express themselves by bringing about disaster. We psychoanalysts think you do not know what a dream is; the dream itself is a pictorial representation, verbally expressed, of what happened. [II: 382]

The message that Bion tries to convey is this: can the birth of a thought or an idea survive in a person long enough to become integrated within their personality? Bion is aware that such an achievement is costly and requires enormous capacity for suffering in facing and respecting truth.

Bion was concerned about how analytic concepts and theories are used as jargon and therefore suffocate or kill a foetal idea or a dream. He was interested to examine how one broke through such jargon. Analysts have the habit of not examining situations with their patients in a new way. To free ourselves from the knots created by jargon requires a movement in a new way. We need to rearrange our ways of knowing so that we are not blinded by new experiences and are able to think in new ways. Jargon often leads to causal thinking, transforming ideals into idols, insisting that internal and external realities correspond with each other.

Bion and Sandler take the reader into an experiential journey. Indeed, we are challenged to observe passionately our own emotional experiences as we read the different characters. The ground is prepared for the reader for potential change. Change is only possible if the reader is interested in being changed. Wittgenstein wrote, "A philosopher is a man who has to cure many intellectual diseases in himself before he can arrive at the notions of common sense" (1980, p. 44). This brilliant understanding of Wittgenstein applies equally to psychoanalysts. Bion is letting us experience, think, and intuit about his own mental processes that are directed towards growth, and his intellectual, pseudo-intellectual, anti-intellectual, and action-oriented processes that are destructive to individual and itersubjective growth.

In inviting the reader on an experiential and imaginative journey, and with his model of container/contained, Bion is telling us that experiences that might lead to change often have to be felt in silence. He understands that freedom comes from acknowledging that one can learn and know more than one can speak.

In *A Memoir of the Future*, Bion has communicated what he has said frequently: one is always becoming a psychoanalyst. He frequently stated that if the analyst is not frightened to be with the patient and is not open to change himself, he has no business becoming an analyst. He demonstrates this by his ability to allow a pattern to evolve, and then to receive this pattern and allow it to develop its own meaningful stories. Without the analyst becoming at-one with the patient's emotional reality, deeper communion would not be possible. Bion's interest was to demonstrate that only a disciplined mind is capable of establishing an I-Thou relation where missed meanings continue to present the possibility of a new meaning emerging that would lead to deeper feelings of communion. For Bion, the disciplined mind had to embody three vertices: scientific, aesthetic, and religious. The scientific vertex allows appropriate distance to observe the evolution of the emotional experience both in the patient and within the analyst. He gives great value to Hume's notion of constant conjunction. The aesthetic vertex needs the aesthetic object, which holds the tension between artistic, religious and scientific vertices until the evolution of the symbol that contains what is meaningful at any given moment. The artistic vertex allows a pattern to emerge and appreciates the "beauty of a harmony and the facts we choose that contribute to this harmony" (Poincaré). The religious vertex is the appreciation of the unknown, the awe, the mystery of the unknown as we tolerate it. The epistemology of not knowing and being able to enjoy the state of waiting.

The Dawn of Oblivion is about the journey from prenatal mind to approaching death. All the major transitions during a life-span relate to the catastrophic "caesura" of birth with its war between Psyche and Soma. Em-mature is the embryo until the time of birth. Em-mature is pressured by the Pre-mature, the false adult who uses destructive jargon, saturated knowledge and self-intoxication to avoid the creation of a Language of Achievement. The Pre-mature is dominated by destructive forces against waiting. At the end of the volume, one reads:

> ROBIN Why catastrophe?
>
> P.A. Because unless the human animal learns to become expert in discrimination he will be in imminent danger of the *wrong* choice.
>
> ALICE Nuclear war, for example.
>
> P.A. There are no labels attached to most options; there is no substitute for the growth of wisdom. Wisdom or oblivion—take your choice. From that warfare there is no release. [III: 576]

Two clinical examples come to mind. Jim is a male in his 50s who had been dominated by what can be called a "Pre-mature" state of mind. He thinks he is a "walking dead" who is unaware of time and space, and has no inner capacity for dialogue with himself. He is frozen in his past failures and dreads the future. The present is killed. He had the following dream: He was dead, lying on the ground to be buried. Waiting, waiting, waiting, and nobody came. He began with both of his hands to bury his body in the soil. Suddenly, he was overtaken by the cells charging stimuli in his body. He could not bear the flooding of sensations in his body. He woke up in panic and for quite some time kept checking his body if the sensations were going to kill him.

Jim's "body" keeps rejecting his "soul". Waiting does not lead to a new idea or a feeling. Many of his "dreams" have been about his body decaying and disappearing and becoming a skeleton. What often remains is his orange coloured hair. He recently asked me about his curiosity about a girl he dated a couple of times when he was in college. He stopped dating her after two dates because he did not know what to say to her. He was very attracted to her and described her as very beautiful. She died of an illness when she was in her 20s, 28 years ago. He asked, "What kind of morbid thoughts do I have? I keep wondering what she looks like now." He first went to the cemetery and only afterwards told me about his thoughts. Jim is the owner of every thought that he has. That way, he ensures that he stays "living dead" and keeps total sameness in his environment. The thought about his curiosity about her skeleton he did not own. Rather, the thought was creating him. However, the shock waves of the sense of catastrophe, "break up, down, in, out, or through", he was sensing and he was able to stop a pattern of thoughts from forming. As morbid as it sounded to Jim, I think that it was a new thought, the birth of a new idea. The beautiful young woman he dated; and that he could not bear tolerating the conflicts triggered by her beauty when she was alive. Now, the thought of a skeleton as a new thought could not be expanded. He sensed the reverberation of the war between beauty, skeleton, longing and mortality in silence, and he had to foreclose.

Norm, a 65-year-old man, has lived a false life most of his life. He has frequently spoken about an internal soldier guiding him. He has realised that the inner soldier uses the jargon of logic, precision and order, in order to make him withdraw from the dreaded contact that would lead to potential disintegration and disappearance in a black hole. Norm feels that only oral sex holds him together. Without someone sucking his penis, he will not survive. He frequently mentions how his mother sucked his soul from him. He reported the following dream: Two lizards were fighting to devour each other. We [referring to himself and myself] had disappeared. Reptiles were the source of the soldier. The reptiles were trying to devour each other's souls. The soldier developed into this ancient animal which had two parts, each trying to devour the other. I was imagining the embryonic thoughts being devoured by the false soldier. The source of the soldier was an ancient underground war between two ancient animals fighting against each other to kill the foetal mind. Now, the penis and the mouth are at war, birth or destruction. Without differentiation, the recurrent destruction of a new birth will continue. He said, "The soul and the body are always devouring each other". His girlfriend, who lives with him, said: "I love you, when we don't have sex it is only temporary, we will have sex again." He started to sob. Her loving tone resonated with an old reverberation of longing to be loved and received totally. In the following sessions he was sad. Through his differentiations, he came to realise that his entire paranoid mind was a misconception based on evading an ongoing agony while growing up.

Bion and Sandler are able to use thoughts and ideas in order to open spaces for other ideas. They are able to allow space for wild thoughts that are not differentiated and are able to wait for future differentiation. They are able to welcome unfamiliar spaces that make one anxious and insecure. Time to pause, time for silence to welcome waiting. Thoughts and words fight such pauses and silences. There is a link between pausing, waiting and madness. Words and forgotten fragments of memories fight to fill up space and saturate the mind away from the potential for the emergence of the new.

Why do analysts fear waiting? Is it an awareness of time in waiting? Is it the awareness of absence of time? Is it the coming of fragments of absence? Waiting is an opening. It inviting that which one does not know. There is a fear of the infinity of spaces. Spaces for the unknown past and future. To keep thinking and to keep possessing our thoughts is to evade the dread of the infinite. To keep thinking is to evade our unknown transformations through thoughts and feelings that make us. To welcome the infinite is to welcome questions without answers. The challenge is to wait and pause so that we are dispossessed by language. The dread of madness is often covered by the need for reason and coherence. These are thoughts that precede emotional turbulence. Inviting the non-rational is inviting madness, which is the centre of meaning. To tolerate staying open is to risk losing and letting go. Forgetting goes with staying open and to forget is to welcome a "Language of Achievement." To stay open is to face the dread of the unthinkable—the not yet. To be able to be open and wait, one has to have some link with the unthinkable and with the acceptance that knowledge comes to us in being able to forget. Waiting and what passes through is not one smooth passage of union. They break things apart, disturb us shake our sense of safety and defy our efforts to make meaning. Waiting calls the unknown, outside and within words. Waiting calls for memories that we cannot remember. We cannot remember because they come to us in fragments. Attempts to recall the origins of our fragmented memories lead to further difficulties in staying open. Forgetting is often that which we never knew. The most difficult thing is to forget what we never knew. What we never knew passes as a loss, not as memory. We forget the unrepresented moments. We both want to forget and are frightened to forget.

In the Trilogy, Bion is struggling to express the complex relationship between sensory, emotional and conceptual elaborations. He knows that through doubting and questioning, learning and growth are possible. He keeps showing us that the words we use are only an approximation. He challenges us to invite our patient's expressive elaborations as ways of understanding the limitations of language. He reminds us that we might be discussing something very similar; but our experience in describing what we are discussing might be utterly different.

Sandler parallels Bion's capacity to be in the "potential space" when fantasy becomes imagination. He allows himself to freely associate from a place of confidence, groundedness and autonomy. He maintains a paradoxical tension and enjoys himself in the process of dialogue with himself as he reads the Trilogy. We witness his passionate encounter with his psychic reality and with its affects of love, hate and curiosity. He welcomes becoming at-one with his emotional truth. An untied truth takes over and he stays committed to his unpredictable journey. Sandler allows us to experience and learn about his own process of becoming a psychoanalyst. He struggles to maintain his emotional and mental growth in the midst of catastrophic anxieties. This is a very comprehensive and informative book.

INTRODUCTION

In the same *ethos* that formed an "underlying mode of writing" of the Trilogy *A Memoir of the Future*, but without any attempt to copy it—for example, this two-volume series contains no dialogues between part-objects—this second volume of *An Introduction to "A Memoir of the Future" by W. R. Bion* allows for a reading in isolation. That is, my supposition is that both works, Bion's Trilogy and this Introduction to it, allow for a reading quite independent of the order of their chapters and even the ordinal sequence of the volumes, while also allowing for a reading along the more traditional, sequential pathway. The first time I saw this particular underlying mode of writing was when I read *Hopscotch* by Julio Cortazar—who explicitly recommended it. It can be read from beginning to end, but it also allows for a patchwork-reading. But it was Bion's surprising and realistic catching of the reader red-handed on the last pages of *The Dream* and of *The Dawn of Oblivion*—the first and the third volumes of *A Memoir of the Future*—that really brought my full attention to this kind of reading (even if my own experience of it was too little, probably due to superego pressures):

> *A Hullo! Here we are again. How did you find it?*
>
> *Q I haven't read it, of course. I was just looking to see how it ended. I'm no wiser than I was at the first.* [I: 217]

> *A I see you turn to the last page as you always used to do.*
>
> *Q Of course. Last time you told me how much it had cost you to publish. Did you find it interesting? How was America—North and South?*
>
> *A Marvellous; a nice change from the Third Battle of Wipers.*
>
> *Q Lots more since then. And more to come—which reminds me; I must rush; I have a date to meet Fate.*
>
> *A Bye-bye—happy holocaust!* [III: 577]

Bion's life ended one year after the writing of the last quotation. I, as well as my family, friends, some patients, and the roster of skilful physicians who helped me during these last seven years, have no pretension to end my life in the next year. Nevertheless, as life is full of surprises, no one can know anything about that now. I am one of those who consider the observation made by Bion to be truthful. As a writer, I recognise the existence of those impelled (for whatever reason) to read this second volume before the first; for them the following introduction may be useful. And, at any rate, it may also be useful as a summary of the last "phase", so to speak, of the first volume "Authoritative, Not Authoritarian Psychoanalysis".

In the latest sense, I imagined that the reader could have experienced, analogically, a "landing" on the firmest space-time ambience that any human being may pretend to achieve, even if partially: Truth, Reality, or, in Freud's terms, a substantial lessening of loyalty to the Principle of Pleasure-Displeasure. The main motive for such a lessening is to provide the very same space-time once occupied by wish and wishful lack of thought (usually known in its commonplace form, wishful thoughts) to allow the inception—and good enough maintenance—of the acknowledgement of the Principle of Reality. The three-word phrase, "space-time ambience" must be apprehended in its fullness: *ambi* is a Latin prefix which means, "two"; the suffix also comes from the Latin, meaning both "being" and "place", or better, an "environment" in which a living entity lives, full of material (sensuously apprehensible) and immaterial (ultra- or infra- or non-sensuously) entities, be they concrete, inanimate things or events; or people—all mutually related, or not. The two-word phrase "substantial lessening" must be taken literally, in both its sensuous or material and psychic or immaterial *nous.* Many—among them, Plato, Luria, Kant, Nietzsche, Darwin, Freud, Einstein, Planck, Klein, Winnicott and Bion—rescued human knowledge about the indivisible ethos of what we, in our seemingly unending ignorance, darkly call, under a split mode, "energy" *or* "matter", or "mind" *or* "matter". Just words, words, words. Is it high time to replace *or* with *and*?

Probably due to our (or the human being's) relative youth on the face of the Earth compared with other animate species, any attempt to search for Truth or, in other words, to achieve a good enough consideration of Reality cannot be made without efforts to face constructive pain—namely, a tolerance of frustration of desire. It has been always accompanied by a contrary force. Searching for Truth was not and is not popular. As I tried to show under the clinical vertex in Volume I and, in fact, in all of my writings until now, in the supposition that I am just following Freud, Klein, Winnicott and Bion (and a host of their intellectual antecedents), enslavement to the Principle of Pleasure-Displeasure continues to be a real fate of humanity. It presents risks to our survival, but the presence of those risks is constantly denied. Even a robust mind like Freud's, which was able to outline at least in entropic terms—in his "Project for a Scientific Psychology" (1895)—the existence of something that countered the primacy of desire, needed more than a decade to discover the real existence of what, for the lack of a better name, he called the Principle of Reality. And then it took him ten more years to discover that that there are sensuous and psychic facts beyond the Principle of Pleasure-Displeasure. Unlike other authors, Fairbairn, Klein, Winnicott and Bion had no qualms about such a discovery. Quite the contrary, they furnished us practical tools to profit from it, in the here and now of our everyday work as practising psychoanalysts.

Conversely, the overwhelming popularity of the so-called toxic addictions, whether material or immaterial, whether legal or illegal—for example, pornography, alcohol, drugs, prejudiced religiosity (different from theology), total dedication to hobbies, consumerism or the vertex of money (Bion, 1970, p. 85), or, in brief, the prevalence of mindlessness—indicates a special difficulty in distinguishing necessary from pleasurable things or activities. Those activities include personal relationships. The difficulty is that real needs are often masked by pleasure and desire, which makes the beholder long first for the latter two. Nourishment is confused with Satisfaction; Need is confused with Pleasure; Possibility with Blind Desire and its siamese twin, Greed—the begetter of Rivalry and Envy. Elsewhere I proposed an analogy for a practising psychoanalyst: to consider a "psychoanalytic compass" (Sandler, 2011). Conversely, Parsimony and Restraint are always unpopular and abhorred to the extent that they can be tools to cope with tolerance of pain and frustration of desire. They demand effort, which imposes difficulties and embodies as a built-in feature the risk of attaining nothing, or something that is much less, both qualitatively and quantitatively, than what Desire demands.

If in our landing we have avoided crashing, the reader may be interested in following the next step, typical of the psychoanalytical endeavour, in this second volume. In the words of Horace, one of the predecessors who gave the clue to Freud: *merses profundo: pulchrior evenit* (plunge it into the deep; it comes out more beautiful). It was not by mere coincidence that Freud also called psychoanalysis "deep psychology" and "psychodynamics": because living matter experiences movements, in psychoanalysis and in real human life.

I called our next step to be expanded in this book, after that thought by Horace, "Diving". Since our method is a critical study of the history of ideas, we must face and deal with many obstacles, well described by a sizeable number of prophets, writers and philosophers, thankfully brought to psychoanalytic practice by the great authors.

I would remark, as a sign of our times, that we live in the over-populated Age of Banality. Where hundreds (of people, or enterprises) were, millions (of people, or enterprises) are now. If in Thomas Browne's, Francis Bacon's, Locke's, Hume's and Kant's time the "mightiest enemy of Knowledge" was dogmatic, authoritarian views, in our age the mightiest enemy is Banality, which pops up in many forms. I would emphasise a seemingly invincible triad: Rationalisation + Little Learning (disguised by easy accessibility to learning, through novel technologies) + the spread of a contradictory, explosive mix of Idealistic Positivism (the idea that reality is just the creation of an individual mind which ideologically dictates, through rationalisations, causes and effects). Even nuclear power is marching resolutely to be within reach of all. New, if short-lived, personality cults propagate a free-for-all, anti-Flaubert motto: *L'oeuvre n'est rien, l'homme tout* (The work is nothing; the individual is everything; Flaubert, in a letter to George Sand, wrote the opposite, *l'homme n'est rien, l'oeuvre tout*). Alas—and this could be a motive in Bion's exclusion—even the psychoanalytic establishment was not free of this, in his lifetime and subsequently. Thirty-five years after his death, one may doubt that his warnings were heard; he was fully aware of this tendency, having written about it in "The Past Presented" and in other texts, published posthumously in *Cogitations*.

For "truth is too heavy a load for rationalisation and explanation to carry". The unavoidable aftermath of this banal mixture, in attempts to communicate in all scientific endeavours, is the inception of what Bion humorously called "Jargonese". Nowadays, despite Bion's warning (borrowed from Whitehead), rationalised, "ingenious manipulations of symbols" prevail, occupying the space where psychoanalysis could be or was. Perhaps the immaterial *ethos* of the psychoanalytic task facilitated the disregard for observation of facts and its consequence, the popping up of non-verifiable "theories". Once some neurologists, enslaved by a concrete (non-)thought, claimed that the Id (a mere model) was located in the limbic system, and the Ego in the brain cortex. They claimed that they could "touch" and manipulate both. Today, the same underlying concrete (non-)thought displays its face when one states that one may "touch" (or smell, or perform theatrically) what Bion called "O". Therefore, this second volume will take a look at what can be called Political Meritocracy—Bion's term for it was The Establishment—and Technical (or Scientific) Meritocracy. As an invitation to the reader, I am reminded of Vaclav Havel and his observations about Exclusion and Truth.

When he was awarded an honorary doctorate at the Hebrew University of Jerusalem in 1990, he said: "The hidden motor driving all my dogged efforts is precisely this innermost feeling of my being excluded, of belonging nowhere, a state of disinheritance, as it were, of fundamental non-belonging". In 1968, after the Prague Spring, he asked: "Isn't it the moment of most profound doubt that gives birth to new certainties? Perhaps hopelessness is the very soil that nourishes human hope; perhaps one could never find sense in life without first experiencing its absurdity." And to his country's criminal dictator, Gustáv Husák and his enforcement gang—today multiplied on a geometrical scale and nullified by globalised Banality—he said: "Your normalisation of society after the Prague Spring only resulted in the calm of the morgue or the grave … in trying to paralyse life, then, the authorities paralyse themselves and, in the long run, make themselves incapable of paralysing life." In *The Power of the Powerless,* he observed that "the human capacity to 'live in truth', to reaffirm man's 'authentic identity', is the nuclear weapon that gives power to the powerless. As soon as the system is no longer able to extract the ritual endorsement from its subjects, its ideological pretensions collapse as the lies they are" (Havel, 1978).

I suppose that any practising psychoanalyst and any kind of group in the psychoanalytic movement to which he or she belongs, or better, feels that he or she belongs, could extract something useful from those observations. More than individual thoughts about transcendent observations, they could only flow into the same ideas already expressed by Freud, Klein, Winnicott and Bion, albeit in different linguistic forms.

DRAMATIS PERSONAE

Q (Questioner, or Reader)
A (Author)
Alice
Rosemary
Tom
Roland
Some military invaders: a driver, a collector, nurses, guards
Robin
An unnamed, unknowable, immaterial godlike entity disguised as a dream, or a dream disguised as an unnamed, unknowable godlike entity
The discoverer and inventor of homo alalu
Big Sister
Small Brother
Small Mo
Half-Awake
Paranoid-Schizoid
Depressive Position
Big Bro
Captain Bion
Myself
Beta
Alpha
Memory
B. Memory (Berkshire memory)
D.O.M. (Deo Optimo Maximo)
All
Voice—seemingly God; or ARF ARF [Our Father]
Nurse
State Psychiatrist
Albert Stegosaurus
Adolf Tyrannosaurus
Bion
Dr Watson
Sherlock Holmes
Mycroft Holmes

Supporter (Military)
Legionary
A Neighbour (Military)
Man
Mrs Mop (card game)
Priest of Ur
Palinurus
Dinosaur
Old Woman
Tonks
Captain
Lieutenant Arthur
O'Connor
♀
Conan Doyle
P(sycho) A(nalyst) subsequently called P.A.
Doctor
Paul (later called Priest)
Edmund (an astronomer)
Thea
Du
Priest
Ghost of Stokes
Ghost of Cliff
Ghost of Keen
Quentin
Padre
General
Clytemnestra
Apparition
Schoolboy
Crowd
All Souls
Gull
Cod
Harding
The Duke of Shehol
Mathematician
Spirit
Classical Singers (Sopranos, Altos, Tenors)
Choirmaster
Big Toe
All Toes
Ghost of Auser
Ghost of P.A.
Leonard
Milton (John)
Krishna
Infancy
Mind
Body
Soma
Psyche
Boy
Girl
Mother
Container
Jenny
Tibs (a cat)
Tree
Cyril
Devil (formerly Du)
Heart
Physicist
Schreber (Judge Daniel Schreber)
All (ante-natal) Souls
All (post-natal) Souls
Germ Plasm
Somites
Somite Three
Four Somites
Somite Eighteen
Somite Twenty-four
Somite Thirty
Somite Thirty-two
Twenty months
Seven weeks Embryo
Pre-mature
Term
Em-mature, subsequently called Em
Six Years
Eight Years

Twelve Years
Fourteen Years
Eighteen Years
Nineteen Years
Twenty-three Years
Twenty Years
Twenty-one Years
Twenty-three Years
Twenty-four years
Thirty Years
Forty Years
Forty-two Years
Fifty Years
Sixty-one Years
Seventy Years
Seventy-five Years
Moriarty
Passing character, quoted only once:
Helen of Troy

References in the text are to the Karnac edition (1991) of *A Memoir of the Future*, and are in the form volume number (I, *The Dream*; II, *The Past Presented*; III, *The Dawn of Oblivion*): page number.

PART I

LANDING .... OR DIVING?

DIVING

If we did not have a crash landing at the end of Volume 1, what could be said about the next step, "Diving"?

CHAPTER ONE

The fumbling infancy: Paradise regained?

> The infancy of psychoanalytic discovery is always brought up against the possibility that psychoanalysis, like infants, might grow up.
>
> [II: 233]

If one adopts the purely arbitrary parameter of "century", which is in any case fairly useful for some purposes, to the point of being taken, in a Western civilisation so accustomed to commonplaces, as if it were pure truth, psychoanalysis has been going on for a little more than one century. If one adopts the year of publication of the Trilogy, psychoanalysis has already been in existence for three quarters of a century. Experience tells us that any scientific or artistic discipline or discovery which can count on just a century of development is still in its "fumbling infancy", a fact repeatedly noticed by Bion in *A Memoir of the Future* (I: 131; II: 233; the issue was expanded in Volume 1).

All generations of psychoanalysts, especially the first three, believed that through the new knowledge which was brought home by psychoanalysis practically all problems and unnecessary—meaning, irrational inter-human struggles—could be avoided and extinguished. Wishful thinking clothed with scientific achievement, exactly according to Vienna's motto. Such a project had nothing to do with Freud's observations. Psychoanalytic aphorisms coined by Freud, such as "make the unconscious conscious", or its improved version, "where id was, there shall ego be", were taken at their maximum under the judgmental, wishful, desire-enslaved vertex of preventive medicine. "Mental hygiene" was seen as the method. Psychoanalysts more obedient or subservient to the establishments of hedonistic societies (Vienna in the late nineteenth century, British, French and American affluent social classes in the twentieth century, for example) duly denied—that is, acted out under a psychotic vertex—other observations of Freud: for example, those included in "Negation", "Analysis Terminable and Interminable", and the one in which he explicitly states that a successful psychoanalysis could replace neurotic anxieties with everyday, "normal" anxiety. Developments provided by Klein and Bion allow us to state that neurotic anxieties correspond to everyday psychopathology, that is, the transitory presence of illusion, delusion and hallucinosis—or, as this writer once proposed, that psychic reality also tolerates psychic un-reality: a good soil for our "psychosis of everyday life" (Sandler, 1997; 2005, p. 782). In colloquial terms: lies. Sandor Ferenczi, Max Eitingon, Adolf Meyer—his "psychobiology" may be considered a forerunner of preventive psychiatry—and a few people in other countries, such as Franco da Rocha, a distinguished psychiatrist in Brazil who first translated some works of Freud in the late 1920s, nourished this kind of hope to save people from illness and suffering and any kind of effort, guaranteeing an unproblematic life. For any problem that might arise would be no problem at all—it would be resolved by this novel "technique" called "psychoanalysis". In some parts of the world, people who had been "analysed" were described as "well-resolved"—meaning, determined, steadfast, wholly healthy, etc.

The function exerted by the innumerable forebears of this posture, which saved people from experiencing pain, allows one to at least hypothesise that later ones would appear. This is not an inductive or predictive approach, but an intuitive view, born from experience, of the future casting its shape now—in the same sense that if a body is illuminated from behind, its shadow is "projected" before it.

Psychoanalysis, backed by enthusiastic people and pioneers who perhaps believed that a Paradise did exist, may have been called to exert, in the name of science (and currently, in the name of literature) the centuries-old "social function" early on attributed to all kinds of

Messiahs. In the Catholic tradition, the "father" who would never forsake his sons, seemingly unlike Jesus's father when he was crucified. The word "cure" comes from the Latin *cura*, meaning "care"; in Latin-language countries, variants of *cura* are used to mean parish priest, one who cares for his flock.

"Late Freud" must be exempted from this attitude. Melanie Klein, Wilfred Bion and, up to a point, Winnicott extended Freud's later contributions, starting with Klein, who emphasised a most basic situation of humankind: the anxiety at annihilation which assaults any baby from his or her birth. Klein's observation is fully backed by neurology: myelination is incomplete in the newborn child, and continues through the first year of life. Bion described Pain as one of the Elements of Psychoanalysis. This is a real fact precociously abhorred, and then ignored and dismissed by a sizeable proportion of the psychoanalytic movement, which was more interested in the ever-popular "soft humanism" (Williams, 1986). This is the border between real psychoanalysis and conscious reassurance and support psychotherapies, ages-old practices used by religions.

Growing pains and psychotic and non-psychotic personalities: countering banality

The human condition means that Pain is unavoidable. Bion reminds us of phrases like "growing pains" which express this reality. At least for some analysts, awareness of this fact was enhanced after the illumination by Freud of what comes "beyond the pleasure principle" (Freud, 1920). Starting from this, there appeared a more explicit and less intuitive distinction between necessary and unnecessary pain. The latter is at the service of desire and embodies a paradox, because there is a disregard for the origin of pleasurable experiences, which can be oriented by sadism and the inhumanity of man towards man—or the "banality of evil", to use a more popular, if apparently non-psychoanalytical phrase coined by Hannah Arendt (Arendt, 1963). After all, Arendt's language is that of a criticism wholly influenced by the political and moral vertices, which are alien to the criticism provided by psychoanalysis.

Do her sociological (or socio-political, or philosophical) studies embody any psychoanalytical insight that might not be apparent at first sight? A critical comparison between sociology and psychoanalysis, imbued with a mutually collaborative transdisciplinary vertex, seems to be a possible task. If the contributions of Arendt are considered under the illumination provided by Bion's integrative extensions of Freud's and Klein's work, especially in "Differentiation of the Psychotic from the Non-Psychotic Personalities" (1957a) and "A Theory of Thinking" (1961—coincidentally the same year that Arendt's reports of the Eichmann trial appeared in the press), as well as what is included in the Trilogy, one may observe that what was hyperbolically expressed in the Hitler phenomenon and in Nazism are built-in features present either explicitly or implicitly in any human being considered—albeit in diminished quantities. The references are implicit in Bion's two earlier papers and explicit in the Trilogy: there are six references to Hitler in Volume I. The initial quasi-novel describes a future development of Nazism. The new millennium showed that Nazism prefigured what may be found in some Middle Eastern and African countries: it is no surprise that many who were among the second echelon of Nazi bigwigs found safe havens in the German Democratic Republic and in Middle Eastern kingdoms and sultanates, helping their modernisation into murderous dictatorships.

The main character of the Nazi phenomenon is critically quoted against the path of humankind with a mixture of sweet and sour humour. In one of the quotations, the same issues approached by Arendt are present in Bion's text, but in a scientific description, not the reprisals of a zealot. One cannot be in doubt about Bion's own opinion, but this opinion is not imposed on the reader. It is stressed in some attempts to display what is psychoanalytic work:

> ROLAND ... Is the supposition that the reptilian age is antecedent to Hitler correct, or is it a feature of our thinking process which has become an aberration which has not been considered, but has become part of what is *observed*? [I: 86]

> PRIEST Gerard Manley Hopkins strove to express an awareness both of a sense of being ideationally or artistically pregnant, and of the reaction, the counter-actions, to that activity. He believed this applied whatever role he played. He might identify himself with the poet that he himself was, or with the priest who hated and feared the fetus, or the poet who feared the priestly fetus. He seemed to be well aware of murderous envy which is born when

the envied idea or person is born. Where? Who knows? The only certain thing, is, *somewhere*.

P.A. You talk about envy in a way that I would expect to hear from one of my colleagues—or even from one of your colleagues predicting the birth of the Messiah. I do not restrict these expectations of a messiah or of envy and hatred to any profession. I am familiar with expectations, even announcements, of the existence of a saviour. Sometimes it is a military saviour; sometimes a scientist who is going to make the world safe for mental defectives of one kind or other. Heaven will presumably then consist of boobies and a number of angel nurses who will save the boobies from liquidation.

MORIARTY That Great and Good Man Adolf Hitler has not been assessed at his true value.

ALICE You are a swine. I don't like saying so, and hitherto I have been saved the necessity by the fact that you are a figment of the imagination.

P.A. I think you may in future have to have a great deal of respect for figments of imagination and take them seriously. I could draw up a considerable list of Saviours of the Nation: for example, Hindenburg, Sir John French, Henry V.

ALICE But surely some of them were good men? Or do you suggest that none was?

P.A. I understand your unease. Mine is perhaps even greater because I am convinced that all the men and women I have ever known have some good in them. Conversely, probably all had some bad. Let me say at once that I am aware of the utter banality of that conclusion, but that this is one reason why I do not wish to regard it as a *conclusion*. I am sometimes consoled by the possibility that the goodness, the capacity for love and concern for our fellows may be a greater force than hate.

ROLAND Possibly. But don't you think it pathetic that when Science and its brood of astronomers leads unmistakably to the discovery of our insignificance in contrast with these gigantic forces—novae, supernovae, black holes and the rest—someone is sure to apply a mental first-aid dressing and hurl us back into the downy comfort of ignorance. Doesn't that depress you?

P.A. No. Down serves the fledgling; mental down preserves us however praise- or blameworthy we may be. The fact that the blackness and absolute cold lies beyond the charming blue of a summer does not make the blue less lovely to me. The vast incomprehensibility of the Absolute surrounding me is not so biting as a toothache. I have not begun to cope with the fear of toothache, whereas God and Devil do not even make my flesh creep.

MORIARTY Splendid! Splendid! Allow me congratulate your perspicacity and courage. *Carpe diem* I say. A good ghoulish murder is worth all the rest of Priest's high-falutin' nonsense—as any reader of the more sensational parts of a newspaper knows. Even Priest knows better than to cut all the spicier bits of the Bible from Sunday reading. "Search the Scriptures" indeed! Why *not*? Instead of that you humbugs search the quotations! No wonder life—real life—doesn't seem worth living. You priests and doctors, and now psychoanalysts, would have made some pretty vile sadistic monsters if you had not been so afraid of your imaginations and the figments to which they would have given birth.

PRIEST Do you suppose we don't know that?

P.A. We advocate knowledge of what we are really like—in so far as we can. But we do not thereby close the options. On the contrary; the options that are there, whether we like them or not, remain open. The patient, who may not have had the knowledge, cannot be regarded as making a truly moral judgement—as he can if he reviews his opportunities when more mature. We do not even know what our nature—bodily, mental, and spiritual—is capable of doing. We can hardly, therefore, regard ourselves as responsible in any true sense.

ROBIN Real human beings are usually so difficult to believe in that we have to be introduced to them, gently, by the medium of the figments of imaginative genius.

P.A. Even so, we do not want to be reminded of our selves.

PRIEST We may want to remind *others* of something they would rather forget; they fear they might not be able to survive the shock of the reminder. Hell is feared—by some.

P.A. I know people who do not need to be told that the kingdom of Hell is within them.

> ROLAND If they do not need to be told, what do you psychoanalysts tell them?
>
> P.A. What *they* tell *me* may remind me of something relevant to what they are saying which is not clear to them. [III: 572–575]

The reader may be familiar with a character borrowed from Conan Doyle: Moriarty, a kind of Devil incarnate. Bion depicted what in psychoanalytic theory is called acting out with Dr Watson as well as with Moriarty. A blend of all—a man who inserts thought between impulse and action and is also able to insert some devilish ways—is depicted with Sherlock.

Experience with sadistic pleasure is hardly restricted to any social class or education. Nevertheless, Hannah Arendt had a fair dose of it, in which an important factor was the specific time in which she lived and the people she had to deal with, either by chance or by choice, such as Martin Heidegger and the Gestapo and SS officials. *And* Jewish-Zionist authorities who shared with Nazi "negotiators" a Nero-like posture in their commercial business dedicated to deciding which Jew would survive or not.

The history of Hannah Arendt's second involvement with SS torturers is well known. She was invited by the editor of a respected weekly, *The New Yorker*, to cover a peculiar trial in Israel. The state of Israel was popular in the Western media and enjoyed sympathy from more parts of the population than ever, because of its newness and moral stature, enhanced by analogies with the seductive Biblical myth of David and Goliath. More than a quarter of a century separated Arendt's two involvements with the Nazis. Both are described by her in the same volume. This time, Arendt met one of the chieftains,[1] former Obersturmbannführer Adolf Eichmann. Being specially gifted in the art of writing, Arendt recorded her first impressions (the following quotations are from Arendt, 1963): "The man in the glass booth was not even sinister (*nicht einmal unheimlich*) ... The deeds were monstrous, but the doer ... was quite ordinary, commonplace, and neither demonic nor monstrous". Arendt felt that Eichmann was "a common man, evidenced in his transparent superficiality and mediocrity". What seemed, at least to this writer, to most impress Arendt was the "thoughtlessness of Eichmann's ordinariness ... it implied an incapacity for independent critical thought". In fact—according to her—there was just a single characteristic that could be seen as differentiating Eichmann from any other type: "a curious, quite authentic inability to think".

She had expected to find just sheer stupidity, probably on the basis of her earlier dealings with such people and of reports from the Nuremberg Trials. Arendt reiterated to many people who met her subsequently[2] that Eichmann incarnated the everyday experience, which became commonplace and thus was unobserved, passing for "normal": an absolute lack of critical thought.

> When confronted with situations for which such routine procedures did not exist, he was helpless, and his cliché-ridden language produced on the stand, as it had evidently done in his official life, a kind of macabre comedy. Clichés, stock phrases, adherence to conventional, standardised codes of expression and conduct have the socially recognised function of protecting us against reality, that is, against the claim on our thinking attention that all events and facts make by virtue of their existence. [Arendt, 1963]

Psychoanalysts who consented to be helped by Freud's, Klein's and Bion's observations about the universality of neuroses and psychosis would not be perplexed at Eichmann's behaviour, either when he was a willing executioner in 1942–1944 or as a kidnapped defendant in 1961. Hannah Arendt and most of her readers, in contrast, were bewildered. People who can couple the reading and application of Bion's methods as exposed in *Experiences in Groups* with a posture that withstands the reading of the Trilogy may question the deeds of compact masses of men and women who, in a socially approved way, are considered "normal".

Nevertheless, normal people are able to behave in such a way that the same people who previously regarded them as normal suddenly change their judgement and condemn them as monsters—initially, those people who are subjected to their acting out. Hitler had been able to take care of his mother when she was dying of breast cancer, a fact confirmed not only by his friend Kubizek but also by her physician, Dr Edward Bloch, who happened to be Jewish (Kubizek, 1955; Kershaw, 1988). Hitler did have some friends and was seen as a kind senior by some of his child acquaintances. Adolf Hitler may have looked for psychiatric help in the 1920s, according to one of his friends, Ernst Hanfstaengl, a Harvard-educated German-American (Hanfstaengl, 1957). There were rumours of a psychiatric report describing him as "incompetent to command people" and "dangerously psychotic" (http://www.nazism.net/about/adolf_hitler; Kershaw, 1988). If true, it shows the error of psychiatrists in the former evaluation and the truth contained in the latter—a paradoxical situation often encountered among psychiatric evaluations which indicates that the fact that they existed may be real. Later, Hitler was hooked on quacks and mystics, which indicates the prevalence of primitive nuclei in his personality. None of this would surprise a psychoanalyst who is used to dealing with the non-pacific coexistence of the psychotic and the non-psychotic (or neurotic) personality (Bion, 1957).

Beyond this murderous historic creature, examples are legion: the ingratitude of a pseudo-friend; the practice of "social lies"; the socialising way of life which is in fact just cheap seduction in order to earn prestige or money; profiteering; the malevolence of the opportunistic "friend"; the Janus-inspired misdeeds of politicians, etc. To this group, the honest person is regarded as naïve or stupid, especially if personal honesty is coloured with phantasies of superiority, a mark of "inhabiting" the paranoid-schizoid position. After all, one cannot be honest if one's encircling environment is decidedly dishonest.

Concern for truth is a hallmark of this transdisciplinary study which unites a central shared area of apparently different disciplines, politics and psychoanalysis. Freud, Klein, Bion and Arendt shared the same goal of "defending … the integrity of the factual truth" (Arendt, 1972, p. 227; also quoted in Lafer, 1979, p. 33). The shared nous belongs to science. A slight deviation may be made when one considers the psychoanalytic vertex applied to Arendt's sociological theory. This vertex of observation deals with the delicate entropic balance between death and life instincts, and one may see that the function of politicians—always under the aegis of morals—would ultimately change. It would now belong, paradoxically, to the "species" of *animal laborans* (Arendt, 1959, p. 234). Therefore, under the psychoanalytic vertex that considers unconscious drives, it is possible to emphasise Arendt's "banality" (appertaining to unconscious proclivities to the principle of pleasure-displeasure) and de-emphasise "of evil" (appertaining to conscious proclivities to morals). Scientifically and ethically (but not morally), banality is inextricably linked, like a Siamese twin, to destruction of truth.

If one accepts a neurophysiological hypothesis, would there be a slight deficit of intelligence (McDougall, 1979) located in the realm of personal ethics—the categorical imperative according to Kant, or superego in Freud's parlance—which is a factor in Arendt's "banality of evil"?

The mechanisms of mental defence were first noticed by Freud in dream work. Aided by his daughter Anna, he expanded the detection to see that the very same mechanisms also appeared in another function, namely, the defending of the ego against dysfunctions in its own entropic status when it is constantly struggling to achieve the lowest possible input of anxiety. To be an agent of "the banality of evil" it is necessary to have psychopathic features, but it is also necessary to have a slight intellectual deficit—not so high as to preclude mental manipulation, which can be done though the abusive use of some of the defence mechanisms, particularly reaction formation, denial, the transformation of a deed into its opposite—also called undoing—and projective identification.

All of these defence mechanisms are swiftly devoured by rationalisation, which is not exactly a defence mechanism, but a psychotic and very early manifestation of un-love for truth (or a mixture of –L and –K, in Bion's parlance about links; on rationalisation, see Freud on the case of Schreber, 1911; Bion, 1962, pp. 42 and 97; review in Sandler, 2005, pp. 406, 475; Sandler, 2011). Armed with these mental weapons, one who has attitudes overtly repudiated by the group may act them out in a rationalised kind of morally defensible behaviour which covers monstrous deeds. This may be exemplified in innumerable works of art: for example, Ingmar Bergmann's *Fanny and Alexander.* This kind of behaviour and its social acceptance—because the agent functions vicariously, saving other people from acting out the same deeds, which are in their imagination anyway—is well described, as a quasi-desperate warning, in Nietzsche's *Also Sprach Zarathustra* and in many literary works, such as Shakespeare's *Richard III* and in some works by Dostoyevsky.

Replacing Myself with P.A.—the maturing author

A most psychoanalytical insight was given in a speech at the opening ceremony of the 1986 Psychoanalytical Congress in Hamburg—the first on German soil after World War II. It was not made by any of the distinguished (at least within the group) analysts present at the event, but rather by one whose external appearance indicated that he was not a psychoanalyst—at least, he was not appointed as such by any psychoanalytical establishment or institute.

The speech was delivered by the lawyer Klaus von Dohnanyi, then Mayor of Hamburg and husband of a German analyst, the psychologist Christa von Dohnanyi. His statements caused trepidation which bordered on commotion in most parts of the audience. In a blunt but sweet form denoting insight he affirmed that if it was fair to present the German people to foreigners with "... our Bach, our Freud, our Einstein ..." it would be necessary to add to this "visiting card" another name: "... our Hitler". Von Dohnanyi had personal experience fully immersed in this environment.

His father, Hans von Dohnanyi, was also a lawyer, a high-ranking officer in the Justice Ministry of the German government from 1929 to 1943. Like very few other people, such as Ernst Jünger and Konrad Adenauer, he was a kind of "untouchable" person in the Nazi Dictatorship despite the fact, usually fateful, that he had not requested membership of the party. Therefore he carried on serving the government after 1933, when Hitler took power. One year later, after the criminal event known as the Night of the Long Knives (the purge of the SA and its leader and of prominent anti-Nazis), Hans von Dohnanyi began to collaborate with the tiny German resistance against Nazism. In 1943, the Nazi secret police (Gestapo) arrested him at his office on charges of illegally transferring funds abroad on behalf of Jews. In 1944, Hans von Dohnanyi was jailed in Sachsenhausen concentration camp. His close links with von Stauffenberg and his colleagues emerged after their plot to kill Hitler failed. Von Dohnanyi—along with the other conspirators—was found guilty by a fake court and hanged with piano wire. The executions were filmed, and Hitler reportedly used the films for his personal amusement until his own suicide (Kershaw, 1988).

This brief account of an aspect of the history of the von Dohnanyi family may highlight the fact that criminals living in a criminal—or untruthful—social milieu are not seen as criminals: they are regarded as ordinary people. The obverse is also true: non-criminals are seen as criminals when living in a criminal social environment (Bracher, 1969; Grunberger, 1971; Bullock, 1991; Frei, 1997; Ayçoberry, 1998; Goldensohn, 2004).

The advent of the Nazi period paradoxically *rekindled* the psychoanalytic movement. The efforts to replace it with a German Nazi psychoanalysis resulted in a flight of many practitioners to more hospitable countries: a true brain drain which replenished universities and art centres in many countries, especially the US and the UK. Nevertheless, it also rekindled the wishful psychoanalysis: a passport to a problem-free life.

Some new techniques were presented, together with hasty promises regarded as derived from psychoanalysis. In fact they were already over-simplifications of Freud's observations, fated to compose a lasting "medical error"—still unobserved. They were temporarily left aside because of the Second World War; among them, what was called "psychosomatics". Full of explanations, looking at medicine with indistinguishable Caesarian arrogance, psychosomaticists vowed to replace medicine with their "teachings"; it was seen as the medicine of the future (Sandler, 2008).

Based on the mindlessness of groups focused on psychotic paranoid beliefs that give an exalted place to placebo effects, "psychosomatic medicine" still flourishes in undelivered pledges. It just adds to the erroneous criticism of real psychoanalysis. Who could demand, in the "fumbling infancy" of the psychoanalytic movement, that lay people must distinguish real psychoanalysis from non-psychoanalysis? This is still a difficult task even for experienced psychoanalysts.

Banal explanations under the umbrella of "psychosomatics" soon acquired the flavour of literature. Untested crude analogies which were no more than mere hypotheses were seen as ingenious by inexperienced, helpless and gullible individuals. They soon gained the social status of proven theses or "theories": the "language of the body" became a favourite bandwagon. Few realise that "Mind" and "Body" are just two words with no counterpart in reality—they show both how little we know and our hate for the unknown, marked by hurried, precocious and unauthorised (by reality) naming (Cagli, 2005; Sandler, 2008). If there is universal truth in what Matthew's gospel says about marriage, "what God has joined together, let no one separate" (Mt. 19: 6), it would be equally true that what man or woman separates would need the invention of a god to be able to be reunited.

> MAN The first thing is to realise that the laws of nature are not formulations or orders which have to be obeyed, but are elements which are constantly conjoined, are conjoined *constantly*. This is true whatever the variables may be and however much the variables dominate, are allowed to dominate, or are encouraged to dominate the object which approximates to the formula of (constant + variable) $\alpha + \beta \times \xi$, or $\beta + \alpha \times \xi$.
>
> ALICE A sign to denote noise, analogous to that denoting the bass or treble clef in music, is required.

> MAN One famed anthropologist says the bone formation of the skull does not lend itself to attachment of the tongue muscle for use in articulate speech. The attachment of the penis to the anatomy, the vagina likewise, is in its own fashion appropriate and beautiful. What God has joined together let no man put asunder.
>
> BION How could we put them together or put them asunder? These are anatomical structures with physiological functions, and I for my part have not in my conscious memory ever known a time when conscious and unconscious aim and ideal have been possible to divorce from each other. Nor have I ever known a time when these constantly conjoined objects were on good terms with each other except for short periods; enough to make me long for more. [I: 164]

Freud, Planck and Einstein did not fall into this fallacy of Western thinking that may have been initiated with Aristotle, St Thomas Aquinas and Descartes, flowing almost uninterruptedly to Auguste Comte's positivism: the false split between matter and mind (or matter and energy).

Wilfred Bion comments on this falsity with good-humoured metaphors and parables; it may be worth noticing that the "Triple Character" (Bion⇔Myself⇔P.A.), which in Volume III is simplified to a "Twin Character" represented by P.A. and Bion, allows the reader to distinguish between them. The importance of the younger, mostly paranoid character Bion diminishes and that of the more mature character P.A. increases, allowing for the concrete disappearance of the character Myself from the text. The reader may notice the precision of Bion's writing: he even remarks that Bion is a less (psychoanalytically) mature and more socialised version of P.A., to whom is left the function of being a real or pure psychoanalyst:

> P.A. According to Heisenberg the fact of *observing* the play of minute physical factors influences the play being observed. I do not know if he is saying that what I have been used to regard as a *mental* phenomenon has an effect on what we call a *physical* fact; I may have been in error in discriminating between "mental" phenomena and "physical" facts. Such an "idea" is perhaps a flaw in the mental apparatus. As a human I have a prejudice in favour of regarding my thoughts as "superior" to the apparently random movements of infinitely minute particles of matter.

ROLAND Are you prejudiced against the random movements of minute particles of matter? [I: 265]

TWENTY-FOUR YEARS Lights out and stop talking now please—

SEVENTY YEARS That's better. If only one could rely on their always going to sleep.

SEVENTY-FIVE YEARS Unfortunately they never do. Sometimes they all speak at once and it is a perfect Bedlam.

P.A. I think it might some day be possible for them all to be awake and carry on a fairly disciplined debate.

ROBIN I doubt it. I sometimes think it saves my sanity that most of them are usually asleep. It's bad enough when it's only two or three talking at once.

ROLAND That's only because they all talk a different language.

MAN I shot you so you would lie down and stay down—and out. And silent. Your friend Robin too—years ago. I don't want any ghostly voices around. Anyone would think it wasn't bad enough with religious nonsense inventing a future life and angel voices to add to the tumult.

ROBIN I can't see that's any worse than P.A. and his crowd inventing minds and characters and psychosomatic disturbances. [III: 443–4]

ALICE What was that? Did you hear it?

ROSEMARY No—I hope you aren't hallucinating or I shall have to get rid of you.

P.A. I should be careful what you do with your voice. Here—suck one of these psychoanalytic pills—slowly. Just let it dissolve in your mind. You've swallowed it! You shouldn't have done that. It won't do you any harm—just a bit of heart ache. But it will spread through your system and be excreted harmlessly by your mind—like cinnamon, or whisky. It was probably the Future casting its shadow before; sometimes disguised as the Past casting its memory forward.

ROSEMARY Thank you; I am most grateful. Do you know what gratitude is?

ROBIN "A lively expectation of benefits to come."[3]

ALICE You are cynical. What is guilt then?

P.A. Ah yes!—the Cynics.

ROBIN No, she asked about guilt. Guilt is "a lively apprehension of rewards to be inflicted".

P.A. For being able to laugh at dirty jokes in school—like "It is I. Come forth—And 'e came fifth—and 'e did 'it 'is eye."[4]

ALICE Oh my God!

ROSEMARY Isn't it awful? Now it has become respectable and is called Psychoanalysis. It hardly makes one anxious to follow Roland's suggestion and become unified.

ROBIN If we could come together we could still preserve our identity—like the hills on a map in which all the same levels could be joined by a contour—

P.A. All right if we could link Somite Three with all the other Somite Threes. Of course, the auditory and optic pits would have to put up with being linked.

DOCTOR The post-natals may want to keep their distance from the pre-natals—and vice versa. We must assume that the pre-natal crowd can adjust to a change from a liquid environment to a gaseous one, the olfactory elements easing the change by bringing mucus with them so they go on functioning even after birth.

P.A. Some of these post-natal people complain of too much fluid. They call it "catarrh" or "influenza" and rush off to someone to "cure" them. You must be familiar with that demand.

DOCTOR Yes indeed, but I would hesitate to tell them they were complaining of too much cure—being drowned in cure.

P.A. Your somitic friends would complain of being immersed in your intellectual, cerebral evacuations—a rarefied, abstract ocean of theory in which they could not taste or smell. If somites could write, the book would be "On the Interpretation of Reality" and the theories would all be what we call dreams. We complain both of the unpleasant warmth of psychoanalysis *and* its arid abstractions.

DOCTOR Poor old body; poor old mind. It is hardly surprising that they do not get on well together and look down on each other, especially if we remember that one is derived from the other. In fact they may derive from a biological atomic plutonium breeder.

P.A. If it is true that living matter derives from the heat engendered by the reaction of oxygen with protoplasm then I can see that brain substance might derive from the "decay" of involuntary muscle, and the mind likewise from the energy released by the degeneration of athletic ability.

DOCTOR I knew some intelligent, "brainy" people who played games for Oxford; they seemed to remain brainy *and* athletic.

P.A. Fortunate people! If only one could see how they did it one might solve the problem of how to produce more energy than beef. I would think I was in reality becoming a psychoanalyst if I could *become* more energetic by *being* more energetic. It might enable others to start that reaction. Melanie Klein seemed to do that for psychoanalysis.

BION What! You don't mean to say you are a Kleinian?

P.A. You remind me of Sir Andrew Aguecheek—"And if I thought he were a puritan I would … !" Your excellent reason, sir?

BION I thought you would appreciate an experience which we could share together. [III: 469–471]

Shakespeare portrayed fools in his plays, particularly depicting people who are made greater fools due to their omnipotence, like Sir John Falstaff, who appears in both parts of *Henry IV* and *The Merry Wives of Windsor*, and is mentioned in *Henry V*. He is matched, in what may be seen as the state of the art of being a fool, by Sir Andrew Aguecheek, a character in *Twelfth Night*. Bion borrows from him to describe his idea of himself when functioning as a member of a group—here called "Kleinians"—and thus risking losing his own real self. The reader may notice that P.A. performs a psychoanalysis with Bion in this part of the text. Bion seems to answer positively, having an insight which displays his own helplessness when put in a situation of having to be responsible for himself. Being part of a group is one of the alternatives one may use when one is unable to be individually responsible for oneself: people look for companions to "share" whatever it may be. This is the case of one who looks for a breast, for a mother, for marriage, and also of one who looks for a doctor.

It was the Nazi phenomenon which brought to the fore the inception of techniques to manage small groups under the psychoanalytic vertex. They were created by two military psychiatrists, S. H. Foulkes, more focused on helping therapy, and Bion, with a definite tendency to describe the inner, non-apparent links which produced clear-cut movements in small groups. Group therapy had increasingly concretised offshoots such as couple therapy, family therapy and Moreno's psychodrama, which in fact preceded the Second World War but had a definite impulse and popularisation after it. Besides having real scientific value, all of them also augmented the assorted verbal promises of a pain-free future life. There was no shortage of pledges and vows, sheltering either the *naïveté* or the bad faith of their proponents.

The *perception* of truth may be obliterated and destroyed. None of this really affects truth itself. Lies that impinge on the whole structure and fabric of society may last for something in the environs of one century until the perception of truth finally emerges. For some learned people, like Hans von Dohnanyi, the perception of truth as regards Nazism took no less than seven years to emerge. Taking into account human life expectancy in Western civilisation, it took at least three or four generations for the majority of people to realise the truth behind these kinds of promises—witness the Soviet empire. For many people, hate against truth underlies a restricted range of options: from subservience to slavery to the principle of pleasure-displeasure. This is probably the best psychic ally that conscious or unconscious demagogues as well as any other promise-making people can have. It is not presently possible, due to the sheer lack of statistical studies, to know if the above-mentioned "many people" form a majority of human beings, or if it is just the case of a ruling elite skilled in imposing their own pleasure-ridden interests. Some facts may indicate a few hypotheses: there are fewer violinists than drug addicts, for example, which indicates the existence of a sizeable number of pleasure-ridden people: at least enough to form a lucrative market, or, in a democratic system, to elect authoritarian demagogues.

Truth, like a phoenix, is robust. Sooner or later the perception of reality re-emerges.

> EIGHTEEN YEARS You will be well and truly educated; never able to draw out again. I look like being educated by one of those solidified nightmares on the Ypres Canal.

> EM Long before my times or yours when I crawled in that primeval slime I was a nightmare and did as nightmares do in nightmare land. Then I was taught and learned to call it "only a nightmare".
>
> EIGHTEEN YEARS It took me a hell of a night time to learn I was wide awake.
>
> TWENTY ONE YEARS I nearly learned that Peter Pan had been our Commander in Chief, but sweet peace came and put me to sleep again and taught me it was "only" a dream. P.A. turned up and untaught me it was "only" real. [III: 432]

> SOMITE TWENTY-FOUR You are prejudiced. If I had known I would grow a soul I would have remained a fetus.
>
> TWENTY-FIVE YEARS If I had known I had such an ugly somitic ancestor I would not have tried to cultivate a soul. [III: 461]

The charismatic entrepreneur, or chief demagogue, or messianic leader may be dead; human forgetfulness and the need to "reinvent the wheel" completes the drama, which, based on the human capacity to hallucinate, may be seen either as a farce or as a comedy—that of the everlasting human error, based on the lack of capacity to learn from experience. Bion dwells on the hallucinosis of the superiority of un-learning *vis-à-vis* learning (or Minus K: Bion, 1962; review in Sandler, 2005).

Lack of charisma makes a profound difference; charisma is not heritable. Disciples, apostles, followers, or anyone else who tries to profit from or continue the farce or comedy, are fated to act as stretcher-bearers: lie is a product which demands constant repair. We may say that the charismatic leaders compose a first generation; the stretcher-bearers compose the following generations. Careerists, flatterers, disoriented people who need to earn a living are conditionally admitted to the "ship", provided that they are endowed with a good enough psychopathic nucleus in their personalities. Bion commented on the issue in *Attention and Interpretation*, with the aid of a model drawn from the New Testament: the story of James and John and their request to Jesus for status (Bion, 1970, p. 113).

As soon as real psychoanalysis begins to emerge in any group we might consider, the stretcher-bearers race towards another promise-maker—and have done so since Freud. He had observed the same phenomenon in the clinical setting: people sought him out for analysis, and as soon as they smelled it or, in the best cases, obtained it, they would refuse to carry on. Conversely, when Freud still had not achieved psychoanalysis, his acceptance by Vienna's medical establishment was increasingly warranted.

Some of the stretcher-bearers, in trying to adapt to the "new times", advocate "modernisation" through transplanting or implanting reasoning or, at best, models stemming from extraneous fields or disciplines. Laxity in one's own analytic education, the unavoidable outcome of popularisation by banality, has another unavoidable consequence: many of the self-styled "admirers" abandon ship when realising the impossible nature of the promises. A great many members of this group display the true face of enthusiastic admiration, passing almost instantaneously to undisguised hate and attack: from idolatry to iconoclasm. Their claims are old wine in new bottles: "Now a better leader, who really knows it all, will replace the earlier one". The cycle is renewed:

> promises of a better life → unfulfilled aspirations → rejection and attack → attraction of new promises (actually just the old pledges in new guises) → (*ad infinitum*).

Real psychoanalysis is duly abhorred—both by the people who make the pledges and by those who find themselves revolting against the unfulfilled pledges. With his characteristic humour, Bion illustrated the issue with a fable in *Attention and Interpretation*. This may be seen as a prototype of one of the basic strains that flow through the whole Trilogy:

> The liars showed courage and resolution in their opposition to the scientists, who with their pernicious doctrines bid fair to strip every shred of self-deception from their dupes, leaving them without any of the natural protection necessary for the preservation of their mental health against the impact of truth. Some, knowing full well the risks that they ran, nevertheless laid down their lives in affirmations of lies so that the weak and doubtful would be convinced by the ardour of their conviction of the truth of even the most preposterous statements. It is not too much to say that the human race owes its salvation to that small band of gifted liars who were prepared even in the face of indubitable facts to maintain the truth of their falsehoods. Even death was denied and the most ingenious arguments were

> educed to support obviously ridiculous statements that the dead lived on in bliss. These martyrs to untruth were often of humble origin whose very names have perished. But for them and the witness borne by their obvious sincerity the sanity of the race must have perished under the load placed on it. By laying down their lives they carry the morals of the world on their shoulders. Their lives and the lives of their followers were devoted to the elaboration of systems of great intricacy and beauty in which the logical structure was preserved by the exercise of a powerful intellect and faultless reasoning. By contrast, the feeble processes by which the scientists again and again attempted to support their hypotheses made it easy for the liars to show the hollowness of the pretensions of the upstarts and thus to delay, if not to prevent, the spread of doctrines whose effect could only have been to induce a sense of helplessness and unimportance in the liars and their beneficiaries. [Bion, 1970, pp. 100–101]

One more prone to studying the history of philosophy or literature—something that may be useful, but not indispensable to the practising psychoanalyst—may notice that Bion wrote this at the climax of the popularity of so-called "post-modernism", dictated by fashion. This researcher may confirm, after a careful perusal of Bion's personal library[5] that Bion was not informed about this "old wine in new bottles", but he was deeply aware, *ad nauseam*, of its ever-present influence. As a telling example of the truth-hater called "the terrorist" knows, just a few people may promote a destructive acting out that immobilises a whole society. On the other hand, any attempt to pursue truth is "conveniently" put aside—a hallmark of humankind, until now. Expanding and paraphrasing Bion's observation that "the mind […] is too heavy a load for the sensuous beast to carry" (I: 38), one may say that "truth is too heavy a load for rationalisation and explanation to carry".

In the psychoanalytical establishment, despite Freud's early warnings (for example, in "On the History of the Psychoanalytic Movement", 1914), the umbrella of psychoanalysis was doomed to shelter different practices—some of them mutually inconsistent. Seventy years later, an acknowledged psychoanalyst, Robert Wallerstein, tried to deal with the conundrum of "one psychoanalysis or many" (Wallerstein, 1988), echoing earlier commentators worried about analytic training (for example, Limentani, 1974). From an early stage the institutes of psychoanalysis contained two activities, separated by a seminal function—one of them could be performed in the absence of a patient. Before that time, patients were the *raison d'être* of psychoanalysis. Many people found it was more pleasurable to pursue the latter kind of activity. Like armchair driving and armchair cooking, which can be illustrated in colourful books that remove the need to do the real thing, armchair psychoanalysis can be done with no patient present—although it is advisable for an analyst to make use of an armchair in the interests of avoiding unnecessary pain.

Pedagogical activities such as seminars and supervisions, first envisaged and then devised by one of Freud's collaborators, Dr Max Eitingon, relieved analysts of clinical work and were the forerunners of all activities which talk about psychoanalysis as opposed to doing psychoanalysis—the latter requires a patient. They may prove to be more pleasurable to very many people, whether they write them or read them. To attain a metapsychological status, according to Freud's definition, a theory depends on empiricism—in an indirect way, it depends on previous work with patients. Conversely, rational manipulations of symbols that construe explanations of mechanisms clothed in a terminology derived from psychoanalysis do not depend on work with patients, which is usually described as "arduous", "hard" and "solitary" by the proponents of this kind of armchair activity.

There is a risk that the psychoanalytic formulations will be transformed into a game of symbols, which belongs to the realm of politics and propaganda—activities dedicated to impressing or dictating conclusions to suitable audiences (Bion, 1965, p. 37). There is a profit, controversial in ethical terms, from the fact that psychoanalysis is done though words and phrases. Psychoanalysis needs verbal *spoken* media as a built-in feature, necessary but not sufficient, because it is a living intercourse maintained between *two* human beings. Dr John Rickman aptly regarded psychoanalysis as a "two-body psychology" (Rickman, 1950). It cannot be a coincidence that Rickman was Bion's first real analyst. Their mutual collaboration began with an analytical contact; it was later both elevated and subdued to the level of a personal friendship.

Supervision and writing up a clinical case: ways to get a mature psychoanalyst?

It is possible to argue that the activity proposed in the second half of the 20th century—until now reserved for teaching—of observing babies, or the mother and baby relationship, could furnish an alternative to this. Its basic condition establishes what is amenable to be observed and eventual conclusions drawn from it. Is this activity to do with what really happens in the interaction between mothers and babies? Or would it just be the case of an observer who is observing a baby and a mother interacting when both baby and mother are the object of observation by a third party? The natural (biological) setting is that of a two-body condition: mother and baby. "Observation of babies" introduces a fundamentally changed state of affairs: one must attempt to deal with a three-body situation. The intimate links possible in two-body situations are irremediably changed in circumstances when another person, the observer, is physically present. Intimate two-body situations, like a sexual relationship, for example, differ from a *ménage à trois.*

Epistemological considerations may help. It is widely acknowledged that the activity of writing up a case is influenced both by the previous theories entertained by the writer and by his or her psychological state. Nevertheless, it is still not recognised by the psychoanalytical teaching establishment that advocates "observation of babies" that the presence of the observer interferes with the object observed and therefore the results obtained. Is there any realistic basis to the renewed protests of positivistic neutrality when one assumes, as a postulate, that there is such a thing as "observation of mothers and babies"? It may be one of the ironies of psychoanalytic history, paraphrasing Deutscher (1966), that avowals of positivist neutrality are occurring, unobserved, in a realm—psychoanalysis—that emerged as one of the two most powerful refutations of the positivistic posture, together with modern physics (Sandler, 1997).

The same situation had already occurred with the invariably flawed attempts to reproduce analytic situations in order to control the analytic situation. The three-body situation may be a manifestation of a syndromic mental triad described by Bion in 1957: the constant conjunction of curiosity, arrogance and stupidity.[6] Members of the psychoanalytic movement became *curious* due to multifarious factors, such as fear of the unknown, fear of personal responsibility and free will, and an unbridled and underdeveloped infantile sexual curiosity that could not transform itself into curiosity about oneself. They became *arrogant* due to the delusional idea that an inner superiority would allow one to impose one's desire on all other people, things and events, above all, on the unknown. The arrogant model is furnished by Oedipus, who wished to know what he could never know: how, when and why he was born. Finally, they became *stupid* or dominated by lack of thinking, as a result of a forced projective identification of their own mind, personality and thought into outside persons, events or things—and a mixture of all these.

Might the triad of curiosity, arrogance and stupidity (Sandler, 2011) be the begetter of the first attempts to record analytic sessions? My medical training told me that often—too often?—the anxiety that encircles those who deal with death is linked to a quasi-maniacal, pseudo-humorous discussion of cases between colleagues. Making the best of a bad job, analysts since Freud have written about what their memory told them was supposedly said during the analytic session.

The supervision provoked a kind of strife in the fumbling psychoanalytic movement. Soon some people were writing about a session while it was still going on, despite Freud's strong warnings against this (Freud, 1912b, p. 113). Some advocated that the writing up of analytic sessions destined for supervision should be done immediately after the session, as an attempt to conserve what they regarded as the "freshness" of memory—openly contradicting, out of little learning, or displaying distrust of, the existence of free associations, a cornerstone of psychoanalysis (Sandler, 2013, p. 89). Some advocated that the patient should not know about it. Others countered with the opinion that the patient should (or must) have full knowledge of what is written about him or using his proprietary data. The arrival of technological novelties exerted initial fascination to the point of creating another fashionable market. The advent of magnetic tape recorders led to their swift introduction into analytic sessions. In the 1950s, to be modern and up-to-date meant buying those contraptions, advertised with the seductive propaganda that people could make their own "recordings".

Propaganda profits from the eternal desire and phantasies of people who feel that they already know what is in reality unknown; it also profits from a lack of common sense. The machines were able to make a rough reproduction of the human voice—which is accessible to just one sense—but were advertised as being able to record feelings, affects and emotions. Psychoanalysis was very marketable at that time, so psychoanalysts could gather money to buy many things, including the novel "tape recorder", an industrial product and name destined for oblivion in a wholly electronic age.

Very soon more complicated problems emerged, again accompanied by byzantine discussions. Was it better to tell the patients about the presence of the machine or not? Some professionals, duly labelled by the psychoanalytic institutions as "psychoanalysts", displayed their lying proclivities by trying to disguise the tape recorders. Some of them were unsuccessful (in lying) and were "betrayed" by the machine, whose tape stubbornly ran out before time, or suffered some mechanical or electrical malfunction, creating a scene which would be better placed in a comic film. In the 1960s, the use of tape recorders declined as the gadget market received a push with video recording. Someone started using rooms with one-way screens or mirrors: for example, a police officer interrogating a criminal could now be observed by "invisible" people behind a one-way mirror. To the most perceptive, it was clear that feelings of persecution were rampant. Supervised group dynamics, psychiatric courses and psychological schools were enthusiastic followers of this "modern" technique, where the policeman was replaced by psychological or psychiatric students and a professor. At the beginning of the new millennium, it is retreating back to police departments: a place where its finality, imbued with explicit persecution, is clearer.

"Early Bion" (1950–57; as contrasted to "Late Bion") tried to furnish clinical data according to the traditional rules, with descriptions in the form "The patient said ..." and "The analyst said ...". This changed from 1963 onwards, when he was trying to adopt a method—The Grid—of verifying the truth value of statements made in the analytic session by both patient and analyst.

> I cannot do justice to the episode because I remember only the general impression and the general impression depending on changes of tone expressing depression, fear, anxiety, confidentiality, and others, was itself intended to give a general impression. The short report is verbally nearly correct; yet as I read it again I see it is a misleading record of the experience. I shall therefore make another attempt to describe this fragment of the session but without attempting verbal exactitude. [Bion, 1965, p. 20]

This was superseded by a more humorous version in the Trilogy:

> BION Once I used to make notes on the session in conformity with my training. I was aware of feeling guilt and anxiety if I had no records to support any argument with myself or my colleagues, or

> real or imaginary accusers. As I became more accustomed to and more familiar with the way I worked, I realised it would be agreeable if I could indulge in the truth (I was, of course, convinced that I always had. I would have been indignant at any accusation that I had not always been the soul of integrity. Even as I realise this, I appreciate that this very account is embellished with certain artistically exaggerated locutions intended to add, in a famous phrase, "verisimilitude to an otherwise bald and unconvincing narrative"). This discovery appeared to emerge over a period of time. The awareness of the discovery varied in intensity—ebbed and flowed. The "notes" I made, the "records" of sessions, turned out to be useful in a way that I did not expect. As a sample I give this imaginary entry:
>
>> Nov, (date) My God, my God!
>> Nov, (date) !!!
>> Nov, (date)
>> Nov, (date) been with her brother!! At last
>> Nov, (date) must (illegible)
>> In so far as the patient's name was correct, the entry could be called evocative.
>
> MYCROFT HOLMES (*yawning somewhat ostentatiously*) Most interesting. [I: 89–90]

Perhaps a biological analogy may help in the conundrum created by the attempts to write up clinical cases and, later, by the so-called observation of babies. What if one compares them with studies *in vitro*? The writing up of cases could be useful to placate an immediate anxiety of the analyst who cannot use or have trust in his or her own powers of free association—because if an experience is real, it stays in the memory and may be recalled in the serenity provided by a friendly and collaborative conversation with other people, whether more or less experienced. Bion, in one of his very few pedagogic and exhorting papers—"Notes on Memory and Desire" (1976b)—dwells on this state of mind. Probably the relative lack of useful practical application that still encircles both practices could be dealt with if the researcher could consider this difference. His or her hypotheses and eventual conclusions could encircle two settings: the former (writing up a case) would serve as a psychoanalytical exercise, like scales for a music student; the latter (observation of babies) could provide some conclusions regarding a maternal couple subjected to observation by a third party. Wild and hasty conclusions and generalisations would be avoided, and the outcome could be something useful in everyday practice with patients. They may be useful for the formation of hypotheses that can be empirically verifiable in the here and now of a real analysis—between patient and analyst: the one and only empirical basis of psychoanalysis, which allows, as Freud indicated in "Constructions in Analysis" (1937b), the testing of hypotheses.

The Trilogy has as an implicit bedrock the observation that some so-called developments in psychoanalysis were not such; their insertion into the psychoanalytic movement produced just more fashionable folklore, resulting in the decay of the very movement.

There are few written works which have a dialogical ethos. In a certain sense, the reader may "talk to them"; conversely, they may "talk to the reader". Sometimes this has fringe benefits—like mystery stories, *romans à clef*, etc.—and sometimes it has none—here, Freud's and Bion's written contributions stand out. The qualification "few" takes into account an arbitrary parameter. It is possible to state that these works are few *vis-à-vis* the immeasurable mass of published media. Paradoxically, there has been no shortage of them through the centuries. In a certain sense, they are made alive by a good enough reader, who is alive. Examples of this kind of literature can be found, for example, in the works of Plato, Pascal, Dante, Shakespeare, Diderot, Goethe and Machado de Assis. The written work is constructed out of words with plenty of counterparts in the realm of reality. Briefly, the words and phrases used to construct the work attain the status of symbols.

In due time, these works allowed the construction of another kind of work. These were—and still are—built with words derived, though imitation, from psychoanalytic ideas and concepts. They resorted to jargon and are fated to be devoid of sense. They are full of disordered and authoritarian meanings; the concepts have lost their conceptual power. Lacking analytically trained intuition, they have extinguished the original meaning. As the terminology decayed in its symbolic sense, it acquired a new quality: it could turn what was dynamic into something static: an attribute of death itself. Bion called this quality a "reversion of perspective" (Bion, 1963; Sandler, 2005).

This process transforms what was in the original writings a symbolic text into an "unsymbolic pseudo-symbol" amenable to be apprehended just in its concrete form. The ratio signifier/signified is distorted, with the signifier becoming supercharged at the expense of the signified. This distortion may be illustrated in the material realm by the use of steroids, which furnish muscular strength but damage other parts of the body, such as the liver and kidneys. Through rhetoric—one of the many fountains from which delusion springs—the signifier grows at the expense of the signified, when people selectively emphasise those parts of the real concept that suit their argument and ignore anything that does not. The semantic field generated by this kind of wording and phraseology is apparently powerful. The latter loses its "truth value". A pseudo-meaning obtrudes in the construed nothingness made from psychobabble, jargon and erudite slang uttered by the secular showman—the expert who discovered the socio-political and commercial value of displaying his theoretical learning in a simplified, palatable form. The expert so enabled gives the onlooker a pseudo-command of the issue, as a hallucinated cover for the same onlooker's persisting little learning. In psychoanalysis, it became a fact that some professionals spend their time giving courses and supervisions, instead of analysing people.

Adelheid Koch, a physician, was the first training analyst in Brazil. She was analysed by Otto Fenichel, who briefly won world–wide fame, mainly due to his book, *The Psychoanalytic Theory of Neurosis* (1946). Being a prolific writer, he saw very few patients.[7] Dr Koch thought in terms of two categories of analysts, the "couch-analysts" and the "writer-analysts". Usually restrained and never outspoken, she showed undisguised preference for the former; having been analysed by a "writer-analyst", her view reflected her experience. This does not mean that all writer-analysts lack the "clinical eye"—for example, Hanna Segal, Paula Heimann and Betty Joseph did not. Dr Koch's idea meant that demands on candidates or analysts to write up cases could be the object of second thoughts: oral tradition, fortunately, continues as the royal road to psychoanalytic learning and transmission—a development of a long history in which Socrates and Isaac Luria stand out. The gift of being able to write clinical cases in a meaningful and lasting way is, like any gift, comparatively rare, and does not necessarily accompany psychoanalytically trained intuition.

Erudition is usually regarded with high appreciation in many fields; perhaps philosophy furnishes the best example of it. According to Popper, there are two criteria that must be met to prove that a scientific theory is good: (i) the same conclusion must be reached by different scientific researchers working in the same conditions; and (ii) later researchers must be able to prove it false. The criteria were known as the reproducibility and falsifiability of scientific data. Even though he was an adamant defender of empirical observation and sided with Humean proofs of validation (Hempel, 1962, 1966; Ruben, 1993), his criteria of scientific validity were well received and met with no criticism. The concepts of hard science and pseudo-science stemmed from him. The criteria of reproducibility established that observers all around the world, dealing with the same subject of study and working in equal conditions, should reach identical results. Falsifiability is a criterion which fired the imagination of some philosophers, especially those from the post-modernist movement. It had deep reflections in the psychoanalytic movement. It was also applauded by many exponents of academic, established science. At that time psychopathy was not known in the scientific field; the exposure of years of false results coming from false researchers deeply compromised with large sums of sponsoring money was left for the future. Those researchers fully met academic conditions, fuelled by large universities and pharmaceutical laboratories as well as other technological enterprises which tried to profit from genetic research.

Professor Popper was not a scientist, but a serious epistemologist. So he did not have the backing of practical, empirical field work; he was more an observer of the everlasting fire than a willing researcher who might burn himself in experimental fire. His theory of scientific knowledge was born from his mind and constructed with selected pieces of the history of science indistinguishable from the process of splitting. It was therefore a judgmental, plausible, rational mythology rather than a construct inspired by observation of scientific facts.

The outcome of Popper's two criteria was the denial of approximations to transcendent truth; the denial of the staying power of scientific facts; and the denial of the very existence of truth. Leon Trotsky's and Mao Zedong's idea of "permanent revolution" found an unsuspecting field to install itself, leaving no stone to erect anything durable. Nevertheless, examples of real science—for example, the discovery and formulation of physical facts such as the wheel, or the illumination of the relationships between mass and energy, or the selection of species, or the Oedipus complex in the human race—as soon as they were discovered, *did* acquire the transcendent power of "staying".

The evolution from the primitive sections of logs to pneumatics or to wheel bearings was a technological one: different and more sophisticated transformations with no change in the invariant "wheel", which can be described by geometrical formulations of Euclidean mathematics. In the psychoanalytic realm, there occurred a still more destructive aftermath of the fascination with "progress in science" which revolutionised and replaced previous knowledge. Due to the obtrusion of non-medical practitioners, deeply enthused with literature, it sufficed to invent "new" theories with "new" names, but with no empirical bearing. Presto: a new, better psychoanalysis was made. Progress with no verification and no hard work, within reach of anyone—a fact pointed out by many, such as Peter Fonagy (2000), a training psychoanalyst who cannot be accused of being a "Kleinian" or "Bionian".

Unlike his early colleagues, who formed the neo-positivist or logical positivist movement, and like the post-modernists—a fact noticed by Professor Adorno and other luminaries from what came to be known as the "Frankfurt school of philosophy"—Professor Popper agreed that the "everlasting fire", or transcendent truth, did not exist.

The neo-positivist movement had nothing to do with Comte's positivism, owing its rather confusing name to the fact that it was born at a time of rebellious revolutions. Due to this factor, it was marked by a specific *Zeitgeist*. It is true that both valued empirical verification, but in this, no science undervalues it. Neo-positivism was practised by the members of the so-called "Vienna Circle". A main representative was Professor Moritz Schlick: in the psychoanalytic movement, Roger Money-Kyrle went to Vienna in order to learn from him. Schlick was assassinated by another former student, Johann Nelböck, a Nazi fanatic. Nelböck shot his professor on the stairs at the University of Vienna, amidst confused accusations of "defilement" in which the criminal mixed the pseudo-cultural Nazi ideology with sexual issues. The most famous member of the neo-positivist movement was Ludwig Wittgenstein; another leading figure was Rudolf Carnap, whose worldly fame was restricted to his lifetime. Popper, Wittgenstein and Carnap migrated to England due to the Hitler phenomenon, although Popper had made a stopover in New Zealand. Karl Popper's probably unwitting *coup de grâce* on the apprehension of truth was increased by his unrecognised heir, Thomas Kuhn, the American philosopher who doubled as historian and science historian. Professor Kuhn did have a real scientific education but did not profit from it. Coinciding with the post-modernist bandwagon, which may have helped him to gain fame, he invented a catchphrase which was instantaneously and uncritically accepted: "paradigm shift", which deprecated the existence of truth and, much more, scientific truth. Popper had public differences which bordered on violence with both Wittgenstein and Kuhn, albeit concerned—at least in appearance—with moral problems, linked to authoritarianism.

Bion used Popper's warning about the pseudo-scientist who looks for *ad hoc* explanations (Popper, 1963); otherwise he was critical of Popper's contributions. His critical mode came from the empirical needs of practical psychoanalysis. A special feature of Bion's criticism was his ability to change his points of view, or better, vertices (his preferred term, justified on page 91 of *Transformations*), an ability born from his clinical posture, deeply embedded in Freud's way.

Freud's ability to change his vertices can be seen in all of his works; to quote just an illustrative example: "Moses and Monotheism" (1939). In using the same "changing vertices" method used by Freud, but made more explicit in *Elements of Psychoanalysis* and *Transformations*, Bion was able to deal, in his next book, *Attention and Interpretation*, with one of Descartes' restrictive and authoritarian sentences, namely, the one about the impossibility of the existence of thoughts without a thinker, well suited to the interests of the Roman Catholic Church. It is not an aurhoritative observation, usually fated to be unpopular and not approved by established institutions. Bion used this phrase in order to investigate its truth value and made a complementary—rather than complimentary—hypothesis: the suggestion of thoughts without a thinker. (Bion, 1967, 1970, 1975; review in Sandler, 1997a, 2005, 2006a).

Notwithstanding the popularity of Popper's reductionist statements, it is possible to use another vertex, furnished by real psychoanalytic clinical practice, to verify the famous philosopher of science's notion of the reproducibility of a scientific event. This is not to denounce Popper's statement as wholly false, but just to point out its built-in one-sidedness—perhaps unavoidable when one deals just with philosophy of science and not science-in-itself. Let us put it into a historically familiar perspective which allows for a paradox *vis-à-vis* Popper's view:

1. A scientific discovery is made by more than one person.
2. The "second" discoverer has not met, and has not heard about the discoveries of, the "first".[8]
3. Both were using *different* methods of research, so if their results are in agreement, this fact would substantiate even more the truth discovered.

For this reason, it would be useful to take care with the term "invention", which would be more appropriately used to describe the situation observed by Francis Bacon as the flights of imaginative fantasy. The reader could consider the hypothesis of replacing it in the scientific and artistic realms with "discovery". This statement has similarities with what Freud once said in a letter to Fliess, comparing himself to Marco Polo rather than to the "scientists" of his day, who were wholly submitted to positivism. A rather flawed paradigm which, like any paradigm, is condemned to be seriously flawed. In the best cases its slight fault is due to its restrictive vertex, as for example in Newton's laws of gravity; in the worst cases it is simply wrong—and murderous to knowledge—due to its simplistic cause-effect relationships. As far as this writer's research has found, Darwin, Freud and Einstein were the first "modern" researchers in practical science to notice the faults of positivism, and contributed to the real advancement of science in overtaking it (Sandler, 1997).

Let us consider the work of Professors Alfred North Whitehead and Ernst Gombrich, two of the most renowned researchers in mathematics, the most developed theoretical science, and art, respectively. They probably never met each other—thus conferring real truth, or authoritative value to their statements, rather than an authoritarian paradigm imposed by politically or economically achieved popularity. Their statements coincide, even though they were formulated under two different realms. Whitehead and Gombrich observed that individuals use their personal gifts both to create and to manipulate symbols—which, according to Gombrich, are things that mean something other than themselves.

Therefore, symbols and their study, augmented by Saussure's linguistics, admit meanings and interpretations of meanings, usually by an extra-scientific and sometimes anti-scientific activity called hermeneutics. This writer has found it useful to distinguish meanings from (vector) senses conveyed by symbols—senses and directions are amenable to be studied by science. In artistic endeavours, this marks the difference between a real artist, as observed by Michelangelo, who looks for something that is already there, and the "installer", one who makes skilled propaganda intended to impose or insert previously achieved meanings into the hearts or minds of others.

In adjoining to Whitehead's and Gombrich's discoveries those coming from early structuralism as practised by Lévi-Strauss from the 1930s to the 1950s, we may resort to his observation of a primitive phenomenon which he called *bricolage*—akin to Freud's discovery of free associations as practised in a social setting (Lévi-Strauss, 1955). In this situation, we may state that when a good enough lack of conscious manipulation exists, the signifier/signified ratio is conducive to the prevalence of neither.

Human life and emotional truth do not submit to the limitations of the Positivist religion's rules, drawn up by Auguste Comte. It is impervious to Cartesian beliefs such as the idea of cause and effect, as well as to ideas of locating events in a given "space"—which is just another deluded idea, when space is regarded as an absolute entity, independent of time—probably a most remarkable error of Kant's (Sandler, 2001). The feebleness that characterises the human condition is one of the factors in the wide acceptance of such belief. There are some individuals, whose appearance is constantly conjoined with due historical (time and space) opportunity, who warn their contemporaries about this flawed belief; but this constant conjunction is rare. Those individuals are usually called geniuses, a name adopted by Freud; Bion called them mystics.

Clothing verbal descriptions in psychoanalytic terms produces a travestied psychoanalysis, plausible to anyone who is restricted to rational, conscious thinking and could not submit him- or herself to real psychoanalysis. It is derived from real psychoanalysis and constitutes a debasement of it. Taking into account that some lies may serve as a path towards truth, in some people who already benefit from a good enough concern for truth and regard for life as it is, the travestied psychoanalysis may function as a negative "lie-stimulus" towards the eventual achievement of real psychoanalysis. This outcome always depends on the "facilitating environment" studied by Searles, Balint and Winnicott.

Nomothetic: two, rather than twin activities

I propose for purposes of nomenclature to provisionally name two activities and consequently two fields of research: on the one hand, an "Archaeology of Psychonalysis", using Nietzsche's suggestion in order to construe a historiography of psychoanalysis-produced ideas and concepts *in vitro*; and on the other hand, borrowing from Bion, "Psychoanalysis Proper" or "Real Psychoanalysis" (1965, p. 160 and II: 307, respectively), which studies *in vitro* psychoanalytic conceptions which can only be experienced *in vivo*. The two are related, not because of their sharing the term "psychoanalysis" but because they both belong to the activity of *talking about*—in this case, about psychoanalysis.

With this nomological discrimination, a Nietzschean psychoanalytic archaeology could be useful to the extent that it may contribute to illuminating the denotation of principles which may resemble laws of biological nature—which are not logically necessary, but just are so. The archaeology could be used as a compass for anyone who might need to talk about psychoanalysis.

Moreover, in performing this denotation (or notation) of principles, it may be possible to relate them, and from those relations may ensue the apprehension of increasingly complex interrelations that can be called syndromic.

It was just this activity that formed Aristotle's "metaphysics"—the group of interrelated principles which came after his studies of applied or practical physics. They allowed him—and others—to think about physics. In due time "metaphysics" allowed the development of practice in physics: a feed-back retro-alimentation between speculation about practice and practice itself. Speculation comes from the Latin term *speculum*, mirror; in Greek, theory, something that mirrors or corresponds to reality as it is.

Centuries later, Freud, inspired by both Plato and Aristotle, took a non-warring, non-partisan posture, integrating some of those two thinkers' valid findings. He proposed a "metapsychology"—that which comes after psychology. We know that Freud equated psychoanalysis to psychology—an equation still disputed by academic psychologists who abhor the realm of the unconscious and prefer to impose an exclusive dedication to the more restricted area of consciousness.

People endeavouring to venture into a Nietzschean Archaeology of Psychoanalysis are not exempted from undergoing a real analysis—before, during and after having attempted to perform this activity. Clinical experience of psychoanalysis over almost four decades, which included an attempt to analyse professional philosophers and physicists, allows this writer to state this fact. This experience showed that the gates to apprehension of real psychoanalysis are opened only in this condition.

There is a shared observation from practising psychoanalysts all over the world of the increasing number of philosophers and epistemologists who look for analysis, constantly conjoined with an initial interest in an "Archaeology of Psychoanalysis". There is no need to be initially oriented by a knowledge of Nietzsche—some of them used Pierce and other "pragmatists". After all, outside the realm inhabited by authoritarian dictators, truth, like oxygen, recognises no owner and cannot be the property of anyone—ever. Truth *is*, quite independent of its possible discover.

The same case occurs if one states that an Anatomist is not a Surgeon even though Surgeons have basic training in anatomy. A given Archaeologist or Historian never talked to Akhenaten—even if they may use metaphors like split stones "talking" to the archaeologist's trained "ears". The reconstruction of Tyrannosaurus Rex skeletons by scholars proved to be flawed—an error that persisted for more than a century.

Freud once compared psychoanalysis to archaeology, but the analogy was lost and a concrete apprehension of the statement gained the upper hand in most quarters. One of the consequences of this is the incitement of outraged reactions when one states that a real psychoanalyst can say nothing apart from imaginative hypotheses about a given patient's mother's or father's behaviour and state of mind—for more often than not the analyst does not know personally the parents or relatives of his or her patient and obviously cannot observe the patient's past.

In this sense, the Archaeology of psychoanalytical ideas is prone to vulgarisation and banality; the scientific activity of psychoanalysis proper is less prone to this kind of debasement. It is not easy to popularise scientific observation. Consequently, it is less prone to following the route of banality. There are exceptions, which occur in the achievement of scientific technology involved in many industries which function under the high finance (money) vertex. They cover a broad range, from the less sophisticated, like the serial production of addictive, illegal psychotropic drugs, to more developed ones, such as automotive production, up to the fabrication of nuclear weaponry. They became banal, first in Latin America, then in Asia.

Jargonese: the aftermath of a banal mixture

L'homme n'est rien, l'oeuvre tout.

Gustave Flaubert, letter to George Sand, 1875

P.A. Allow me to conduct you round the cages of my psychoanalytic zoo. Of course the names are somewhat forbidding, but the creatures themselves are beautiful and ugly. Ah! Here is Absolute Truth—a most ferocious animal which has killed more innocent white lies and black wholes than you would think possible.

ROLAND You muddle it with your puns.

ROBIN Call it paronomasia—more scientific.

ALICE It sounds like a very attractive flower.

P.A. Only a flower of speech. Throw hither all your quaint enamelled lies that on the green turf suck the honied showers.[9] "Blind mouths", as Ruskin showed you, would have to learn to read.[10]

ALICE I learned to read years ago.

P.A. That is what we all think, but in fact the greatest thinkers are very difficult to read unless you find great readers to read them.

ALICE But I was a *great* reader as a child.

P.A. You may have been—but now you are a grown-up and have an enormous amount of knowledge—or is it bilge?—to fall back on.

ROLAND Please don't insult my wife.

ROBIN He was only referring to Longfellow's poem. You will make him so nervous he won't dare to say anything.[11]

ROLAND Good job too.

P.A. I had no intention of monopolising, but I certainly think that as one falls silent someone else who may know even less will occupy the vacant space.

ALICE "The anarchs of the world of darkness keep a throne for thee"[12] and then no one will be able to fill the vacant space.

P.A. For fear of the turmoil—the turbulence that obeys no man-made "laws of nature". Far worse than any zoo. We were just coming to the twins, Absolute Space and Absolute Time.

ALICE They sound perfect pets.

P.A. They do; but if I were really showing you round my psycho-analytic zoo I would warn you not to get *too* near the cage because

> these long names—especially when you read them in broad daylight—give you no idea of the meaning—
>
> ROBIN The meaning often seems the worst part.
>
> P.A. It depends so much on what the "facts" cover up. They are not so misleading as the scientific language, but Absolute Space can terrify even robust minds like Pascal. Conversely, a harmless personality—indistinguishable from Descartes—finds a key like Cartesian Co-ordinates, and Euclidean space is exposed.
>
> ROBIN And decent people like me cannot even think of the roars of cosines and the bellowing of tangents and the whistling of borogroves— [II: 239–40]

> ROBIN You were going to talk about mathematics as potentially affording a precise and short method of communication.
>
> P.A. You remember we talked before of the way in which Cartesian Co-ordinates proved to be a key that released Euclidean geometry from the tyranny of visual imagery. [II: 250]

Before Lobachevsky and Riemann it was assumed that formal logic was the only form of thinking—an idea that endured for some centuries. A thinking person was equated to a chess player. In this sense, chess players would be the model of mental health. Bion reminds us, in a transdisciplinary approach, that algebraic calculus disentangled the whole field of geometry from its former prison, namely, the sensuously based representations contrived mainly by Euclid. In any case, both mathematical methods were based on Euclidean formal logic. This does not mean that Lobachevsky or Riemann were "anti-Euclidean", or that Freud was "anti-rationalist"; they demonstrated the limits of applying formal logic or rationalisation in mathematics and psychic functioning, respectively. Bion's illustration is just a *model,* rather than a piece of advice. Bion's import of the Kantian concept of models to psychoanalysis was made in *Learning from Experience* and *Elements of Psychoanalysis;* a complete review appears in *The Language of Bion* (Sandler, 2005).

The fact that continuous progress in mathematics took centuries to occur could be used by members of the psychoanalytical establishment in a hurry to find new theories. The study of the *history* of mathematics and of the *philosophy* of mathematics (which could be called "metamathematics"), rather than the study of mathematics-in-itself, may be useful to those hurried professionals. Therefore, study of what is currently called the history of the theory of numbers displays how the existence of (for want of a better name) "negative", "infinite", "irrational" and "imaginary" numbers was discovered. "Negative numbers" were added to "natural", "positive" numbers, which also included the "rational" numbers—that is, numbers which allow the operator to extract roots: in arithmetical notation, ½, ¼, etc. The name "natural" is misleading, but tradition must be respected when a name sticks and finds generalised use. To change it would just increase confusion.

The expansion did not end with the discovery of the possibility to operate with negative numbers—something that really expanded mathematical operations on what could not be *concretely seen*. As Bion notices in *Learning from Experience, Elements of Psychoanalysis* and *Transformations*, in the light of observing patients with disturbances of thinking processes, from this time on, mathematicians were able to deal with (mathematical) objects (defined by Aristotle) with no need for their concrete presence. Later, "rational" numbers were expanded with "infinite" and "irrational" numbers; the former were made when mathematicians tried to calculate what was happening with the circumference of the circle and discovered the necessity to make *approximations* to the number 3.14159 … or π. Approximations to the infinite are important to psychoanalysts willing to undertake explorations into the unconscious. It is possible to state, in the light of the history of mathematics, that psychoanalysis occupies a place that mathematics occupied at the time of Euclid.

"Imaginary" numbers—another unfortunate name that has stuck—made it feasible to extract square roots from negative numbers. It required courage to challenge the establishment of mathematicians at that time. The same courage was needed by those who challenged or criticised the limits imposed by Euclidean geometry and formal logic, to discover—rather than to invent—the possibility of a non-Euclidean geometry. The consideration of probability calculus, the emergence with Brouwer's work of the Intuitionists, Russell's and Whitehead's paradoxes, Gödel's theorems, and da Costa's paraconsistent logic which goes beyond Euclidean logic, all displayed failures in the idea of absoluteness in all fields of knowledge, including thought processes. The development of the epistemology of mathematics, or how mathematics could contribute to the theory and practice of knowledge and its possible transdisciplinarity with psychoanalysis (or usefulness to psychoanalysts) are explained and expanded elsewhere (Sandler, 1997).

The Intuitionists thought that mathematics is based on special intuitions which demand first and foremost a definite rejection of the Euclidean law of the excluded middle. They challenged the then dominant schools of mathematical thought, Formalism and Logic.

> Sequential thought "stretched out" what it purports to describe. But may it not be a peculiarity of thought, of the deductive system which has become detached and confused with the reality that approximates it? If so, it could be an illusion like some foreign, alien object not really part of the thing-in-itself, the noumenon. [I: 85]

Mathematical Intuitionism observed that there are self-evident truths which may be intuited; those are the real foundations of human knowledge. Like psychoanalysis since Freud, they observed a kind of "force"—in psychoanalysis named instinct, or in the German language, *Trieb*—awareness of which can be obtained neither though deduction, as Kant warned, nor through induction, as Hume warned.

> ROBIN You are as bad as the Intuitionist mathematicians who seem to disparage logic.
>
> P.A. The Intuitionists would say that logical and intuitionist mathematics can exist happily with one another provided the logicians admit the reality of another approach. Quantum mechanicians do not deny the existence of wave motion. [III: 553–4]

Bion resorted to this unpopular school of mathematical thinking: Brouwer's Intuitionism, which he elevated as a new analogical model for psychoanalysis as regards approximations to truth. Its main aspect is the rejection of the Euclidean law of the excluded middle. He observed that human attempts to pursue "truth-O", as he first called it in *Attention and Interpretation*, are seemingly inevitably accompanied by a proportional counter-movement: human attempts to move away from "truth-O". This feature of the still fumbling human mind was expanded by Freud in much of his work—for example, "Studies on Hysteria" (1895b), "The Interpretation of Dreams" (1900), "Totem and Taboo" (1913), "Moses and Monotheism" (1939) and "An Outline of Psychoanalysis" (1940). Through a more detailed examination of the biblical prohibition on knowledge, Thorner (1981) also added to Bion's expansions of Freud concerning moving away from "truth-O".

Bion's appeal to the philosophy of mathematics—rather than to mathematics itself—was not apprehended by some of his readers. The misapprehension was disguised as "understanding" of his work, originating from a concrete approach whose appearance mixed with idolisation and its opposite, iconoclasm. "Understanding" means a mental attitude contrary to the psychoanalytic posture, as was illuminated by Bion in 1967, in "Notes on Memory and Desire"—which also warned about the deleterious effects on psychoanalytical practical work when an undisciplined use of understanding was rampant. To understand precludes the use of models and analogies.

This kind of understanding was counteracted by statements against the "mathematisation" of psychoanalysis. As an example of this, one may quote a renowned foreign analyst visiting a South American psychoanalytical society. He told a public supervision group that "mathematising" psychoanalysis was "one of Bion's many errors".[13] When this comment was translated for the supervisee, a senior member of the local society whose admiration for Bion bordered on fanaticism, the atmosphere became tense. The supervisee dismissed the comment, saying that he had said nothing to do with mathematics. He accused the supervisor of not having understood what he had said, claiming that he had understood everything the supervisor had said. Completely disregarding the complaint, the supervisor quoted *Transformations*, claiming that "Bion used Poincaré and the infinitesimal numbers in order to catch what was going on in the session" in order to prove his thesis, and finished with a self-eulogy: "When I was a schoolboy, I was keen on mathematics. Bion was wrong to try to adapt Poincaré's infinitesimal numbers to psychoanalysis". A warring group, rather than a working group, was instantaneously formed under the three basic assumptions of fight-flight, messianic leader and pairing. The fight-flight group appeared first, around a disputed messianic leader: a hallucinated "Bion" versus a hallucinated "foreign supervisor". One member of the audience spotted an error in the supervisor's quotation of Poincaré, who, according to him, was quoted by Bion only regarding the concept of the "selected fact". The audience member was right, but his warring and triumphant mood debased his argument, which was immediately followed by comments for and against from many pairs formed in the audience. The chairman, who had previously been analysed by the visiting supervisor and later befriended him, and had been responsible for inviting him, immediately leapt to his defence. Like any group that cannot achieve the level of a working group, this group was divided between two warring parties, "for the supervisor" and "against the supervisor". Pandemonium ensued, with neither side listening to the other. Both parties were unwittingly united in a common, unobserved mistake (in Bion's terms, an invariant), namely, a confusion between the model and the reality that the model purported to illustrate. Observation of the history of psychoanalytical ideas shows that *no* theory is safe from this kind of concretisation, because its apprehension (or lack of it) depends on the onlooker or beholder. It was Bion himself who observed this in the year before he died:

> These primitive elements of thought are difficult to represent by any verbal formulation, because we have to rely on language which was elaborated later for other purposes. When I tried to employ meaningless terms—alpha and beta were typical—I found that "concepts without intuition which are empty and intuitions without concepts which are blind" rapidly became "black holes into which turbulence had seeped and empty concepts flooded with riotous meaning". [II: 229]

One of those in the audience who supported the "anti-foreign supervisor" party felt that "only through the study of Mathematics would analysts be able to deepen their knowledge of psychoanalysis". Disguised as an open posture, his attitude contained an underlying severe restriction indicated by the word "only". He dismissed psychoanalytic training, albeit unconsciously. The same restriction, implying the same kind of exclusivity, was earlier attributed to the obligation to undergo other kinds of training: "only" if one had a literary education, "only" if one was a child analyst, "only" if one had had an analysis with "the famous Dr X" (who could be locally or internationally famous), "only" if one had followed a particular course, etc., could one be considered a psychoanalyst. Freud's observations stemming from his medical training were increasingly dismissed. All of this composed, within the psychoanalytic movement, one of the seemingly infinite variations in the phenomenal realm of the human prohibition of knowledge (Thorner,

1981a), and, like any prohibition coming from above, it betrayed the presence of phantasies of superiority—one of the rules of transformation in hallucinosis (Bion, 1965). The member of that South American psychoanalytical association who felt that only the study of Mathematics could enhance and warrant his alleged "psychoanalytic powers" (his exact words) acted out his wish by embarking on a postgraduate Mathematics course—only to quietly abandon it in a matter of few months. This South American experience may serve as a representative example of the whole psychoanalytic movement as regards unanalysed phantasies of superiority, primitive group politics, shared hallucinosis, and their behavioural (phenomenal) manifestations.

There was a failure to apprehend the philosophy of mathematics used by Bion, leading to a concretised view which led to just mathematics-in-itself. The absolute view, as usual, won popularity, and has remained popular at least up to the present, unavoidably adding other phenomena: concretisation, idolisation and iconoclasm—idolisation in the minus realm. Those factors led to a misapprehension of Bion's contributions and a blindness to his appeal to the *philosophy* of mathematics. As far as this writer has found, the only author fully aware of this was Parthenope Bion Talamo (1996). The difficulties were soon seen by some authors, such as Grotstein (1981) and Matte Blanco (1981). The Trilogy has many passages that unequivocally address this misapprehension, like the following:

> ALICE Hello, Robin. We were just thinking of Cartesian Co-ordinates.
>
> ROBIN Good heavens! I hope you aren't suggesting that I should use those. I would have my farm overrun with co-ordinates—they would grow much faster than the seeds of thought would germinate in my mind.
>
> ALICE Here's the padre. "Thou art the man". Our scientific pagan needs baptism. Let me introduce our latest brain child—Cartesian Co-ordinates—as yet without a literary or religious naming.
>
> TOM They are triplets in fact; the first-born is real and distinct, the second, real and co-incident, and the third, conjugate complex.
>
> ROLAND As initials I would say R. D. for the first.
>
> P.A. R. C. and C. C. for the next two.

PAUL The parents usually tell me what are their wishes. I only commend them to God.

ROLAND Guessing at their dispositions I would expect the first to be a bit obstinate. "I am *not* you," I can almost hear him say as he looks angrily at himself in the mirror.

P.A. "I got here first. This is my place," I hear the second say.

ROLAND And complex conjugate is an intellectual snob, as Man, our aspiring politician, would be sure to say. You can rely on our intellectuals to be wrong—always.

ALICE I think you are being very hard on our brain children. This is a religious christening at which the wicked fairy is being allowed to have the last wish. What characters!

TOM Well, the line cuts the circle in a liberated and highly franchised manner. Uncle Riemann will be delighted.

P.A. And godfather Lobachevsky likewise.

ROLAND And Uncle Tom Cobley too true.

TOM But seriously, Cartesian co-ordinates set geometry free. We were no longer imprisoned—restricted to what we could see.

ALICE Wordsworth talked about the inner eye which was freed by the sight of the daffodils dancing in the breeze. He little knew "what wealth to me" the sight had brought.

ROBIN Or as some wit put it, the chance of another slim volume at three and sixpence.

P.A. He would not become wealthy with three shillings and sixpence today. Eric Gill prayed that England might become poor.

ROBIN He must be a happy man today. Perhaps we are not allowed to be happy in the "blessed Kingdoms of joy and love".

P.A. "So much the rather thou, Celestial light, the mind and all her powers irradiate. There plant eyes; all mist from thence purge and disperse"—

PAUL —"that I may see and tell of things invisible to mortal sight". [II: 224–5]

Most analysts who already are somewhat familiar with Bion's previous work would be reminded of one of Freud's observations, given in a letter to Lou Andreas-Salomé, about blinding himself artificially in order to really see what might be invisible to "mortal sight".

Would it be opportune to re-examine, perhaps more precisely, what those invisible things might be? They belong to the realm of what is *not* a thing. One cannot properly name them—this is what "ineffable" means. Anthropomorphism cannot help, to the extent that it "materialises" and "concretises" what is pure energy which, nevertheless, conveys pure matter. They contribute, like a kind of immaterial "plasma"—single words are deceptive—to the aliveness of everything that must be kept alive. There are some words that reflects indirect expressions of what those "no-things" are: mitochondria, DNA, RNA, anxiety, depression, love, hate, affects, emotions and emotional experiences.

In this dreamy construction, Bion reminds us of the biological bearing—an issue dear to Freud. An allegiance to the biological nature of the instinctual life (and therefore, as a matter of consequence, of the unconscious phantasies) is emphasised in this part of the Trilogy. Even though Karl Abraham's contributions are not explicitly quoted in the Trilogy or in Bion's earlier contributions, it is clear that his medical education and his analysis with Klein allows the hypothesis that Abraham's "embryonic" findings may be seen in this quasi-artistic original formulation. The term "soma" is less saturated with the prejudices of psychosomatics.

No reader would deny that Bion appeals to any means available to him in order to intone the words-without-a-tune that call to be expressed when the issue is to achieve good enough communication of the ineffable unconscious. In the excerpt just quoted, Descartes, Euclid, Lobachevsky, Milton and Wordsworth are hand-in-hand with the part-objects of Wilfred Ruprecht Bion.

It is fair to state that Bion was the first psychoanalyst who drew the attention of the psychoanalytic movement to the knowledge obtained by the Intuitionists. It is also a kind of knowledge, among so many others, that has hitherto been dismissed by the majority of the psychoanalytic movement, who are more interested in fashion: today exemplified by discussions about gender, *in vitro* fertilisation, and so on. Fads in the psychoanalytic movement are the rule. Professionals tend to make chaotic runs chasing fashionable comets whose duration can be equated to that of neutrinos. In Bion's time, "borderline" was the hit; in the late 1960s, psychodrama attracted a number of psychoanalysts; Lacanian and Kohutian analysis competed for the limelight in the late

1970s; the 1980s saw the pseudo-theatrical election of "enactment" as well as pushes towards pre-psychoanalytic, consciously based, positivism-biased "research", in parallel to "neuropsychoanalysis", another newfangled "last word" and an aping of "neuroscience"; women's lib, "intergender", "homoparental family" and transsexuality are taking their places as newfangled leanings in the beginning of "the new millennium"—in itself an arbitrary measurement of time.

A historical detour may be useful. In 1967, Bion—as often occurs with "men of achievement"—was encircled by a complex mix of real friends, idolaters and their counterparts, iconoclasts. It seems that he was not as lucky as Melanie Klein, who could count on collaborators—such as Joan Riviere and Elliott Jaques—who exchanged ideas with her about the content of her writings. They were duly heard: for example, she changed the title of her last book from *Envy* to *Envy and Gratitude*, after Dr Jaques's timely warning. The opposite happened with Bion: he had no one who could tell him, for example, that his book *Transformations* (1965) might well be more properly called *Transformations and Invariants*; or that his paper "On Arrogance" (Bion, 1957b) could be better apprehended if it were called "On Arrogance, Curiosity and Stupidity". Also, his "Notes on Memory and Desire" (1967b) would be better apprehended if the title were "Notes on Memory, Desire and Understanding".

In the latter case, all of his warnings about the need for personal discipline over memory and desire apply to understanding too. When a tendency to "understanding" prevails, both in an individual analyst and in the psychoanalytic movement, there is an embodiment of an anti-analytic or pseudo-analytic posture, expressing hate towards the unknown. As time passed, the term "unconscious" acquired the nature of jargon, and turned into a kind of slang: two vicious habits of language which indicate a lack of thinking. It now has the ethos of a prejudice or postulate: it is felt as a term already understood in the psychoanalytic movement. Thus it requires no further scrutiny. There was a denial and consequent oblivion of the very original meaning of "unconscious". It has become a shibboleth. Nevertheless, as we saw earlier, "unknown" is just a synonym of "unconscious". In the German language used by Freud: *unbewußt*.

The oblivion reached a telling point that can be illustrated by a book written in Portuguese by Frank Philips, a psychoanalyst already mentioned in Volume 1 of this work, in the last years of his life, with the help of collaborators. It was entitled *Psicanálise do Desconhecido* ("Psychoanalysis of the Unknown", 1997), and was made up of selected recordings of his past lectures at the Sociedade Brasileira de Psicanálise de São Paulo. Mr Philips, a multilingual globetrotter, was known as an experienced clinical psychoanalyst, having attended Freud's lectures in Vienna in the 1930s. He participated in the foundation of the SBPSP in 1936, and played an influential part in its local politics. In 1959 he moved to London for analysis with Melanie Klein; two years later she referred him to Dr Bion. He had a seminal role in dealings with Ernest Jones, both in the sending of German expatriates who were the first training analysts and in the recognition of the SBPSP by the IPA in 1951. Eight years later he interrupted his analysis with Bion, and from then on they enjoyed a real friendship which included their families and lasted the rest of their years. He returned to São Paulo in 1968 and resumed his previous political position, with whiffs of commandeering, as the principal analyst who could provide re-analysis to senior members. He chaperoned Bion on his visits to Brazil, acting as his interpreter in conferences. Like Bion, Philips was not spared having flatterers full of reverence (greed and envy displayed in their negative or minus realm) and acerbic critics full of hate (greed and envy displayed in their positive realm—as regards –L and –H, see Sandler, 2011). As distinct from Bion, he was at least partially responsible for stimulating, if subtly, a posture of partisanship among followers and foes, which included phantasies of idolisation around what he saw as "Bion" as well as around himself. He was also said not to have written either papers or books before,[14] but as ever, hearsay is not a reliable source of information. Careful research conducted by this writer (1997b) showed just two papers published abroad: one in English, at the request of Dr James Grotstein, to tell people about his own personal memories of Bion, the man; and one in French, about Imitation and Hallucination, offering original ideas which encompassed a new way to look at identification. The title of his first book—*Psicanálise do Desconhecido* (Psychoanalysis of the Unknown)—was felt as charming by some readers, elitist by others, and containing the re-invention of the wheel by yet others. He made explicit his feelings about the existence of at least two psychoanalyses, one of which he called "classical psychoanalysis" and compared in derisive tones to "true psychoanalysis", unleashing a witch-hunting group situation. In his many public conferences he adopted a partisan posture, stating in pedagogical and political tones a definite preference for the latter. It seems to this writer that he mixed Bion's formulation about the existence of "real psychoanalysis" with judgmental, Manichean values. This posture gained him both adoration and abhorrence—a dark chapter in the history of the Brazilian psychoanalytic movement, completed by external intervention from the International Psychoanalytical Association. He continued with this attitude until his last days; for him, "classical psychoanalysis" merited contempt because it had no regard for the unknown.

Therefore, "classical" acquired a different sense, if compared with the one used in Volume 1 of this work. This is in addition to the sense given to it by Bion himself, in his deep transdisciplinary approach, which includes the study of projective identification and the paranoid and the schizoid aspects pervading immobilisation in the paranoid-schizoid position:

> P.A. The difficulty is not only with the galactic centre. It is as difficult to see the centre of one's own personality. Distracted and fascinated by what is *not* one's self, the periphery is substituted for the centre.
>
> EDMUND You've said this before.
>
> P.A. Have I? I had forgotten.
>
> ROBIN Outer darkness or central darkness—it is the wrong thing in the wrong place. Any sphere whose centre is occupied by some segment of the surface is sure to wobble uncertainly about its "centre".
>
> EDMUND Like eclipsing variables. Nowadays some are beginning to think that the less obtrusive partner in a binary may be a black hole, that there are signs compatible with two black holes.
>
> ALICE Only two—in the whole of the universe of universes? That sounds—
>
> P.A. —like Classical psychoanalysis. Two parents or—according to one of the parents of psychoanalysis—two breasts.
>
> EDMUND Or one proton and one electron. They proliferate masses of offspring all circulating like hadrons round the nucleus or suns about a galactic centre.
>
> PAUL Or gods around a theocrat.
>
> DOCTOR Or diagnoses round a turbulence, as P.A. would say.
>
> P.A. Or what happens when two people meet.

ROLAND How dull.

ROBIN What bores psychoanalysts are! It isn't just sex.

P.A. It never was. It is its meaning that we do not know or understand, not our environment. It is not in our stars since we are underlings with ambitions to be overlings. We want someone or something authoritative to tell us we outshine these beauties of the night. [II: 254–5]

Other authors, such as Dr Robert Wallerstein (1988), noticed a similar fact occurring in the psychoanalytic movement. Nevertheless, Dr Wallerstein had put it in a way that can be seen as leaning to both the scientific and the historic realms, and avoiding the inclusion of political issues within the movement (Wallerstein, 2000). To him, it was a question to be investigated, rather than accepting *a priori* that there was, in fact, more than one psychoanalysis.

The pretended "elevation"—in reality, a downgrading debasement—of Bion's contributions as making a better or different psychoanalysis, endowed with undisguised elitist postures, fuelling and fuelled by phantasies of superiority, was—and still is—seen the world over; one may consult Grotstein (1981) and Matte Blanco (1981), for example. It is possible to elicit at least one of its foundations: the attempt to understand, be it conscious or not—a feature typical of the tendency to be immobilised in the paranoid-schizoid position. It disregards Bion's warnings about the necessary discipline over memory, desire and understanding. The "understanding" occurred within the minds of some readers of his work, especially after the publication of *Transformations*. Bion had already advanced the theme before: for example, when he introduced the mathematical model of factors and functions in psychoanalytic practice. It may sound to some readers that Bion was a kind of reversed Mendelssohn or Vieuxtemps: he was able to write *paroles* without a *chanson*. Because the *chanson* will depend on the analyst, or any interpreter, who must add the words to a *chanson* built into each analyst's experience in life and analysis. In Chapter Seven of *Transformations*, Bion quotes Pirandello's *Six Characters in Search of an Author*: some psychoanalysts utter words and phrases to some patients, who are able to hear a song.

Are there members of the psychoanalytic movement who contributed to building the psychoanalytical establishment who could profit from the following fictitious discussion between Paul (a priest), Robin and his friend Roland (two ordinary men), Doctor (a physician), and P.A. (a run-of-the-mill psychoanalyst)? Is there such a thing as a real psychoanalytical level of observation which allows for reflexive self-criticism with no fascination for extraneous disciplines biased by exclusive interest in consciousness (Archard, 1984), excluding research in other realms of the mind, such as the unconscious?

> PAUL What shall we discuss today?
>
> ROBIN I feel I can't remember what we were talking about before. It is curiously like dreams, for I know that I have dreamt and though I couldn't say what the dream was, I know that I have not forgotten it—it has gone. On these occasions it can come back; I don't *remember* it, but it is there, all in one piece. It is quite whole and quite absent.
>
> ROLAND I can't say I have that experience, but then I rarely dream at all. I do remember some dreams which I had as a child and some were very frightening, but others were not.
>
> DOCTOR It sounds as if we were going to talk about dreams. But what about things that could be easily explained if they were dreams, but the patient has them—I'm thinking of a particular man—when wide awake? I don't think I would call them hallucinations; there is no adequate name.
>
> PAUL What would you call the vision clearly seen and verbalised by Isaiah?—he describes it clearly in the sixth chapter as he would any other fact and date.
>
> P.A. I think of visions as coming from a "level of mind", or a "time of life", although I always *hear* of them in the present and *described* in articulate terms. This is one of my difficulties; because I use ordinary English it is assumed that I am saying something already known to all of us, and at the same time that it cannot be anything as ordinary as to be comprehensible to ordinary people.
>
> ROLAND Couldn't you say something that is neither?
>
> ROBIN According to the Intuitionists you can't, because there is no excluded middle. Why, as someone asked, does logic apply to anything but mathematics?
>
> P.A. I certainly do not intentionally exclude, or include, any topic, although I can see that if one topic can be said to be "included" then

> other topics are "excluded". A responsible person must exclude the topics which he does *not* discuss. To that extent he is not allowing some aspect of his personality to express itself and is thus incurring his self-hatred—whatever grievances he may consider also to be inflicted upon him by forces or people *not* himself. We include dreams as a part of thinking. Do you call that *in*cluding or *ex*cluding logic?
>
> ROBIN Hasn't Brower already pointed out that there may be a mathematics in which classical, mathematical logic is irrelevant?
>
> ROLAND I'm no mathematician. [II: 246–7]

The advent of Kant, who rescued and amplified early advancements first provided by Aristotle, namely, the distinction between the object of study and the methods used to study that object, had a number of important consequences. Among them, the illumination that formal logic is useful when one looks to the final products of thinking—which focus the objects of study—in favouring the material and concrete realm.

Kant's re-opening of the Platonic realm allowed for a renewed, more detailed study of the processes of thought—which includes, perforce, the methods used to study the objects, responsible for the final products of the same processes of thought. Nevertheless, the study of the methods was dimmed and dwarfed due to a growing confusion about the original etymological meaning of the word "metaphysics". The confusion developed along centuries and ran in proportion to the increased dismissal of awareness about the immaterial realm. It was left to mysticism and religiosity, rather than to scientific endeavours. Formal logic or Euclidean logic was the backbone of the contributions of Aristotle and Descartes, and made up the framework of Comte's Positivism. They are not wrong; they appertain to a small part of the infinite ways opened to real thinking—now encompassing non-Euclidean logic, such as relativistic and quantum physics, and later developments like string theory and theories of complexity. The facts that appertain to the immaterial realm demand intuitive training. The paradoxical material and immaterial allow for making relational hypotheses that connect expressions of fact. They may at first indicate an event or a fact not yet found in any sensuously based, corresponding event in reality, but they have counterparts in the ineffable immaterial and material reality. The issue was explored by Freud many times, reaching its climax in "Constructions in Analysis" (1937b) and "Moses and Monotheism" (1939). It seems that Bion expanded this, mainly in *A Memoir of the Future*—with no resorting to flights of imagination that are a main feature of naïve idealism and relativism.

Is Jargonese the consequence of mixing up logical thinking with non-introjected, undigested technical words?

CHAPTER TWO

Love it or leave it: transformations and invariants again

The previous volume quoted a dialogue involving the characters Alpha and Big Bro. Let us return to them:

ALPHA And even myself, whose thoughts and feelings linger on long after I have woken up and remain active and alive in my waking life long after it is expected or supposed (by whom, pray? Shut up!) that I should be dead and buried (where?) In the land of nod, the unconscious, the forgotten, the … wherever else I am to go to—the Future will do for a sort of royal cemetery, as well as the past. Below the Thalamus. The royal cemetery at Ur, Newton, Shakespeare, Descartes. But some are so deeply buried, forgotten, even their names swallowed up, that they need exing the cave. Even metaphors come alive, otherwise the words that are needed achieve the qualities of "life". (More bloody metaphors! Who ever could sort out a mass of verbiage like this?) You could try calling it "Paranoid Schizoid" after—a long way "after"—Melanie Klein. Good idea. Good dog paranoid schizoid, here, here is a nice piece of jargon for you. Suspicious are you? Take *that* then! Another great lump of free associations, dreams and their interpretations, poetry, ("all lies," said Plato, sly, suspicious old dog that he was) is hurled at the poor, new-born baby. "Intelligence" they call the puir, wee thing. Where is that Anarch of the stops and dashes and never-ending Parentheses?—Sterne, they called him, wasn't it? The Anarchs of the world of darkness keep a throne for thee, puir, wee Intelligence. A rose by any other name … might just as well be a stink that smells as foul even if you call it a "salubrious environment".

Come here bad, baaad dog!—Hitler dear, *such* a nice Hitler, *such* a *benito*, such a sweet, rosy little boy! Here, here's a nice salubrious environment! Washed, nay bathed, in our Auschwitz showers. They smell—aah! You can't think how sweet and refreshing those showers are. Now *here* is a brand new *mind*. It is far superior to the nose as an instrument for discrimination. You just have to attach one of our "minds" to the old apparatus and this tiny adjustment, fitted to the nose and any of the no nonsense organs, to obtain a really superior organ of discrimination! Yes: but how can I tell quackery—use it! Why discriminate?—from truth? Can I tell by it, for example, if this mind you talk about is any better than all the previous gadgets I have been invited to attach, at enormous expanding cost, to my various existing battery of gadgets? I knew a delightful old stegosaurus who thought he had found *the* answer to the tyrannosaurus. But the "answer" was so successful that it turned into a kind of tyrannosaurus itself and loaded him with such fame—not to mention exoskeleton—that he sank under its own weight. In fact, he was so loaded that the only trace of him left was his skeleton. Yes, but those same dead bones gave birth to a mind. Because while all eyes were fixed on the conflict between Fate and armour (there is *no* armour against Fate) the attacker got through disguised as a bomber. Now, the Mind … you just try it. Just attach it to your sensory perceptions! How do I know it won't just turn into extrasensory perceptions—s.p. → e.s.p.? The animal, meaning you, who reads this and I that write it and all biological living constructs, have an inborn mechanism for self-disposal. This dogmatic, definitory hypothesis shares the character of the character it represents. On this definitory hypothesis is built the hypothesis and the construct of which it is the foundation.

The tyrannosaurus provokes intrinsically an equal + opposite reaction—the stegosaurus. The stegosaurus sinks under its own "maginot line", its defensive armour which is its own weakness and makes its own armament, its own weight, under which it sinks. The self-destructive elaboration is blind to the quality which is to lead to its own destruction. If ξ is felt to be the successworthy quality, to be producer of progress, ξ is also the character unknown and auto-destructive. If the Oedipus story is the weapon that reveals homo, it is also the story that conceals, but does not reveal, that by which it will destroy itself. What happened to Delphi? and Socrates? If man is a tool-making animal he will not observe that that same capacity will be more than he can protect himself against. Superficially it may become clear that he is a clever monkey who can produce an atomic bomb that is a potential menace to his existence. While his gaze physiological is directed to observation and "detoxication" of the menace *represented* by the atomic bomb it will, by the same token, be directed away from the growing annihilating force, the "helpless infant". "Too much learning will make thee mad ..." Too much "tyranny"—freedom, food, armour, defensiveness; the list can be extended—but the only reality that matters is that which is denoted by "too much". Quantity, + and –, requires awareness. In the language suitable for communicating, it would be called a capacity for discrimination of quantity and quality. But in the domain that concerns us there is nothing that lends itself to the exercise of discrimination; there is no quality, no quantity to be discerned. Relativity is relationship, transference, the psychoanalytic term and its corresponding approximate realisation. Mathematics, science as known hitherto, can provide no model. Religion, music, painting, as these terms are understood, fail me. Sooner or later we reach a point where there is nothing to be done except—if there is any exception—to wait. The "impasse" is itself a word which, in the context of this writing, is known to denote a feeling.

BIG BRO Using some schoolboy mathematics I make a model, thus:—I cannot take five from three using only natural numbers. Natural numbers are the kind of numbers I use if I see a pile of oranges and want to know how many oranges there would be if five were removed from the pile. I would say "one, two, three, four, five" as I separated the oranges from the pile. Then I would do the same with the remainder and count thirty. So, given the fruit and the technique I have described, what would happen if I took thirty oranges away from five? First, it would be very improbable that I would want to know anything so ridiculous, and I might be afraid of doing anything because the people round me might be very cross if I wasted their time, and mine, dreaming. In fact, I have just dozed off which shows you … What?

MEMORY I dreamed I was taking thirty oranges away from five. In the dream I didn't see anything extraordinary about taking thirty oranges away from five. The five were very fat, big and greedy and had lots of oranges. I was angry that they should have such masses of oranges when they *were* oranges themselves already! So I suppose I did not see why they should not have thirty taken from them. It was really rather funny—really! What's so funny about it, said one of the big ones. I felt frightened. Well, put like that, what *was* funny? I remembered one of my patients telling me, "I tell you … I never woke up so fast in my life, I can tell you!" So I thought I had better do the same. I *woke* up. What a funny way you laugh. Arf, arf, ARF you go … do wake up. What was so funny about it? I told her I had forgotten and couldn't remember. But it was—very funny. I wish I could remember it!

Well, as I was saying, of course you can't take thirty from five—not in reality; not with real numbers. If someone invents negative numbers and you add them to natural numbers, *then* you can take three from five and get minus two! What's the good? Is that not just playing tricks with numbers? It doesn't mean a thing. *No*. It is pure mathematics. If it's pure mathematics it's all right because it doesn't have to mean a thing. Daft, I call it. There are lots of people who don't think. *They* must be daft too. No: because someone—Lobachevsky or Riemann—invented a daft geometry and now they find it quite useful in space—not the space which Euclid geometrised about; infinite space, space that has no end. Like "world without end Amen", you mean. Ye-es, perhaps; you mean religious space? I think it's more like the "space", if there was such a thing, made out of adding conscious space to unconscious space. How? Well, if you have a new kind of space, call it mental space, then you may have to invent a new addition to go with it. Or, if you invent new numbers you have to invent new mathematics. They have: they have invented negative numbers and a new geometry in which there are imaginary points and tangents which have coordinates of two points, one which is real and contingent, rather like

> ones that are real and separate or real and distinct, and other lines which don't cut the circle at all and are conjugate complex. What the hell is that? I understand points that are real and distinct, or real and coincident, but not points that are conjugate complex. If you weren't so proud of being sane, someone would be sure to notice how frightened you were of "insanity". You wear your "bravery" as a cloak for your cowardice and things you are afraid of—it must be terrible to have a parasympathetic and a "voluntary" nervous system so close to each other! What dreams, what thoughts, the other system has! Which is the other? Look at your skin; but I suppose you wouldn't dare to go more than skin deep. [I: 59–63]

There were some readers—either previous pundits in the then available psychoanalysis or young learners—who felt that the double concept of transformations and invariants was too abstract to be apprehended. In a not exactly peaceful coexistence, there were also other students who felt that there was an astounding, or at least a good enough quantum of "aliveness" in the practical examples given by Bion in *Transformations* (Bion, 1965). Those examples cover a remarkable range, because they were drawn, under a constant conjunction, from (i) everyday life—like the model of an image resulting from a painter looking at a landscape and then painting it (p. 1); (ii) philosophy of science (just to quote one example: p. 12); (iii) philosophy of religion (p. 45) and theology; and (iv) poetry (for example, pp. 15, 133, 162).

The reader may see that these items fit perfectly into the Trilogy. The spinal cord used to integrate all those models was furnished by his psychoanalytic clinical experience, mainly illuminating the phenomenon of hallucinosis and its contrapuntal function in the apprehension of reality *as it is*—the noumena, which Bion called "O". This is both the initial and the final point of any Invariant, a fundamental immaterial "part" that must be at least partially apprehended in a communicable form to cohere the scattered elements—a kind of gluing kernel to the many constant conjunctions that may be drawn from the clinical material, which may form a discernible pattern. The pattern may or may not be known from previous experience. Returning to one of the origins of the Trilogy, that is, *Transformations*, Bion still used a more traditional mode of writing *vis-à-vis* his chosen form in the Trilogy, and furnished many clinical vignettes spread through the book. A few examples can be drawn from the first three chapters: the case of the psychotic breakdown in an analytically controlled situation (p. 7), the feelings about a casual or habitual handshake (p. 13), Pepper (p. 16), and the milkman (p. 30). The vignettes, as if they were a preview of the content of the Trilogy, encompass—to the surprise and abhorrence of many readers—the history of theological and mathematical philosophies, using models taken from the work of Meister Eckhart and Saint John of the Cross (pp. 158, 170) and from the diatribes between Bishop Berkeley and Sir Isaac Newton (p. 157). Seminal contributions from them are applied in the Trilogy. Do Bion's applications of them elicit in a fuller way their mythical nous?

Bion noticed at least two kinds of reaction to his psychoanalytical writing *tour de force*. His source was either covert or open communication from some of his contemporaries. It seems that he was not annoyed with those who expressed their lack of comprehension: he never took it personally, and being understood was not the purpose of his writing.

Nevertheless, not being annoyed is not the same as nourishing contempt. There is evidence that Bion was able to apprehend what was going on and took the comments seriously—this is made clear in his introduction to *Seven Servants* (1977c), and much more so in the Trilogy (III: 578). All of this is very clear in the transcript of Bion's last talk, recorded three months before his death (Bion, 1958–1979, p. 374).

As a matter of consequence, Bion tried to make the concept of transformations and invariants more "alive", more "vivified" in the Trilogy. After all, he had an uncanny sense of the direction taken by the "arrow of time", as he made crystal clear the first time that he had the thought that he had finished the writing of his Trilogy. This seemed to occur a few months before his death, of which he had no inkling, despite the fact that he was an octogenarian. Anyway, it is a common fact that some people intuit when their days are close to finishing. In an imaginary conversation with an eventual reader—in the manner of Freud "holding conversations" with prospective critical readers—Bion gives a humorous summary of the dawn of oblivion (where A is the Author, or Bion, and Q is the Questioner, or Reader):

> *A I see you turn to the last page as you always used to do.*
>
> *Q Of course. Last time you told me how much it had cost you to publish. Did you find it interesting? How was America—North and South?*

> *A Marvellous; a nice change from the Third Battle of Wipers.*
>
> *Q Lots more since then. And more to come—which reminds me; I must rush; I have a date to meet Fate.*
>
> *A Bye-bye—happy holocaust!* [III: 577]

The references are to his critical view about his globe-trotting life in later years, as compared with his war experience in the last criminal non-sense battle waged at Ypres, Belgium, commonly referred to by British troops at the time as Wipers. This summary expresses Bion's yarn to thread the whole tissue of his Trilogy text with the immaterial but highly audible cord made of transformations and a set of basic invariants.

Man, for example, is a continuous source of transformations. In the beginning of Book I, *The Dream*, he is capable of performing a kind of psychoanalysis which strips off all the other character's belongings, which in their turn epitomise upper-class aspirations, mainly expressed by personal effects and worldly goods. Like any good enough Man, a model that serves to express some invariants of any male human being who merits the name, Man deprives other people of their resources; he displays unequivocal sadistic features, assisted by his collaborators. Some of them have the external appearance of people dedicated to the profession of nursing, but are skilled just in causing unnecessary pain when examining people, especially women. There are hints that Man is a leftist revolutionary. Robin thinks that he is a Nazi invader, while Roland considers that the Nazis were inept compared with Man and his armies. Roland, the educated farmer, acquires a "schizoid" smile—which may reveal his truthful self—when describing a famous picture with a phraseology more typical of automated people who perform automated jobs, such as museum guides. By the way, as soon as Wilfred R. Bion died, museum managers, aping small businesses who were already using answering machines to replace human beings, also adopted such a machine to perform the act of guiding people around their museums. As Roland, "becoming more and more academic, in guide book style", continues his sleep-inducing discourse, revealing that "the real name of this famous painting is 'Saint Athanasius chased by a wild boar'", the boar "loses all its ferocity and trots peacefully out of the picture" (all quotations, I: 187), in a way not dissimilar from a scene in *The Purple Rose of Cairo* (Woody Allen, 1985). The painting was owned by the family of the farmer Roland, but now it is revealed that the farmer was, in fact, owned by the picture. In other words, animate non-entities are enslaved by inanimate, dead concrete things. This is the consequence of the infinite greed that makes people search for infinite material comfort—an unwinnable struggle, like any struggle against reality, under a continuous denial or lack of perception of the immaterial realm. This aspect was covered by the concept of "forced splitting", an outgrowth from Freud's and Klein's concept of splitting, illuminated by Wilfred Bion in the fourth and fifth chapters of *Learning from Experience*.

Bion's distrust of authoritarian personalities moulded his scientific allowance of doubts and continuous, increasing avoidance of falling into dangerous, delusional states of "owning absolute truth"—mainly after his renewed service in World War II and the loss of his first wife. His second marriage gave him his final chance, which he did not waste (Bion, 1979, 1982, 1985). It can be subsumed in more than twenty quotations from Maurice Blanchot that one may find in Bion's later works. He became extremely interested in André Green's remark on Blanchot's aphorism *la réponse est le malheur de la question* (the answer is the misfortune of the question)—an undesirable side-effect of any answer. Bion kept quoting Green on Blanchot from first hearing the aphorism (around 1970) until his last work—the Trilogy.

> THEA And what conclusion have you come to?
>
> PAUL The conclusion that the conclusion is the start of the problem. [II: 264]

The discarding of a theory must be done in the light of empirical evidence. The reaction of politically minded and of relativistic readers appears in a different guise: they have a tendency to inflict a fundamental transformation on Heisenberg's Principle of Uncertainty, a principle very dear to Bion. This kind of reader transforms the Principle of Uncertainty into a Principle of Ignorance, inoculating it with a disguised absolute truth whose paranoid motto could be "If I don't know, nobody knows", enshrining the darkness of ignorance on the high altar of absolute truth. This introduced a serious decay in the apprehension and application of Bion's seminal theory of observation, that of Transformations and Invariants, by privileging Transformations at the expense of Invariants. Enshrining personal opinions, and dismissing any attempt to pursue truth-O, the naïve idealist or relativist reader believes that *all* transformations are valid.

The enshrining of personal opinion, fuelled by rhetoric and the group's adhesion to messianic and other group assumptions such as fight-flight and pairing (Bion, 1961), makes for a symbolic equation—a concept developed by Melanie Klein and Hanna Segal:

personal opinion = psychoanalysing people

It proved to be a successful political enhancer in the psychoanalytic movement, winning wide support for its over-simplification of what was originally a scientific attitude. Relativists and idealists do not need empirical research, and came to despise it. Freed from reality testing, a term coined and much used by Freud, the mind is able to make "flights of fantasy"—a term first coined by Francis Bacon. The same problem is highlighted in many parts of *A Memoir of the Future*; in *Transformations*, Bion had already observed

> ... one advantage that the psychoanalyst possesses over the philosopher; his statements can be related to realisations and realisations to a psychoanalytic theory. What psychoanalytic thinking requires is a method of notation and rules for its employment that will enable work to be done in the absence of the object, to facilitate further work in the presence of the object. The barrier to this that is presented by unfettered play of an analyst's phantasies has long been recognised: pedantic statement on the one hand and verbalisation loaded with unobserved implications on the other mean that the potential for misunderstanding and erroneous deduction is so high as to vitiate the value of the work done with such defective tools. [Bion, 1970, p. 44]

One may state that Bion's way of writing, as well as the content of his writings, can be seen by some readers as demanding. After all, Bion's Trilogy proposes that the reader should make the effort of maintaining absolute attention—the initial step of a caring, respectful attitude—and continuously demands the reader's own free associations. To other readers, the demand is internal, from their own instincts, and the writing functions as a "free association generator".

Bion's writings confront potential readers who are prey either to naïve realism or to naïve idealism with a dilemma: "love it or leave it". His writings require intense attention, attempts at interpretation, and transformations which vary from time to time.

The thought-inducing or thought-evoking[1] qualities have similarities in the greatest authors of Western civilisation. A 19th century Brazilian author, Joaquim Machado de Assis, is currently becoming better known to English-speaking readers not acquainted with Brazilian literature. In his novel *The Posthumous Memoirs of Bras Cubas* (1881), whose title and contents remind us of Bion's Trilogy, one may see the fictitious musings and reflections of a character who is already dead. Is it coincidence? Or is it an indication that both writers turned their attention to the human mind and human reality? Wilfred Bion visited Brazil three times and helped at least three Brazilians[2] to gain their analysis, as well as furnishing supervisions to a number of others.

Sources: surprising verbal formulations?

The endless flow of "new" theories (often old theories clothed in new names) made Bion observe that practising psychoanalysts need few real theories, provided that they know those theories well (Bion, 1962, p. 42; 1963, p. 2). Are those "new" theories really necessary? If the ages-old idea about the existence or creation of a "new man" through the application of social, or psychological, or religious doctrine is right, the new theories would be a matter of necessity. Anyway, there is historical evidence that in its most basic features, the human being has challenged evolution. Biologically speaking, a "new man" would take more than fifty thousand years; cultural changes are epiphenomenal.

> Is the supposition that the reptilian age is antecedent to Hitler correct, or is it a feature of our thinking process which has become an aberration which has not been considered, but has become part of what is *observed*? [I: 86]

None of Bion´s quotations in his later contributions (post-1970), whether coming from papers or books, from analysts, or from great thinkers, is in the usual standardised scientific presentation—a form which he had previously defended (Bion, 1962, p. 38). But even in his earlier works, there were comparatively few quotations *vis-à-vis* the works of his colleagues. His quotations from the medieval thinker Isaac Luria, a Kabbalist, and Dr Kurt Eissler, an analyst, in *Attention and Interpretation* left some readers surprised—in the wake of his earlier quotations from the mystic thinkers Meister Eckhart, John of Ruysbroeck and St John of the Cross in *Transformations*.

In the Trilogy, Freud and Klein are the most quoted; if we add André Green (twice, in Volume III) and Roger Money-Kyrle, we have the only four analysts from whom Bion derives concepts and ideas. There are nine quotations from Melanie Klein in Volume I, and five in Volumes II and III, almost all of them dealing with projective identification. A most telling quotation about Melanie Klein, unavailable in her own works and much less in references to her work made by any other analyst is that "in the domain of human comprehension Melanie Klein could not reconcile herself to the fact that whenever she had made herself understood, that fact rendered what she understood no longer 'alive'" (I: 88–89). As regards quotations and affiliations:

> ROBIN I thought you would call yourself a Freudian psychoanalyst. Or are you a Kleinian?
>
> P.A. I can recognise and would like to acknowledge my debt to Freud and Melanie Klein, but they might be affronted by such attribution. I would acknowledge my debt to others, but I am aware that many would think such an acknowledgement more a liability than an asset; they would not wish to be thought my mental forebears. Nor do *I* wish to wear the plumage of the peacock when my true colour should be the feathers of the sparrow. [II: 360–1]

For one of the few living authors quoted, there is a compliment embedded with hope: "I think James Strachey's achievement in translating Freud may yet come to be valued at its worth" (III: 541)—a compliment earlier given in the flesh: the completion of the Standard Edition was coincidentally achieved under one of Bion's tenures as President of the British Psychoanalytical Society. Due to influences already mentioned, linked to commercial interests from publishing companies which led to rivalry, Bion's hope, like most hopes, was destined to be unfulfilled.

In contrast, past generators of *idées-mères* are extensively quoted: Socrates, Plato, Pythagoras, Milton, Shakespeare, Leonardo, Locke, Hume, Pascal, Poincaré, Bacon, Meister Eckhart, St John of the Cross, Luria, Joyce, Pound, Carroll, Heisenberg, Einstein, Wordsworth, Keats,

Shelley, Ruskin, Browning, Hopkins, Rimbaud, and so on. All of them contributed to the writing pattern increasingly favoured by Bion that reached its climax in the Trilogy, regarded as another unwelcome feature by the psychoanalytical establishment.

Bion offered the reader a dialogical form, having seemingly become fed up with many years of experiencing the heavy use his colleagues made of jargon and pre-patterned formulae construed with pseudo-psychoanalytic wording. Jargon and easy formulae had proved to be mesmerising and hypnotic to many members of the psychoanalytic movement. Nevertheless, the dialogical form chosen by Bion is another revival of Freud's working method—after all, psychoanalysis is done though a living dialogue between two people.

Summing up the more detailed comments made throughout this book, Bion added to the dialogical form a revival of the aphoristic and metaphorical traditions typical of the Enlightenment era, intermingled with a most important venture stemming from the Romantic Movement: one of many attempts to take care of human emotions. Enlightenment acquisitions were epitomised by Denis Diderot in France—who wrote in the same dialogical form. Even though Bion did not quote him explicitly in any of his written works, this author's research in Bion's private library when writing *The Language of Bion* showed that Bion was very fond of Diderot and read him extensively. Mrs Bion herself nourished deep respect for Diderot's work and confirmed her husband's admiration for him.

Both in the Trilogy and in his preparatory papers, published posthumously in *Cogitations*, Bion quotes Alexander Pope, Dr Samuel Johnson and William Blake. They were the main representatives of the two movements in England. The influences stemming from the Romantic Movement came from Wordsworth (Volumes I, II), Keats (Volumes I, II), Shelley, Goethe and Nietzsche (Volume I). Independently of explicit quotations, the informed reader can detect their pervading and all-encompassing scent; sometimes the quotations are just phrases extracted from their poetry.

The dialogical form is remarkable due to its colloquial nature, though some readers may regard it as somewhat dated now. It contains a number of idiomatic expressions common in the English language in the post-Edwardian era, as well as formulations such as "Boche", the pejorative denomination used by the French for Germans during World War I.

Other features, such as the use of slang, Cockney speech and dirty words, proved to be timeless, even if felt as obnoxious by readers not accustomed to facing truth but more accustomed to socialising. Or rather, accustomed to socially accepted hypocrisy—the thing the French call *politesse*. Some of them may feel outraged when they come across those parts of the text—which, in their turn, are valid under psychoanalytic, scientific and even literary vertices. Bion had used the same form of writing in a short paper, "Emotional Turbulence" (1977d), when discussing the term "bloody cunt".

All of this added to the unmistakable lack of popularity of the Trilogy. It is fair to state that from 1981 to 1989 the Trilogy was one of the least read works in the English-speaking countries; the few exceptions were very hard to find. Letters from the so-called leading Kleinians, and conversations with some of them who visited São Paulo at that time, left this author with the idea that there was a precocious dismissal of those writings. The Trilogy was barely mentioned in English-language psychoanalytical papers. References to it include a brief excerpt from Volume II quoted by Donald Meltzer in his obituary of Bion (1981), some remarks by Grotstein and Matte Blanco (1981), and unpublished manuscripts from Meltzer's lectures at the Tavistock Clinic in 1984.

An exception to that scarcity of interest appeared in the *International Review of Psychoanalysis*, a short-lived, green-covered, and commercially unsuccessful "cultural" younger sibling of the *International Journal of Psychoanalysis*. A creation of the South African-born Dr Joseph J. Sandler, it published a paper by Meg Harris Williams, a gifted literary critic. She was a solitary voice who stated, with the authority given by her own perception, that the Trilogy was Bion's "most vital legacy to the human condition", showing "his individual model to the potential growth of every mind" (Williams, 1983). Mrs Williams is today better known in the psychoanalytic movement than she was at that time due to her collaborative work with Donald Meltzer (*The Apprehension of Beauty*, Meltzer & Williams, 1988) and her own books (such as *The Vale of Soulmaking*, 2005). Her appreciation of the worth of Bion's Trilogy increased in the ensuing years.

Other contemporary comments did no good as regards public acceptance of the Trilogy. Many people regarded—and still regard—Bion's written works as "obscure and difficult", and the Trilogy is an outstanding example of this. It was around that time that comments about the author's state of mind emerged, indistinguishable from prejudiced badmouthing. A more detailed description of this atmosphere around Bion's contributions can be found in Volume 1 of this work, in Grotstein (1981), and in the introduction to *The Language of Bion* (Sandler, 2005), so it seems fair to spare the reader's time now.

Bion looked for a form of communication embedded with what, for the lack of a better name, can be seen as the sense and the soul of the psychoanalytic clinic. Nevertheless, many readers felt the need to obtain written clinical records of the type "The patient said this and the analyst said that". There is a belief that what may at best be a mere caricature, built from the raw material extracted from memory, desire and understanding about moments which are now already dead, can convey the sense and the soul of clinic. This is a wishful belief based on another belief: that one should learn psychoanalysis through the method of reading, dispensing with personal analysis. If we need to "set a poet to catch a poet", and if the transplantation of this observation to psychoanalysis proves to be homologous, it results in "setting a madman to catch a madman" (J. Sandler, 1973). This possibility is hinted at in Bion's description of a psychoanalytically controlled breakdown, which characterises a catastrophic change (*Transformations*, Chapter One), as well as in his observation about the need to "participate" in the hallucinosis displayed by the patient (*Attention and Interpretation*). Extensive reviews of these concepts and observations can be found in *The Language of Bion* (Sandler, 2005). This posture was already adumbrated by experienced psychiatrists. In any case, it is not possible to do this without previous analytic training, except by practising "wild analysis".

Freud's misgivings about selling psychoanalytical papers and books to the general public reflect the impossibility of learning analysis by reading texts. He thought that only people who had been analysed could grasp what he had written. He agreed to the creation of a publishing house after World War I for a practical reason: to save his progeny from the indignity of famine, which haunted the impecunious inhabitants of the defeated "Central" countries. Bion's writing—like Freud's and Klein's—demands the previous analysis of the reader. Lack of analytic experience makes for blindness and deafness to apprehension of the phenomena described by their texts.

The same had already occurred previously with the work of Melanie Klein. Her communications were seen in a range extending from improbable to crazy. They were paradoxically seen as both too abstract and too concrete—at least by people who did not, or could not, realise though analytic experience the phenomena which are both physical and mental, that Mrs Klein tried to describe though verbal formulations drawn from psychiatry.

Physical and mental, rather than physical or mental

There is a serious—due to its hallucinated nature—conundrum that afflicts Western civilisation's attempts at thinking. It can be called the "first world war against truth": renewed attempts to split mind from matter (a review of this subject for psychoanalysts can be seen in Sandler, 1997a, 2001a, 2001b, 2013). The same fact can be seen in the history of physics: the attempts to split energy from matter. Modern physics allows the observation that such as split is a fallacy, a product of a special form of hallucination: self-deception. Psychoanalysis, together with modern physics and mathematics, has shown that a factor nourishing this fallacy is the limited range of apprehension of the human sensuous apparatus coupled with impatience: a hurried human desire to understand what in a given moment cannot be understood.

The split was heightened with Aristotle's juvenile revolt against his master Plato—a move he later regretted. Perhaps too late: the split or "first world war against truth" was made still more noxious to the processes of real thought by part of the work of St Thomas Aquinas—to the political benefit of the Roman Catholic secular establishment. Aristotle's attack on Platonic forms continued with René Descartes, whose work proved to be the climax of this split. It enshrined what can be called the delusion of "rational thinking". It resulted, a couple of centuries later, in the Positivist Religion founded by Auguste Comte, which claimed to be the one and only method to obtain knowledge.

The same split was responsible for considerable worldly or secular achievements, as well as a remarkable impoverishment in the processes of thought in Western civilisation, as Freud pointed out in "Civilisation and its Discontents" (1930). This kind of reasoning was criticised by Kant, who in turn was indebted to Hume's observations. Kant recognised, albeit reluctantly, that Hume awoke him from his "dogmatic slumber" (Kant, 1783). The "Chinaman of Königsberg" discovered the possibility to construct a method of "criticism", or critical method (Kant, 1781).

In Kant's parlance, the split between matter and energy planted into human soil the specimen "naïve realist": someone who feels that his or her sensory apparatus will suffice to get *the*—rather than just *an*—idea of what reality is all about. The naïve realist abhors what in his or her eyes are just complications, as observed by Kant with due help from some of his teachers, mainly Johann Georg Hamann (1759). Both saw that what was seen by the naïve realist as a disposable complication was in reality a fundamental constituent of human reality: namely, what Bion later formulated as "ultra- and infra-sensuous".

The Romantic Movement valued other events and features that the naïve realist felt as unimportant, such as those appertaining to the emotional realm or, in Freud's terms, to the psychic reality. France is a country which fairly occupies a central role in the emergence of the Enlightenment and Romantic movements: the *Siècle des Lumières* was born in France. The influential French academic philosophical tradition attributes to Jean-Jacques Rousseau the discovery of the importance of emotions in human mind. The fact that Immanuel Kant kept a book by Rousseau at his bedside, out of respect for parts of Rousseau's work, was used as political propaganda to display the superiority of French culture. Nevertheless, like any phantasy of superiority, it was at the expense of other human beings. This phantasy was a contributing factor to three bloody wars (1870, 1914 and 1939) between France and Germany. Apart from linguistic hurdles, German authors, taken as representatives of German culture, were kept hidden from non-German audiences. In consequence, the influence of non-French authors was not emphasised in the struggle to gain world dominance of ideas. Many countries were deeply influenced by this biased approach. Researchers worked—consciously or not—in a climate which a Brazilian author described as that of a French overseas department (Arantes, 1994). A version which can respect truth could state that Rousseau and Voltaire were busy, buzzing, over-exaggerated heralds of what was until that time a hidden realm of human emotions. The former would be a news-monger; the latter, a speaking trumpet.

In the 1960s and 1970s, there were many philosophical authors working in this climate who inferred that Freud had been influenced by Rousseau. This inference was authorised by a profound ignorance of the depth of Freud's quotations from Rousseau: they were used just to display the French master's destructive behaviour as reflected in his sexual postures, as well as some word-play by just one of Freud's patients, rather than any influence or inspiration, as is the case with

Goethe (on destructive behaviour: Freud, 1907, p. 36; 1915, p. 299; 1930, p. 125; on word-play: Freud, 1905a, p. 193; 1905b).

It became acknowledged that Rousseau epitomised the decay of the Romantic movement—despite the fact that he can be seen, under the vertex adopted by academies and universities, who prefer a chronological vertex, most of the time proven to be false, as the founder of the Romantic movement. It would be fair to state that he is the founder of a political and ideological movement, Romanticism, or the decay, though concretisation, of Romantic achievements. In hindsight, it is fair to correlate the facts known about the life of Rousseau, which reflected, albeit roughly, parts of his personality which displayed unmistakable features of bestiality—a most typical feature of humankind, only comparable to its paradoxical sublimity. Unfortunately, in most individuals, it is a real possibility that there are no compensations in the quantitative endowment of the two features in a given personality, for an entropic steady state must be pursued.

Conversely, in a very few individuals one may confirm the presence of the two features (bestiality and sublimity) in quantitative terms, as in the composer Richard Wagner. In other words, to most people, the heights of bestiality are mandatorily accompanied by a lowering of sublimity, respecting Fechner's principle. A quantitative imbalance between the two features seemed to be the case in Rousseau. David Hume, who knew him well and was responsible for many acts of kindness that helped Rousseau to stay afloat, said of him: "He seems to be skinless". Rousseau's personality proved to be prophetic to idealistic and relativistic followers in the next three centuries. They displayed a similar imbalance, as one gathers from a scrutiny of Deleuze's and Althusser's life. What matters for the purposes of this book is that it shows that at that time, philosophy still tried to deal with mind and truth.

Other "complications", under the vertex of the naïve realist, are the formulations of the mysterious infusion that permeates human life: formulations pervaded with doubt—or human reality as it is. The naïve idealist fully profits from them, to fuel in infinite quantities his or her capacity to hallucinate. Even though this second type of reader expresses sympathy towards works similar to the Trilogy, his or her use of it condemns the writing to the same type of dismissal, travestied with liking. Both readers extract pleasure from certainties, and for the naïve idealist, doubt is transformed into certainty—that of the enshrining of personal opinion. *Both types of reader replace what Bion and other authors, such as Isaiah Berlin, called "sense of truth" with absolute truth.* The naïve realist develops an unconditional love of the purely hallucinated absolute truth. A factor in this kind of love (in fact, minus love) is his or her submission to greed, which produces an envy of truth in its most fundamental mode hitherto discovered: the truth of the feeding breast. Both follow Bion's rules of hallucination, the first of them being the hallucinated self-feeding breast, which "belongs" (in hallucinosis) to the person rather than to his or her mother. Thus they "own" the breast, dissociated from the mother, dissolving and then "resolving" (in hallucinosis) the paradox, making an irresolvable split between the good and bad breast.

In this sense, they "own" just the good breast. In the naïve realist, due to the prevalence of schizoid mechanisms, it constitutes a concrete, external breast (or penis), a fetish-breast in the external world. In the naïve idealist, due to the prevalence of paranoid mechanisms, it constitutes an inner, hallucinated breast, wholly constructed by hallucinosis and delusion, dispensing with the real breast. The same split occurs, or the integration of the object cannot be achieved, because the good breast is owned by his or her imaginative fantasy. In analysis, both have an impoverished capacity to dream, to freely associate, and to get hold of their own unconscious phantasies (Freud, 1909; Isaacs, 1948). The naïve realist has, or tends to have (I use the term in the sense that mathematicians use) no willingness to play or to phantasise, while the naïve idealist tends to have an open door to hallucinosis. Thus both replace unconscious phantasy with pure fantasy. In the psychoanalytic movement, the naïve idealist is prone to enshrining artistic means and gifts at the expense of clinical observation—both in his or her practice and in theoretical approaches.

Realising the books—with Bion's help

Wilfred Bion provided a series of descriptions, sometimes construed with colourful, witty, rich, both humorous and sad metaphors, aphorisms and short parables which constitute the external tissue as well as the framework of the Trilogy. They can fairly serve as explanatory guides to the variegated built-in senses of the writing—sometimes hidden, sometimes in overt form. The descriptions colourful, witty, rich, humorous and sad must be coupled with colourless, dull, drab, humourless and happy. It is open to the reader to decide which description applies in each case. It is also open to the reader to read the text in its entirety from the beginning, or to begin at the end or at any intermediate point. It is possible to split the text into parts, as if dismantling a piece of fine clockwork. Yet there is something that is not a matter of choice: the Trilogy demands a reader willing to pay due attention to those descriptions. This kind of reader will easily grasp the multifarious senses of Bion's writing. The "attention rule" is valid for the whole of Bion's written work, but it reaches its climax with the Trilogy. After all, it is not by mere coincidence that the title of his previous book (1970) was *Attention and Interpretation*.

As if he were experimenting with a prototype, Bion included in this very work just one colourful, witty, rich, humorous and sad metaphoric parable—one that could be entitled "The liars and mental health", quoted in Chapter One. A brief note about conventions: "sense", in this book, may be understood as an indicator—like a vector in physics—giving the direction of any determined human function.

Until now we have focused on the seemingly novel form of the Trilogy—at least, novel to the psychoanalytical establishment—that was described by some observers as a "new genre". It may be a genre of its own, but the description "new" is questionable. Bion mixes theatre, fiction, history, science and epistemology coloured with maieutic overtones. Not very new, is it? And not very far from Freud's way of writing, at least if one focuses on the principle rather than the external form. In contrast to Freud's writings, which were precociously debased though copying and repetition—due to their "flowing nature" which enables people to understand the texts but not apprehend them—Bion's mode of writing challenges copyists and imitators.

In the last thirty years (1979–2009), at least according to the observation and experience of this author, there appeared very few attempts to copy the formal presentation of the Trilogy: just one was published. Not aping, but profiting from inspiration, just one author, Dr Antonino Ferro, used Bion's way to write a small illustrated book in the Italian language, *Prima Altrove Chi* ("Who Elsewhere Before", 2000),[3] which could mean personal freedom rather than idolisation. His book met the same fate as Bion's Trilogy—it was destined to remain largely unread.

Brothers in suffering, resilience and fortitude

At least according to the (perhaps limited) research undertaken by this writer, there is just one contemporary researcher who used similar methods of investigation: Professor Hans Günther Adler. He worked in the field of history and sociology, and was not known to Bion. Both used their painful, life-threatening experiences to construe scientific works which could successful reflect—or better, express—the embodiment or incarnation of personal suffering as an example of the inhumanity of man towards man.

Bion and Adler made theoretical and practical contributions which had striking underlying similarities but no superficial kinship—with the exception of war experiences. If one accepts social references, Bion was on the militarily victorious side. On the other hand, Adler, as a prisoner in Theresienstadt and Auschwitz, was not. Both lived in London after World War II. Human helplessness emerges in undisguised form in war—or, in other words, human strife. Some of its origins are depicted right from the start of the Trilogy, in a way not dissimilar to that described by Isaac Bashevis Singer in *Satan in Goray* (1935).

The character Robin, hidden in a pigeon cote, thought he was safe:

> "It's all very well to say 'Get to hell out of here.' How?" said Robin angrily. "You'll know quickly enough if you stay and have one of these bloody things crashing a hole through your skull—that will leave a way out!" "That won't be *less* likely if you start walking around here."
>
> "You're caught either way—stay or leave."
>
> The voice seemed familiar.
>
> "Who are you, pray?" said Robin and Roland together. The wind was rising. The crash of the bullets seemed to be heavier, to become merged with the storm. "God damn it! They *are* shells!"
>
> "You use my name in vain! … in vain, in vain in vain …"
>
> The words were echoing round the storm.
>
> "Christ! I must be hearing voices now! Who are you?"
>
> "Christ—" The voice echoed round and the storm dropped suddenly, to a whisper—"All Mighty."
>
> The silence was so sudden that the words were clearly and shockingly audible.
>
> "What the devil was that?"
>
> "At your service!"
>
> Though no one was visible, the voice seemed to be so clear that you could almost see it bow with elaborate and ironic courtesy. "I told you I had come didn't I? … come …" The echo was almost

gentle, like an invitation. "… to my arms … come … come … my beamish boy … come. Not in terror, like Ozymandias, but kind and good, like Hitler who chortled in his joy. Is that you Cap'n? Down below? Keep … till I come again."

"Who *is* that?" Roland sat up to listen more clearly. He smiled a schizoid smile. Such a gentle smile. "There! Don't you hear it?" He lifted a finger to signal silence.

I am the discoverer and inventor of homo alalu. I and my fellow homines with our opposable thumbs learned how to give birth and life by opposing penis to penis, vulva to vulva, till one of us began to swell up and up till the whole earth and sky was filled with the swelling and the roaring. It was decided that the monster should be destroyed. But some were lying and deceitful and resolved in their lying and deceit to continue their evil practices in secret and contribute their knowledge of pleasurable feelings to each other by rubbing. Some resolved to find this secret by learning from the secretive ones to do likewise, and others resolved likewise to deceive and lie so they could learn who and what they were that did these things so they could kill those who practised and taught these practices, and so confusion grew and it became impossible to tell good from evil. Some learned to talk, but again the same thing happened, for the language was used by some to perfect the arts of lying and deception and others to increase pleasure, but they could not agree which was which nor which was the sign by which what thing should be known. The monstrous swelling and roaring grew till the world was almost about to come to an end, but then it ceased. There came peace and quiet and the man was seen to be holding a deformed "thing". And he lied and said it came from inside him. And some said this was so and some said it could not be so and some sought to destroy the evil thing and some said, "Let us wait and then we shall be able to tell whether it is as they who say it is evil are right, or whether they who say it feels nice are right." But no one could say because sometimes even those who said it was good admitted it was an evil brat, but they were not constant and the decision became so late that the brat, if it were evil enough, could slay those who came to kill it and so again confusion grew until even the confusion of tongues, even the counsel, was darkened until it covered the earth. And fear made men worship what they did not know and some said—Let us

> worship it in ignorance and fear—and some said—Let us worship it in daylight when we do not fear—and some said—Let us make ourselves afraid or we shall not fear—and some worshipped the sun and some the moon. Some likewise worshipped fear itself and some happiness and joy and light. And again they could not agree. And some worshipped what they made and some worshipped their cleverness, saying—We are the highest and best of all animals because we are tool-making animals—and some worshipped that part of themselves which they thought enabled them to make tools, the tools that made tools, but again they could not agree what that part was or how it should be treated. [I: 40–42]

This may perhaps represent a most beautiful verbal presentation of the human's perplexity, born from hate for the reality presented by the supreme human creative act, the one performed by mother and father, as illuminated by Melanie Klein, Bion's second analyst. He pays homage to his forebear, emphasising that the origin of human strife may be in the hate aroused by the most fundamental truth still waiting to be discovered—that of parenthood. Which, or what, or whom do the characters represent? They embody in a more living form a part of Bion's personal myths.

Unlike Bion's, Adler's work caught the attention of famous naïve idealists. The diatribe between the highly educated Theodor Wiesengrund Adorno, an ideology-ridden thinker who enjoyed worldly fame, and the more experienced Hans Günther Adler, a truth-lover, an independent researcher who never enjoyed worldly fame, vividly exemplifies the damaging effect of naïve idealism.

A reader familiar with Brazilian literature could find similarities with Professor Adler's work in the writings of a good-humoured, sensitive, sharp, and deep observer of human truth: Joaquim Maria Machado de Assis. His enlightened, truthful prose makes him the most complete Brazilian writer ever—in the same league as the greatest writers of all times. Like any great literary work, his books call for a dialogue with the reader. I have previously mentioned one of his novels, *The Posthumous Memoirs of Bras Cubas* (*Memorias Póstumas de Bras Cubas*, 1881), whose subtitle in the English-language version at least partly conserves the paradox: *Epitaph for a Small Winner*. It is the history of Bras Cubas, who relates his memoirs from beyond the grave. There are many similarities to the Trilogy, especially in the serious humour. Another of Machado's many works is the novella *The Alienist* (*O Alienista*—an old word for psychiatrist, 1881b), about the tribulations of Dr Simão Bacamarte (*bacamarte* is Portuguese for "blunderbuss"): an imagined psychiatrist who is head of a lunatic asylum. The novella has many similarities to the Trilogy, with questioning observations about the real existence of clear-cut distinction between madness and sanity.

Fame: a mix of illusion, hallucinosis and delusion?

Bion spent a great deal of his analytic time researching the idea that established the existence of geniuses—another aspect that he shared with Freud. His final results were first presented in *Transformations* and expanded in *Attention and Interpretation*; he added to the better known denomination "genius" that of "mystic". The development of his research was displayed in the Trilogy.

Was Bion a genius? There were heated discussions about this. To those who think that he was *not* a genius, we may say that in the light of his own writings, this was an idea to which he would give his unquestioning agreement. In his introduction to *Seven Servants* (1977c), Bion writes:

> I had recently overheard two people debating whether to go to a paper that was to be given by Bion. "Oh, I've heard all his stuff. It's always the same anyway". The speaker I have quoted probably did not realise that he had thus learned something about himself—how much he already knew. That is what I call a fringe benefit. What about my "fringe benefit"? I likewise learned what I knew already, namely how little I knew and how often I repeated that small amount. It also stimulated, as is often the case, my curiosity about the vast, the infinite, and the domain of my ignorance. [Bion, 1977c]

Most "helpers", people devoted to the "caring professions", as they were named by Donald Winnicott, are probably endowed with a good enough perception of their irrelevance in worldly terms. Helpers are more often than not toasted with oblivion; gratitude never won anyone prizes in popularity. Bion shared this unenviable lot with other authors who met with strong, sometimes murderous resistance during their lifetime and whose work is extensively appreciated by subsequent generations: Wilde, Rimbaud, van Gogh, Bach. At least one of them—Goethe—thought it was better to leave the reading of his last work to future generations! The caring professions are not socially valued; the truth-speakers are safely hurled as memoirs to the future: "Are we … prepared to tell our children, or our children's children, what price they would have to pay if they served their fellows?" (III: 508)

This observation has already been quoted before, and refers specifically to Bion's experience in World War I. The following warning is attributed to one (among many others) who is often called a genius and undoubtedly was a helper of humankind in the disciplines of philosophy and methodology of science, Immanuel Kant: "God protect me from my friends; from my enemies I can protect myself". Who will protect psychoanalysis from the psychoanalytical establishment?

In any case, both praise for and accusations of genius are associated with secular fame, "no plant that grows on mortal soil", according to John Milton (*Lycidas*). Bion, like Freud, seemed determined to issue serious warnings against the idea of "fame". Much more in the Trilogy than in his earlier works, he left written testimonies to display its hallucinated nature:

> Poor Newton! Poor Shakespeare! Poor Galileo, Descartes, Freud, Milton: whose are they—the faces, faint revealed, yet sure divined, the "famous ones"—ante Agamemnona multi—the mute, inglorious ones? They saw the promised land, the mirage, the fame which is man's last and first infirmity of noble minds. [I: 55]

Bion, like Freud, was accused of being an erudite, both by idolisers and iconoclasts—two sides of the same unworthy coin, whose stuff is either an implicit or an explicit destructive attack. To them, and also to those who were prone to not looking for this kind of hallucinated attribute, he brought home his human fallibility and his personal opinion about the Sisyphean search for fame.

He shows himself as one who can be displaced and dislodged from his own psychoanalytical office by three fictitious characters, Dr Watson, Sherlock Holmes and Mycroft Holmes, in one of the author's own multifarious explanations about the Trilogy:

> MYCROFT HOLMES (*yawning somewhat ostentatiously*) Most interesting.

WATSON Shall I shut him up?

SHERLOCK HOLMES My *dear* Watson!

BION (*outraged*) What the devil do you mean by butting into my serious discussion? Are you not aware that I am raising serious issues?

MYCROFT (*in no way impressed*) Go on Sherlock. This is more your line than mine. *You* tell him.

WATSON (*before Sherlock intervenes, which he appears unlikely to do*) My dear Sir, Mister Holmes and his brother really must not be interrupted; it's a private and important matter.

BION But, my good man, are you not aware that you are entirely fictitious characters? I am a qualified doctor!

WATSON So am I; and an M.D.

BION Nonsense! Purely imaginary and not very bright even in the estimation of your fellow spooks. I am a past President of the British Psychoanalytical Society and past Director of the London Clinic of …

MYCROFT & SHERLOCK (*together burst into a gale of laughter.*)

WATSON (*contains his mirth with difficulty, but manages to be civil*) Excuse me, sir, but I must admit that I have never heard of your existence. I do not want to hurt your feelings or to appear to boast, but although Mycroft has always been of a retiring disposition, Sherlock, and to a lesser extent myself, has a world-wide following. You yourself were admitting that there are imaginary characters who are infinitely better known than countless generations of nonentitites. Now excuse me. I am a very busy man—allow me to suggest that you get on that couch there and sleep it off quietly.

BION (*with a gesture of despair, abandons his office to the three intruders and goes to sleep*)

SHERLOCK I hope you weren't too rough with him, Watson.

WATSON Real people have to be treated roughly if the universe of discourse is to be made safe for imaginary people. If you remember, this problem cropped up before with real numbers. Quite impossible for the simplest mathematical problem even to be formulated till negative numbers destroyed the tyranny of being confined in the restricted space of addition—just more real numbers. [I: 90–92]

And in a much less oblique way:

> SHERLOCK You seem to me to be deprecating fame itself.
>
> MYSELF Holmes, you did not begrudge Lestrade his need of fame. But who, think you, decided between you and your begetter? When was the award made? Who is more famous: Nelson, or his "blind eye"? Fame is no plant that grows on mortal soil. [I: 126]

The ubiquitous Dr Watson makes his usually showy appearance, typecasting the "pure action" actor. Sherlock is used by Bion, according to his perception of Conan Doyle's contributions, as an "in-between" actor, fully capable of matching deductive reasoning with corresponding actions: compare his actions with those of his brother, Mycroft.

In Western civilisation, one may affirm that there is global knowledge (long before the coining of the fashionable label "globalisation") of the characters created by Sir Arthur Conan Doyle. It would be fair to state that the popularity of Conan Doyle's novels is beginning to wane in some parts of the world and within some age groups. It is not possible to know what may happen in the future—revivals and nostalgia are things that happen cyclically—so the Sherlock Holmes novels may return: something already predicted at the time that the novels were written. The public refused to accept that Conan Doyle decided to get rid of Sherlock Holmes, "killing" him at the Reichenbach falls. He was seemingly fed up with writing detective novels and badly wanted to reach higher "levels", and saw it as his only option. Poor sales of his other literary ventures, coupled with the angry reaction of his captive audience, gave him second thoughts. His capitulation to the group's reaction took the form of *The Return of Sherlock Holmes*—received with fanfare by the readers.

Truthful things and events may have this kind of course in the group: initial perplexity is replaced by catastrophic change. From then on, oblivion colours the scenario, due to the human hate for truth. Truthfulness allied with sheer necessity look for a chance; when it arrives, some people (or sometimes just one person) press for the return of truth. A renewed cycle displays its face. For this reason, many experienced people conclude that human beings "never learn".

Sherlock Holmes, Arsène Lupin, Inspector Maigret, Inspector Morse, Rabbi David Small and The Saint[4] are perennial best-sellers.

Regarded as second- or third-rate literature by most of those who form the intelligentsia, mystery novels are their favourite dismissed subject. "He who disdains it, wants to buy it" goes a popular saying in Brazil; the works of the intelligentsia rarely sell well. There are exceptions: Umberto Eco, a semiotics expert, became world-famous when he constructed two sophisticated detective stories, *The Name of the Rose*, with undisguised admiration for Conan Doyle and homage to him in the characters William of Baskerville and Adso of Melk, and *Foucault's Pendulum*. Luiz Alfredo Garcia Roza, a Brazilian philosopher who teaches theoretical psychoanalysis at Rio de Janeiro's university, is a part-time writer of detective stories.

Bion, the commonsense man, was adamant in stating that literature helped him to keep his mental health in good order when he was faced by very difficult times. He singled out Sherlock Holmes as his preferred real-fictitious character, who had revelled in his real world fame despite never having enjoyed (or suffered) concrete existence. It is widely known that many letters are still sent to 221b Baker Street—an address that did not exist at the time the novels were published, though Baker Street was subsequently extended. Baker Street Station (London's oldest underground station) is decorated with silhouettes of Sherlock Holmes, copied from the profile of the most successful actor who performed the role: Basil Rathbone.

Conan Doyle's writing proved to be inspirational for Bion. Hostile critics may accuse him of plagiarism. A different way to put it was heard by this author: some readers say that he misquotes Conan Doyle, in the same way that earlier critics said that he misquoted Kant. Envy and rivalry know no limits. Those destructive critics cannot see that Bion was able to get the most from the nous of those authors.

Conan Doyle constructed the character Sherlock Holmes with a built-in companion, the faithful and mostly thoughtless but action-prone friend, Dr Watson. Bion borrows those personae in order to better illustrate reality, hallucinosis and thought processes, paying homage to something that—according to his own public and private testimony—enhanced his mental health in difficult times. Meg Harris Williams spoke loudly in support of the idea that literature has healing effects on the mind; references to the fact that fictitious characters can be more real than real living non-entities have been made at least since Shelley's famous comment about the uniqueness of Shakespeare's gift of writing, and were echoed by people such Aldous Huxley (1960).

The reference to Conan Doyle's seemingly immortal creations brings with it something that has been very popular since the inception of psychoanalysis: namely, an equalisation between the two activities, that of the detectives and that of the psychoanalysts.

Bion, part of what is here called the Triple Character, somewhat infatuated with his secular titles, pretensions to immortality and self-importance, is caught in a diatribe against Watson. Bion accuses him of being an unreal character. Watson strikes back, refuting Bion's argument with a real fact: he is known, whereas Bion and psychoanalysis are not. Sherlock enters into the conversation, and Watson reminds him that "real people have to be treated roughly if the universe of discourse is to be made safe for imaginary people".

> MAN … The grey seas, the grey mists and the grey hairs. Leonardo da Vinci drew those writhing coils of hair, those swirling masses of water, to remind you of the from that lay concealed within the formless infinite. He could see them and draw them for you. What he could not see or help was that you would not be made to look even if he did draw them for you. You, if I may say so, are a "consequential idiot". "And the consequences were …" You remember the game? Still at it, still playing it. Cause and effect!
>
> BION I don't see how you are so superior and what makes you think you are so wonderful.
>
> MAN I have not supposed you would. Although you had enough capacity to know your legion of honour, and D.S.O., and mention in dispatches were baubles, glittering toys, you have worshipped them with great tenacity. If Krishna told Arjuna, if Newton, Shakespeare, Bach, Mozart, Meister Eckhart, Plato, Socrates, Dante, Job told you, you could "remark the ruck and reel[5] which coil, keep and tease the simple sight", because you are blinded by the effulgence of your glory, you are condemned for ever to admire the evacuations from which you cannot free yourself. What is most worthless about yourself—*that* is what you admire.
>
> BION Oh, shut up!
>
> MAN Very well: I shall. [I: 156–7]

Later, Bion called psychoanalysts "gas bags" (II: 343). Some analysts may be used to being seen as rough, rude, dispassionate, cold, controversial or even crazy people. Freud used to compare the psychoanalytic posture with that of surgeons, who are also often seen as sadistically dispassionate people. The laymen's view is tainted with idolisation—out of fear of death—and its opposite, iconoclasm. In other words, omnipotence, be it projected outside or not, is prevalent.

Human sympathy, tending attention and care—meaning passionate love—are intrinsically present when a real medical posture is involved. Without them, medicine loses its *raison d'être*. This applies to any medically inspired activity in all fields in which medical doctors can no longer act, where, due to the immensurable amplitude and depth of knowledge available, they must work in collaboration with others. The Renaissance polymath is a thing of the past. When a medical doctor could no longer tend his patients, nursing was born. Psychoanalysis also had to appear, by sheer necessity, when physicians could not take care of the human soul. Clinical psychology, occupational therapy, physiotherapy, speech therapy, and so on, were marks of the continuous limitations that plagued the exercise of medicine, in its increasing moves towards more specific knowledge and increasingly subdivided specialities.

The attitude of a real scientist, who tracks down like a detective where and how truth underlies (and/or overlies) any kind of external, disguising appearance, may appear rough and lacking in tact. What matters is the possibility of performing an intuitive quantum leap in the most precise possible terms, in order to detect where and when truth displays its real face out of seemingly humdrum reports made by patients. It turns the apparent scenario in order to elicit a real fact, if one exists: psychoanalysis itself happens to be during the decisive moment of a particular session. Nothing that is endowed with real value—whether in Art, Science, Medicine or Psychoanalysis—is given directly to the senses; it cannot be dealt with exclusively by the senses. In other words, conscious, external appearances are deceptive. Conversely, appearances matter a lot in placebo, reassuring, empathetic and other conscious alternatives to psychotherapy.

Negation and reaction formation are names created by Freud on the basis of his empirical observation of phenomena not previously described, in the absence of any other available names. Their prevalence indicates the presence of psychosis: a dysfunctional state when the task is the pursuit of truth-O. A most common external appearance that betrays the presence of negation can be seen in those who describe themselves in a rosy way. Out of self-indulgence, they try to hide their true self from the perception of onlookers when they deny their "other side". The mechanism through which they do this is projective identification: they deny and split the perception of the "other side" from their own awareness, and they try to do the same with other people. The ensconced paradoxical "other side" was depicted in the words of *Canto de Ossanha,* a song by Vinicius de Moraes and Baden Powell de Aquino: "The one who claims 'I give' doesn't give, for the one who really gives doesn't say so; the one who claims 'I am' is not, for the one who already is would say 'I am not'; the one who claims 'I'm the boss' is not, for the one who's really in charge isn't there because he wants to be ..."[6]

Bion's views about those who form academic or university groups exemplify the same situation. There is a self-attributed superiority born from intolerance of the unknown and denial of the basic helplessness of the human condition.

> ROBIN If I understand P.A. correctly you are lucky not to be carrying a heavy burden of preconceptions, even if they are respectable preconceptions hallowed and sanctified by a university qualification—
>
> P.A. By "university" I think you mean a number of individuals gathered together and self-endowed with the privilege of declaring who is, and who is not, worthy of joining their association. [II: 247]

The character Bion displays features akin to Winnicott's "false self" (Winnicott, 1960). In comparing the three guises of the Triple Character—Bion, Myself and P.A.—Bion is the least important. Paradoxically, as if betraying his false (or minus) self-attributed importance, Bion is resigned to being the target of mocking commentaries. He is the most despised part of the Triple Character. No other character, with the exception of Roland, is as despised as Bion in the whole text. Roland is a character who displays striking similarities to a young man once named Wilfred R. Bion.

Personal fame, manifested both in large social groups (as with some physicians who look for prominence among their peers and "other mortals") and in small, parochial or familial groups, is one of the many phenomena that indicate the presence of primary narcissism and the inborn cycle of primary envy-greed. It exhales omnipotent phantasies whose basis is denial, or challenge, or control of death and illness (sometimes these appear together in a triad), as well as omnipotent depressive phantasies whose basis is unconscious guilt of violence against one's objects, first illuminated by Freud. This kind of personal fame dismisses the presence of the other, the patient, as if any kind of treatment (therapy) did not depend on the characteristics of the person who is ill. So personal fame must be seriously considered in the analysis of anyone who is willing to go into the "caring professions".

The external appearance more often than not disguises and therefore reveals nothing about inner motivations—like any external appearances, which are given directly to our human sensuous apparatus, by the way. Nevertheless, it may be seen as a paradoxical pointer to the corresponding motivations that belong to the unconscious, numinous realm. One may say that of the people who consciously and unconsciously dedicate themselves to the "caring professions", and specifically those who pursue medical and psychological activities, most are prevalently immobilised in the paranoid-schizoid position. This manifests itself, obviously, through the development and emergence of paranoid traits: phantasies of superiority, persecution, hallucination and delusion.

A most eloquent manifestation of these phantasies of superiority takes the form of denial of death. It becomes impossible to face their dread of the basic human condition of helplessness. Professionals in these fields are subjected to primitive hopes and expectations, which in their turn fuel hallucinated demands. These were illuminated by Freud's observations about transference. The state of denial and the impossibility of facing human helplessness manifest themselves in calls for the presence of an Almighty Saviour. This Saviour traditionally assumes the form of a replacement Mother and/or Father who could guide the person "back" to a hallucinated Paradise (Freud, 1939).

Bion refers to Admiral Nelson (I: 56), who gained secular and historical fame for winning a naval battle against no less than the then all-powerful Emperor Napoleon Bonaparte. Nelson was half-blind; in Bion's view, this characteristic was essential in his successful campaign against an apparently invincible foe. In other words, it seems that Nelson was more able to obtain a true idea of reality itself than the over-infatuated—a psychiatrist could say paranoid—French Emperor, who could be pseudo-nourished by ideas of grandeur and superiority.

Bion's observation in his analysis of psychotics (1957b) allowed him to state that people in this condition feel that they are precluded from resorting to projective identification, and their inability to do this in adulthood is expressed by a triad or syndrome made up of three factors, arrogance, stupidity and curiosity, with the factors present in varying proportions. Phantasies of superiority emerge in this behavioural triad (Sandler, 2011). Experienced analysts who were able to analyse their narcissistic nuclei attained a good enough condition to observe that many people who look for analysis believe that the most important person in the analytic setting is the analyst, rather than themselves. They besiege the analyst with intensive questioning about his or her personal life. The same triad drives non-analytically trained psychologists to submit the patient to queries. The issuing of queries by the analyst or psychologist is usually linked to an arrogant, omnipotent posture, full of curiosity (driven by the analyst's desire), which is conducive to stupidity. The interviewer is limited by an arrogant prejudice: the patient *has to* tell him the truth. On the other hand, real analysts make comparatively few queries. Instead of hoping that the patient can answer queries about his or her personality, the analyst looks for hidden answers contained in the patient's free associations, which include non-verbal manifestations. All of this is spontaneously issued in the first interview. According to Virginia Leone Bicudo, Melanie Klein used to say that the patient "tells" the analyst how his or her analysis will be right from the first interview. If patients were able to face their inner truth, they would never be patients. Anyway, patients are entitled to display the arrogance included in their own queries when they ask something as if the analyst *had to* answer—this is why they are patients. In the same fashion, making arrogant queries includes a posture of sexual curiosity; the triad is completed with a sense of stupidity: the very issuing of one question after the other indicates a mindlessness. The patient behaves as if he or she were empty of thoughts and intuition.

The observation obtained through the application of the psychoanalytic method allows for a more precise apprehension of a social event, usually called "Romanticism", which promoted the decay of an outstanding achievement of the Enlightenment: attention to the individual was mistaken for individualism. In social terms, Western civilisation's social systems had to distinguish the individual-oriented procedures of the Enlightenment, which introduced care for the individual being, from the narcissistic individualism that characterised Romanticism, the decadence of the Romantic Movement. If the spectrum of observation goes from the individual and reaches the social level, a middle level would consider family organisations; the term to describe the emergence of phantasies of superiority could be the spoiling of a child when there is no distinction between personal care and personalism. This may be further complicated by the imbalance between what Bion, after Freud, called "social-ism" and "narcissism": returning to the socio-historic level, an illustration can be seen with human scourges who heavily sponsored (or still sponsor) and promoted "personality cults"—the socio-cultural embodiment of phantasies of superiority. The Trilogy quotes Hitler; one may also be reminded of Stalin, Mao Zedong, Fidel Castro, Osama Bin Laden, Enver Hoxha and Kim Il Jong. The social surge of those phantasies, which terrorised entire generations—including Bion's—was foreseen with uncanny precision by philosophers such as Nietzsche and later observed by many others, such as Freud (1915, 1939) Niebuhr (1941), Russell (1946) and Schorske (1961).

> P.A. We consider the attempt to improve humans both worthwhile and urgent. [III: 528]

> FORTY YEARS You are too personal, Twenty-five. You've learnt that from P. A. He is always being personal.
>
> FIFTY YEARS Not personal—specific.
>
> P.A. I have great respect for the individual. Do you think that is wrong? [III: 461]

The delusion of fame can be seen in Bion's resorting to a metaphorical construction by a remarkable author whose work matches that of Shakespeare, though he is less known outside the literary milieu: John Milton. In his monody *Lycidas*, he foretold the downfall of the corrupt clergy who encircled his life and asphyxiated his people. This group was then at the height of their political power and secular fame:

> Fame is no plant that grows on mortal soil,
> Nor in the glistering foil
> Set off to th'world, nor in broad rumour lies,
> But lives and spreads aloft by those pure eyes
> And perfect witness of all-judging Jove;
> As he pronounces lastly on each deed,
> Of so much fame in Heav'n expect thy meed.

There are readers who are either suspicious or self-righteous; usually they deny those features in themselves, split them from their awareness, and project them outside, creating conditions conducive to projective identification. This assumes the form of accusations: that Bion wanted to occupy a position of prototypical excellence. In the same sense, the present book would be just a eulogy, rather than an appreciation of truthful observations which are useful in the everyday clinic. Nevertheless, there are many statements by Bion that challenge this idea:

> P.A. There is no such thing as a "well-known analyst"; an analyst is one who at one stage of fashion is famous, at another infamous; the barrier between "famous" and "infamous" is as slight as the verbal "in". It is unimportant—except to the psychoanalyst who cannot afford to be unaware that it is a "built-in" part of his profession. [III: 520]

> ROLAND If you want the doctor to be honoured he should also be recognised as the source of the knowledge that enables the addict to inject his veins with heroin.
>
> P.A. I did not mean to be advocating honours. Perhaps, if I were to do so, I should advocate "dishonours", statues erected to the Marquis de Sade for his services to cruelty.
>
> ROLAND Are you then opposed to "honours"?
>
> P.A. "Honours", as part of institutional organisation, is not a matter on which I am qualified to speak. I do not remember anything in the course of my experience with small groups which provided me with material for interpretation. Even a social conjecture becomes hazardous if, when I am speculating or privately discussing a few speculative phantasies, it is assumed that it carries the force of a scientifically derived formulation. But I *would* be prepared to express an opinion in a psychoanalysis and to be held responsible for what I said. In that context there is evidence that a patient must respect himself. If this sounds too obvious I can only regret that I have to use words which have become debased and for which there is little respect. Here it is easier to see that we must respect each other. I knew a successful and wealthy farmer who had great and justified respect for a drunken and illiterate cowherd when he spoke of any matters relating to cattle. "Honour thy father and thy mother" is an injunction which lacks validity unless the father and mother are worthy of respect. The general principle has to be worth applying in

> a precise instance. The individual is always a particular instance to himself; whether he can respect himself is a matter which *he* must decide. I do not know if this bears on the question you ask, but I think it is related to it. There are good grounds for supposing that the character of a group would be revealed by individual people or activities or achievements it chose to honour + or −.
>
> ROBIN By "honour + or −" I suppose you mean honour or dishonour.
>
> P.A. Yes. Part of the ambiguity and uncertainty of psychoanalytic interpretation is that we have to speak spontaneously and cannot at such short notice express ourselves with precision. However accurate we may try to be there is the ambiguity of imprecision of the language we use. [III: 529–30]

Morals "without morality" is one of the main tools of phantasies of superiority. The reader interested in becoming acquainted with psychoanalytic research into the prevalence of the moral vertex, as elicited by Bion in his studies about the schizophrenic thought, might find further readings useful:

> Omniscience substitutes for the discrimination between true and false a dictatorial affirmation that one thing is morally right and the other wrong. The assumption of omniscience that denies reality ensures that the morality thus engendered is a function of psychosis. Discrimination between true and false is a function of the non-psychotic part of the personality and its factors. There is thus potentially a conflict between assertion of truth and assertion of moral ascendancy. [Bion, 1967, p. 114]

Developments in the psychoanalytic study of the moral vertex can be seen with the discovery of the "minus" realm (Bion, 1962, p. 89; Green, 1973, 1986, 1997a, 1997b, 2000, 2003; Sandler, 2005, 2011).

Old friends revisited …

It is a fact well known to psychoanalysts that the re-reading of real texts—or texts written by the so-called "great authors"—may furnish a rewarding recognition of what may be called "old friends". As time goes by, the "revisited old friend" seems to appear invigorated. For example: a young boy first read *A Study in Scarlet*, the first Sherlock Holmes novel, at fifteen. Within twenty years, after having undergone medical training, he recognised that this novel was his initiation to scientific research. The same occurred with Bion's resorting to Conan Doyle's characters, and the same may occur with some readers of the Trilogy.

The generators of *idées-mères* of the past who so impressed Wilfred Bion compose what the statistically-minded reader would call a significant sample of the history of ideas in Western civilisation, with mild tinctures from thinkers of Eastern civilisation: Socrates, Plato, Euclid, Francis Bacon, John Milton, William Shakespeare, Gerard Manley Hopkins, Robert Browning, René Descartes, John Locke, Immanuel Kant, Johann Wolfgang von Goethe, David Hume, Bishop Berkeley, Isaac Newton, Samuel Johnson, Alexander Pope, William Wordsworth, William Blake, John Ruskin, John Keats, Percy Shelley, Arthur Conan Doyle, Rupert Brooke, Friedrich Nietzsche, Arthur Rimbaud, James Joyce, Ezra Pound, Sigmund Freud, Albert Einstein, Omar Khayyam, Melanie Klein, Werner Heisenberg; and in between, the Old and New Testaments, little bits of the *Bhagavad Gita*,[7] and Sufism. As a time-space table, the clock ticks from Edwardian England, complete with Scottish, Welsh and Indian friends and their contrapuntal German relatives, with a fascination for France and Italy, reaching the decay of British Empire and a sojourn in the (North and South) American Wild West. A pageant of knowledge? The reader may or may not be familiar with the written contributions of those authors. In the latter case, he or she is free to make their acquaintance.

> MYCROFT So do I. Your treatise on a hundred or so cigar ashes. Who on earth could possibly remember Myself on psychoanalysis or sex—whatever that may be! I'd give the lot of them for Irene Adler. She was at least fun. Even God didn't spend the whole of his time obsessed with religion. You would think he was fascinated by being worshipped like one of the psychoanalysts. *That* religion has to be a whole time job worshipping psychoanalysis and singing hymns to the ruling psychoanalyst and his divine attributes. Now: let me show *you* something. I'll give you sight of—the promised land! Listen!—it's Browning speaking. "Now the cloud rift broadens, spanning earth that's under, wide our world displays its worth, man's strife and strife's success. What! They smile! Our names, our deeds so soon erases time upon his tablet where one hundred thousand are spread out!" [I: 120]

Irene Adler was Sherlock Holmes's one and only love interest. The same excerpt contains a warning: Bion will not make concessions to a novel form of pseudo-religious rituals, clothed with terms derived from psychoanalysis and profiting from the hallucinated fact that Freud called "transference" (Freud, 1912a).

> MAN One famed anthropologist says the bone formation of the skull does not lend itself to attachment of the tongue muscle for use in articulate speech. The attachment of the penis to the anatomy, the vagina likewise, is in its own fashion appropriate and beautiful. What God has joined together let no man put asunder.
>
> BION How could we put them together or put them asunder? These are anatomical structures with physiological functions, and I for my part have not in my conscious memory ever known a time when conscious and unconscious aim and ideal have been possible to divorce from each other. Nor have I ever known a time when these constantly conjoined objects were on good terms with each other except for short periods; enough to make me long for more.
>
> MAN Rosemary and I realise that. I was only a little while back saying to Rosemary—was I not Rosie?—
>
> BION Rosie! Good God! Rosie!
>
> MAN That is what I said. You do not approve, so you sneer; if our terms of endearment are not yours, your hostility is at once in evidence.
>
> BION That is me. I did not choose my education or my personality. I would rather I were tolerant. What you say and do is not my business, but what you say and do stimulates disagreeable feelings in me, as in this instance; feelings are aroused in me which I would rather did not come together. Yet they constantly *do* come together. I can do nothing about your arousing such feelings. I can do nothing about the feelings that in fact are aroused. [I: 164]

... and older friends put in abeyance due to pragmatism

In letting Bion provide his own hints to the reader, one may be reminded that, according to him, "Mathematics, science as known hitherto, can provide no model" (I: 61). This may come as an unwelcome surprise to at least some of Bion's readers around the world: both to the idolaters who like to applaud what they see as his "great erudition" and to the iconoclasts who like to denounce what they see as his attempt to "mathematise" psychoanalysis. Both, by the way, have serious reservations about the Trilogy, as observed earlier. Bion's fondness for mathematical philosophy, mistaken for an alleged mathematisation of psychoanalysis, plays a role here. The quasi-mathematical tools, in fact inspired by the philosophy of mathematics rather than by mathematics-in-itself, that he used in *Learning from Experience*, *Elements of Psychoanalysis* and *Transformations* are virtually abandoned, with few exceptions: in the same way that he used the quasi-biological (or quasi-genetic) signs ♀♂ to better present his hypothesis about container and contained, he still uses quasi-mathematical formulations, resorting to the better impact of graphical signs *vis-a-vis* the lower performance of single words or unpoetical phrases (Bion, 1962, 1963; a review appears in Sandler, 2005 and a clinical application in Sandler, 2011).

Being interested in the philosophy of mathematics, or metaphysics, the first attempt at epistemology, Bion coupled his own foray into it with a few seminal observations from Kant. The first time he did this in a published work was 1963, with his amendment of two Kant-inspired categories in The Grid, his operative tool to verify any existing truth value in the statements made in an analytic session. These were definitory hypothesis (Column 1) and Ψ, or lies (Column 2). The former corresponded to Kant's pre-conceptions; the latter to the whole of Kant's endeavour, namely, his questioning about the existence of pure reason (Kant, 1781).

To achieve this aim in the simplest way possible, Bion tried to resort to what seems to be the most compact form hitherto available, again furnished by mathematical notation. In creating the quasi-mathematical symbol O, Bion wished to denote the numinous realm of the unconscious: the space-time where and when human and individual truth resides—ultimate reality, absolute truth. It was an integral part of the introduction of the theory of transformations and invariants to psychoanalysis (Bion, 1965, p. 12). Here the psychoanalytical establishment had at its disposal a theory created to enhance psychoanalysts' powers of observation. It was Bion's contribution to highlight the importance of the act of observation in psychoanalysis, which had sunk under the load of prejudiced pseudo-theories applied both *a priori* and *ad hoc* on lower-grade data, empirical material.

In Bion's epoch, there was a growing dominance of the idea that it would suffice to learn "officially approved theories" and try to find them in one's practice. This posture paved the way to what can be seen as the creation of yet more jargon. Learning the psychoanalytical lexicon could give someone a qualification to be a psychoanalyst—a tendency later emphasised by André Green (Green, 2003). One may philosophise about the Oedipus complex. One may know by heart the pages of the *Standard Edition* or the myriad new editions that are emerging today due to commercial reasons. But one must be a real analyst to be able to observe and discriminate, and more than that, to specifically name and communicate the peculiar, microscopically specific evolving way in which each patient may experience and phantasise "Oedipus". This "learning by heart" posture dismisses a fact: that the full realisation of theories is only possible if one undergoes a personal analysis with a real analyst, and has a good enough experience of that which the theory attempts to formulate. In this case, the practitioner learns through his or her own experience. Then he or she may have a chance to introject that which the theory (any theory) formulates as a caricature (an exaggeration of a particular parts of the whole in order to aid identification), an attempt to keep alive its counterpart in real experience. No book would explain how or when this living, real counterpart occurs, because it occurs on the spur of the moment of an analytic experience. Sigmund Freud and Melanie Klein never knew that particular patient who comes to any given psychoanalyst, who is neither Freud nor Klein. Moreover, with very few exceptions, most of the people who actually met Freud and Klein are dead, like Freud and Klein themselves. Therefore, their clinical examples, even when they attain a heuristic and universal—scientific—value, cannot be applied *in toto*, or worse, in a mechanistic way, to any other patient. Rather than being the desired examples of "how to", their case studies show that "it can be done". In this sense, the best analytic sessions or insights are those which are amenable to being forgotten: they are "the dawn of oblivion". In being forgotten, they have a chance to be introjected into the individual unconscious, and may be recalled in different forms, naturally, through free associations.

Bion seemed to think that a two-pronged way out of the then prevailing adoption of *a priori* and *ad hoc* theories and the use and abuse of jargon would be (i) an attempt to develop a theory of observation in psychoanalysis—or psychoanalytic observation; and (ii) a more precise approach to theories of psychoanalysis proper. This way out was not new—it was, again, a revival of something that Freud did (Bion,

1965; the introduction to *The Language of Bion*, Sandler, 2005, dwells on this subject). Bion was not alone in this attempt: he quotes Drs John Wisdom, Joseph Sandler and John Bowlby, among others, as professionals involved in the development of theories of psychoanalysis proper. Bion's appeal to literary-artistic formulations was another way to introduce his theory of psychoanalytical observation.

Forty years later, the tendency to adopt *a priori* and *ad hoc* theories and the abusive use of jargon proved to be insurmountable. It easily won political backing in the psychoanalytic movement, due to its apparent simplicity and infinite provision of catchwords, mantras and shibboleths—the indispensable tool of politicians. The existing considerable stock of psychoanalytic "theories" was augmented. Where there was "id", there are now "empathetic self", "neuro-psychoanalysis" and "enactment". Conversely, to Bion and Winnicott—and according to reports left by Freud's patients (for example, Wortis, 1954)—any use of jargon constitutes an abuse.

In *Transformations*, Bion furnishes a model to display the analyst's task: a painter who tries to depict a given landscape. One of the features of the analyst's task is "public action": to make available to himself and to others both his and his patient's "fight for an insight". The eventual insight is a product of a "language of achievement", a concept that Bion introduced five years later with the help of another man of literature, John Keats (Bion, 1970; Sandler, 2005).

Bion adds to his attempt quasi-mathematical signs other than "O": T to represent Transformation; Ta to represent transformations stemming from a psychoanalyst; Tp to represent transformations stemming from a patient seen by a psychoanalyst; Tα to represent a specific *process* of transformation as well as a general symbol to represent any process of transformation—therefore denoting a living, dynamic movement; and Tβ to represent a specific *final product* of a given transformation. Therefore, Tβ denotes static, concrete or solid stuff, amenable to be vivified later, after having initiated a further cycle of transformations. It is implicit that Bion is encircling the mystery of the origin of life, something that would not surprise any real psychoanalyst, who is always dealing with this. The Trilogy may be regarded as a practical lesson, or, in today's parlance, a master class, in much of the content of *Transformations* and *Attention and Interpretation*.

In construing the Trilogy, Bion develops his previously introduced system of theories of observation (Bion, 1965, p. 34; 1970, p. 87), and also the theories of psychoanalysis already available, previously developed by Freud and Klein. An analytical review of those theories *vis à vis* the system of theories of psychoanalysis can be seen elsewhere (Sandler, 2005, pp. 533, 743, 833). The practical lesson on those theories allows—like any practical lesson—increasing transient glimpses of aspects of eventual emanations that present immaterial, psychic reality, "O", among the variegated phenomena that can be observed throughout an analytic session. It is not by coincidence that Bion called the first book of the Trilogy *The Dream*: this is the first and foremost, *primus inter pares* method of psychoanalysis, the one that marked Bion's most important extensions to Freud's contributions.

Anyone who has done a practical lesson, or experienced a practical activity, like psychoanalysis and medicine, as well as any artistic endeavour, learns by experience the meaning of the term "realisation". Bion created other quasi-mathematical symbols in addition to "O" in order to represent the realisation. Let us return to his model of a painter who tries to paint a landscape:

> A sign to represent the realisation would denote … the landscape as a thing-in-itself, and therefore distinguish it from both $T_2\alpha$ [the painter's processes of transformation of that which he saw] and $T_2\beta$ [the completed painting]. The sign would denote something that is not a mental phenomenon and therefore, like Kant's thing-in-itself, can never be known. I introduce the idea of the thing-in-itself in order to make clear the status of $T_2\alpha$ and $T_2\beta$ as signs for mental phenomena.
>
> The use of these signs may be clarified by an illustration: The patient enters and, following a convention established in the analysis, shakes hands. This is an external fact, what I have called a "realisation". In so far as it is useful to regard it as a thing-in-itself and unknowable (in Kant's sense) it is denoted by the sign O. The phenomenon, corresponding to the external fact, as it exists in the mind of the patient, is represented by the sign T(patient)α. [Bion, 1965, pp. 12–13]

Where the quasi-mathematical notation symbolises the numinous realm, in the case of "O" (after Kant, 1781), the non-sensuous experience, the thing-in-itself, it corresponds to Plato's Ideal Forms. Where it symbolises the phenomenal realm, in the case of Ta or Tpα and Ta or Tpβ, it represents what is ultimately unknowable. Therefore, all of them correspond to psychic facts as they are, appertaining to the numinous realm of the unconscious system and of the id—in the case of "O"—and to the phenomenal realm of the pre-conscious (Ta or Tpα) and conscious (Ta or Tpβ).

Taking into account that a large part of the text included in the Trilogy exemplifies what the variegated transformations are all about, let us return to the invariant, or in its most compact formulation, "O", the main goal of the book. Or, more precisely, an attempt to describe and depict a number of "O"s of humankind found by a person named Wilfred Ruprecht Bion in his path through his own life. "O" corresponds to "origin". This is explicitly stated: "I shall therefore assume that the material provided by the analytic session is significant for its being the patient's view (representation) of certain facts which are the origin (O) of his reaction" (Bion, 1965, p. 15).

At least once, in the Trilogy, Bion referred to it as "zero", probably in order to stress its elemental ethos of origin, in a humorous guise (I: 36). One may evolve from it or to it. One should not be identified with it, one cannot describe it verbally, and one cannot know it. One can, through *becoming* (Bion, 1965, pp. 140 ff.; 1970, p. 26), be O. "O does not fall in the domain of knowledge or learning save incidentally; it can 'become', but it cannot be 'known'" (Bion, 1970, 26).

It is not, as it would seem, a theoretical formulation *per se*, but rather a practical one which seemed to allow more practical extensions—the purpose of the Trilogy. Bion states it in many parts of his work, stressing its usefulness during an analytic session, as something to be pursued. He adds it to descriptions of the analyst's task as established by Freud:

> The psychoanalyst tries to help the patient to transform that part of an emotional experience of which he is unconscious into an emotional experience of which he is conscious. If he does this he helps the patient to achieve private knowledge. But since scientific work demands communication of discovery to other workers the psychoanalyst must transform *his* private experience of psychoanalysis so that it becomes a public experience. The artist is used here as a model intended to indicate that the criteria for a psychoanalytic paper are that it should stimulate in the reader the emotional experience that the writer intends, that its power to stimulate should be durable, and that the emotional experience thus stimulated should be an accurate representation of the psychoanalytic experience ("Oa") that stimulated the writer in the first place. [Bion, 1965, pp. 32–33]

The obstacles to intuiting it are sometimes seemingly insurmountable. It depends on the activity of feeble beings—human beings—using a new tool, psychoanalysis. What slowly emerges in *Transformations*, a book that presents a theory able to be presented in a more practical sense, is that the very inaccessibility of "O" is its betrayal not to the senses, but to our fleeting apprehension. To deal with resistances, lies (Column 2 categories of the Grid) and hallucinations are ways of glimpsing "O" transiently, exactly in the sense depicted by Freud in *The Interpretation of Dreams* and his grasping of the paths to the formations of symptoms (Freud, 1933a).

In dispensing with the signs Ta and Tp in favour of more detailed descriptions of the many Tas and Tps he stumbled on during his life, Bion seemed to be more free to use "O":

> I want to discuss man, but as soon I say that, I realise the word "man" has a definite, perhaps misleadingly and frustratingly definite, meaning. [I: 87]
>
> O is by definition indestructible and not subject to, circumscribed by, beginnings and ends, rules, laws of nature or any construct of the human mind. In the domain of human comprehension Melanie Klein could not reconcile herself to the fact that whenever she had made herself understood, that fact rendered what she understood no longer "alive". [I: 88–89]

It is easy to show that Bion's appeal to the philosophy of mathematics has a particular purpose: namely, to talk about psychoanalytic practice though the use of psychoanalytic observations:

> ROBIN Is there an analogy in the relationship between group analysis and psychoanalysis proper?
>
> P.A. It is a seductive possibility. Detailed psychoanalytic scrutiny reveals movements, up and down, of the individual particles composing a group; the "up and down" movement would give an illusion of waves, as when the sea is compared visually with the drops of water in it. Visual images penetrate deeply in the way that a capacity for sight extends the range of the infant; it is not limited to what it can grasp or touch. Mobility does not extend as far as the eye can reach.

ROBIN What about the range of visual images in geometry? That was extended by algebraic, not visual pictures of lines and circles.

ROLAND Desargues extended the grasp of mathematics even though his diagram was visual.

ROBIN The development of projective geometry which followed was not visual.

P.A. The person concerned with conic section falls back on the operation of an inner eye. Psychoanalytically individuals still seem to rely on the existence of a diaphragm analogous to that separating the lungs from the digestive canal. There is a survival of that mentality in the "division" which is made between pre-natal and post-natal—as if *birth* were of great significance—

PRIEST And death which, as I have remarked before, you also speak of as if it were obvious to anyone except possibly stupid people like priests. We are assumed to deny death because we are afraid of it. It seems to me to be a naïve example of psychoanalytical misinterpretation and ignorance of religious teaching and experience.

P.A. It is not naivety that is limited to psychoanalysis. I would not defend myself against such a charge, but the tone you employ when you formulate your observation invites a response which becomes either an admission of guilt or an aggressive repudiation.

ROLAND Admission of guilt? You don't say what crime.

P.A. I am not bringing the accusation. I am merely trying to draw attention to the way in which a feeling of guilt is evoked or created; it is basic, fundamental. The crime—rational, logical—and the feeling of guilt are natural partners. It is a matter to which justice, morals, intellectual ingenuity can be devoted for so long as anyone can spare the time and energy.

ROLAND The psychoanalytical view is an invitation to create a lawless and undisciplined world.

P.A. There is no "psychoanalytical" view. But there are people who can use psychoanalytical theories to support any activity they choose. That is why we try to train people who are not only able, but who also wish to help, not hinder, the individual.

ROLAND Individual burglars, robbers, murderers as well?

P.A. The occupation or the philosophy of individuals is not usually—in the culture with which I am acquainted—believed to be the concern of doctors or surgeons; they are usually expected to confine themselves to medicine and surgery. I have an idea of how I ought to run my own life, but what I consider to be appropriate for me has nothing do to with an individual "not-me". I choose to train people I wish to help, but my ambition is not psychoanalysis—it is me.

PRIEST I could not watch a child putting its hand into a fire to grasp a live coal. If I saw adult behaviour likely to have similarly evil consequences I would intervene.

ALICE Anyone would.

P.A. These are hypothetical situations and the problems posed can be solved logically. In real life problems appear in a form which is not susceptible to solution theoretically; you have to act or refrain from acting. These discussions are important not in themselves, but because they promote readiness. Psychoanalysis is a kind of action which is a *prelude* to action. In the individual a nerve impulse is a prelude to action; it is not a thought. "Tell me", a neurologist will say, "if you feel anything when I touch your foot." I do not need to ask such a question because I can see for myself if the patient feels anything when I touch his sensory apparatus with an idea, or a grimace, or a tone of voice. That is one reason why a psychoanalysis is not a social conversation or vice versa; the behaviour of a psychoanalyst conversing in a psychoanalysis is *not* the same as the behaviour of a psychoanalyst conversing at a dinner party. Confusion occurs because that important distinction is not observed. [III: 554–6]

CHAPTER THREE

Is there an object-alienated science?

Any contact with the unknown is mostly abhorred. Among the many manifestations—symptoms—of this abhorrence is the precocious naming of unknown things, facts and events, be they material or not. This gives the beholder an impression of knowledge about what remains unknown despite the fact that it is named. Unborn children already receive a name—and many of them dislike it. The step from naming to labelling is too short; very soon labels are transformed into jargon—which is liable to be misused by people who do not have direct experience of seeing or using those things, events or facts.

Bion had at his disposal the experience of a multitude of predecessors, over at least two millennia, in unsuccessful labelling approaches to "O": myth-makers, theologians, philosophers, literary authors, neurologists, psychoanalysts. They coined labels like "psyche", "phrenes", "spirit", "soul", "humanity", "man", "heart", "mind", "brain", "psychoanalysis", "id-ego-superego", "love", "woman", "child", and so on.

The labels are used in a method of reasoning known as deductive logic, which is trapped in a circularity: the self-feeding proof of its own assumptions, furnishing no way out to the discovery of anything new (Davies, 1992; Penrose, 1989, 1994; Sandler, 1997a). Those who claim that there is no need to find eventual empirical verification of statements and reasoning fall into the epistemological trap, due to their heavy leaning towards idealistic approaches. Theirs is a factory of variegated beliefs travestied with unscientific "explanations", which obeys a special kind of self-feeding logic, issued by complicated minds which, under a trained psychiatric vertex, are indistinguishable from hallucinosis.

Freud and Bion were ingrained with, or introjected by, Aristotle's concept of the mathematical object, in a sense similar to that maintained by Kant, Schopenhauer and Nietzsche. Before writing the Trilogy, Bion had already suggested the existence of a psychoanalytical object (Bion, 1962, pp. 67–68; a review can be seen in Sandler, 2005, p. 592). He seemed to spare no efforts to add formulations that could help the unceasing approach to reality, stemming from other disciplines such as poetry, theology, epistemology, music and painting. One may consider that Bion was a person who abhorred authoritarianism and seemed to be fashion-proof from the time he had overcome his protracted adolescence. He warned through all his written contributions that that the purpose of what were, after all, ancillary methods was radically different from the purpose of psychoanalysis. Keeping the difference firmly in mind may prevent the confusion of means with ends:

> The practical point is—no further investigation of psychoanalysis, but the psyche it betrays. *That* needs to be investigated through the medium of *mental* patterns; *that* which is indicated is *not* a symptom; *that* is not a cause of the symptom; *that* is not a disease or *any*thing subordinate. Psychoanalysis itself is just a stripe on the coat of the tiger. Ultimately it may meet the Tiger—The Thing Itself—O. [I: 112]

Perhaps it would be opportune to examine the whole formulation in "analytical" terms—a method which was successful in scientific branches such as chemistry and inspired Freud in his attempt to name his discovery. "No further investigation of psychoanalysis" means that any object-alienated science is doomed to failure. Thus debased, it is condemned to be a pseudo-science. Epistemology and its later development, the theory of science, always run the same risk. Karl Popper is one who tried to warn us of the existence of this approach, even though he was limited by a positivistic view of science. He could not see that the enemies of science were within his own movement.

"*That* needs to be investigated through the medium of mental patterns" can be seen as a way to emphasise Kant's approach with a specific amendment to psychoanalysts, in the sense that Bion's statement finely discriminates the object of research from the methods used to research the object.

"Mental patterns" can be seen as a shorthand formulation of "psychoanalysis" in a Wordsworthian use of colloquial language—even though the single term "mental" is liable to be dealt with in such a way that its meaning may be taken for granted—like jargon or slang.

"Psychoanalysis" is regarded by Bion as a field of investigation spoiled by the actions of members of the psychoanalytic movement. Bion's warnings were similar, even if couched in different words, to those coming from many authors such as Karl Menninger, John Wisdom, Kurt Eissler, Robert Wallerstein and Otto Kernberg, to quote a few. All of them echoed Freud, who tried to cope with, for example, the misunderstanding of Alfred Adler and Otto Rank—due to their simplistic approaches—and of Carl Gustav Jung and Wilhelm Reich—due to their political approaches. All of them flowed into the turbulent river of underrating real psychoanalysis. Rivalry travestied as criticism created different attacks subsumed by some invariants, for example: "Freud was too inclined to reductionism"; "everything is sex"; or "everything is just intra-psychic, Freud discarded socio-cultural influences", and so on. The rivals wanted to erect a superior psychoanalysis: the best example of which, inspired by Jung, was enforced by Matthias Göring, an elder cousin of Hermann Göring.

"*That* which is indicated is *not* a symptom; *that* is not a cause of the symptom; *that* is not a disease or *any*thing subordinate". This formulation can be regarded as a serious warning against causal hypersimplifications modelled on positivism, pervaded with morals and expectations. The final part of the quotation (Tiger, Thing Itself) brings with it the numinous realm—the purpose of real psychoanalysis.

> P.A. Mystery is real life; real life is the concern of real analysis. Jargon passes for psychoanalysis, as sound is substituted for verse, verbal facility for literature and poetry, trompe l'oeil representations for painting. Real self-murder is not observed, and accidental suicide passes for the real thing which is planned, worked out in detail economically to create real effect. [II: 307]

CHAPTER FOUR

The royal road

In *The Interpretation of Dreams*, Freud observed that dreams are the "royal road to a knowledge of the unconscious processes of the mind"—for example, one may know something about dream work. Freud did not observe that one might have the royal road to a knowledge of the unconscious—or, more precisely, the unconscious-in-itself. That would constitute a denial of the existence of the unconscious—the unknown—because one would know what is unknown. Many—too many?—readers entertained no second thoughts in omitting the last part of the sentence ("processes of the mind"). When this is extracted, the original sense, which translates the original concept, is irremediably ruined. Bowing to the popularity of the Internet at the expense of quoting from particular books and papers, three examples, drawn at random from the Web, may serve as a representative sample of the state of affairs in the psychoanalytic movement. Whether this is sad or not, readers may decide for themselves. Supposed authorities misquote Freud; those who were able to spot the misquotation add to the confusion with renewed misquotations in a different guise. This progression or regression—each reader is allowed to make his or her choice—began in the 1990s: that is, fifteen years after the publication of the Trilogy. One already has at one's disposal a half-century's worth of misquotations: a serious indication that Bion's warnings about the future of psychoanalysis were—in general terms—not heard.

At www.freudfile.org/psychoanalysis/dream_interpretation_and.html, signed by J. Jones, one may read:

> Dream analysis, in psychoanalysis, provides the possibility to decipher the mystery of neurotic disorders, specifically hysteria, and secondly, it opens the road towards unconscious. Freud's phrase: "The interpretation of dreams is the royal road to a knowledge of the unconscious" has become famous.

Any observant reader may spot the flaw in the quotation, where "unconscious processes of the mind" is replaced by just "unconscious".

At www.encyclopedia.com/doc/1G2–3435300386.html, signed by Roger Perron one may read:

> For Freud, the interpretation of dreams was the *via regia*, the royal road leading to the unconscious. On several occasions, in *The Interpretation of Dreams*, he noted that the procedure should be carried to the extreme, yet the examples he provided could hardly be said to adhere to this recommendation—presumably because these are for the most part his own dreams, and he may have been reluctant to expose the most intimate aspects of his personal life. It is in any case doubtful that such an exhaustion of meaning is conceivable or even desirable. Dream interpretation may well be the royal road to the unconscious, but the unconscious is inexhaustible. Nor is it desirable for either patient or analyst to claim that the moment has arrived when there is nothing more to be said.

As has occurred before, Freud is criticised on the basis not of what he said, but of misunderstandings based on misreadings of what he said.

Hanna Segal's credentials in the psychoanalytic movement need no description. After the death of Melanie Klein, according to some sources (for example, Grosskurth, 1986) she became the crown princess of the "Kleinian" movement. After Anna Freud's death, the "Kleinian" establishment lost some of its role and reputation as outsider, being gradually more accepted and inserted into the mainstream of the psychoanalytic movement. This roughly coincided with a disillusionment due, at least in part, to impossible promises of cure obtained through the application of psychoanalysis—or what those people understood to be psychoanalysis—made by members of the psychoanalytical establishment. Simultaneously, there was an increasing social demand for a "better psychoanalysis", based on doubts about its therapeutic value. The therapeutic value was measured by the ability of analysts to provide socially adapted behaviour and the extinction of psychiatric symptoms, now as defined by the DSM classification. The demands stemmed from critics oriented by positivistic and therefore concrete criteria. Was the thing subjected to criticism real psychoanalysis or not? An interview with Hanna Segal by Daniel Pick and Lyndal Roper at www.psychoanalysis.org.uk/segalhwj.htm may reflect this:

> Daniel Pick: The first thing that we wanted to explore was the significance of Freud's Interpretation of Dreams for psychoanalysis today. As we reach its centenary, does its original interpretative model still provide "the royal road" to a new understanding of dreams and of the unconscious in the way that Freud believed?
> Hanna Segal: Yes and no. Freud is often misquoted; he never said that the dream is the royal road to the unconscious; but he did say that the interpretation of the dream is the royal road to the unconscious. In present-day analysis people vary greatly in how much attention they pay to the dream. I belong to those that like to work with dreams, but the whole attitude to the dream has changed.

A second misreading added to the first misreading means confusion and chaos of knowledge. Forty years earlier, Bion formulated this question:

> What part of England or Shakespeare was it that forged the England that is eternal and will be for ever England? What is foreign soil? Which part is Rupert Brooke, Shakespeare, Milton? Which part will be for ever foreign? [I: 42]

Replace England and Shakespeare with Psychoanalysis and Freud: unscientific psychoanalysis is fated to be foreign to real psychoanalysis. There is a difference between being free from a rigid, concrete, literal reading of the text and a reading that is so "free-for-all" that the reader puts his or her personal meanings on the text instead of intuiting the ineffable meaning and sense that lies beyond the concrete form of the text. Does Dr Segal's answer to Mr Pick prove that an authoritarian remedy is worse than the disease? That no learning is less damaging than little learning? Due to unknown factors, Dr Segal's statements never were checked. This writer observes the damaging effect on science of the tendency of human groups towards idolisation of certain individuals, well described by Hans A. Thorner (1981). Again and again, one may see the truth conveyed in Bacon's observation about religion: "all colours will agree in the dark".

Bion was able to elicit Freud's then forgotten mode of practising psychoanalysis, which had a living push from Melanie Klein: a perpetual, dynamic "going to", paradoxically linked to an ever-changing trial that strives to be near to what remains unchanged—the variable invariant. Bion's term for this living movement is "pursuing truth-O" (Bion, 1970, p. 9).

> PRIEST The Kingdom of Heaven is not "on earth" and nor is the place that chap from Hippotades was when Augustine wrote the City of God. Plato knew that; Socrates was not so wise.
>
> ROBIN: "... as if of hemlock I had drunk," said Keats.
>
> PRIEST: He should have tried peyote; the Aztecs knew better.
>
> SHERLOCK HOLMES Even they had to wait till the Supreme Court recognised the Native American Church—
>
> PRIEST Which recognised the Holy Spanish Church of Cortes, the Holy Catholic Church. As I was saying, Plato did not lack wisdom to the point of drinking hemlock.
>
> SHERLOCK HOLMES Nor, I gather, did you take the draught you offered the Court assembled in the Death Pit of Ur.
>
> PRIEST: There is no evidence.
>
> SHERLOCK HOLMES *That* is the evidence. My business is facts and I have to respect all kinds of evidence including negative evidence—
>
> P.A. Which you have to interpret. I interpret—do not dispense—facts.
>
> SHERLOCK HOLMES I do not argue against your vertex. I only argue against the favouritism you show for one fact rather than another and one vertex rather than another.

PRIEST So do I. God is not mocked, but you behave as if you do not have to bother with God because you cannot be confronted with a particular category of a fact. Isn't that music hellish?

P.A. You give a perfect example of applying a religious category appropriate to religious categories of localisation.

PRIEST I do not. Like you, I have to use topographical terminology to describe categories and locations when I am discussing, as here, a subject which has no known locality. One prophet said, "The Kingdom of Heaven is within you".

ROLAND Psychoanalysts deprecate these Kleinian statements.

ROBIN Good Lord! Don't say you have psychoanalysts in Heaven.

ROLAND You rush to conclusions. I didn't say I was in Heaven—or Hell. I did say I was dead.

ROSEMARY I never regarded physical death as a necessary qualification for being dead.

PRIEST: The classics are dead.

P.A. It has become a sign that a person or theory is dead when it is called a "classic". Classic Art, Classic Religion, Classic Science are states of those activities and people when they have reached the stage where no one regards them save as objects. This music—

PRIEST Not music yet, surely? Should there not be some structure, some sign of mental discipline about it?

P.A. If that is what you think, should there not also be some discipline to which religion conforms? In psychoanalysis, though we do support the idea of "freedom", we also preserve a mental discipline—a rigorous one.

ROBIN Where is the line between licence and freedom?

PRIEST There has always been discipline in religion. Dogma is a succinct statement of religious law. Terms like "dogmatic" are employed in an undisciplined manner by those who use dogma as a pejorative comment on a scientific statement. We are familiar, from personal experience, with "life-preserving" religious experience, but we do not and cannot impose that fact on others who have no such experience.

> ROLAND The band is playing a jazzed-up version of "For though the Body dies the Soul shall live forever". Do you call that blasphemous?
>
> PRIEST: No; it gives a sombre note to a boringly hilarious evening.
>
> ROBIN: Aren't you being intolerant of hilarity?
>
> PRIEST I think it would be boring without that tincture of solemnity which the reminder of death gives.
>
> ROBIN: Why? What is solemn about death?
>
> P.A. Nothing; but people think so if they suppose they are doing something for the last time. I suppose one would think it doubly solemn if it were felt to be the first. Women have more reason than men to fear death as they know they can die in giving birth.
>
> ROSEMARY Reason has nothing to do with it. If it had, many people would fear pregnancy who don't. [II: 408–9]

The stillborn analytic couple cannot learn anything from experience. The insight is turned into an "outsight"—a text printed in books. Partial and transitory facets of the numinous realm (or "O") cannot be apprehended because they have become "knowable" by established theories. The issue can be subsumed by a few points: the psychoanalytic movement may be unwittingly murdering psychoanalysis through the continuous electing of repeaters who may be skilled in manipulating jargon:

> ROLAND Why all the mystery? Cut out the dramatic suspense and come to the point.
>
> ROBIN: Give him a chance. I'm interested even if you aren't.
>
> P.A. Mystery is real life; real life is the concern of real analysis. Jargon passes for psychoanalysis, as sound is substituted for music, verbal facility for literature and poetry, trompe l'oeil representations for painting. Real self-murder is not observed, and accidental suicide passes for the real thing which is planned, worked out in detail economically to create real effect. For this the patient—a good name for him—has first to suffer, in collaboration with psychoanalyst or family, to achieve success, to be worth murdering. The danger of death does not become acute until it is clear to every beholder that a resounding success is at hand. Then comes the not-so-blind Fury with the abhorred shears. This kind of man or woman

> resembles a self-murderer only superficially. "Ay, in the catalogue ye go for men …" Shakespeare was not deceived by counterfeit; it would be a "brave" psychoanalyst who thought he could not be deceived. But there are such people amongst us. [II: 307–8]

Readers familiar with Shakespeare's plays will instantly recognise the Bard's help, in a popular extract already quoted by Bion in the second edition of *Transformations*: the hiring of a murderer by Macbeth, who tells him:

> Ay, in the catalogue ye go for men,
> As hounds and greyhounds, mongrels, spaniels, curs,
> Shoughs, water-rugs, and demi-wolves are clept
> All by the name of dogs. [*Macbeth*, III i]

The Trilogy calls to be intuitively perceived, rather than understood. It is written in such a way that it provides an experience of reading which embodies the mind's and life's outstanding features, which are not usually put onto paper. When they are, the reaction of the audience can be summed up with the name first given to the theatrical contributions of Ibsen, Beckett and Arrabál: "absurdist drama". A few decades later, what was called "absurdist drama" came to be seen as "naturalist drama". Perhaps a better name could be "reality drama"—at least until the very word "reality" began to mean its opposite, as in "virtual reality" and "reality show" that are currently fashionable. Ibsen, Beckett, Arrabál and Bion, and before them, Shakespeare, Goethe, Racine and Dante, tried to express in written form paradoxes, disconnections, causeless love and hate, sudden loss of meanings that that had barely been won, doubts, disquiet, phases of not understanding, and the all-pervading feelings of persecution which can no longer be seen as "pathological" in the history of knowledge. They are linked to the basic hostility coming from the material and immaterial environment that awaits the human the moment it is born, and even before. Children's "anxiety" and "fear of annihilation", as elucidated by Freud and expanded by Klein, always underlie what is seen as socially accepted behaviour. One may experience those aspects typical of the paranoid-schizoid position as one proceeds with the reading of *A Memoir of the Future*. Conversely, one may experience evolving meanings throughout one's own life: the sense of being found by or of finding whatever it is in truth. There are transient moments of a *sense of reality*, as Isaiah Berlin put it, or a *sense of truth*, as Bion put it before writing the Trilogy (Bion, 1961b, p. 119; Berlin, 1996).

The reader can try not to resolve paradoxes, but instead find a still unknown synthesis between the poles. He or she can find constellations and connections of relationships between intervening factors and functions—known or not. One would be allowed to find love and hate as springing not from external causes, but from the unexpected, unknown parts of the mind. One may find a way to get a good enough tolerance of doubts, transient serenity, lessening of persecution, and a clearer sight of realistic guilt in whatever it is. That is, the reader can experience a movement towards the depressive position in order to realise Bion's text—like any text that appertains to real psychoanalysis. Analogous to a Beethoven symphony, the serenity is suddenly replaced, in the next paragraph, or the next page, to the disquiet of the first set of sensations. The writing characterises the living tandem movement between the paranoid-schizoid and depressive positions.

Bion observed that the psychotic personality (Bion, 1957, 1962, 1965) clothes itself with a neurotic appearance. Rationalisation, a travesty of rationality—described, for example, in Freud's "Paths to the Formation of Symptoms" (1916c)—is the most usual way to weave this "cloth". Careful detection of rationalisation, in order to discard it as soon as it is discovered, must be carried out if one needs to have a glimpse of the processes of functioning of the unconscious. According to Freud, rationalisation is typical of secondary processes (1895, 1900, 1911b, 1920). It still is an unclassified concept, and can be defined in terms of what it is not: it is not a mechanism of defence, and is not an unconscious phantasy (Freud, quoted and expanded by Jones, 1956; Laplanche & Pontalis, 1967).

> ROBIN The whole of psychoanalytic theory seems to be vitiated … by favouring only those phenomena which appear to conform to classical logic, the sort of logic with which we are already familiar.
>
> PAUL Timidity is a fact of our nature. We cling to anything which gives us the chance of saying "Thus far and no further". Any discovery is followed by a closure. The remainder of our thoughts and endeavours is devoted to consolidating the system to prevent the intrusion of yet another thought. Even any roughness of our system that might facilitate the lodgment of the germ of another idea is smoothed and polished. [II: 265]

Dreams offer a good challenge to rationalisation—even though there is the debris of unsuccessful rationalisation in dream work, which tries to serve two masters, the principle of pleasure-displeasure and the principle of reality. Dreams are not hermetically sealed against the powerful rationalistic trends in the psychoanalytic movement, which continue to create empirically untested rational "interpretations" of dreams. During the day, dream activity remains mostly unseen, unless one pays attention to free associations. Both have a kinship with hallucinations, such as their appeal to visual manifestations. The presence of delusion and hallucination in a personality otherwise conserved is better known by its psychiatric name, hallucinosis;[1] those delusions and hallucinations remain unseen and unheard by most people who are more accustomed to social customs, and they pass for normal. Disturbances of thought and language consequent to hallucinosis, hallucination and delusion are successfully disguised by rationalisation in social settings. Nevertheless, what governs things is the *underlying*, unconscious and unseen prevalence of psychosis. Its *underlying* nature—that is, not given directly to the senses, demanding to be intuited—is decisive. Clothed with the overt appearance of rationality, it was perceived by Hume's refutation of pure reason, later expanded by Kant (Hume, 1748; Kant, 1781, 1783). Hume's discovery is implicit in Freud's description of free associations and dream work. It was brought to the awareness of psychoanalysts by Bion: *reason is the slave of passions*. It is *psycho-logically* necessary, but has nothing to do with truth (Bion, 1965, p. 73). This theoretical formulation is put in a living, practical way throughout the book.

Truth is a term that here in this text is understood after Freud, Klein and Bion: it means the material and immaterial truth which occurs both in the internal world—the truth about oneself—and in the external world, described by quantum and relativistic physics. Those disciplines are still looking for a mutual integration; nevertheless, even if this future integration remains to be made, it is acknowledged that both encompass phenomena that occur in the quantum micro-environment as well in the great universe.

A Memoir of the Future embodies centuries of development of human knowledge that tried to make approximations to truth or reality as it is. The impressive array of scientists, philosophers, thinkers, musicians, mystics, poets and psychoanalysts who "populate" the book try to elicit underlying, governing non-rational facts which are a road towards the numinous realm, or truth. Non-rational is not to be confused with irrationality; compacted in the very title is the canon and the organon of the three books, each named in a non-rational, albeit apprehensible mode: *The Dream, The Past Presented* and *The Dawn of Oblivion*.

In the history of the ideas of Western civilisation, rationalisation is confused with reason. Rationalisation is a slave of the passions. Its main function is to brush truth aside; from rationalisation arose a series of terms such as "an unwanted truth". It can be seen with the help of a paraphrase of a well-known saying usually attributed to Abraham Lincoln. Namely: one may deceive oneself about unimportant things for a long time; one may deceive oneself about important things briefly; but one cannot deceive oneself about important things for a long time.

The word "ratio" was drawn from the theory of numbers in mathematics: it means that one may extract roots of what mathematicians call "natural numbers". This ability gave the impression that the mathematician knew the most elemental truth about numbers. That impression lasted for more than a millennium. Nevertheless, the perception about the "real realm" of numbers was expanded by new discoveries: for example, "infinite", "irrational" and "imaginary" numbers. Euclid's formal logic was expanded by Bernhard Riemann's, Nikolai Lobachevsky's and Newton Da Costa's non-Euclidean and para-consistent logic, which did not abhor what was hitherto considered illogical. Descartes' causality was shown to be false by Hume (1748) and Kant (1781). It was realised that rationality is a very limited method as regards "pursuing truth-O". Newtonian mechanics was expanded by discoveries made mainly by Albert Einstein and Max Planck in relativistic and quantum physics. Just like psychoanalysis, which displayed the timelessness and lack of formal logic of the unconscious, modern physics goes beyond the senses—in using the immaterial parts of matter—and formal logic, which is seen as the climax of the rational method of research on truth.

Nevertheless, some of the most irrational social events and, in a most obvious way, individual behaviour occurred in the name of what was felt as rational, such as the eugenics movement, whose aftermath was genocide. Rationality is felt as a reassuring weapon. Like a weed, it appears in renewed and more resistant forms, as for example in the resurgence of the positivist movement, which believes in predictions as well as in linear causal chains, as a reaction to almost a century of development brought mainly by modern physics and mathematics and, in a more limited sense, by psychoanalysis.

Rationality is in the basis of the justifications and explanations given by human beings to their basest, unrecognised human aggression. Its psychological foundations can be found in the most illogical psychic trait, which Freud called narcissism, and Klein expanded to what she called, for the lack of a better name, the paranoid-schizoid position.

Alpha function

The prospective reader of the Trilogy will not encounter any of the previously furnished definitions of the concept of "alpha function". He or she may consult Bion's works from 1959 to 1963, subsumed especially in *A Theory of Thinking* and expanded in the first chapters of *Learning from Experience*. Perhaps a summary of all these in a compact form may be useful (Sandler, 2005). Instead, as occurred with the theory of observation of Transformations and Invariants, the reader of *A Memoir of the Future* may contact the theory of alpha function in still more vivid form through its actual functioning. In its original form, the theory stated that each baby's alpha function is enabled, or at least enhanced, through the mother's reverie (Bion, 1962, p. 35; review under the vertex of the history of Bion's ideas in Sandler, 2005, p. 643).

In this sense, one may see that the printed pages of books by a deceased man, taken in their concrete external aspect, can function as the initial sensory data, or external data that may be apprehended or not by each individual reader. So far, no novelty is involved. Nevertheless, Bion's Trilogy is intentionally constructed in such a "living" way, imbued with truthfulness and experience, that it offers the likelihood of awakening each reader's alpha function—if the theory of alpha function is valid. This statement was made by this writer in 1981 (and published in 1983). Experience with reading groups at an institute of Psychoanalysis from 1988 and at a post-graduate course in a state University from 1998 confirmed this idea. In 1995, the idea was discussed with Parthenope Bion Talamo, who had reached roughly the same conclusion by her own means.

The coincidence of the conclusions reached by two different observers who did not know about each other's work points out that their conclusion was near to truth. As we have seen before, such an epistemological remark differs from that made by Karl Popper, who insisted that the reproducibility of scientific facts observed in the same conditions would be one of the only two ways to confirm that a statement has scientific status. The partial aspect of this statement condemns it to untruth; it is valid that the same conditions of research may be useful in some areas of knowledge, but they are not universal. For example, Einstein and Poincaré came to the same conclusion—known as the theory of relativity—through the use of very different mathematical tools.

CHAPTER FIVE

The numinous realm

Roland rubbed his eyes. "My eyes do trouble me rather. Do you know, I think I must have fallen asleep. I do that sometimes; it goes in a flash. Mostly people don't notice but sometimes I think they do because they look at me so queerly. Or perhaps it is the dream that I have and forget. It goes in a flash." Tom seemed to be changing every second into someone whom he knew well, but could not remember. It was awkward that he did not know his name. One of his colleagues too! "Call him 'Colin' to myself, but must remember not to say it out loud. It will do for the dream or whatever this is. If it isn't too high-falutin' it reminds me of the shadows on the walls in Plato's cave. You remember", he said aloud, "that Plato had an idea that what we call reality were really shadows cast on a wall of a very dark cave in which men were sitting, chained, with their backs to a bright light entering the cave from an opening that they couldn't see, but only were aware of by the shadows that they thought were reality. Well, Plato thought that 'things', as we call them, and people are really a kind of precipitation of the 'Forms'. The Forms (either the concept, or, in so far as concepts cannot be called 'empty thoughts', the 'things-in-themselves'), the 'noumena', were not understandable. Plato seemed to think that the

Socratic Greeks might at least understand the parable of the cave. But between then and now many hundreds of people have tried, oh, 'ever so hard', to understand what it means. And some people, like Jesus, have continued the naive idea. 'If you can't understand the parable, what am I to tell you?' he complained when his disciples were not stupid enough to be simple. All that they could do was to decide that Jesus was God and shut him up under a tombstone of heavy, cold, religious adoration. I suppose they were foolish enough to suppose that they could get their shot in first before the opponents, who said they had known him from childhood and he was a carpenter's son and they were all so fond of him—why! They were his loving brothers and sisters! It was just brotherly love, and no less an authority than Jesus himself had admitted you couldn't have one who loved you more than a father or brothers or sisters. (Though even *he* preferred a Father in Heaven and not one at too close quarters.) They had only come to save him because he was beside himself. Or in plain Aramaic, 'nuts'. Well, since then that story has been taken up, whenever it has one of its periods of volcanic activity, by the scientists and the protagonists of the looney bin, the tomb robbers and the tomb builders, the religious outfit and the scientific blackguards who try to keep the humanists and artists and poets under control by murder; sometimes with 'loving adoration' and sometimes with Herodic anxiety to find out where the dangerous embryo is, so that they can worship it to death. Of course, they were crude, but methods have become refined. The 'tool-making animal' found out that tools were very useful and anyone could learn to use a tool and no one need know *how* the tool was being used if it could be covered and hidden. That is where women were so clever. They had an invisible tool and the man had a visible and useless prick. Come, let us find it so we can worship also. So ... well, some genius had to discover some way in which lying, deception, evasion and their opposites could be used without detection and how 'truth' and noumena-robbing were to be kept inviolate and inviolable. The 'discovery' was, in its early stages, difficult because it was so vulnerable. Lying and deception were exposed, usually by some blundering child who could see that the emperor had no clothes, until it had been educated to know better. Hullo! Hullo! No one here? Must have been talking to myself. Well, it's all practice I suppose!" [I: 46–8]

Ultimate reality, or the numinous realm, is a concept linked to questioning of its very existence, due to its immateriality. It was unearthed by Kant and some of his followers, such as Goethe, Hegel, Schopenhauer and Nietzsche, from the achievements of the Ancient Greeks, mainly Socrates and Plato. It is the source of the philosophical conundrum of realism versus idealism, already mentioned in this work under the more generalised label of the Two Naïvetés. If the very existence of a counterpart in physical or material reality of the concept of ultimate reality as it is were put into doubt, what could be said about its perception and, moreover, about its possible usefulness in the practice of psychoanalysis? In this aspect, the psychoanalytic movement, increasingly dominated by unscientific tendencies, constructed a path which puts it more at ease with current philosophy than with the scientific disciplines which do not deny the existence of truth and reality, such as biology, physics and chemistry.

Freud's implicit use of the concept of ultimate reality proved to be effective for its practical value. That is, his use was not restricted to the philosophical concept, but profited from its counterpart in the realm of reality. It is in this area that the truthfulness of any concept *occurs* in the exact moment that it happens to be. This moment was called by Freud the *here and now*—and has a remarkable similarity to the discovery of space-time by Einstein. Bion called it becoming. As far as the psychoanalytic vertex is concerned, a most basic human situation is anxiety about personal annihilation, out of human helplessness against the hostility (to the preservation of life) of the environment. It is linked to life instincts in infancy. It may be distorted, through the prevalence of the principle of pleasure-displeasure as age increases, turning into phobias, obsessive anxieties and paranoia.

> There are many formulations of dread, unformulated and ineffable—what I denote O. Plato named it "forms", of which sensuous objects are the unreal, but sensible counterpart. Saint Augustine resorted to using the equipment of religion, which is available in many Religions, to express the separation of good from evil. The systematic separations into two objects, good and bad, conscious and unconscious, pain and pleasure, ugly and beautiful, has provided a framework which seems to have facilitated the development of knowledge, but the element of growth appears to have escaped formulation especially since it resembles maturation. [I: 77]

This is the most important advantage of psychoanalysis over written communications about psychoanalysis. A psychoanalysis is an event—rather than a thing—that constitutes a happening, whose raw material is facts. Therefore a psychoanalysis does not need the help of belief, because the patient and the analyst make it happen: (a) human instinctual needs, destructive and constructive: Death (expressed by Hate), Love, and Epistemophilic, as a specialisation of the former two; (b) principles of human mental functioning: Pleasure-Displeasure and Reality; (c) systems and structures of the mind, later encompassed in a unitary whole: Unconscious, Pre-conscious, Conscious and Id, Superego, Ego; and (d) concepts derived from (a) above: Oedipus, object relationships and their vicissitudes, from (b) above: dream work, unconscious phantasies, and from (c) above: the ego's defence mechanisms.

The list is not exhaustive; it was made with the purpose of furnishing an illustration. Nevertheless, the psychoanalytic movement soon found its own controversies, to the same extent that it distanced itself from psychoanalysis proper through psychoanalytically unwarranted transplantations from other disciplines.

Wayward tendencies were studied by different authors in different disciplines, with different motivations. These nevertheless kept their spontaneous, unsought but real interdisciplinarity, such as the research of Aichhorn (1925), Reik (1948), Cleckley (1941) and Schorske (1961). They shared a transcendent invariant: the old philosophical conundrum, realism versus idealism. We have seen that this conundrum displays the existence of hate for truth, bordering on psychopathy.

The conundrum precociously installed itself in the psychoanalytic movement, mistaken for psychoanalysis proper. Among many examples of this was a covert refusal to continue research into the unconscious. A socially safer bet was the foundation of divergent tendencies and paths, such as Ego Psychology and its offshoots. For this reason, extensions to the study of dream work and its manifestations in waking life, and extensions to the theory of instincts—in itself, another source of theoretical controversies which, at least since Max Eitingon, could ruin the previous theoretical edifice built by Freud—became increasingly rare. The rarity led to stagnation and poverty of thought, due to being starved of truth. The usual, unsuccessful attempt to avoid certain death (of the field of research) is the building of established pseudo-truth enforced by establishments or institutions.

This is multiplied in the individual attempt of the person shipwrecked in the sea of truth: one adopts a system of judgements full of arbitrary morals, devoid of any ethics. One phantasises that one is exempt from distinguishing reality from falsehood, or truth from error. Truth is replaced by "right"; error, or hallucination, is replaced by "wrong". Since it is an arbitrary decision, weight is always given to the search for Pleasure (or Desire) and the avoidance of Displeasure (or Pain).

Dr André Green, in a talk at the Sociedade Brasileira de Psicanálise de São Paulo (2003), stated that in some institutes of psychoanalysis in the United States, whose functioning was authorised and sponsored by the IPA, the study of Freud was seen with serious distrust. Students (or candidates, in the old classification) were strongly advised to leave Freud's work aside in order to make a correct analysis. The psychoanalytic movement became more interested in new fashions destined to replace what the psychoanalytical political establishment viewed as "outdated" psychoanalysis. After Freud's death, the existence of a Death Instinct, which had already met with initial resistance, was submitted to pseudo-controversy: the two customary parties, "pro" and "con", emerged, the former resorting to unfounded praise and the latter to destructive criticism. It passed unnoticed that one of the manifestations of the death instinct had been revealed within the psychoanalytic movement. The concept was increasingly outlawed—albeit unwittingly and unconsciously—in clinical practice, to the point where the so-called neo-Kleinians denied the existence of a remarkable manifestation of it, namely, the self-feeding cycle of envy-greed, which can sometimes be a kind of perpetual motion. In this sense, their denying ideas equalled those expressed by Dr Walter Joffe twenty years before (Joffe, 1969).

Successive alternatives to real psychoanalysis emerged, with no scientific evidence of their alleged theoretical or practical superiority: the so-called "dissidences", a sociological name for what is known in psychoanalysis as denial of reality and splitting. They included analytical psychology, with the idea of a "collective unconscious" and its archetypes (Jung); trauma of birth (Rank); inferiority complex (Adler); sociocultural causality (too many authors to quote; a review may be seen in Sandler, 1982); psychosomatics (Alexander); ego psychology and self psychology (Hartmann and Kohut); the "patriotic nationalisation" of psychoanalysis that "justified" attacks on the analytic setting due to "cultural" variations; intersubjectivity; enactment. All of this was encircled by difficulties in the apprehension of what the great authors had discovered, immersed in a sauce whose name could be "banality". To quote a single example: as soon as Donald Winnicott died, his name began to be bandied about as the "new saviour" of psychoanalysis. Idolatry, based on misunderstanding and banality, encircled his work: "good enough" mothering was transformed to mean the maximum mothering, rather than the minimum.

This wave or vogue was felt in Freud's time with the decay of Goethe's *Naturphilosophie* into Schelling's "Naturalism". It marked the escape to mysticism—which at least believed in immaterial facts. The scientific posture dispenses with beliefs:

> ALICE I thought you were a scientist.
>
> ROSEMARY I thought scientists spoke the truth and believed in facts.
>
> P.A. I wouldn't waste my capacity for belief on facts—I only believe when there is no fact available. [II: 294–5]

The dialogue carries on, displaying an attempt to reach a non-positivistic scientific posture in the psychoanalytic realm:

> ROBIN You mean that when there is nothing factual you fall back on beliefs—like the Christian religion and such rubbish. No wonder psychoanalysis is such a tissue of lies.
>
> P.A. No, I don't mean that. I mean I am careful to choose what I know and what I believe and, to the best of my capacity, not to mix them up. Because I do not take to be true what humans tell me are the facts, it does not mean that I fall back on "believing" a lot of twaddle as if I had to keep my mind full at all costs. Or the reverse—empty—like a kind of mental anorexia nervosa.
>
> ROLAND I thought anorexia nervosa was supposed to be mental.
>
> P.A. Not by me. It is reputed to be a fact like all these masses of psychoanalytic theories which are not facts at all though their representations, like the pages in a book, are facts. They fill a space as paramnesias fill an amnesia.
>
> ROLAND Then you must be a liar and a fraud.

> P.A. No; a few psychoanalytic theories or formulations are typical of the kinds of thing in which I believe. From my vertex they are not facts; they are beliefs of mine.
>
> ROSEMARY Were those facts when you said all that about "masochistic cravings"?
>
> P.A. No, they were attempts at formulating a particular instance of belief. If I were an artist I would try to formulate it in terms of painting or music. [II: 295]

It seems to be a fine discrimination between pseudo-scientific beliefs and psychoanalysis. It is possible to separate real psychoanalysis from the attitude of "thus far and no further", the basis of the non-scientific capitulation that precludes investigation of the unknown, attracting the attention and practice of members of the psychoanalytic movement, whose path may go either to hermeneutics or to positivism.

The attentive reader may have noticed the high frequency use of the word "No" that Wilfred Ruprecht Bion attributed to the character P.A. in this "dialogue"—or, better, inner dialogue. It seems that the experience of *not having understood*—or misunderstanding—filled him. As a peculiar consequence, P.A.—or a good enough psychoanalyst, one that the man, Wilfred Ruprecht Bion, aimed to be—seemed not to have given up; he did not make a capitulation which could risk his own ethical codes. Freud, who never forgave himself for finally giving up and surrendering to the politically powerful people who encircled him and were refusing to give him his professorship (Jones, 1953–6; Schorske, 1961), could have given the prototypical example—in this case, a negative example. At least from the reading of this text, Bion always profited from misunderstandings in order to carry on in his attempts to furnish chances for any of his interlocutors to apprehend what he was trying to say. This corresponds to the experience of the people who underwent an analysis with him as well as with the experience of his family and friends. To most readers, this could be a most valuable lesson of practical psychoanalysis, albeit given in a written form.

A different idea was given by Meltzer, in *The Kleinian Development* (1978). To his mind, Bion used a "military technique" full of tactics such as pincer movements and retreats in order to defeat the enemy. In the view of the present writer, this idea, embedded with innuendo, attributes political violence to Bion and belongs to the domain of psycho-history based on appearances. It links Bion's military experience with his later approach as a psychoanalyst. According to Carl von Clausewitz, "war is the continuation of politics by other means". Using military strategies and tactics includes a purpose of containment hardly distinguishable from an aim to defeat—something that sees enemies. In this case, the hated enemy is the unknown as it emerges in any analytic session. In contrast, as the text just quoted makes clear, the reader is exposed to a loving and caring aspect stemming from Bion's writing. The character P.A. is one who refuses to be drowned in the "sea of troubles" referred to by Hamlet. The only exception appears to be in what can be seen as Bion's premonition of his own death, in his concluding comment about the Trilogy, included after his death by Mrs Bion (III: 578). Despite this, he entertained no hatred for truth, as one may see in the comment recalled by Dr Oliver Lyth, which Bion made a few days before his death. Seeing how distressed his friend was, Bion reminded him that "Life is full of surprises—most of them unpleasant" (Lyth, 1980).

Many readers try either to nourish or to poison—they make their choice according to their preferences or their experiences, respectively—their own life with too much "giving up". Those readers are usually filled with doubts about psychoanalysis.

It seems that the numinous realm, in its most elementary form, functions with pairs of opposites, or elements in a dialectic relationship, prone to develop into a hitherto unknown third, the synthesis; this in turn will, in a complex chain of developments, have its own opposite, and so on. The model can be of two contrary forces. The most basic elementary pair may be the instincts of life and death. There is no "absolute life" or "absolute death". Klein called this opposition the possibility of annihilation. If some entity, event or thing exists, there is also the possibility that it cannot exist any longer. There are people who cannot wait for the time when Physical Death comes by itself (in other words, "naturally"). Those people, enslaved by the pleasure-displeasure principle, give in to their own omnipotent wishes and "decide" to choose that Psychic Death must come before than Physical Death—a desperate attempt to split what in the end cannot be split.

> ROSEMARY Even women risk death. In childbirth …
>
> ROLAND You did not risk childbirth.
>
> ROSEMARY What do you know about it? I believed a man and his promises once. I don't now, but I did once. I didn't die, but something died in me—mentally, I suppose you would call it.

BION Most people experience mental death if they live long enough. You don't have to live long to have that experience—all you have is to do is to be mentally alive.

ALICE You speak as if it were simple to be mentally alive. That is hardly my experience. It is true that a person does not, as far as we know, have to "do" anything to be physically born. It seems easier to think that he has to "do" something to *keep* physically or mentally alive. You have to have a partner for one thing—even in opposition.

ROBIN How do you mean? I can see that I have to be "opposed" if I want a contest. But suppose I don't.

BION Doesn't it depend on what use you need a contest for? This very discussion is a contest. We are talking about something. I think there is a sense in which we need, and are even feeling aware of the need for contest, or for opposition.

ROLAND (*sarcastically*) This gentleman (*indicating Man*) has obliged.

ROBIN I don't feel at all grateful. I had plenty of trouble with the weather and the crops without the need for invasion too.

MAN I don't think any of us like the "opposition" we have. We feel we should appear in a better light if the opposition were different. I can't do what I want; I have never known a time when I could. But there has always been someone or something against which I could rage.

BION If all else fails you could rage, as I too can, against yourself, your youth or your age, your strength or your weakness. It is one of the uses you can make of God—if you can believe in God.

ROBIN Well, can't you?

BION Which god are you referring to?

ROBIN Allah Akbar!

BION I don't think you are being serious. I shall use psychoanalytic licence to take jokes seriously. To start with, you show you are aware that you have a choice.

ROBIN You think of me as joking; it would not be so easy to suppose that, if I were in fact a member of a Muslim culture. Nor would you suppose that you could "choose" to take it seriously "because" you are a member of a psychoanalytic group. You would be compelled to take it seriously. It has nothing to do with being a member of a particular group, profession or culture, but that the particular "culture" has a great deal to do with some underlying, unobserved, constant conjunction of beliefs; an actual God of which the various religious formulations are only approximations to the underlying configuration of facts.

BION You are asking me to suppose that there is a "thing-in-itself", noumenon, Godhead, which, using Kant's terminology for my purposes, becomes "manifest" as a phenomenon; "God" as contrasted with "Godhead"; "finity" as contrasted with "infinity"; "won", as Milton says, "from the void and formless infinite"; a geometrical, Euclidean figure, a triangle with sides of 2, 4 and 5 units, as contrasted with an algebraic deductive system. But a rational fact gives no scope for "belief". Belief itself is destroyed if is transformed to find a "reason" for belief. [I: 178–80]

The reader may see that Bion's mere reference to "opposition" evokes abhorrence from the character Robin, who refuses to have anything to do with it. The attentive reader may also remember that earlier Robin was described as taking refuge in a pigeon cote (I: 29). Robin (or "the Robin part of Wilfred Ruprecht Bion") had refused to get out of what he saw as a sanctuary, despite the fact that bullets from invaders were zipping around him. In risking imminent death he felt safe due to denial of reality—a mechanism discovered by Freud as a fundamental of psychosis.

The whole of this time we saw none of the infantry officers. Hauser and I now began to wonder what to do. It seemed imperative that we should get to our men. For my part, as I said before, I cared too little about the whole business to mind the idea of getting killed. This, and, I think, a curious kind of excitement that used to come over us in action, combined to influence me. I told Hauser that I thought the only thing we could do if we were to be of any use at all was to get out of our place and get with our men. He agreed. I may well say now that from the point of view of sheer unadulterated lunacy what followed was the maddest and most dangerous thing I ever did. I must have been very nearly mad to do it. But I never *thought* more clearly in my life. [Bion, 1919, p. 106]

Bion constructed Robin's and Roland's situation out of his memories as a teenager eager to enlist in the British Expeditionary Forces in France, mixed with his battle experiences in World War I.

> P.A. ... I am supposing that the gifted child has tried, even when a foetus, to be without "feelings" or "sensations". It cannot be rid of its inborn, inherent genealogical inheritance; it can possibly get rid of what used to be called "acquired characteristics", what I have called phenomenes—phenomena as contrasted with genotypes.[1] So it remains the gifted, inherently gifted, person. Since this is so, it is able to learn what is expected of it, how to be what Mother or Father, or both, want. It learns the difference between what Father and Mother call right and wrong, what will one day be called The MacNaughton Rules.[2] All this, however, is split off from its fundament, its base, its real self. So there you have a civilised, apparently well-adjusted moral being; its armoury of accomplishments is daily augmented in the way that a really intelligent animal learns to augment its repertoire of parlour tricks. "Die for your country", the fond dog-lover says to her pet, who obediently lies down on its back and wags its tail. In due course the young patriot learns to die for his country but may get killed in the process—unless one of these powerful but anaemic emotions breaks through the caesura and causes the young man to have "shell-shock", or to have his brain washed according the fashion prevalent in the culture current. His intelligence hardly need cause a ripple in the depths of his personality even though engaged on what would be a difficult task of maintaining his shell-shocked, brain-washed personality in good repair if he had to do it with the conscious skill of an actor playing a part. [III: 563–4]

Let us go back to the above quotation from *The Dream* (I: 178–80), when Robin and P.A. find themselves immersed in an unwanted, but real discussion—or oppositions of vertices. The reader can see this where the character Bion questions Robin's refusal. He does it with the phrase: "Doesn't it depend on what use you need a contest for?" The author, Wilfred Ruprecht Bion, returns again and again to the psychoanalytic vertex: the attempt to encircle and focus the function of what is indicated by the verbal speeches and non-verbal manifestations originating from both interlocutors in any analytic session.

There is tendency in the human being—at least in those who are the inheritors of knowledge acquired by Western civilisation—to deny the existence of what is put into the mouth of the character Man: "I don't think any of us like the 'opposition' we have". In other words, the struggle for life, the existence of pairs of opposites—which philosophy calls dialectics. The external environment harbours "opposition" to the point of being hostile to survival. Many—most?—people make a desperate appeal to religious belief. The two delusions which may be called "safety" and "satisfaction" are expressed by the many chases after lottery prizes and the accumulation of money. With a remarkable prescience, Wilfred Ruprecht Bion talks about the effects of Muslim beliefs forty years *before* they emerged in their most violent form. Would it be a coincidence that Lawrence of Arabia was an Englishman? A perusal of Bion's library, carefully maintained by Mrs Francesca Bion, reveals that he had a copy of the Koran dating from the 1930s. Bion also nourished interest in the ideas—and not the self-righteous practical work stemming from them—of the Muslim dissidence called Sufism (Bion, 1970, p. 83).

The hallucinosis of personal satisfaction

This writer thinks that Bion's project is the same as Freud's: to get a more effective approximation to reality, with no concessions to desire—which has a long, damaging history as regards science and art.

When subservience to the principle of pleasure-displeasure prevails, social and personal interests are indistinguishable from what may be called the hallucinosis of personal satisfaction. It is conducive to prejudice; at its climax, it characterises either delinquent or psychopathic behaviour—which closes the cycle, "legalising" subterfuge and evasion of pain to the beholder. This posture has indelible damaging effects in many social endeavours: science, art, economics and politics. It hampers and in the end renders useless disciplines whose practical purpose is consideration for life, for the hallucinosis of personal satisfaction has as a built-in factor a profound disregard for truth. When one is functioning in accordance with the principle of pleasure-displeasure, there is a tendency to enter into illusion, hallucination, hallucinosis and delusion.

It seems that from truth there "emanates" a kind of paradoxical mix of light and darkness that some people may find unbearable. Guilt may be felt as persecution; repair of damage though gratitude seems impossible. Getting in touch with the psychotic personality (Bion, 1956) that exists in any human being is felt as if one were staring at a bright sun, which might make one feel blind. The psychotic personality is able to notice where and when truth exits, but cannot bear it. Thus the psychotic personality creates a situation in which it can neither sleep nor be wide awake, as Bion described in the so-called "clinical papers" republished in *Second Thoughts* (1967a). In the Trilogy, Bion focuses on the same issue with the help of many characters and fictitious situations:

> The dreamless sleep ended. The day was as empty of events—facts proper to daytime—as the night had been empty of dreams. Meals were served to both girls. It occurred to them that they had no memory of the food; the "facts" of daytime and night were defective, mutilated. They were having dreams—mutilated dreams—lacking a dimension like a solid body that casts no shadow in light. The world of reality, facts, was no longer distinguishable from dreams, unconsciousness, night. Thoughts with and thoughts without a thinker replaced a universe where discrimination ruled. Dreams had none of the distinguishing characteristics of mind, feelings, mental representations, formulations. The thinker had no thoughts, the thoughts were without thinkers. Freudian dreams had no Freudian free associations; Freudian free associations had no dreams. Without intuition they were empty, without concept they were blind.
>
> Rosemary said, "You are nice, Alice. I prefer you to Tom." Alice felt a voluptuous glow steal over her. "Oh thank you, Ma'am," she replied humbly to her maid. "Will that be all now?" "No, lay out my finery; then you can go." Alice found herself ranging over the wardrobe of exquisite shoes.
>
> Thoughts, whore's apparatus, schooling ... As she collected these objects she was carried away by an immense love and adoration. Unable to contain herself she said, "Oh Ma'am, can't I see you wear them? It would be wonderful to be able to give them all to you. I shall call Roland. He will make a better husband for you than for me. You will make him a better man than I could." She fell at Rosemary's feet, anointing them with her tears which themselves turned to a precious ointment as they fell. How does she come to waste all her treasures like this? Does she not know what manner of ... servant this is? Does she not know what the value of her gifts

is—the education, the health, her beauty, our beauty? Does she not know that we were Penelope's suitors? That Homer celebrated us? That we died even before there was a poet to confer immortality upon us? Ronsard knew of us when we were beautiful. Why does she not send them away? Why are we sent away empty? Why are even our thoughts emptied and our concepts denuded of their contents, our concepts and thoughts denuded of their apparatus, equipment, without which they are blind? Did not Kant, our Browning, tell them? Why do they choose Cant, the Barabbas-like thief? I before 'ee except after see?

Alice, adoring, looked up. "Who are you? May I not see you as you are?" "I have told you. I am your maid—your servant—poor, despised, needy, the whore. It was I who sent Tom to you, deprived you of Roland. You can't give me anything." She spoke without bitterness. Alice looked up expecting to find she was being mocked. There was no mockery. "But tell me who you are; I shall wrestle with you from dawn to dusk; from dusk to dawn, from O to God; from God to science; from science to God; from security to the infinite that is man's infinity; from the infinite confines of stupidity, from stupor to the bigotry of certitude; from infinite hate to infinite love; from infinite coldness, indifference of the absolute, to the intolerable infinitude of absolute love. Show me." "No." "Show me."

"Because of your importunity I will lift the veil. I will not give you sight, but I will give you insight so your greatest will be able to see me in a glass darkly; me in whom there is no shadow cast by turning. You will pay as even your greatest had to pay—'from that time on the balance of his mind was disturbed.' He was condemned to live imprisoned in everlasting sanity."

"Who are you?"

"I am compassion."

"Who are you?"

I am your maid—but even then you did not see."

"Open my eyes."

"No. I sent you prophets but you would not listen."

"Open my ears."

"I sent you Bach."

"He had perfect pitch."

"He tempered the clavier well."

"Send me a batter one."

"No, I sent you Mozart."

"You took him back too soon."

"I sent you Beethoven."

"He was flawed."

"You flawed him: you would not look at the flaws I made."

"Show me."

"I sent the spirochaete."

"I could not see."

"It was beautiful."

"I could not see its beauty."

"I sent you Thais."

"Who are you?"

"Only now do you give a home to curiosity, but to make it sleep."

"I will awaken it."

"I have done that, but you strive to put it to sleep."

"Tell me who you are. Let me see."

"I will show and tell. And you will use what I show and tell to stupefy, to drug yourself."

"Try me!"

"See then: I am Thais. I am Helen of Troy. I caused mankind to see Beauty. I launched a thousand ships and burned the topless towers of Ilium."

Rosemary and Alice have swooned away, but Rosemary still talks.

"Who are you?"

(Shadowy Figures disguised as S.F. take over.)

"We are Science Fiction. Who are you?"

"I am the Artist who made the ram caught in a thicket beautiful in gold. I am the hunter who caught the ram in a thicket. I am the thicket in which the ram was caught. Who are you?"

"I am Science Fiction I am S.F. I am the Fiction which became Science Fact. I am the tomb robber. I am the drug that stole your senses away. I am the tomb, ugly and frightening. I am the thief that made you bury, in the golden ram and its golden, golden thicket, the work of Art. I made you bury it in the death pit of Ur. I robbed the death pit of its terrors. I am the S.F. who, disguised as the holy fool, appeared as the Silly Fool. I am S.F. But who now is this?"

"I am what I am. I am God. I am Satan. I am hell fire. I am the burning bush. I am the fire that all men worship. I am Satan. I stole your thicket and refined it in the fire till it burned so brightly that all men worshipped me. I am Mammon. Who is this?"

"I am Strife. I set God against Mammon. I set the vulva against the penis, the container against its content. I caused the lean to devour the fat. Who are you?"

"I am the dreamer. I dream a dream. I am the den in which I was buried. Who are you?"

"I am the thought that found a thinker. Who are you?"

"I am the robber who drugged you so you would not know you were being conceptualised. I am the dream that drugged you so you would not know I was a concept that would be so nice that you would never be the same once I had conceived you. You would not know that the direction in which I was robbing you would lead from nothing to unconsciousness to sleep to dream to waking thoughts to dream thoughts to nothingness to O = zero, from O = zero to O which is O = oh! to O which is a picture which is a picture of a hole or greedy mouth or vagina which offers perfect freedom which is death which is perfect freedom which is perfect pitch or absolute colour or Eternal Life or Eternal Death or Perpetual Motion or Perpetual Inertia or Absolute Space or space like mental space in which there exist objects so compact that they are like white dwarfs or so sparse and rare that they can only be grasped by finite means like Poisson's law governing exceedingly infrequent events or so absolute a space that your mental life is itself destroyed as in a body which is anaemic because mind is lost like blood in a body whose capillaries are so greedy that there is not enough blood to be shared. Who are you?"

"I can see you are waking. You will be so blinded by day, by sight, because you are so blind you detect the faintest light of an object so dark that increased light is too much. You oscillate, back and forth."

"No. Round and round. The diameter is so vast that you cannot see the opposite side."

"No. you oscillate, with so small an excursion that you cannot discern that the excursion would have to be beyond your time to make the journey round the circle. You cannot even detect that the circle and the diameter are signs denoting the same object. You argue … who are you?"

"I am strife. I cause you not to agree and the strife wakes you out of darkness. I am confusion. I cause confusion of tongues. I am Babel. I am the Tower that all men are made like. Who are you?"

"I am the garden into which the serpent found entry."

"I am the beam by which I found a way to enter."

"I am Urania."

"I am divine wisdom by which pagan disguise I entered as Urania."

"I am Palinurus by whom the fleet of lesser helmsmen were able to sail."

"I am the many-wiled leader who gave Palinurus his orders. Who are you?"

"I am the disguise robbed from Odysseus who is so wealthy in wiles. I flung reason from his throne. Who are you?"

"I am rationalisation who is Reason disguised so that I may appear as the slave or the master of the passions. Who are you?"

"I am the king in whose dream you are but the furniture. If *I* were to wake you would go out bang!—like a candle. You are?"

"I am a funny story. I am a child's book. I am wonderland. I am a children's story. You are laughing in your sleep. You are waking up. The funny story which makes you laugh will make you cry. The child's dream will grow up to become adult, the night mare will carry you, like Shakespeare's sonnet, sluggishly away from home but fast, back to where you came from: which is the same place as the one you go to. Godlike, I shall fling you and your tiller back to the domain from which you came disguised as Palinurus, Urania. As men like trees walking. Rooted as trees disguised as men walking. Your root is already in its grave; your flower is already so brave, so fiery red. You slept. Who are you?"

"I am the horrendous dream that turned Science Fiction to Science Fact. I turned hideous night to even more hideous day. And you?"

"I am the Refiner's fire. The glorious sun who was the revolutionary flame disguised as R.F., the republique française, the public thing, the thing that turned the hidden thing to the public thing; who robbed death; who robbed the secret of its cover and exposed it as the monster that it is. Who are you?"

"I am thought searching for a thinker to give birth to me. I shall destroy the thinker when I find him. I am the Odyssey, the Iliad, the

> Aeneid. I prevented Mars from destroying me but I ate away Mars from inside, from outside so he died. He is a memory and a desire: I am the eternally alive, indestructible, indispensable, adorable. I am the force that makes the books. My last triumph is the Mind. The mind that is too heavy a load for the sensuous beast to carry. I am the thought without a thinker and the abstract thought which has destroyed its thinker Newtonwise, the container that loves its content to destruction; the content that explodes its possessive container." [I: 33–38]

If one tries to stare directly at the sun, one probably will feel blind before becoming really blind—something that may take years to occur, as with fakirs in India. They believe in a personal development called "transcendent vision", which calls for continuous, unrelenting staring at the sunlight for years. They have a conscious intention to destroy their own retina in order to obtain that kind of "vision". The advocating of such acted out measures to people other than those who are deeply immersed in the ages-old Indian tradition would hardly be the task of any psychoanalyst. With the exception of this case, real blindness occurs when human beings attempt to look at a solar eclipse. Psychosis, psychopathy, lack of dreaming and dream work equal the eclipse of the mind.

One of Bion's favourite quotations from Freud was taken from Freud's now widely known exchange of letters with Lou Andreas-Salomé. Namely, the psychoanalytic discipline of blinding oneself artificially that enables the practitioner to perform the quantum leap from the manifest content to the latent content—the transient messenger of the unconscious. Bion also took from Milton and Wordsworth analogies about the need for an "inner eye". We can see from those examples the need to lessen contamination from the senses in order to have a glimpse of what appertains to the ultra- and/or infra-sensuous level: glimpses of the noumena, the unconscious, the psychic reality, O.

Many parts of *A Memoir of the Future* are filled with technical hints that were used by Bion himself when he was trying to help people who went to him for analysis. In those parts, he is wholly sincere in describing the various reactions coming from people who either submitted or refused to submit to analysis by him. As the reader may have seen before, the psychological origins of religious thinking appear conjoined with the everyday practice of psychoanalysis, to reiterate Freud's discoveries about the idea of God being the projection of each one's omnipotence (for example, "Totem and Taboo", 1913, expanded in "Moses and Monotheism", 1939)—due to the basic human helplessness in the face of the unknown. At least when the analyst makes attempts to "pursue truth-O" in order to elicit the unfolding truth in the multifarious and complex interacting "micro-moments" that compose any analytic session. As the analyst does this, it is possible to profit, via attention, from anything—in principle, considered here as just an ideal goal—that comes from the patient, in order to continuously regain the analytic vertex.

Attention includes giving due respect to attempts coming both from the patient and from the analyst to dismiss or undervalue the analytic vertex. A very common way of doing this is to call people "mad"—including the analyst and the activity he or she is carrying out. The main invariant of this is probably the personal factor.

The following quotation differs in its form from most of the others to be found in this text: it includes emphasis which does not appear in the original text. The relevance of the parts this author has emphasised is centred on the importance attributed by him to the toleration of paradoxes—and the reaction of most patients who have tried to undergo an analysis, as well as the general view of lay people about analysis:

> MYSELF ... I could try to escape the problem of discretion by using material drawn from myself and making it truthful. I cannot—I know myself too well to be honest. There would be no discretion or privacy unless I remained silent about my own affairs. There is a further problem. Non-artistic methods of communication are less accurate than those used by artists. For example, I could use a camera to take photographs, or a recording machine and video tapes to record the audible and visual. I can watch a television picture and see men landing on the moon. My impression is that the photographic representation is inadequate and even if improved by mechanical means I and others would still regard it as "flattening". I can say this with conviction of the psychoanalytical experience also. I cannot describe this experience in any convincing way to someone who does not share it, any more than the moving picture of men landing on the moon tells me what it feels like. It is delusory to suppose that contemporaneity makes the experience

communicable. Even while it is happening I may not succeed in drawing attention to the experience, less still with an experience which I know I have had, but cannot now "remember".

I can remember, faintly, what it is like to go into battle in a tank. I know enough to be able to describe it in terms of terror. I know a companion had the experience of being invalided out as schizophrenic; another never regained his skill as a soldier. He was said to have been delinquent although he wrote to me in terms of affection years afterwards. Another became disillusioned and desperate and in his last battle was destroyed with the rest of his companions and burned to death. I know that some people, while not having the same experience as myself, were confident that I knew what they felt; some believe I know what it is like to be a psychoanalyst; others neither know what it is like to come to me for analysis nor how it might feel for me to be their analyst. They can learn to pretend they are familiar with psychoanalytic experience as a clever animal learns tricks: the human animal can learn how to play tricks which might convince the ignorant. If trickery were enough, no harm would occur. In a group trickery might afford a solution of the problem. An interpretation appropriate psychoanalytically cannot be right in a room where others are present; the interpretation addressed to a group is witnessed in a way which differs from the psychoanalytic interpretation. In what does the difference consist? Some differences spring to the mind at once. In psychoanalysis "common" sense—I am talking about physical sense—suggests that two physical beings only are present; in a group a number of people can be physically "sensed" (literally) to be present. Wilfred Trotter, in *Instincts of the Herd in Peace and War*, suggested that the group as a whole is greater than the sum of its parts. I feel that I, who am writing this (and thinking before I am writing it), am less than the whole of me. I can "think" the possibility that my ideas, valued as cultural achievement, are insignificant, "stuck on" a part of my group reproductive functioning which I choose to ignore by identifying with my sexual life and other functions which have been emphasised through the over-elaboration of the individual by psychoanalysis. Thus, I can argue that the mind and its works are of great significance; the rest, a total, inchoate mindlessness to be called "the unconscious", is lumped together and glorified and idealised as a further tribute to the mind. Are the gametes mindless, unconscious, mentally active, or do they belong to a category so different that the mind has no apparatus for dealing with them? I put forward, herewith, a theory of ξ with a recently proliferated sense organ known as the "end", in which various functions, usually associated with psychoanalysis (the Oedipus situation, aggression, rivalry) are supposed to be observed (on the model of forms of dis-order, dis-ease, sex, fear, love). In reality they are patterns, configurations, insignificant in themselves but, if delineated, indicative of an *underlying* reality by their perturbations, regroupings, shifts in pattern and colour; they reflect a category and kind that the human mind cannot formulate or conjecture in their presence. If so, these Oedipus situations, impulses, instincts and characters could be made opaque in the way in which patterns in X-rays are revealed by the use of sensitised plates. The personality or mind, as portrayed psychoanalytically in detail, is a recent photogram of some long-existent reality, of significance only as an archaic physical anatomy might be. Psychoanalysis would appear as an ephemeral phenomenon, betraying forces on the surface of which the human race flickers, flares and fades in response to the unrecognised but gigantic reality.

The practical point is—no further investigation of psychoanalysis, but the psyche it betrays. *That* needs to be investigated through the medium of *mental* patterns; *that* which is indicated is *not* a symptom; *that* is not a cause of the symptom; *that* is not a disease or *any*thing subordinate. Psychoanalysis itself is just a stripe on the coat of the tiger. Ultimately it may meet the Tiger—The Thing Itself—O.

BION If I had heard you say this a few years back I suspect that I and my colleagues would have been shocked and thought you were turning against psychoanalysis and were guilty of dishonesty. Indeed, I would be interested to know how you justify the fact that you are still practising—do you call it psychoanalysis or some other term like psychotherapy?—and charging people fees. Can you expand this?

MYSELF Thanks to memory I can make a comparison. The comparison causes change, and on some occasions the change obtrudes. When this happens you feel the change deserves to be recorded and the dialogue between me and me might just as well

> be conducted between me and a fictitious character. The fiction can be so rhetorical as to be incomprehensible; or so realistic that the dialogue becomes audible to others. There is thus a double fear: that of the conversation being so theoretical that the thoughts might be taken for meaningless jargon; and that of the seeming reality. *Having two sets of feelings about the same facts is felt as madness and disliked accordingly*. This is one reason why it is felt necessary to have an analyst; another reason is the wish for me to be available to be regarded as mad and used to being regarded as mad. There is a fear that you might be called an analysand, or reciprocally, that you may be accused of insanity. *Should I then be tough and resilient enough to be regarded and treated as insane while being sane? If so, it is not surprising that psychoanalysts are, almost as a function of being analysts, supposed to qualify for being insane and called such. It is part of the price they have to pay for being psychoanalysts.* [I: 110–113]

The analytic vertex is the one which allows the analyst to observe what is happening. The goals and limits of a psychoanalysis are continuously presented in the text. This feature allows some readers to appreciate the "aliveness" of the same text, because the "end" of an analysis is an ever-present situation, as is the continuing possibility of its being "alive", through the "everlasting"—as long as personal life still exists—issuing of free associations and free-floating attention. In the following quotation, the outstanding characters are Priest (formerly known as Paul) and P.A. (formerly known as Bion and Myself) as the standard-bearers of thinking processes. The quotation, again, is done differently from the rest of this book in that it is peppered with commentaries:

> PRIEST Where's the P.A.? I've had a horrible dream. God! I've forgotten it already!
>
> P.A. It's not a dream. We are just going to start our weekly meeting. [II: 328]

The "weekly meeting", which implies that it reflects an actual session of psychoanalysis, is about to begin: the dream makes its appearance again.

Bion recommended many times that any analyst could do the same thing that Freud did when he was confronted with an analysand's report of dreams. The analyst should try "to dream the session" and deal with the report uttered and performed by the patient as the manifest content of a dream which is being dreamed in the here and now. His first observations about the feasibility of doing this are in *Cogitations* (1958–1979, pp. 38–39, 43). An earlier work (Sandler, 2011) tried to focus on this subject in reports of clinical sessions.

Most of the time, psychoanalytic sessions display a dream-like nature. Nevertheless, the term "display" depends on the range of perception and the ability to apprehend it. Proper analytic technique, learned through experience of analysis (as was pointed out in the works of Freud, Karl Abraham, Sandor Ferenczi, Melanie Klein, Ella Sharpe, Ernest Jones, Donald Winnicott, Harold Searles, Theodor Reik, André Green, James Grotstein, Hanna Segal and Irma Pick, among others), pays due attention both to classical dream analysis, which focuses on night-time dreaming, and to waking dream activity, which may occur anywhere and everywhere, following the timelessness of the unconscious. The patient's consciously verbalised material is akin to the manifest dream content, and can be dealt with as such.

The whole scene was already drawn in volume I: the characters Roland and Alice had lost their farm to invasion forces commanded by Man; the social background enables a reversion of social roles. The former maid Rosemary, the daughter of a whore from the lower classes, is now the mistress of Alice; she sponsors the "analysis", or the free conversation between the characters. Alice, her former employer, is now her physically and mentally subjugated servant. The previous chapters display a still cloudy and misapprehended reality: is Man armed with a weapon? Or is his weapon just a fake, made of chocolate rather than steel? Is it a case of illusion, delusion, socially shared hallucinosis or apprehensions of a dangerous reality?

As for any human being in this world, it is a matter of necessity for all of the characters, in order to survive, to gain a good enough grasp of the encircling or outer reality as well as of their own inner reality. This inner reality is shaped by and paradoxically also shapes the outer reality.

The environment is confused, so that one cannot know if one is wide awake or sleeping and dreaming. It is an environment where and when dreams and reality are not easily discernible: dreams are very similar to reality and reality seems to be just a dream. Who is the person who has never had this kind of feeling? Sometimes the "dialogue" goes on like any social interchange could go; sometimes—like any real analysis and real life—it entails real risks. The extract continues:

> PRIEST How did I get here then? Have I been walking in my sleep? It feels a bit like that. (*To Alice*) You have torn your dress, haven't you?

ALICE Where? So I have. More darning. *She* is very particular.

ROSEMARY I don't care in the least—so long as you are neatly turned out when I want you.

ALICE That's what I meant; I didn't mean—

ROSEMARY That will do. Go and darn it.

ALICE (*submissively*) Yes, Miss.

MAN Don't let her be insolent, darling. Dismiss her if she argues.

ROSEMARY She won't argue with *me*. Well, who's going to start?

PRIEST I wanted to ask P.A. something, but I have forgotten it … Rosemary … forget it! Who's next?

ROLAND I was thinking about Man's chocolate bars. Would you think them much use in war?

MAN Of course, most powerful in war. In peace people don't know how to use them. The division which was supposed to be defending this area surrendered without firing a shot.

ROLAND That was because it was starving and its commander knew that the rest of your army had landed in overwhelming force. You could hardly claim that to the credit of your chocolate bars.

MAN I do; not a particularly brilliant example, of course, but if our commander hadn't used that weapon we would have had endless trouble. Our mistress, Rosemary, is brilliant.

ROLAND She didn't have command of your hordes; she depended on their victory.

MAN When your lot had surrendered she knew how to *use* our victory. Brilliant, I call it. You saw how she just sent her mistress out of the room to smarten herself up.

ROBIN She has *you* where she wants you too.

MAN It is possible.

ROSEMARY I spent years leaning to do much with little. Alice will learn—the hard way—after I have finished with her. Pity she hasn't got a brat as my Mum had, but I expect Tom or Priest will see to that.

ROBIN You are a bit coarse aren't you?

ROSEMARY No—realistic. I don't bear her any ill will; she can come for my cast-offs when I have done with them.

ROBIN Your cast-off man too?

ROSEMARY (*angrily*) I wouldn't go out of my way to keep any trash I've had hanging round me.

ROBIN Does that include Alice?

ROSEMARY Alice is right where she is—while I am satisfied. When I'm not she will have to go. Where? Where did my Mum have to go? I don't know or care. At present she's quite pretty; what you men are good for I've no idea.

ROBIN We had to fight.

ROSEMARY You had to win and that you failed to do.

ROBIN We can still try.

MAN I doubt it—and don't forget I am taking great risks allowing these meetings which Rosemary encourages.

ROBIN Who could know? [II: 328–330]

The answer is obvious to a psychoanalytically minded and experienced reader: *knowing* is a conscious activity; intellectual musings are conscious activities. According to Freud's observation, making the unconscious conscious, or later, but meaning almost the same thing, "where id was, there shall ego be". There is an extremely synthetic approach to it by Freud in the first chapters of the last version of "Moses and Monotheism" (1939). Let us see how the "dialogue"—in fact, the inner dialogue that Wilfred Ruprecht Bion maintained with himself—evolves:

ROSEMARY You, Robin, the P.A., Priest—even Alice. Tell lies and you don't even have to spy.

ROBIN You are right. You put ideas in my head!

ROSEMARY Be careful what you do with those ideas. *I* had to keep my mouth shut—

ROLAND In free England? Nonsense!

ROSEMARY Free England?! Roland, you must be a fool. [II: 330]

That is, there is no free land without free citizens. As Freud observed in "Civilisation and its Discontents" (1930), one is not free without a free apprehension of one's instincts, which are always translated in the realm of phenomena as necessities waiting to be met rather than desires to be fulfilled.

The renewed attempts to meet human necessities in a good enough way is a manifestation of a good enough appreciation of the principle of reality. They include an ability to tolerate frustration and the pain eventually involved in it. Conversely, the failed attempts to *fulfil* necessities are just a disguised form of subservience to the principle of pleasure-displeasure. Roland is a fool because he believes the conscious claims of the social authorities and the conscious claims of an individual submitted to a given establishment—social and mental. In doing this, he falls into a situation carefully avoided by Rosemary, who has a good enough appreciation of her unconscious needs.

Let us resume the conversation: Bion re-introduces the character P.A., making the best of a bad job, profiting from a clue and an opportunity to express his living experience in the here and now—just like any run-of-the-mill practising analyst would do. In doing this, Bion furnishes one of many treasures to the interested reader. One who is familiar with Bion's earlier work will recognise a compact version of the stuff already presented in *Learning from Experience* (1962):

> P.A. Being aware of facts has, I am sure, had an effect on me analogous to that of food on my physique. The experience is "like" being changed—as one ultimately feels changed if one survives.

The ever-present religious vertex is brought to fore:

> ROSEMARY That begs the question. Priest believes one survives even after death; don't you?
>
> PRIEST Survival after death is a belief which has undergone many transformations. May I ask to which belief you refer?
>
> ROLAND Alice has changed since she became a servant in her own house. Rosemary has changed since she became the mistress here.
>
> PRIEST Alice worshipped Rosemary; I have known many women who have been god to other woman. In Ur of the Chaldees—

ROLAND You are surely not going to maintain that in those barbarous days there was a standard *we* should emulate?

PRIEST *Those* barbarous days? I have lived through many civilisations, yet I wonder if I shall survive this. I daresay there is some saving quality even in today's barbarism—"civilisation", you'd call it.

ROBIN I don't call the "saving quality" civilisation.

MAN You are prejudiced since I and a couple of my friends used you for shooting practice. We only ringed you with heavy-calibre bullets—they weren't explosive. *And* we weren't incompetent. [II: 330]

Summing up, the characters are nearing the discovery of an unwanted truth: the imminent death of a character gifted with "too human" features, to whom Bion ascribes important functions in the text: Roland. The discovery is represented in this part of the Trilogy by a discussion of the real nature of Man's weaponry.

The various characters are divided in their views: Man tells them that his holster contains just a bar of chocolate; Robin supposes that he is not telling the truth. Roland takes it as a challenge to his manly self. P.A. offers a cautious interpretation, issued as a warning, that the holster may well contain a real gun.

The conversation dwells on the many expressions of resistance displayed by us, human beings, when our endeavour is to face truth without subterfuge and evasion. Which, in their turn, hamper or even preclude any kind of attempt to deal with truth, especially truth which is felt as a source of displeasure. Bion introduces the real nature of a psychoanalytic intercourse, which always includes issues of life and death. Taking into account that those issues were and still are dealt with both by religion and by literature, it is coherent that Bion appealed to the character Priest as well as to transcendent authors:

P.A. … Messages intended to convey profound truth—*The Iliad, The Aeneid, Paradise Lost, The Divine Comedy*—have all in turn become famous as gorgeous settings for the precious "stone" which is outshone by its attendant splendour. Krishna warned Arjuna that he might not be able to survive the revelation of the godhead which he, Krishna, was prepared to vouchsafe. Dante has only

> rarely found a reader able to discern the vision to which he points in Canto XXXI of the *Paradiso*. Milton's mind was overshadowed by a doubt whether he could pass beyond the "evil days" on which he had fallen; it was indeed his tragedy.
>
> PRIEST The most profound expression of despair known to us was "Why hast thou forsaken me?"
>
> P.A. This discovery is one which all are afraid to make. A theory that the human animal is not going to call on God to do for him what he must do for himself in loneliness and despair cannot be formulated; any formulation is a substitute for that which cannot be substituted.
>
> ROLAND Do you suggest that *that* psychoanalytic interpretation is the explanation of Christ's reported call on the Cross?
>
> P.A. You show that I have failed to make it clear that I attach the utmost importance, in the practice of analysis, to the presence of analyst and analysand at the same time and in the same place in conditions in which the consciously discernible facts are available to both people. These are the *minimum* conditions, not the maximum. Only *then* does psychoanalysis become an activity open to the two participants. You suggest that I am making a statement about events reported to have taken place almost two thousand years ago; if you believe that to be the gist of my remarks, what might you not say about my opinions when I am not present to defend them? [II: 333]

There would be no doubt for the reader of this text that it refers to an ongoing analytic session. It emphasises one of the many misunderstandings about psychoanalytic practice which keeps to the tradition inaugurated by Freud and maintained by Klein and Bion: namely, that it is "hard", and that analysts who profit from their contributions are hardened or callous people. Conversely, other practices which took on the name of "analysis" or "psychoanalysis"—for example, the practice attributed to Winnicott by others, such as Masud Khan—were seen by some to act under the ethos of "soft-humanism". Freud, Schopenhauer and Nietzsche—and others before them—were easily labelled "pessimists". The nourishing origin of what seems to this writer to be a specific misunderstanding is enslavement to the principle of pleasure-displeasure—a feature that characterises a large number of human beings, as is indicated by observation of modern social systems prevailing in Western "civilisation".

Let us continue with the conversation. The precise typecasting allows no manifestations of authoritarian views from the character P.A. He adamantly tries to hold the observational—scientific—and contributive—medical—view. The reader may see that projective identification strikes again; P.A. avoids being caught in verbal diatribes—a very real attack in the analytic setting. It would become clear that invectives—judgmental values—from the patient may try to destabilise the analytic view stemming from the analyst:

> ROBIN I don't see why you are angry. Roland's mistake seems to me to be natural and understandable. *I* had not observed that he was misrepresenting you.
>
> P.A. As I see the situation I would be lacking in proper feeling if I were not angry.
>
> ROLAND That's your opinion.
>
> P.A. That is what I said. Who else's should it be? Yours? Well, why not? I hope I am not doing anything to obstruct your freedom.
>
> ROLAND Your answer is hostile and I can detect, even though you may not, impatience, sarcasm and irony in it too.
>
> P.A. I shall not deny or confirm your observation; I think you want me to be so impressed by the facts that you observe, that I would not dare to make an interpretation at all.
>
> ROSEMARY Like your interpretation of Man's holster.
>
> P.A. I still think it would be wiser to interpret it as containing a gun that to accept his offer to interpret it as containing chocolate. [II: 333–4]

The reader familiar with Bion's earlier contributions may find the same situation expressed in different terms in *Transformations*:

> The link with the analysand should be K, not H nor L. He should not express himself in any terms other than those used by an adult; theoretically this excludes certain categories (notably column 2) but, as I have shown, it is possible to regard the patient's statements in different ways, so that sometimes one dimension is thrown into relief,

> at other times another, and it is equally open to the patient to do just that. It is because he does so that his response to an interpretation may appear anomalous. Therefore although the analyst is under an obligation to speak with as little ambiguity as possible, in fact his aims are limited by the analysand who is free to receive interpretations whatever way he chooses. In a sense it can seem that the analyst is hoist with his own petard: he is free to interpret the statements of the analysand how he will; the analysand retorts in kind. The analyst is not free except in the sense that when the patient comes to him for analysis he is obliged to speak in a way which would not be tolerable in any other frame of reference and then only from a particular vertex.
>
> The patient's response would also be intolerable if there were no psychoanalytic indulgence to excuse it, or if it were not for a psychoanalytic vertex. [Bion, 1965, p. 145]

What is the vertex attributed to Roland, whose function is to be a man who needs analysis but refuses to be a patient? Roland is the one who believes that Man has a chocolate bar in his holster. The vertex furnishes another clue to the whole dialogue: hallucinosis. Again, Bion had attempted to write about this earlier, using a theory of observation rather than the colloquial-dialogical mode which he used in the Trilogy:

> When the presenting problem in analysis is hallucinations of the patient a crux has been reached. In addition to the problem that the patient is attempting to solve by transformation in hallucinosis is the secondary problem presented by his method of solution. This secondary problem appears in analysis as a conflict between the methods employed by the analyst and the method employed by the patient. The conflict can be described as a disagreement on the respective virtues of a transformation in hallucinosis and a transformation in psychoanalysis. The disagreement is coloured by the patient's feelings that the disagreement between patient and analyst is a disagreement between rivals and that it concerns rival methods of approach. Unless this point is made clear no progress can be made. When it has been made clear the disagreement still continues but it becomes endo-psychic: the rival methods struggle for supremacy within the patient ... It follows that it is a matter of difficulty for the analyst to conduct himself in such

> a manner that his association with the analysand is beneficial to the analysand. The exercise, in the patient's view, is the establishment of the superiority of rivalry, envy and hate over compassion, complementation and generosity. [Bion, 1965, pp. 142–143]

Let us return to the conversation between the characters in Book II, where an anticlimactic environment is construed through the use of seminal psychoanalytic issues. Namely, the analyst's state of mind—or, more precisely, the analyst's purposes when he is under the aegis of a personal availability to apprehending and dealing positively with other people's pain. This is usually given by a complex constant conjunction of (i) the medical roots of psychoanalysis, and (ii) the encircling social milieu, in itself a very complex conjunction of different levels of natural needs ruled by the principle of reality, further complicated by non-natural interests fuelled by the principle of pleasure-displeasure.

The underlying configuration of the facts is also an observable, albeit immaterial fact clothed in material appearances. There are instantaneous, kaleidoscopic changes in the constant conjunctions which may unfold: one may partially observe the transient moments, in order to participate in them. Each one hints at its correspondent vertex, pervaded by the personal interests—clothed in epiphenomena given by their social class and religious beliefs—of the people involved. Underlying the epiphenomenal appearances there is a scientific observation of real facts in order to attain glimpses of "O":

> P.A. We have many facts available; if we interpret each one in isolation the facts and the interpretation do not amount to much; taken together the "gist" can be interpreted. The Mathematical sum cannot be mathematically expressed, yet the "gist" can be.
>
> ROLAND What is your definition of "gist"?
>
> P.A. I have none, because a definition would add to an already overwhelming vocabulary of formulations that seem to be precise where no precision exists. If you listened to my talking you could probably feel that the "gist" of what I meant when I used the world "gist" was a constant conjunction of your impressions. Your interpretation of my communications might be something you could formulate.

ROLAND Can you give me an example of something—an interpretation, say—which expresses the "gist" of an idea?

P.A. I was called to see a patient who was suspected of being "schizophrenic". As I approached his bed I was aware of a flurry of movement. When I reached his bed he had hidden himself beneath a blanket so that only one eye was visible. With this eye he observed me intently. He maintained silence for weeks—it may have been a month or more.

ROLAND Yes, but can't you give me the "gist" of your definition? I don't want to be rude, but our time here is very limited.

P.A. That is why I said "intently". Sometimes, as in this instance, the gist of an experience may take a long time to grasp. An eye seen in isolation conveys nothing; seen for some weeks as I saw it, "intently" is a fair summary of what I saw—the "gist" of the experience. Psychoanalysis may convey the "gist" of what two people are doing if both are satisfied that the name "psychoanalysis" conveys enough meaning for immediate needs. But what I want to communicate to you would require other conditions and time which you will not spare.

ROLAND Go ahead then. What about your dotty patient?

ROBIN Have we time to discuss dotty patients?

ROSEMARY Yes, I'm interested.

ROLAND These aren't the days for pursuing interests.

ROSEMARY Not for you perhaps. When I was the servant here I never had time for anything that might have interested me. You can think yourself lucky that I allow you and the rest to participate when *I* am following my interest. Go on, P.A. Alice—you may stay in case I want you; it may do you good.

P.A. One day, after I had given many interpretations apparently without effect, the man suddenly said, "I want help".

ROBIN I suppose you thought that was the result of your interpretations.

P.A. The only result that I *know* about was that I felt hopeless; the minimum conditions did not exist for psychoanalysis as I understood it and as I had been taught it. My faith in the interpretations was being eroded to a point where I could hardly summon up enough interest to persist. But I reminded myself that my duty was to the patient.

ROLAND It sounds most laudable.

ROSEMARY Never mind him—go on, P.A.

P.A. I wondered if my interpretations were some use after all. I suppose this showed for when I asked him what help he wanted he at once shut up. My heart sank; I felt I would have to go on for weeks, months, years, and then maybe he would repeat his remark.

ROLAND What about your definition? How many months before you get *that* out?

ROSEMARY Alice, I can see now what a terrible pair you and Roland were as master and mistress. Were all your governing class friends as bad as this? I prefer to have you where I want you.

MAN Shall I shoot him?

ROSEMARY No, darling—not yet.

ROLAND Darling! My God—not yet!

ROBIN Did you hear that? Shoot chocolate bars!

MAN I didn't say I always wore chocolate bars.

ALICE Rosemary, don't—

ROSEMARY Alice, this is not a game. I want a servant who knows her place. That will do for tonight. (*They disperse*) [II: 334–6]

Autobiography or not?

Despite his determination to keep his personal issues in strict privacy, to the extent that his personal experiences both reproduced and reflected, as a kind of representative sample, features shareable with his "fellow humans", Bion resorted extensively to what may easily be seen as an autobiographical account—which it is not. Such a function was left to *The Long Week-End*.

One of the many paradoxical situations that pervade the text is the fact that it is *not* an autobiography and at the same time it *is*. To put this in other words: it is personal rather than "personalistic". A necessary digression about the style purposefully used by this author: he avoids resorting to the commonplace term "great authors". This has a penumbra of meanings that often includes the presence of idolatry and phantasies of superiority between us, "fellow human animals"—in this case, much less fellows than animals. Anyway, the real psychoanalytic authors' most reliable research can be compared to a double-tracked gizmo: it contains their own personality coupled with their own personal experience used to make universal—that is, non-personal—discoveries. Is it any different from any other human activity? In Psychoanalysis, perhaps, as in its parental predecessor, Medicine, this apparatus reaches a climax due to the fact that there is an intrinsic mix of the *tools* used in the research and the *object* of research. They are the same: currently called the human personality—or character, mind, soul, *Geist*, unconscious, whatever name one attributes to it.

In the psychoanalytic realm, a certain disclosure of personal data is unavoidable. This constitutes an advantage as well as a drawback. Psychoanalysts who dare to write about their clinical experience are always running the risk of writing about themselves, however unwittingly. Perhaps a good enough personal analysis, which enhances their capacity to entertain second thoughts—in this case, on what they are writing about—may give a partially successful antidote. If the analyst makes a good enough use of his or her personal life and experiences in order to discover shareable and universal facts about the life of any human being, he or she will be able to write a real analytic communication. The scientific quantum leap from "individualistic" to "individual", meaning something that avoids what is "exclusively personal" ("personalistic") and reaches something "universal", warrants some transient and partial glimpses into the unconscious. This is a universal attribute of human beings. A disclaimer must be made in order to avoid unnecessary confusion: "universal unconscious" differs from Jung's "collective unconscious"; the latter concept abhors paradox and loves uniformity and concordance. It abhors scientific generalisation which encompasses individual cases. In this sense, the universal unconscious is *never* collective.

An individualistic or personalistic work might potentially be boring for most readers, except for those moved by scurrilous curiosity or, paradoxically, those motivated by the same pushes (or instincts) that pervade anyone involved in Winnicott's "caring professions", such as any psychoanalyst, especially in his or her everyday work, or for any close relative or friend of the personalistic writer. A universally applicable text will more often than not constitute a real psychoanalytic contribution which is felt by most readers to be "thought-provoking" or "interesting", even though there is no "interesting" text or subject, just interested readers or researchers.

Hard-core examples may be useful to some readers: Oedipus constitutes a most telling one. It would not be an exaggeration to state that all seminal texts by Freud contained at least part of his life experiences, submitted to his own analytic scrutiny in order to make them ample enough to constitute scientific theories. For example: "Formulations on the Two Principles of Mental Functioning" (1911a), "Mourning and Melancholia" (1917b), "Negation" (1925), "On Transience" (1916b), "Beyond the Pleasure Principle" (1920) and "Moses and Monotheism" (1939). Some observers criticised both Freud and his works due to this fact. The same criticism was made against the whole body of psychoanalysis. The critics claim that unverifiable conclusions drawn from single case histories were unduly amplified to the whole of humankind. Nevertheless, case histories build medical knowledge; statistical verification was something that came much later. Our times reveal the undue overvaluing of statistical results—which includes other activities, such as economics and finance, weather forecasting, and physical research. Those who deal with statistical data with no other intentions than just the apprehensions of truth (economic, atmospheric, etc.) are familiar with the limitations. Statistical correlations have no power to provide knowledge about constant conjunctions and motive networks. Statistical methods are of little use to individual beings; *in extremis*, they do not apply. The issue may be neither overvaluing nor undervaluing whatever it is. The various financial "bubbles", linked to the greedy posture of investors and manipulators of world financial markets, were based on the misapplication of statistics in those markets. Is it possible that in the future, if humankind is able to develop its state of mind such that it is not enslaved by the principle of pleasure-displeasure, there will be an end to belief in authoritarian data based on fashion and pseudo-science clothed in statistical authority? If statistical methods and case histories are coupled with gifted intuition and ability to learn from previous failures, due to an unblemished scientific posture, they will contribute to everlasting achievements. They are endowed with a "transcendent nature". It is fair to state that Freud had exactly this kind of sound scientific posture: an intuitive, unabashed love for truth. Therefore his extensions of his own personal data as well as of the personal data coming from his patients allowed him to make apprehensions increasingly close to psychic reality as it is. As soon as the transcendent "germ" is achieved, scientific generalising theories may appear—quite independent of the position assumed by the observer.

Did the same occur with Melanie Klein's empirical discoveries about the features of the paranoid-schizoid and depressive positions and with the very discovery of the existence of the positions? The discoveries stemmed from her insights about the behaviour of her own progeny, Hans and Melitta. The moralistic, religious approach to depression, greed and envy regards them under inhumane labels. It precludes forbearance and patience towards them. In the history of ideas in Western civilisation it was supplemented—and in the analytic session, replaced—by the psychoanalytic comprehensive apprehension of them as mental phenomena. This allowed for the study of their specific functions and eventual developments (positive and negative) in each person's mind, as well as their consequences in each person's social milieu.

How can one make effective, truthful extrapolations that may encompass whole classes of people, and perhaps the whole of humankind? If one resorts to external features, given directly to the senses, it would seem easy. For example: any human being is in possession of a nose, eyes and ears. It would not leave anyone perplexed if one stated that all people possess a nose. This kind of knowledge will do for most practical uses. Obversely, data belonging to the mental (psychic, personality, etc.) realm offer added problems that challenge the human belief of knowing—they demand a good enough grasp of the functions exerted by them. In that sense, Bion suggested that human reality and the realities lived by the human being do not call for understanding, but for "being" the very realities which are observed. To know a person, he or she must be denuded of social appendages and be as free as possible—or naked—from sensuously based data and distorting social hypocrisy—"clothes" material and immaterial.

The complex situation begins with the very terminology one may use, characterised by ambiguities and utterly different points of view that the observer may have assumed as an intrinsic condition of performing the very act of observing. To return to the act of knowing an individual as he or she really is, one should say that a more accurate conclusion about what a person is can be obtained if the observed data come from different observers who occupy different "places" (or better, "space-times") in the world. If the majority of such people suppose that there is something that they know about the person observed, there is a high probability that the conclusion is right. This differs from shared unanimity which comes from people who occupy the same "place" and use the same methods to arrive at the same conclusion. In this case, there is a high probability that they may be sharing a common hallucinosis. In medicine, placebo effects can be quoted as an example of this situation—a most recent example is the anti-depressive effects of serotonin reuptake inhibitors. The proposal is to have a large sample of observers who *do not* share mutual contact with each other. This is the negative of Popper's criterion of the reproducibility of facts (Popper, 1963): if and when many different observers sharing the same methods and observing a fact under the same conditions find the same thing, the thing observed may be regarded as having successfully passed the test of scientific verification. "Negative" is not the same as being "anti-": it belongs to the realm of minus; analogically, the realm of negative numbers. The present proposal does not replace Popper's but adds to it, by emphasising that the many different observers may have many different methods of observation—if they reach the same conclusion, that conclusion is a good enough reflection of truth. A telling example is given by Einstein's and Poincaré's conclusions about the theory of relativity; or Malinowski's final conclusions about the existence of Oedipus in the people of the Trobriand Islands. To apply this proposal to the Trilogy: Francesca Bion pointed out that it was only at the scattering of her late husband's ashes that she, her children and her grandchildren realised how well they knew Wilfred Bion. When they talked about someone who was under various vertices a Husband, a Father or a Grandfather, they found that they were talking about the same person (F. Bion, 1981).

Psychoanalysts have an opportunity to know their patients, because they attain what Lucian Freud tried to attain when he painted—the naked human being. The "analytic setting" and the analyst's artificially trained discipline in self-containment allows the patient to issue his or her real free associations, which reflect his or her inner truth. The patients share the same opportunity to know their analysts. This is not a social happening intended as a pleasurable diversion; its medical orientation endows it with the sense of a one-way vector—just like the sense of the arrow of time—because it is intended as an attempt to help uniquely the patient, rather than the analyst. In the end, it is unavoidable that the patient unwittingly helps the analyst, by giving him or her the living function that makes him or her an analyst. In the same sense, a baby biologically furnishes the mother with the ways and means that make her a mother. As Winnicott observed, there is no "mother" as a separate entity; paraphrasing him, it is possible to observe that there is no physician without a patient and therefore no analyst without a patient. If such a hallucinated being were possible, it would be a pseudo-theoretical analyst without empirical support. Autism is an attempt to achieve this state of mind. People are usually afraid of the costs involved in undergoing analysis—the real cost is the Churchillian blood, sweat and tears, which reach their climax in war, but are no less present qualitatively in any useful human endeavour in the struggle for life. For this reason, pain is one of the few "elements of psychoanalysis" (Bion, 1963). We are familiar with the saying "time is money"; a patient this writer saw for many years, whose profession was linked to money exchange, observed that "time is life".

Pseudo-science, on the other hand, demands just rationalising reasoning applied over unverifiable hypotheses. Often they instantaneously acquire the value of theses if they are approved by the group, under the whims of fashion and idolatry. Kuhn's theory of scientific paradigms is an example of this (Kuhn, 1970).

Some reactions among the comparatively few people who read the Trilogy without taking short-cuts or giving up the effort are that they, like Bion's family, think they could know the man better, due to his sincere and honest way of writing, which builds the ethos of truthfulness in the whole text. There is a danger: the readers may have the opportunity to meet themselves in this verbal, graphical reproduction of "what psychoanalysis is all about".

It would be fair to say that some of the texts written by the experienced eighty-year-old Bion in the third volume of the Trilogy are candid accounts of the seemingly inexorable "inhabiting" of the paranoid-schizoid position. Ontogenetically and phylogenetically, the paranoid-schizoid position corresponds to a natural human need, coming from human frailties. It can be seen as "normal", not in a Panglossian posture, but in dealing with reality as it is: paradoxically hostile and propitiatory. Therefore to "inhabit" the psychic "space-time" called, in the absence of a better name, "paranoid-schizoid" is a matter of principle, on both the macro (racial, social, cultural) and micro (individual) levels of observation. Lack of development through good enough mothering and a good enough working through of Oedipus leads to "sticking" and immobilisation in it, making the living movement towards the depressive position *and back* to the paranoid-schizoid position an impossibility. To become chronologically older without having minimally learned from experience means that no wisdom is acquired. This seems to plague humankind, and especially the male of the species.

For the Male is anthropologically and psychoanalytically just a collaborator, but not the real creator. He cannot provide an inner shelter to what is really new, the embryo and the foetus, the really new human being, despite the paradoxical fact that what is really new needs his intimate collaboration to be created. The Male is able to *represent* life (visually, acoustically, verbally, etc.) and to collaborate with the Female to make life; the Female is not his medium, because he does not have an inner shelter for life (a uterus). The Female makes life with the collaboration of the Male, and therefore does not need to approach life through representations using predominantly concrete media other than the Male. Hers is a living medium. Does this natural state of affairs shed some light on the fact that in Western civilisation there are no female classical music composers, painters, sculptors, conductors and scientific explorers at the level of Hippocrates, Praxiteles, Michelangelo, Bach, Beethoven, Goethe, Nietzsche, Freud, Einstein, Planck, Dobzhansky (the list would be too long to enumerate here)? And, just as important, that there are no females at the level of Nero, Tomás de Torquemada, Stalin, Hitler and Mao Zedong, whose willingness to provoke a nuclear war made the Soviet post-Stalinist leaders tremble? A roster would necessarily include personal choices; the reader is free to complete it with his or her own choices. Would the answer be that females do not need this kind of sublimation, because the predisposition to creative sublimity is their real material and immaterial built-in feature?

> EM-MATURE This book is a psycho-embryonic attempt to write an embryo-scientific account of a journey from birth to death overwhelmed by pre-mature knowledge, experience, glory and self-intoxicating self-satisfaction. [III: 429]

This is quite independent of personal confessions printed on paper, consciously or unconsciously made—such as the fashionable writing down of the "analyst's mistakes" in the form of public confessions of countertransference, something that worried Melanie Klein and ruined her relationship with her former protégée, Paula Heimann (Grosskurth, 1986). Mrs Klein, like Dr Freud before her, was sensing that if the psychoanalytic movement went along this path, psychoanalysis could be extinguished. Old wine in new bottles appeared again under the apologies of "enactment"—in itself, another apology. Who in this world—outside the realm of psychopathy—is really exempt (self-spared?) from having to take the intra-psychic personal responsibility to be his or her own judge? Some of them, the criminals from a sense of guilt, are examined by Freud (1916a, p. 332). Kant called this condition the personal acknowledgement of the "categorical imperative"—a human preconception to which the human being *needs* to be submitted. This level of apprehension has to meet a condition to exist: namely, one must be able to have a good enough perception of one's natural needs. Freud called this a good enough awareness of a minimally developed superego. It is no coincidence that *A Memoir of the Future* follows a similar path to that initiated by Freud: one with the least possible commitment to evasion and subterfuge. Therefore it displays experiences of lie, that is, hallucinosis and error, in confrontation with the opposite though "reality testing"—a term used by Freud at least since 1895 and widely used since 1911 (see also Freud, 1911a, b; 1917a, p. 217). It emphasises the artistic and scientific legacy in the search for truth that could have a motto devised by Bion: "from that warfare there is no release" (III: 576: also I: 83).

Language and its discontents

To state, as this work has already stated, that the English language as used by Bion has many peculiarities means nothing in itself. After all, any responsible individual sometimes uses peculiarities of language; in literary circles it may be regarded as a sign of virtuosity. It also happens often with schizophrenic and pedantic personalities. It is necessary to put down on paper what those peculiarities are—something that I have tried to do in this work. In the practice of psychoanalysis, peculiarities both in verbal formulations during an actual session and in attempts to write something linked to them—including the theoretical working through—may be an indicator of how far the writer is either free from or enslaved by jargon.

One of the main features demonstrated in their writing by Bion, and earlier by Freud, is their capacity to convey a kind of universal language which includes the transcendent features of the unconscious—which is, in itself, universal, timeless and "spaceless". Let us fall back on discoveries made by the researchers who participated in the Human Genome Project, a trans-national scientific research project initiated in 1990 to discover the sequence of base pairs which make up human DNA. To do this, the researchers tried to identify and map the 25,000 genes that compose the human genome, from both their material (physical) and their immaterial (functional) standpoints. The genome of almost any given individual—with the exception of identical twins—is unique. The attempt to map the human genome involved the examination of multiple variations of each gene as well as their natural sequence. This research pointed out that the centuries-old established view of the existence of different human races was a flawed one.

The concept of the timeless human unconscious preceded the findings of the Human Genome Project by a century. After all, historically speaking, it is a definitive fact that psychoanalysis is an heir of medicine. Any practising physician already knew that there is a universal liver, a hypothalamus and a pituitary gland; the nose, ear, arm, kidney, or whatever, are universal too. Their individual variations—which may be described as *transformations*—are infinite. Even within a specific individual, the composition of the internal body systems, and therefore their form and functionality, may vary over time. Nevertheless, the invariant—liver, hypothalamus, pituitary gland, nose, ear, arm, kidney, etc.—remains the same. The invariant belongs to the Platonic theory of "ideal forms", which in fact describes the function. If one perceives the natural ethos shared by concepts like "liver" and Oedipus, one may easily grasp that all of them share human transcendence. This will be true until the time when a new being, by definition not human any more, may be discovered or invented—if human cloning and genetic manipulation ever prove to be real facts. The fashionable bandwagon at the dawn of the 21st century about the existence of "new families", "homoparentality", and the pretence psychological effects of artificial insemination allured many people when this book was written. At the same time, another new-fangled, incoherent term, "virtual reality", whetted the appetite of the news-seeking, unscientific masses to whom the message of this book must be anathema. Again and again, the intuitive grasp of immaterial facts escapes human apprehension: like the search for the Higgs Boson or the Higgs Field, is psychoanalytic research a case of hubris or nemesis? Freud, and Susan Isaacs after him, stressed the reality of unconscious phantasies. To be condemned to inhabit the conscious realm fuels belief in concrete superficial features—is this an expression of denial of the possibility of using a "third ear", and of a contemptuous posture towards psychoanalytic research (Reik, 1948; Winnicott, 1965)?

Freud and Bion insisted that their written works demanded a reader who had experience of analysis. People who had previous clinical experience of the issues described by Bion in the so-called "clinical" and "schizophrenia" papers of the 1950s were captivated almost at once by the latent contents he was able to communicate without resorting to the established clinical descriptions traditionally written in the form "the patient said this, the analyst said that".

Remaining aloof from the frequent political wars waged in the name of different analytic experiences, like the "Controversial Discussions", some authors, such as Kinston and Cohen (1986), emphasised that despite the different analytic theories espoused by practitioners, the outcome of analytic treatment did not vary. The same conclusion, from a more theoretical approach, was implicit in a most peaceful contribution by Robert Wallerstein, whose political function helped the wide dissemination of his epochal work about "one psychoanalysis or many" (1988)—the legacy of which is the search for "convergences and divergences" between the multifarious and continuously sprouting fashionable "theories".

In *Transformations*, Bion emphasised that under the theory of psychoanalytic observation (formerly known as the theory of technique),

> ... the invariants would be different so the meaning conveyed would be different even if the material transformed (the analytic experience or realisation) could be conceived of as being the same in both instances ... Further particularisation is achieved, for one Kleinian analyst's transformation and therefore interpretation would differ from another's. [Bion, 1965, pp. 5–6]

In other words, it may well be possible that the same "wars" may occur between "Kleinians" when the issue is a given clinical material. Usually those wars are "resolved"—extinguished—by established "authorities". In *Attention and Interpretation*, Bion returned to the same point in a more explicit way:

> Most analysts have felt at some time that the "universe of discussion" in psychoanalysis is expanding so fast that we no longer maintain what a soldier calls "lateral communication". To take one instance about which I am able to have an opinion: the gap between what some regard as analysis and what I, as a Kleinian, regard as analysis is very wide and widening. This is attributed to differences in theory. I do not believe that what separates scientists is their difference in theory. I have not always felt "separated" from someone who differs from me in the theories he holds; that does not seem

> to me to afford a standard of measurement by which the gap can be measured. Conversely, I have felt very far separated from some who apparently hold the same theories. Therefore, if the "gap" is to be "measured" it will have to be in some domain other than that of theory. The differences in theory are symptoms of differences in vertex and not a measure of differences. [Bion, 1970, p. 86]

A most operational tool, albeit immaterial, for the practising psychoanalyst is construed when the analyst improves his apprehension of the transcendent universal language of the unconscious—which always encompasses what is non-verbal. Perhaps the more complicated terms "inaudible music", "odourless scent", "impalpable touch" and "the ineffable language of the unconscious" could give a less imprecise account of the bone of contention.

To apprehend the inaudible music, the odourless scent, the impalpable touch and the ineffable language of the unconscious in the complex and heterogeneous specific moments of the space-time of any analytic session—the "here and now"—would correspond to an increasing precision in approximations to an invariant—the unconscious. Whose processes and therefore functions may be expressed in assorted ways: according to Freud's more concrete term, "roads". Among these are dreams, considered by him to be the "royal" one. In the increasingly improved apprehension of the unconscious processes, the analyst is proportionally more "loyal" to the existence of the unconscious. Freud's observation—rather than just a mere opinion—was that the person who displays such allegiance to the fundamentals of psychoanalysis deserves to be called a psychoanalyst.

CHAPTER SIX

Towards truth: glimpses of the numinous realm ("O")

Dashing into religion: failure to apprehend analogies?

Among the comparatively small number of people who have displayed an interest in Bion's work there is a remarkable sub-group, about which one cannot fairly say that in current times it composes a minority. They did not—and still do not—hesitate to describe Bion's written contributions to psychoanalysis as belonging to the mystical realm; in consequence, they suppose that Bion was a "mystic".

Perhaps a good look at his writings—especially in the Trilogy—may help those who entertain doubts about such labelling. The same applies to those people who compose the sub-group, who have religious interests and have the habit of reasoning under pre-patterned approaches.

> PRIEST ... From what I see of psychoanalysts they do not know what religion is; they simply transfer their allegiance from one undisciplined, desire-ridden system of emotions and ideas to another. I have heard psychoanalysts discussing; their discussion itself betrays all the characteristics which I have recognised as pathognomic of religion of a primitive, undisciplined, intellectually unstructured kind. They argue heatedly, adducing national, racial,

> aesthetic and other emotionally coloured motivations in support of their particular brand of activity.
>
> P.A. I would not deny that we do all these things, but we do in fact continue to question ourselves and our motives in a disciplined manner. We may not succeed; neither do we give up the attempt.
>
> PRIEST I hate to appear to sit in judgement but I have to judge, to appraise such evidence as I have as it touches my private life and my responsibility for my own thoughts and actions. You have as many sects of psychoanalysts as there are in any religion I know. You have as many psychoanalytic "saints" with their individual following of devotees. [III: 544–5]

The phrase "individual following of devotees" brings to light a point to ponder. It may reflect—perhaps in the vast majority of cases—naïve idealistic tendencies. The basis of naïve idealism is a religious state of mind illuminated by Freud: one projects one's omnipotence and omniscience outside onto a chosen divinity. It is doubtful that idealism is an attitude fully accepted by all theologians of the mystic tradition. Bion's respect for the contributions they have made to humankind can be seen in his differentiation of the mystic tradition, which belongs to the realm of thought, from bigotry, which belongs to the professional area of group politics—which some of the former call "secularism". Lack of the discrimination provided by Bion can be exemplified by the political motto *Die Religion … ist das Opium des Volkes* (religion is the opium of the people), a critique of customs uttered by Karl Marx and his disciples, and upgraded by its author, who was not shy to make the self-interested claim that his journalistic tirade had attained sociological status. Nevertheless, its hating tone puts it at the level of a psychological denial of the kind that adolescents make. Through this and other political drumbeats, Marx created another religious practice called "communism".

In nominally non-religious micro-social organisations, labelled by their associates in a variety of ways, such as artistic, philosophical, psychoanalytical and sociological, the same feature presents itself. One specific expression of it may interest us now: one reads a work written by an author and replaces the author's meanings with one's own—disregarding John Ruskin's guidelines on how to deal with the writings of the great authors (Ruskin, 1865). The same action was described in Freud's "Moses and Monotheism" (Freud, 1939): he describes it as a noxious bias when using tradition to study the history of religion—which turns it into a religious story.

How many readers are able to pay attention to the *discoveries* made by an author rather than to the *author* him- or herself? The discoveries, the facts illuminated by the original author remain outside the reach of this kind of reader and his or her group. Projective identification of one's omnipotence and a concrete anthropomorphism are factors in the lack of discernment between a person and his or her work; there is confusion between allegiance to *discoveries* and allegiance to a *real person*. The Apostle Paul of Tarsus furnishes an example: he did not actually know his idealised master, as is usually the case. What this text classifies as the naïve idealist posture was known through the centuries under at least three names: subjectivism, idealism and solipsism. Freud referred to it extremely clearly in his paper "On the Question of a *Weltanschauung*" (1933b).

One may assume that the scientific and/or artistic posture states that there must be a counterpart in reality of truthful statements, as discovered and established by Spinoza, Bacon and Kant: for each artistic and/or scientific formulation—be it verbal or not—there is at least one corresponding counterpart in reality as it is (Bacon, 1625; Spinoza, 1677; Kant, 1781; Gleizer, 1990).

Naïve idealist readers dismiss both the scientific and the artistic postures, sometimes due to the naïve idealistic mindset: in that case, they unwittingly cannot try to assess whether a given concept—their idea about a given thing, event or person—formulated by them can have a rationally coherent counterpart in a written text, but no counterpart in reality. Idealistic readers only get as far as the rational internal coherence of their ideas with their own mind's functioning. As Bion described in his clinical papers of the 1950s, these readers become baffled when the laws of natural science do not follow their own laws—or better, decrees. Their ideas are single, isolated, and cannot be matched with reality as it is. In brief, they are "homo-": inevitably uncreative due to their isolation preventing them from making a creative pair with reality. They are enslaved by their own ideas, with no way out. They suppose and feel a false way out of nothing—after all, just a fantasy: they *imagine* that there is *just one* way out of this solitary state: hallucination, hallucinosis and delusion. The same case occurs with naïve realists. A different case occurs in psychopathic personalities: there are purposeful, conscious steering areas which are used to avoid at all costs stumbling into truth.

How many readers leave aside the tendency to construe hasty conclusions, not allowing themselves to keep the subject "in the air" and not tolerating the lack of conclusions? How many are willing to wait a good enough span of time before reaching any kind of conclusive statement? This was the case of Freud—and Bion, as one may see in the clinical cases recorded in *Cogitations*. To wait for a real follow-up may take years. The so-called therapeutic effects of psychoanalysis display no difference from the therapeutic effects of drugs, like the now fashionable idea that serotonin reuptake inhibitors may "cure" depression (Kirsch, 2009). Both are indistinguishable from the therapeutic effects of placebo.

> P.A. I think there is something to be said for differentiating *knowledge* and *wisdom*—at least for purposes of this discussion. Then I would say that whatever *knowledge* each of us has must be augmented by *wisdom*. However intelligent, the chance of survival is decreased if the character cannot rely on being wise.
>
> ALICE Is it not also true that the wise person's chance of survival depends on intelligence?
>
> P.A. Certainly. Part of the problem is that intelligence, as a capacity for collecting knowledge, needs to be distinguished, isolated—defined for purposes of this discussion—from wisdom. In real life the problem cannot be solved as simply as it can be conversationally. "Acts" do not arrive clearly labelled. Projected acts are not like a medicine in a bottle.
>
> ALICE Do you remember Prince Andrei in *War and Peace* feeling in the course of a discussion as if an inner voice said, "That is sooth; accept it". [III: 497]

There are at least three sources of misconceptions about Bion's writings: (i) his use of borrowed terms; (ii) the reader's analytic experience or relative lack of it, which allows for the use of analogies and models, and (iii) the difficulty of observing, and therefore finely distinguishing that Bion either profited from or avoided the penumbra of meanings allowed by certain terms.

Firstly, Bion pointed out that *he borrowed some terms from other disciplines*. He preferred not to resort too much to neologisms, and even less to indulge in jargon. He intentionally borrowed in order to profit from the penumbra of associations which some already existing terms have. He usually emphasised when a specific term was already endowed with some well-known and widely accepted meaning and connotation. He explicitly wanted the reader to be reminded of them—for example, "transformations and invariants" or "hallucinosis". Sometimes he used a term giving specific warnings that the reader must see that the term is used differently in his work—for example, the non-hyphenated term "preconception". And sometimes he created new terms, such as "O", "α" and "β", precisely to avoid any associations with existing ones. Sometimes he stressed some meanings that the term allows and stuck only with them, such as "hyperbole". It seems that many did not and still do not pay enough attention to his warnings and explanations about the use of the terms which are specific to his work. Perhaps Bion is in good company: in the preface of the 10th edition of *The Interpretation of Dreams*, Freud commented that people were not really reading it.

The disciplines that furnished terms and conceptions for Bion are science, mathematics, physics, art and the mystic tradition, mainly the Jewish-Christian Cabbala. More misapprehension and consequent misunderstanding occurs with the confusion between the mystic tradition and mysticism. The use of those borrowed terms has the purpose of facilitating communication. Nevertheless, some readers cannot see that the use of those terms does not mean that Bion used transplanted models from other sciences.

> Relativity is relationship, transference, the psychoanalytic term and its corresponding approximate realisation. Mathematics, science as known hitherto, can provide no model. Religion, music, painting, as these terms are understood, fail me. Sooner or later we reach a point where there is nothing to be done except—if there is any exception—to wait. [I: 61]

Secondly, in 1970 he was still trying to make it clear that he hoped *practising* psychoanalysts would realise that *reading about* psychoanalysis differs from *practising it*. He could only represent the practice "by words and verbal formulations designed for a different task" (Bion, 1970, p. 1). Like Freud, Bion supposed that his readers should have a personal analysis and analytic experience. The lack of analytic practice makes the reader unappreciative of Bion's heavy use of analogy.

> The psychoanalytical approach, though valuable in having extended the conscious by the unconscious, has been vitiated by the failure to understand the practical application of doubt by the failure to understand the function of "breast", "mouth", "penis", "vagina", "container", "contained", as analogies. Even if I write it, the sensuous dominance of penis, vagina, mouth, anus, obscures the element signified by analogy … [I: 70–71]

Thirdly, mystic tradition, mathematics, art and philosophy tried to serve humankind before the obtrusion of other scientific branches; as a matter of obvious consequence, this includes psychoanalysis. The issue raised by all of them concerns the negative realm of the noumena (Sandler, 2011). Bion followed Freud's hint; *Transformations, Attention and Interpretation* and *A Memoir of the Future* represent the climax of his attempts. More specifically, in the negative realm of noumena, the mystic tradition, as well as mathematics, art and philosophy, were *earlier modes that expressed human attempts to approach human nature and the mind's functioning* (Sandler, 1997). To do this, those disciplines demanded that one must go beyond the sensuously apprehensible appearances. There are differences between artists and philosophers on the one hand and mathematicians on the other hand, who are the predecessors of science and still perform the most scientific mode of apprehension of reality at the disposal of human beings. They increasingly learned the advantages of diminishing the penumbra of meanings allowed in the modes in which they formulated their discoveries. Artists and philosophers sometimes have an "artistic licence" and "philosophical licence"—akin to the well-known "poetic licence".

In his peculiar mode of formulating all his writings, and especially in the Trilogy, Bion mixes the two ways: sometimes he goes along with a given penumbra of meanings and profits from it; sometimes he uses the same term emphasising a specific aspect indicated by another penumbra of meanings. In those cases, he usually resorts to a graphical resource: he hyphenates the specific term. This transdisciplinary issue is discussed in detail elsewhere (Sandler, 1997–2003).

Bion's relative familiarity with the attempts to gain transient glimpses of the numinous realm of the unconscious allowed him to grasp a fundamental truth: the unconscious—the real "psychic reality" (Freud, 1900) independent of place, time and nationality. It challenges what Hegel and most of his German and Austrian followers called *Zeitgeist*. Is

Bion's formulation that people such as Shakespeare were great analysts before there appeared a Freud to think the thought-without-a-thinker "psychoanalysis" an exaggeration? Or is it a true assertion—even if one cannot know today whether or not Shakespeare was really interested in helping individual human beings with his plays and poetry? André Green (2002) thought that to put things in this way was a *boutade*.

In *Transformations*, Bion plainly states that Plato was a patron of Melanie Klein's internal object (1965, p. 138). This issue was expanded elsewhere, in a work focusing on the relationship between Hegel and the work of Melanie Klein (Sandler, 2003a). Other transdisciplinary contributions may be seen in Carl Schorske's *Fin de Siècle Vienna* (1961), which collects the work of authors fated to (temporary?) oblivion, such as Adalbert Stifter, Hugo von Hofmannsthal and Ferdinand von Saar, who contributed to forming a cultural environment permeable to the apprehension of the real, albeit immaterial and non-sensuously apprehensible stuff of the unconscious. Its negative nature shares the features of the noumena.

The same occurred with Schopenhauer's and Nietzsche's work. Both acquired social fame but their works were and still are subjected to misapprehension and misunderstandings. Theirs was a non-religious approach. Obversely, mysticism had the upper hand in Fichte, Schelling and also in many parts of Hegel's work. Freud avoided using terms such as "intuition" due to realistic fears of his work being confused with Shelling's *Naturphilosophie*—a fashionable trend which unfairly copied Goethe's earlier attempts. This fashion has returned in our times with the "eco-exaggerations" of those who extol the virtues of what is natural and abhor what is artificial, failing to distinguish between the product of human skill and the product of hallucination. The persistent prevalence of naïve idealism and its twin brother, relativism, keep the same love affair with mysticism. This is one of the many manifestations of the ages-old prohibition of knowledge, studied in Hans Thorner's expansions of Bion (Thorner, 1981). Many readers take Bion's words as if they were used in artistic, religious, mathematical or neo-positivist senses *per se*, as if Bion were an artist, religious man, mathematician or neo-positivist trying to impinge art, religion, mathematics or neo-positivism onto psychoanalysis.

Do these readers fail to see the analogical value of Bion's writings, and confuse means with ends? Many did not hesitate to state that Bion was crazy, deteriorated and senile: for example, Joseph, 2002; that he was incomprehensible and non-psychoanalytic: for example, the chairman of the IPAC's panel on schizophrenia in Edinburgh in 1961 is reputed to have said "This is not psychoanalysis any more!" and thrown away his manuscript of *A Theory of Thinking* just after its public presentation (Bicudo, 1996); that the concept of thought without a thinker has no psychoanalytical value (Segal, 1989); that he was just a theoretician whose work had no clinical application (Joseph, 1980); and that he had a poor grasp of Freud's work (Sandler, J. J., 1992). Bion himself addressed those critics in some parts of his work (for example, 1958–1979, p. 377).

Apart from the semantic and terminological issues, Freud's psychoanalytic task of approaching psychic truth and reality did not differ from any other similar attempt as regards the difficulties it entailed. Equipped with the psychoanalytic method, Bion emphasised (or rescued) Freud's observation that psychotics displayed similar difficulties—put in an extremely clear form in many works up to the last ones, such as "Moses and Monotheism" (1939). Bion included clinical expansions, in which one may see those difficulties greatly augmented. His seriously scientific statements, which may provoke a smile in some readers, were adumbrated in *Transformations*, and were expanded in the Trilogy.

> The situation of the psychoanalyst dealing with psychotic transformations is similar to that attributed to the nuclear physicist. He has to deal with relationships of a domain that has no finite limitations. The terms psychoanalytic invariant, variable and parameter are meaningful in a universe that has in one important respect no realisation corresponding to it; his interpretations have characteristics of relatedness that are applicable to his universe of discourse, but not to phenomena they represent, since those phenomena possess a relatedness, if there is one, appropriate to an infinite universe. If a patient says that he knows that his "char" is in league with the postman because his friend left white of egg in the bathroom, the relatedness implied by his statement may differ from forms of relatedness to which I am accustomed because his statement represents phenomena related to each other in an infinite universe. [Bion, 1965, p. 45]

To this writer's knowledge, no other author since Freud, with the exception of Melanie Klein, was able to precisely focus the realm of hallucination, hallucinosis and delusion as Bion did. Like Delacroix, Bion was not searching for new ideas, but focused on his intuitive certainty that "what has been said is not enough". With Whitehead's history of mathematical philosophy, he stated:

> BION ... If the "universe of discourse" does not facilitate the solution of 3 minus 5, then real numbers are no good, but must be enlarged by "negative numbers". If the mathematical "field of play" is not suitable for the manipulation of "negative numbers", it has to be extended to provide conditions for "games" with negative numbers. If the world of conscious thought is not suitable for playing "Oedipus Rex", the "universe of discourse" must be enlarged to include such plays. If serious psychoanalytic discussion cannot take place in the domain which Freud found adequate, it must be enlarged. In fact, Freud did enlarge it when he found that he could not believe what his experience with patients seemed to suggest—that they had all been assaulted sexually. He had to entertain the idea that events which had never taken place could have serious consequences. If I cannot "believe", I cannot act or think. I need "thoughts without a thinker". I may have to create a domain which is not a serious paper, not a game, not a murderous rival. If this is true of "childhood", "mathematics", why not of other thematic apperceptions including "psychoanalysis" itself? A "field of play" must be found on which to play our "game". I once asked a group, "What is the interpretation of that?" and I pushed a chair into the forefront of the discussion. It took almost twenty minutes before anyone ventured a reply to my question. [I: 175–6]

"Events which had never taken place" correspond to hallucination, hallucinosis and delusion. Paradoxically, they may also correspond to dreams, intuitions and hunches. At the same time, as Shakespeare noticed though Polonius, "Though this be madness, yet there is method in't" (*Hamlet*, II ii).

Mathematical thinking and physical research are disciplines accustomed to formulating real events whose factual—concrete—existence has never previously occurred and thus could not be sensuously observed. For example, the formulation of a flying machine by Cayley; the relationship between matter and energy formulated by Einstein; the attempts to observe the Higgs boson. In psychoanalysis, Bion's statement that the analyst must participate in the transformations in hallucinosis first made by the patient in order to be able to interpret (Bion, 1970, p. 36) is an expansion of Freud's discovery of the possibility to elicit "latent contents" though the conjoined work of patient and analyst (Freud, 1900, p. 277), later improved with his quotation of Goethe's witches (Freud, 1937a, p. 225). Freud also stated:

> I protest, however, against being misunderstood to say that the world is so complicated that any assertion one may make is bound to hit upon a piece of truth somewhere. No. Our thought has upheld its liberty to discover dependent relations and connections to which there is nothing corresponding in reality; and it clearly sets a very high value on this gift, since it makes such copious use of it both inside and outside science. [Freud, 1939, p. 108, footnote]

This writer supposes that Freud was making reference to material reality, while "a piece of truth" includes material and psychic (immaterial) reality. He was impressed with the engineering achievements of Leonardo da Vinci, which were formulated with no precise mathematical or concrete correspondences in reality at the time. Centuries after Leonardo, Freud witnessed the emergence of Juan de La Cierva's "autogyro" and Hanna Reitsch becoming the first female helicopter pilot. Bion mentioned the existence of thoughts without a thinker. Some thinkers could formulate thoughts with no correspondence in material reality at the time of their formulation. Kekule's work on the structure of benzene, Planck's constant and Einstein's equation describing the relationship and connection between mass, energy and the square of the speed of light, are telling examples of this. In other words, the precise unconscious and conscious (both!) discrimination between the seemingly related hallucinosis and dream, delusion and intuition—or, in the simplest colloquial terms hitherto found by this writer, the eliciting of lack of truth, untruthfulness and lie—does have the most serious consequences. This is not a moral issue; this is a scientific issue, fully understood by real artists and theologians. Therefore, hallucination is a lie one tells oneself. A student attending one of this writer's courses about the apprehension of psychic reality given at the Sociedade Brasileira de Psicanálise de São Paulo asked, on his unhasty personal path to conclusions: "Is psychoanalysis the history of our lies?"

Bion's first published attempts timidly appeared in *Learning from Experience* and were expanded in *Elements of Psychoanalysis*; they "took off" in *Transformations*. It would not be far-fetched to infer that at that time Bion was attracted by Rudolf Carnap's work, that is, the neo-positivist attempts to establish the truth-value of scientific statements (Sandler, 2006a). Therefore Bion tried to establish the truth-value of psychoanalytic verbal formulations made by the analyst both within and outside the sessions, as well as the truth-value of the patient's verbal formulations. He came to state that the analyst must avoid at all costs making lying statements—a possibility allowed to patients, up to a point. In his particular mode of noting those verbal statements he assigned them to column 2 in the Grid, his novel psychoanalytic instrument to be used outside the analytic session.

It took at least three years—if we consider the time span between the publication of *Learning from Experience* and *Transformations*—for Bion take the path which started from Hume and reached the so-called "mystic tradition". In *Transformations,* he recognised the limitations of the Grid in performing such a task. His next step was an appeal to other traditions of apprehending reality as it is, in order to preserve the analytic view—mathematics and the Christian mystics: Meister Eckhart, John of Ruysbroeck ad St John of the Cross. The numinous realm, which in *Transformations* he calls "O", should be the compass of the analyst. This tendency is enhanced in his next book, *Attention and Interpretation,* which can be seen as his last-but-one attempt at attaining the analytic view under a commonsense vertex. He specifically quotes the Lurianic movement (Scholem, 1941; Yates, 1979). The analytic view is closely related to the analyst's ability to dream the patient's material—which would be the stuff of his last attempt, the Trilogy. To analyse equals the "pursuit of truth-O": becoming. It is necessary to go from what he had earlier called "transformations in K" onto a path towards "transformations in O".

What has been known for millennia, that is, the records from many civilisations under many names, such as the Bhagavad Gita, the Old and New Testaments, the Talmud, the teachings of Zen Buddhism and the Koran, are descriptions that in principle allowed students of those records to perform "transformations in O". In all of them, either explicitly or in metaphorical, implicit ways, there are recommendations to eschew memory, desire and understanding—as an ultimate, probably unattainable point. Those are not tools specific to and much less the preserve of any given religious tradition, even though the history of humankind shows that those ideas were used to implant ideological, political and moral teachings. Thus they unavoidably swerve into violent, revengeful, "monotheistic", "absolute truth" dictatorships—religious absolutism. Would this use constitute a debasement of what began as a "monistic" pursuit of truth-O? In any case, Bion's respect for the wisdom contained in the mystic tradition is outside either prejudice against or favouring of religious rites and religious submission. Lest any doubts remain about Bion's ideas on religion, one may read one of his last formulations:

> BION ... I wonder how many plausible theories have been used and bewildered the human race. I would like to know. I am not sure of the ease with which "plausible" theories are produced. In this context of "plausible theories" about which we are talking, the plausible theory, or "convincing interpretation", may be hard to come by. It can be plausible and false. Witness the idea that "the sun rises"—what trouble that has caused! We do not know the cost in suffering associated with the belief in a Christian God, or the god of Abraham's Ur, or Hitler's Germany, or peyotism—or god of any kind. [I: 172]

In the Trilogy, which tries to be "a description of psychoanalysis" (I: 86), Bion makes clear his—and science's—relationship with religious manifestations with the help of the fleeting characters Edmund, an astronomer, and Paul, who is later transformed into Priest. Bion ascribes to Paul priestly functions, albeit leaning towards the history of religions and theology rather than as a run-off-the-mill, parochial priest.

> I have to employ an extremely inadequate apparatus to discuss it. I have to manufacture the apparatus as I proceed. I claim that it is artistic though the art has not yet been created; it is religious though the religion has not been and never can (without ceasing to be a religion) be made to conform to any of the dogmata and institutions hitherto regarded as characteristic of religion. [I: 88]

> P.A. Suppose astronomers could convince the majority of human beings that the sun showed signs of imminent catastrophe; that at any moment we would be enveloped in whirlpools of immense

temperatures. Would you allow that to be broadcast when nothing could be done?

ROBIN The religious people have already issued warnings that the end of the world is at hand; that God is a consuming fire and so on.

P.A. Nobody minds God's being a consuming fire. They either say that He does not exist or that He is really rather a Decent Chap, a Good Fellow, a Good Sport.

EDMUND Even the earliest religious people we know, the Egyptians, regarded the Sun as a powerful god. Milton, to come nearer our time, had an idea that "Heavenly Light" should be treated with respect.

ROBIN In passing he touched his cap more than respectfully, as Blake pointed out, in The Other Direction—"the Void and Formless Infinite".

PAUL Many people think religion should include respect not only for God but also for the powers of Evil.

ROLAND Yes, but no one believes in religion nowadays.

PAUL There is much muddled thinking. Religion, the human impulse, is often confused with God or the Object to which religious adoration is directed. I say that all mankind is religious, just as Freud said all mankind is sexual. But the expression of religious forces in the individual is coloured by each person's character and mental quality. Someone who prides himself on his no-nonsense unbelief is sure to show that in fact he has a religious belief of the most fanatical and intellectually contemptible kind.

ALICE Oh, you mean addiction to sport and such like—that's not religion.

P.A. I agree with Paul and disagree with Alice. The addiction, as Alice calls it, is not religion if it is obvious to the person that he or she is addicted. I have, however, observed by using scrupulous care in my attention that the behaviour of an individual displays qualities which can be felt to be correctly described as "religious" and *not* to be correctly described in any lesser terms.

ALICE I don't call that religion.

P.A. I do not mean that it is "religious" in the sense of something worthy of general or absolute respect, but that the phenomenon

> observed is correctly characterised as religion. Whether that particular religious characteristic is being worthily or adequately deployed is another matter. There may well be differences of opinion as regards the exercise of the religious faculty by an Aztec or Voodoo or Roman Catholic or Jew or Protestant. These differences are not evidential material either for the existence or non-existence of religion.
>
> ROLAND I don't see what you mean.
>
> P.A. A man may be exercising a sexual fetishist capacity. That does not mean there is no such thing as sex or that the object is that towards which sex should be properly directed.
>
> ROBIN What is "properly"?
>
> P.A. In a manner which is capable of development rather than decay.
>
> ROBIN At that rate an old man whose capacities were decaying would not be properly sexual.
>
> P.A. The decay you talk of is nothing to do with sex; it is "to do with" anatomy or physiology, and should be distinct from decay or development which "originates" in sex. Similarly, development or decay of religious impulses which originate in religious forces should be distinguished from those which originate elsewhere. [II: 285–7]

It might be opportune to dedicate some space (and for the reader, the corresponding time) to dwell on some terms which were used by Bion. It is possible to hypothesise that his posture was the least prejudiced possible, because at least in his written works, an invariant emerges: namely, the respect he paid to the activity of apprehending anyone's vertex. Obviously, this included the theologian's vertex. There is a perception that readings which take some statements out of their context can result in wrong apprehensions, in the sense that a given part of the text is taken as if it were the whole. As regards Bion's writings, due to their plentiful quotations, sometimes subliminal, this kind of error may be heightened.

> ROLAND If you cannot believe in a religious solution I at least cannot "believe" in *facts*. Facts do not offer an outlet for a religious impulse—only for scientific curiosity.

P.A. Might they not be the same? The religious people I know certainly think they are concerned with the Truth and nothing but the truth. It is often difficult to retain a sense of awe in the face of what we are more likely to think of as humdrum daily trivialities rather than facts which deserve to be treated with respect.

ROLAND "With respect" I could manage, but not "with awe".

ALICE I would have thought that "awe" is more appropriately left to people who are religious. [III: 514]

P.A. I do not deny the possibility; my prejudice in favour of a scientific or "factual" approach has not led me to any mystical experience. Perhaps one day in my room I might experience such an illumination. Even so I should expect it to have an endo-psychic origin.

ROLAND "Endo-psychic"! Pardon me, but that is only one of the technical terms which darken counsel rather than throw a beam through the realms of darkness and brutish ignorance in which we labour to exist.

P.A. I am sorry to have used a term which disturbs your understanding of what I am trying to convey. Technical terms in fact save a lot of time in conversation between colleagues who are familiar with the language of which they are part. [III: 522–3]

Reverence and awe

Bion uses this term in one of his Brazilian lectures (1973) and also in a previously unpublished draft, later included by Francesca Bion in *Cogitations* (1958–1979, p. 284). He points out a difference between the attitude of reverence and awe on one side, and imitation or projected omnipotence on the other side. Bion had already used this differentiation in 1965 and returned to it many times—for example, in his references to Meskalam-du in Ur (in *The Dream* and in "Emotional Turbulence", 1977c) as well as in his autobiography, when he referred to the *lack* of a "communion" kind of "relationship" with God as reported in an unhappy way by his parents (Bion, 1982, p. 22). His written references dispel any doubt about his own orientation. They allow for a discrimination about his contributions to psychoanalysis and they back anyone who casts doubt on the religiosity attributed to his work by some readers.

Would it be useful to distinguish between what Bion actually wrote and the reader's view of what he wrote? There is no rule that precludes anyone making their own contributions to psychoanalysis, but there would be doubtful value in attributing one's own ideas to Bion or any other great author: a kind of negative plagiarism or profiting from another's fame. If one's thinking is empirically based in the clinic, rather than impressionistically stated, one's ideas could turn into real contributions to psychoanalysis.

ROBIN Why? Did you have nightmares too?

ROLAND No. But Alice was tossing and turning and moaning all over the place.

ALICE Perhaps it will be your turn tonight.

ROBIN Geo-centric night of course.

P.A. Geocentric night is only a particular sample of ego-centric time. Absolute Night is part of human thought about Absolute Time.

ALICE Like the Abominable Snowman.

ROLAND I thought that was an exploded myth.

ROBIN If you mean vastly and suddenly enlarged so that it becomes far too frightening, I would not object to your epithet "exploded". You should include the myth exploding the scientific "fact". I haven't been up Everest, or Nanda Devi, or the source of the Seven Rishis, but just fooling around the pathways of the milder Alps I have been terrified.

P.A. This, Alice, is one of our tamer animals. Even if it gets out of its cage it is really quite friendly. Not an explosion like the one that blew the top off Krakatoa. But these geocentric affairs are alarming only to Ephemera like us.

ALICE I understood Mont Pelée killed a lot of Ephemera.

P.A. Of course we dislike it, but I do not see why we should get above ourselves and indulge in our megalomanic sense of our own importance—there could be something between the extremes of religious abasement and religious exaltation.

PAUL Don't call it religious *please*—it may be psychoanalytic abasement and psychoanalytic exaltation, but don't drag in religion. I believe in God and in God's Truth and in God's Wrath and God's Love, but I don't see why anyone has to confuse their undisciplined human thinking with God. Men are always worshipping their own image and calling it God.

P.A. You are not far away from expressing something to which, as a psychoanalyst, I frequently try to draw attention when I interpret an actual human statement as betraying an omnipotent phantasy. You would be surprised how often it is supposed that we are casting doubt on God. All I purport to do is to give the individual a chance of observing his God-like assumption of God-like attributes. It is not surprising that he finds it difficult to be awestruck by God, though not doubtful about his own God-like qualities.

ROBIN They must be a conceited lot, your patients.

P.A. Yet they are humble enough to submit to non-devotional observation by another ordinary human animal.

PAUL By "non-devotional observation by another ordinary human animal" you mean a psychoanalyst?

P.A. I mean myself—

ROBIN Then why don't you say so?

P.A. Because at that moment it seemed to me that a particular aspect of myself had been lost to conscious awareness of my company.

ROBIN All of us?

P.A. No, not all of you—not even all of any single one of "us".

ALICE Surely it is clear enough—he means us.

P.A. It is true that if we use conversational language for the purpose for which is has been invented, the "meaning" could be said to be clear enough. But we are not using it for that purpose, and ordinary language may sometimes seem to us to be inadequate. Just now Alice seemed to feel ordinary language *was* adequate and only became inadequate because we were, perhaps perversely, *not* listening to the ordinary meaning but to something else. [II: 241–2]

Caesura

The term caesura was used by the mystic tradition as an indication of the theological ability to be detached from any sensuously based "illusion" of the presence of a being in order to see, or feel, the "real presence" of the same being—usually a manifestation coming from the presence of a divinity or a divine "work". This is a concept referred to by the Romantics, from Kant to Nietzsche. From this remarkable shoulder, Freud offered a step forward, in his discovery of the paradoxical integration of material *and* immaterial reality—"two different forms" of one and the same "existence" (Freud, 1900, p. 695). The terms "forms" and "existence" are from Freud. The sense—rather than simply the meaning—of those words may perhaps be seen more clearly with the aid of Bion's proposal to adopt Sylvester's and Cayley's observational theories of transformations and invariants—a proposal similar to that made by Paul Dirac in Physics (Sandler, 2006a). Therefore, material and psychic (immaterial) are the two transformations around a single invariant: reality itself—or reality-in-itself. The early Romantics, like Kant, called it "the thing-in-itself". In fact is not exactly just a concrete, material thing. It embodies the immaterial no-thing: a paradox to be tolerated, not resolved.

Freud avoided the risky posture which usually flows, in the so-called "humanities", into inhuman naïve idealism, which backfires into Manicheanism and pedagogic moral overtones. The same splitting occurs in so-called "hard science", though in the other direction, equally inhumane: towards naïve realism. Through Freud's integrative observation, one may give due consideration to the "monistic", rather than "monotheistic", nature of truth and reality—a discovery parallelled by modern Physics, which discovered the real indivisibility of matter and energy, previously considered as different "natures" or entities. They are related ("communionised") through the speed of light. Freud's discovery gave him the practical tool to describe the differences between the "manifest content"—dependent on epiphenomenal, sensuously apprehended forms, immanently transformational—and the "latent content", a dynamic, evolving truth in the here and now of the session, glimpses of the transcendent invariants conveyed through the disposable "manifest content". Again, Freud's monistic observation was destined to be debased by members of the psychoanalytic movement, who insist that there are two different "natures" or entities and are blind to the paradoxical monistic nature of nature itself. Under a psychoanalytic vertex, the subject is deep, because it involves a good enough realisation of the impossibility of dealing with solitary, "homo-" entities. Nature is creative, based on the communion (relationship) of at least two—"twoness", to give birth to a "third".

Freud observed, and since him many psychoanalysts observe, are equipped by and deal with unique emotional interactions between a patient, who issues free associations about and around a given dream, and an analyst, who makes use of his or her free-floating attention and memory and knowledge of the patient. Freud emphasised the identical importance of both and their interlinking and paradoxical relationship.

Freud also observed another natural, obvious event which had not previously been brought to human awareness. Namely, the formidable continuities between pre-natal and post-natal life. This perception can be hampered if and when one mesmerises oneself with the "formidable caesura of birth". Bion would expand the concept in his paper "The Caesura" (1977a).

In the same "monistic" sense described above, caesura is an event that simultaneously unites and disunites. It tolerates what Freud, and later, Melanie Klein and Fairbairn, called "splitting", but does not let it take the upper hand. Bion took the concept of caesura from Freud and developed it to deal with the paradox in a more explicit way. Bion, like Freud before him, does not try to resolve the paradox. He tries to apprehend it and use it. The paradox is the caesura itself. Caesura embodies something that flows continually, and at the same time, because of its formidable sensuously apprehensible appearance, seems to undergo a total change. There are changes, but they are not all-encompassing, as they seem to be to the appearance-addicted, flawed observer. The apprehension of the concept of caesura depends on the apprehension of previous concepts: contact barrier and transformations and invariants (Bion, 1962, 1965; review in Sandler, 2005). Caesura can be seen as the mode of functioning of the contact barrier, and is responsible for the continuous flow of transformations and invariants.

The following conversation continues to be put in the form of free associations. P.A. has just made an ironic statement, inspired by John Ruskin, that people "*of course*" read the classics. Roland says "Touché", signalling that he has not read them properly, but has got the message to go and read them. The free associations carry on, centring on an extremely clear definition of caesura:

> PAUL I don't know why, but you reminded me of a cartoon which I once saw in the *New Yorker* in which a duellist, having just delivered a mortal stroke, says "Touché".

ROLAND I saw a horrible photograph of a duel between two people armed with sabres in which one had decapitated his opponent in one stroke. I was not really claiming to have been so completely separated from my nervous system, or the seat of my intelligence.

ALICE You often talk as if, because I am a woman, I can't ever have had intelligence from which to be separated.

P.A. Perhaps that is because he has never been completely separated from his primordial mind and is still dominated by the belief that as a woman has not got a penis she cannot have a capacity for masculine thinking.

ALICE Does the caesura connect or separate? He often behaves as if he were not a male sexual animal.

ROLAND That's not fair! You're behaving like a female sexual animal and I can hardly be blamed if I am cautious—sometimes.

PAUL This is not an occasion for display of the matrimonial experience. But if I say so, it will be assumed that I and my nominally saintly predecessor are opposed to sex. The biological creator does not appear to be on good terms with the creator of morals. Verbal intercourse is not granted the freedom that sociologically we are supposed to have.

P.A. Freedom often seems to be driven "underground"—or should I say "subterrane"?

ALICE Please yourself; but suppose both the dictator and liberator go underground and meet there.

P.A. I shall avail myself of your permission to say "infra-conceptual".

PAUL Well, *that* is horrible enough to escape durability as an artistic expression. The world of thought shrinks its boundaries in inverse proportion to the length of the verbal weapons it uses; the shorter the "bayonet" the wider the empire it sways. [II: 248–9]

Thanks to splitting and concretisation we usually think in terms of the mind-body conundrum. Hence Paul's first sentence in the conversation. As happens with free associations, in a way not unlike *bricolage*, the cartoon of the American weekly magazine furnishes the form, the "body" that is clothed by and thus expresses his thinking. It is meaningful that it is a priest who assumes the careful posture of trying "not to put asunder that which God has united". The cartoon's duellist kills: the factual actuality, the concrete, material existence ceases to be. Life's immaterial nature is not separable from material survival; in the cartoon it may express a kind of gentleman-like aplomb that would sound ridiculous and misplaced if life itself were at stake: "Touché". The common man, Roland, takes the clue: he remarks on how difficult it is *not* to separate mind and body. Alice enters into the debate—which up to this point may be seen as a "male" affair. Or, in other words, the caesura between male and female "cannot be stable" (I: 196).

Alice's contribution seems to be enlivening, as only females can be with male issues. It is now that analysis comes to the fore: envy of the breast, contempt for women, displays its face. The dialogue goes on, displaying the caesura as an event that is characterised by simultaneous union and dis-union. Its earliest roots—Freud's three essays on sexuality—are taken up in P.A.'s intervention: "Perhaps that is because he has never been completely separated from his primordial mind and is still dominated by the belief that as a woman has not got a penis she cannot have a capacity for masculine thinking." Alice goes on, making the issue explicit: "Does the caesura connect or separate? He often behaves as if he were not a male sexual animal."

Now we enter into the area of two-person relationships: female and male. This is the external appearance enclosing and encysting the mystery that encircles (pro)creation. Paul, the priest, intervenes now, quoting Christ, and warning about the murderous superego and the existence of morals. P.A. supposes that freedom—sexual freedom, mental freedom—is a manifestation of psychic reality, more than skin deep: "Freedom often seems to be driven 'underground'—or should I say 'subterrane'?"

Freud, after all, suggested—as a model intended to be understood—that the unconscious and the id belong to the "deeper" strata of the human mind. Alice is now able to furnish a kind of social counterpart to the apparent split between the dictator and the liberator. In reality this is a caesura: they meet in the "underground", meaning in their minds. It is a well-known fact that the worst dictators thought highly of themselves: they thought that they were just liberators (or benefactors, etc.). Significantly, both leftists and rightists buy their weapons from the same vendors.

Paul, the priest and mystic, is a character more prone to having glimpses of the "infinite", the invariance, the transcendence. Transcendence is that which gives the immaterial "substance" to formulations that prove to be valuable. They are valuable if the meaning that they convey is truthfully real. But to be so, they must be immaterial. They must transcend the factual form or formulation; the shell, the phenomenon.

Paul seems to be more able to warn about the limitations of verbal formulations to express "O". His warning begins with an admonition to the character P.A. that his attempts at scientific formulations lack elegance. Splitting is the one and only real fact when the otherwise unconscious phantasy, projective identification, is at work. In this sense, caesura has its deepest roots in projective identification. When projective identification is at full bore, there is a near absolute non-toleration of caesura. An unabashed mind proceeds to splitting—the one and only real fact that may occur in projective identification, an otherwise unconscious phantasy.

Atonement, at-one-ment

Atonement is a well-known—perhaps weary—ritualistic term in the Hebrew-Christian theological tradition. This term may have influenced the idea of some readers who claim that Bion was a mystic.

Bion used to hyphenate some of the words that he used to construe his concepts, in order to emphasise a hidden, underlying aspect or aspects which could be brought to the awareness of the reader. At-one-ment is one of those hyphenated concepts which emphasise a twofold meaning; it also warns that the concept differs from one already used with a specific meaning in religious practices. Like many of his other warnings, this one was not widely heard.

At-one-ment is a verbal (written) indication describing situations that are experientially alive and truthful, with no taints of lies. It formulates an evolving ultimate reality during the here and now of the session. It is not a tool to *know* one's own psychic reality, but *to apprehend* it in a transient way. A given reality as it evolves and becomes amenable to be formulated under a series of guises: literary or musical, among others. This is done partially, as a glimpse. At-one-ment is a passageway to insight. It is not a tool for knowing psychic reality due to the fact that psychic reality, like any form in which that reality may eventually present itself,

> ... is not something which lends itself to being known. It is impossible to know reality for the same reason that makes it impossible to

> sing potatoes; they may be grown, or pulled, or eaten, but not sung. Reality has to be "been": there should be a transitive verb "to be" expressly for use with the term "reality". [Bion, 1965, p. 148]

Reality-O, or "truth-O", is the *Leitmotiv* of analytic pursuit (Bion, 1970, p. 29). It can "become", but it cannot be "known" (Bion, 1970, p. 26). The analyst "becomes O"; being expressions of O, the emotional experience as experienced by the patient and analyst, towards the reality of the patient as he or she really is. "In so far as the analyst becomes O he is able to know the events that are *evolutions* of O" (Bion, 1970, p. 27).

Therefore the experience of atonement or at-one-ment cannot be described. It can be lived. It is not a matter of mere feelings, that Bion ascribes as appertaining to the realm of inner sense impressions. As a preparation for the concept of atonement, he paves the way: "people exist who are so intolerant of pain or frustration (or in whom pain and frustration is so intolerable) that they feel the pain but will not suffer it and so cannot be said to discover it" (Bion, 1970, p. 9).

Bion states that mystics are people who seem to have had some kind of contact with "O". Taking into account his sparing use of quotations, it would be fair to conclude, when examining his selected quotations from St John of the Cross, that this contact with "O" is closely related to an increased ability to tolerate paradoxes. When St John of the Cross tried to describe "repellent" qualities, Bion remarked that they "may be an unconscious tribute to his identification of absolute real evil with absolute real good" (Bion, 1970, p. 139).

One may see that Bion matches the use of this term with one easily found in undoubtedly secular authors, such as Wordsworth. The matching pair does not mean that Wordsworth was a mystic or that the religious mystics were poets. What Bion seemed to be trying was just to express a given posture which is seminal to the practising psychoanalyst. For example, in *Cogitations*, he writes:

> If psychoanalysts can abandon themselves to analysis in the psychoanalytical sessions, they are in a position when recollecting the experience in tranquillity to discern their experience as part of a greater whole. Once that is achieved, the way is open for the discovery of configurations revealing yet other and deeper groups of theory. But the discoverer must be prepared to find that he has started another round of group oscillations. Persecution⇔ Depression. [Bion, 1958–1979, p. 285]

The word "tranquillity" is used by Wordsworth to convey his "sense of poetry" (1798). At-one-ment is an observational concept belonging to the realm of the psychoanalytic posture. It describes both the psychoanalytical view and the gift of furnishing formulations at the decisive moment of the here and now of the session. It borrows a term from the mystic tradition that can be found in the Jewish and Christian Cabbala, as well as in some postures of the Reformation. This is done in order to depict a mental state. It is a tool for attaining "real psychoanalysis". To grasp the meaning of the concept one must have an idea of that which Bion named "O", a quasi-mathematical notation for the realm of the noumena, the unconscious, the id. Bion proposed the symbol "O" to denote "ultimate reality, absolute truth, the godhead, the infinite, the thing-in-itself" (Bion, 1965). The clinical vertex was emphasised; Bion stated that the "central postulate is that atonement with ultimate reality, or O, as I have called it to avoid involvement with an existing association, is essential to harmonious mental growth" (Bion, 1967a, p. 145).

A Memoir of the Future does not put aside the concept of "O". One may find many parts in which Bion resorts to another colloquial term which is also reminiscent of something usual in religious rituals as well as in romantic literature: namely, "compassion". It was already used by Bion in previously unpublished drafts later united in a single volume, *Cogitations.* It seems to this writer that his final verbal formulation is more apt—not needing to resort to theoretical terms, it benefits from the compactness embedded in colloquial language:

> P.A. I do not think we could tolerate our work—painful as it often is for both us and our patients—without compassion. [III: 522]

> The interpretation should be such that the transition from *knowing about* reality to *becoming real* is furthered ... The interpretations that effect the transition from knowing about O to becoming O are those establishing ... the material through which the argument circulates. [Bion, 1965, p. 153]

A failure to apprehend the use of analogy may hamper the realisation of the scientific nature of atonement and, by extension, of psychoanalysis:

> The scientific approach, associated with a background of sense impressions, for example the presence of the psychoanalyst and his patient in the same room, may be regarded as having a base. In so

far as it is associated with the ultimate reality of the personality, O, it is baseless. This does not mean that the psychoanalytic method is unscientific, but that the term "science", as it has been commonly used hitherto to describe an attitude to objects of sense, is not adequate to represent an approach to those realities with which "psychoanalytical science" has to deal. Nor is it adequate to represent that aspect of the human personality that is concerned with the unknown and ultimately unknowable—with O.

The criticism applies to every vertex, be it musical, religious, aesthetic, political; all are inadequate when related to O because, with the possible exception of the religion of the mystic, these and similar vertices are not adapted to the sensually baseless. The realities with which psychoanalysts deal, for example, fear, panic, love, anxiety, passion, have no sensuous background, though there is a sensuous background (respiratory, pain, touch, etc.) that is often identified with them and then treated, supposedly scientifically. What is required is not a base for psychoanalysis and its theories but a science that is not restricted by its genesis in knowledge and sensuous background. It must be a science of at-one-ment. It must have a mathematics of at-one-ment, not identification. There can be no geometry of "similar", "identical", "equal"; only of analogy. [Bion, 1970, pp. 88–89]

Faith, act of faith

Faith is a term used in many religions. Bion uses it to describe a "scientific state of mind" (Bion, 1970, p. 32). It was devised to use at the decisive moment of interpretation, referring to a sense of experiencing the existence of reality and truth. Even though truth is not wholly reachable, comprehensible or amenable to being uttered or owned, its existence can be intuited and used. The experience of an evolving truth or reality as it is, is a transient one—but unmistakable. Is it a mystical posture? Or is it an acknowledgement that trained intuition can be developed and put into practice? It expresses a faith that truth exists.

It may be wondered what state of mind is welcome if desires and memories are not. A term that would express approximately what I need to express is "faith"—faith that there is an ultimate reality and truth—the unknown, unknowable, "formless infinite". [Bion, 1970, p. 31]

The issue is not the particular truth(s); even less "the truth"; but truth itself. There is a hope that truth is strong and will prevail. Faith, here, is faith in the existence of truth and reality.

Does lack of attention to these warnings and explanations of the use of a term arouse confusion and therefore an inevitable polemic? Do prejudices hamper the full realisation of Bion's use of terms derived from mystic experience, such as reverence, awe, caesura, faith and atonement? The use of a known term facilitates communication without resorting to neologisms. Concrete-minded people cannot grasp the fact that the mystic tradition, like art and philosophy, was an early human attempt to approach human nature and the mind's functioning before the obtrusion of science and psychoanalysis.

Some of the mystics' insights gained durability, to the extent that they were truthful, quite independent of time and of the forms in which they were first couched and then conveyed. Does the concrete-minded reader take these words literally, as if Bion had used them in their religious sense, or with religious purposes? Was he trying to impinge religion on psychoanalysis? Bion did not attack religion; nor did Freud. This statement runs contrary to the current prevailing (religious) belief that attributes an anti-religious posture to Freud. This belief turns the psychoanalytic movement into another form of religion. It would suffice to read with real attention what Freud says about religion in "On the Question of a *Weltanschauung*" (1933b). The Trilogy pushes forward Bion's descriptions of the religious states of mind that characterise human mindlessness (I: 172, quoted in "Dashing into religion"). Bion also dwells more extensively on the danger that religious states of mind represented a real capacity for faith or belief that truth exists:

> BION If all else fails you could rage, as I too can, against yourself, your youth or your age, your strength or your weakness. It is one of the uses you can make of God—if you can believe in God.
>
> ROBIN Well, can't you?
>
> BION Which god are you referring to?
>
> ROBIN Allah Akbar!
>
> BION I don't think you are being serious. I shall use psychoanalytic licence to take jokes seriously. To start with, you show you are aware that you have a choice.

> ROBIN You think of me as joking; it would not be so easy to suppose that, if I were in fact a member of a Muslim culture. Nor would you suppose that you could "choose" to take it seriously "because" you are a member of a psychoanalytic group. You would be compelled to take it seriously. It has nothing to do with being a member of a particular group, profession or culture, but that the particular "culture" has a great deal to do with some underlying, unobserved, constant conjunction of beliefs; an actual God of which the various religious formulations are only approximations to the underlying configuration of facts.
>
> BION You are asking me to suppose that there is a "thing-in-itself", noumenon, Godhead, which, using Kant's terminology for my purposes, becomes "manifest" as a phenomenon; "God" as contrasted with "Godhead", "finity" as contrasted with "infinity"; "won", as Milton says, "from the void and formless infinite"; a geometrical, Euclidean figure, a triangle with sides of 2, 4 and 5 units, as contrasted with an algebraical deductive system. But a rational fact gives no scope for "belief". Belief itself is destroyed if it is transformed to find a "reason" for belief. [I: 179–80]

It would be right to state that Bion was inspired by some findings of people popularly called mystics, who seemed to be the first to emphasise that this kind of intuition mentioned by Bion is exercised during the experience of deprivation—in other words, the experience of what may be called "nothing". Before deciding to continue writing what would became the Trilogy, Bion was especially interested in the warnings issued by St John of the Cross, who in his "Dark Night of the Soul" warns that this deprivation includes, first and foremost, a finely attuned discipline over memory, desire and understanding:

> The "act of faith" depends on disciplined denial of memory and desire. A bad memory is not enough: what is ordinarily called forgetting is as bad as remembering. It is necessary to inhibit dwelling on memories and desires. [Bion, 1970, p. 41]

The term was introduced further to differentiate "knowing about", something that the erudite may do, and "being" whatever it is, which requires a practical posture. It deals with attempts at apprehending reality as it is. It was devised, albeit in an implicit way, in

Transformations, where an appeal to the wording used by the mystic tradition was made for the first time. The trend continued in *Attention and Interpretation* and reached its most vivid form in *A Memoir of the Future*. "Faith" is a term used for the attempt to depict a "welcoming mind" under the aegis of disciplining oneself from memory, understanding and desire.

More specifically, "faith" allows one to make, analogically, a journey from K to O. Those who are open to accepting Bion's resorting to symbols may find palatable his own compact formulation of such a journey: K⇨O. Some readers found his use of this and other symbols annoying: one of them perceived it as a "maze of symbols". For them, the reading of the message "at length" should be an alternative. Therefore, they would realise the journey from processes of knowledge to the numinous realm (O), or origin, ultimate truth. In the Trilogy, Bion abandoned the symbolic formulation.

Its intuitive nature is akin to what must be done by the infant who, equipped with a pre-conception of a breast, looks for a real breast to match it. The real matching is possible when the baby tolerates the "no-breast" part of the experience. Therefore the concept of "faith" in the work of Bion has nothing to do, in its ethos, with mysticism or the mystic tradition; it is a development of Bion's theory of observation of alpha function.

> It must "evolve" before it can be apprehended, and it is apprehended when it is a thought just as the artist's O is apprehensible when it has been transformed into a work of art. But the "act of faith" is not a statement ... [and] has no association with memory or desire or sensation. It has a relationship to thought analogous to the relationship of a priori knowledge to knowledge ... It does by itself not lead to knowledge "about" something, but knowledge "about" something may be the outcome of a defence against the consequences of an "act of faith". A thought has as its realisation a no-thing. An "act of faith" has as its background something that is unconscious and unknown because it has not happened. [Bion, 1970, p. 35]

It is a "pure Freud" approach as regards Bion's constant attention to psychodynamics and the interplay of a mind's movement forward, followed by a counter-movement backwards, known since Freud as resistance—the defence mechanism most used by the ego against emerging anxiety and onslaughts on the mind's steady state. It is judged by the beholder as the best one under the sway of the pleasure-displeasure principle and denial of the reality principle.

Perhaps it would be useful to echo a small part of the text just quoted: "It does by itself not lead to knowledge 'about' something, but knowledge 'about' something may be the outcome of a defence against the consequences of an 'act of faith'." For "the analyst whose aim is O" (Bion, 1970, p. 29), Bion suggests:

> A term that would express approximately what I need to express is "faith"—faith that there is an ultimate reality and truth—the unknown, unknowable, "formless infinite". This must be believed of every object of which the personality can be aware: the evolution of ultimate reality (signified by O) has issued in objects of which the individual can be aware. The objects of awareness are aspects of the "evolved" O and are such that the sensuously derived mental functions are adequate to apprehend them. For them faith is not required. For O it is. The analyst is not concerned with such sensuously apprehended objects or with knowledge of such objects. Memories and desires are worthless but inevitable features that he encounters in himself as he works. He *is* concerned with these objects in his analysand because he is concerned with the working of the analysand's mind. His analysand will express his awareness of O in people and things by formulations representing the intersection of evolutions of O with the evolution of his awareness ...
>
> There can be no rules about the nature of the emotional experience that will show that the emotional experience is ripe for interpretation ... I can only suggest rules for the analyst that will help him to achieve the frame of mind in which he is receptive to O ... then he may feel impelled to deal with the intersection of the evolution of O with the domain of objects of sense or of formulations based on the senses. Whether he does so or not cannot depend on *rules* for O ... but only on his ability to be at one with O.
>
> My last sentence represents an "act" of what I have called "faith". It is in my view a scientific statement because for me "faith" is a scientific state of mind. [Bion, 1970, pp. 31–32]

This experience can be felt by some people as fearful, and allows for catastrophic change and atonement:

> ... by eschewing memories, desires, and the operations of memory he can approach the domain of hallucinosis and of the "acts of faith" by which alone he can become at one with his patient's hallucinations and so effect transformations K⇨O. [Bion, 1970, p. 36]

Adding to the solipsistic/relativistic trend, some readers prefer to see Bion's contributions as indistinguishable from those of religious writers. It is possible to see that he was not a religious writer, at least when writing those texts: "An 'act of faith' is peculiar to scientific procedure and must be distinguished from the religious meaning with which it is invested in conversational usage" (Bion, 1970, p. 34).

The term is simply an attempt to express just "approximately". It conveys Bion's observations on a state of mind that is conducive to scientific (that is, truthful) interpretations and insights in the analytic setting and is not to be taken as a concept. To echo Bion's writing one more time, which may—hopefully—preclude preconceived interpretations of his work: "A term that would express approximately what I need to express is 'faith'—faith that there is an ultimate reality and truth—the unknown, unknowable, 'formless infinite'... But the act of faith is not a statement". It is not a learnable statement to be improved in the session, nor is it a theoretical or technical statement; it "approximately" depicts a posture.

Bion's reverence and awe before the investigation of what is still unknown in order to get some transient glimpses about its unfolding phenomenal expressions equals that of Einstein, Freud and Heisenberg, to quote a few. Was his posture before the numinous realm—or "O"—the basis of the idea at that time that Bion was gaga (Meltzer, 1981; Joseph, 2003)? Did those commentators fail to see the analogical value of models in psychoanalysis?

Taking into account the scarcity of better terms, made more scarce by the way the psychoanalytic movement debased into jargon the original psychoanalytic formulations of Freud and Klein, it should be no surprise that one resorts to verbal formulations derived from other realms. The catch here is that resorting to verbal formulations more apt to describe expressions of truth drawn from seemingly extraneous realms does not mean also resorting to their methods. They are not indications of Bion's alleged siding with mysticism or religiosity. Let us examine an earlier statement regarding approximations to O, that "the religious mystics have probably approximated most closely to expression of experience of it" (where "it" means "O"; Bion, 1970, p. 30).

Is this a hint at the necessity to differentiate mysticism from the mystic tradition? If one reads it in a respectful, "Ruskinian" way, one will notice that Bion clearly states that mystics are more successful at elaborating an "expression of experience". This definitely encircles the subject: it is as a matter of verbal formulations, analogical expressions intended to communicate an "eventful" human event, endowed with the gift of keeping in good enough form the event itself. Namely, the ability to apprehend reality:

> Verbal expressions intended to represent the ultimate object often appear to be contradictory within themselves, but there is a surprising degree of agreement, despite differences of background, time and space, in the descriptions offered by mystics who feel they have experienced the ultimate reality. Sometimes the agreement seems close even when, as with Milton, the individual seems to know of it rather than to have experienced it ... The process of binding is a part of the procedure by which something is "won from the void and formless infinite"; it is K and must be distinguished from the process by which O is "become." [Bion, 1965, p. 151]

Some readers would like to prove that the whole work of Bion had as a pivot the Indian tradition as it may be found in the *Bhagavad Gita*. The Trilogy does not leave any doubt about this; Bion carries on in his unprejudiced resorting to anything that may help him to communicate what he must communicate. The one central origin of his work is a "pursuit of Truth-O", not a siding with a specific "truth" which is always a submission to an ideology. In psychoanalytic terms, this behaviour betrays a paranoid-schizoid clinging to ideas of "owning" absolute truth.

"Late" Bion, as his work has been called in England in the last ten years, never allowed a given specific vertex to gain the upper hand. The scientific vertex is always put into constant conjunction with at least two other vertices, the mystic and artistic traditions. The value of appreciating a resort to analogy is emphasised in the next quotation. Nevertheless, current readers carry on failing to use the analogy as a means and transform it into an end-in-itself. Their attitude is the same as that of photographers who value the instrument they work with—a contraption—more highly than the photograph itself, the end product of their activity:

> ROLAND's VOICE (*the enunciation is clear and precise. He is himself not visible and as he talks he becomes progressively more a disembodied thinker and finally pure thought without a thinker*) Krishna makes the point quite clearly; he shows Arjuna that his depression is part of feelings of compassion which are unworthy of thought, still less of God-head. That kind of thing may be appropriate to reception and emission in the range of sensuous perception whether perceived directly or mechanically by constructs like radio receivers, X-ray films, musical instruments and, in their very crude and gross manifestations, by animals and creatures in the biological range. Very sensitive animal organisms may then be able to interpret or transform the disturbances in the waves which render them opaque and obstructive. St John of the Cross was even able to point out that an analogy can be found which may be serviceable in the process of vulgarisation intended to make the grosser crudities even grosser, till they impinge on elements which are still within the spectrum of the infra-sensuous and ultra-sensuous, though not outside that very narrow and limited band. He uses, it will be remembered, the analogy of dust particles which can render perceptible a ray of light that traverses it. Recently, by mechanical means, it has been possible in the biological range (human sub-category) to detect disturbances of great violence which have completely escaped detection by animals dependent on sight, even when sight is augmented by instruments such as telescopes, spectrographs, cameras and preparations of film coated with fine grain receptors—all macroscopic. Yet these perturbations are matters of the greatest crudity and violence!
>
> Though extremely rare and scattered over a huge range of temporal space, they only appear to be extremely rare because of the crudity and triviality of recorded time as an instrument of measurement. Time as a concept is as inadequate as topological space to provide a domain for the play of such enormous thoughts as those liberated by freedom from dependence on a thinker. The breakdown is as trivial, though made to appear vast by the inadequacy of the framework, as, to take a very gross but simple analogy, that which occurs if a simple operation such as the subtraction of five

from three is attempted with sensuous objects or even a relatively sophisticated mathematics best limited by being exclusive of negative numbers though well stocked with real numbers.

The failure to grasp the trivial range of the biological spectrum, even when the field of the living is extended by the dead, the animate by the inanimate, has been matched with the vastness of the extent of the relatively minute. This is due, in part, to the failure to grasp the nature of relativity, in particular the fact that it includes paradox. The restriction imposed by the limitation of thought to thoughts with thinkers implies the polarisation "truth" and "falsehood", complicated further by morals, uninvestigated "moral" systems, and extensions of Plato's thought to moral views of the function of poets and artists. A similar seepage from the domain of religion may likewise be traced to the inability to respect the "thought without a thinker" and, by extension, the "relationship without related objects". How this has affected even so-called practical thinking is seen in the difficulty of the "public" to grasp that an analogy is an attempt to vulgarise a relationship and *not* the objects related. The psychoanalytical approach, though valuable in having extended the conscious by the unconscious, has been vitiated by the failure to understand the practical application of doubt by the failure to understand the function of "breast", "mouth", "penis", "vagina", "container", "contained", as analogies. Even if I write it, the sensuous dominance of penis, vagina, mouth, anus, obscures the element signified by analogy …

ROSEMARY (*yawning*) Oh my God.

VOICE Why drag me in?

ROSEMARY (*imperiously*) Alice! Come here at once.

ALICE (*submissively*) Yes miss.

ROSEMARY Why can't you keep that crashing bore in order? Why did you marry him if you didn't know how to keep him on a lead? You at least should have learned that the factual exercise of a relationship is not the two objects related, like the cunt and the prick, but keeping one thing inside another. (*Laughs contemptuously*) The container and contained! My God, I believe he has driven me as mad as he is! I'm even talking this crazy nonsense. I'll get locked up if this goes on much longer!

ALICE Yes miss. Excuse my saying so, but—*you*'ll be contained in a container then!

VOICE ARF, ARF, ARF. Very funny. Very funny indeed!

ALICE & ROSEMARY (*together, hushed suddenly*) *That* was a joke-without-its-fun, a joke *with* a vengeance.

ROLAND (*frigidly polite, resuming his discourse*) The joke with a vengeance differs considerably from the joke with fun. To the superficial observer they can appear similar. Poor Robin. To some extent, if I could compare myself even remotely to him, "poor me". Just now, when we left Munden … will you ladies excuse me if I continue my discourse? [I: 69–71]

These considerations mark the existence of limits in our mental apparatus that proved to be resiliently hidden from general awareness throughout the centuries. Linked to the human "felt need" for material, concretised comfort and denial of the basic human condition, helplessness, what is here rated as "limitation" was and still is not seen as such by many people. Through all those years it was called secularism by the theologians; materialism, futurism, consumerism, and technocracy by philosophers and social scientists in the present century and in the previous one.

This also does not mean that other vertices and their corresponding methods of apprehending reality and truth, like artistic forms, especially music, or the Cabbalist tradition, as well as psychoanalysis, are wholly effective for the task. There is evidence that they are less ineffectual, due to features highlighted in Bion's text quoted above: namely, the tolerance of paradoxes, the nature of relativity and the inadequacy of judgmental values.

The quotation may be useful at least to the unwitting protagonists of what is currently a fairly frequent situation in the psychoanalytic movement. What was seen as an awful mistake made by the pioneers—examples being Freud, Wilhelm Reich, Melanie Klein and Hermine Hug-Hellmuth—allowed the second and third generations of analysts to learn from their sad experience: namely, attempts to analyse members of their families, which ended in disaster. At that time, there was an embryonic tendency: an increasing number of "married" couples among the members of the psychoanalytic movement, which added in some cases an unwise addiction to attempting to analyse not only the progeny, but also the spouses. Why slot into technical talk that which should remain in the realm of a free human relationship? The final part of the excerpt just quoted addresses this subject. Another way to read it could take into account that the text tries to embody

> Years of education at a public school, years in an army at war, years at Oxford University, years being psychoanalysed, years of medical training and a year at the University of Poitiers. The last three sentences were served concurrently. [I: 217]

In addition, approximately 80 years of life, two marriages, two daughters and one son, medical training, a non-conformist religious education, as well as a propitious (in the eyes of many) trajectory in the psychoanalytic movement.

Ineffable

Yet another term which already had theological and mystical connotations means that the description of an event cannot be confined to the limits of any verbal formulation known to humanity. Strictly speaking, all subjects appertaining to human life, including human beings, challenge human abilities to build a language that may remotely deal with this task. Again it was used by Bion to talk about the numinous realm, or, in his quasi-mathematical notation, "O".

The term "ineffable" had been viewed as alien to the established psychoanalytic nomenclature. It would cause surprise to a reader endowed with a free mind, less prone to judgmental values legalised by the ruling elites regarding what *must* be said and what it is *forbidden* to say. As soon as they are socially seen as legal, the perception of their prejudiced ethos is attacked. As a matter of consequence they are paradoxically both reduced in importance and upgraded; the former occurs in the area of conscious awareness through repression in the unconscious; the latter occurs just in that repressed realm, where and when it is continuously upgraded under a paranoid view of an "all-conquering, know-all" posture.

Four years after the publication of Volume I of the Trilogy, *The Dream*, Bion and his dedicated wife decided that some hints might be needed. He decided to write a "Key" to the whole Trilogy, which was destined to be published posthumously, as was Volume III, *The Dawn of Oblivion*. He also wrote an "Introduction ..." (also variously called, at the choice of the reader, "Prelude ...", "Overture & Beginners ..." or "One, Two ..."), to be placed, like any introductory text, before the whole Trilogy. For the end of Volume III, there was an "Epilogue". The "Introduction" may be not suited to its purpose, but in any case it furnished to the attentive reader a straightforward *explanation* of what the Trilogy was about as well as of its attempt to address what is ultimately "unaddressable"—or ineffable:

> Within this book there are changes of meaning that are obvious, communicated and interpretable according to the rules of grammar and articulate speech. There are changes of rhythm that are not so obvious, but if detected they are similarly communicated and interpretable. The rules to which they conform may be more difficult to detect, as would the key of a musical composition written without the statement of the key signature. There are changes detectable only by those willing to make the effort. If no existing human mode of thinking provides a model, an approximation could be found in astronomical space. There may be modes of thinking to which no known realisation has so far been found to approximate. Hallucinosis, hypochodriasis and other mental "diseases" may have a logic, a grammar and a corresponding realisation, none of which has so far been discovered. They may be difficult to discover because they are obscured by a "memory", or a "desire", or an "understanding" to which they are supposed—wrongly—to approximate. Unless the obscurity can be circumvented or penetrated it will remain unobserved, as the galactic centre or the origin of the universe remains unobserved.

Obversely, there are readers—the "willing" ones, as previewed by Bion—who were and are reminded of Freud's firm Kantian basis, as expressed, for example, in his statement in *The Interpretation of Dreams* (p. 690) that "the unconscious is the true psychic reality". Those are the readers at peace with Kant's and Freud's indications about the ultimate unknowability—and hence its ineffable character—that afflicts human knowledge. This encompasses even material reality—something that remains ultimately unknowable to our sense organs. Materiality gives just the impression of ultimate knowability; a deceptive appearance, like any appearance.

Models in science are constructs that purport to depict some parts of their counterparts in reality. It is a limited and acknowledgedly flawed task. Even to scientists, ultimately, the word "ineffable" does apply. In Plato's terms, that which appertains to the Demiurge's work is, in its perennial reformation, an attempt to utter the ineffable. Ineffable means just that: some event or fact that cannot be put into words. Emotional experiences are ineffable; that which is intuitable and "experienceable" is ineffable.

Ineffable, in Bion's work, has no links either with esotericism or with mysticism, even though the mystics were among the first, after Plato, to recognise the existence of that which is not amenable to be put into words—by any religious, artistic or scientific formulation. For example, the conception of death:

> ROLAND We used to hunt. But mostly it was the fun of rough shooting round the farm. Alice visited us. I liked her. Till one day she flared up at going to church and said she had told her parents she did not like the parson because he gabbled away like an old cockatoo. I liked her fiery spirit and we agreed, privately, that we would marry one day. But war came. It was marvellous, especially when I went into action and didn't run away—the first time. I found I had to go into action again that same day. That I hadn't expected. I knew I would have to go into action again, but I did not expect that the second battle, only a few hours after the first, would feel so different.
>
> ROSEMARY (*examining her toe nails*) Alice, you look positively interested.
>
> ALICE I am. I haven't heard any of this before.
>
> ROSEMARY (*yawning with affected indifference*) Well, get on with it. I don't expect you to be listening to voices when you have my feet to attend to.
>
> ROLAND The next day I was lying in a dugout because the strafing was so bad. Everything was going up. At first I was frightened. Then I realised I could run away. I had not realised that before. You couldn't even be brave!
>
> ROSEMARY What on earth has this to do with Munden?
>
> ROLAND It has this to do with it: Munden occurs many years after. In fact Munden lies far in the future. Also far in the past.
>
> ROSEMARY Oh my God! Can't we have a little whoring? That also lies far in the past. And far in the future. Also, it is at least

interesting and not this boring Roland stuff. Alice! Give me that whip. I'll teach you what it is to be my maid. Now; lick! Not like that you fool! Beneath, under the toes. And between. Now the soles of my feet. You will never make a whore the way you are going on. Now—concentrate. Carpe diem, as we used to say and will say again when my client and slave arrives. I am Thais. I am Berthe au grand pied—you never heard of them I suppose?

ALICE Oh yes: I had a question on Villon—le Grand Testament—in my certificate exam.

ROSEMARY Really? How boring you are. It comes natural to you I suppose. And just wake up that husband of yours will you? What about Munden?

ROLAND (*pale and sweating*) Those heavy bullets. They crashed like the slamming of train doors in a tunnel. Robin and I flattened as low in the mud as we could get. Slam! Slam! Slam! Grand slam! The rat hunt. Someone was trying to get me in a corner and club me to death. But thanks to reversed perspective I could cower in the corner where the angle of the walls protected me.

ROSEMARY What happened then?

VOICE 'E fell on 'is arse! Arf, arf, arf!

ALICE What was that?

...

ROLAND I believe it's clearing. God, but that was a heavy shower! Nowadays they use computers. Hard to see what fun they can get out of sports in which you use computers to work out the position—the exact position of your blows. This rat uses it to aim his blows exactly so they just miss. The wheels of God roll slow, but they roll exceeding small. Slam! Slam! Small! These are so close that I can feel the hot air as they pass. It has started again. You can't just have machines. There still has to be some kind of vestigial brain to programme the computer. The tiny vestigial scrap of human cruelty. Small, vestigial, but tough and resistant like a spore—a spore of malignancy. Where's Robin? "They" must have got him. Ah, the sea at last. The salt marshes and the peewees calling and the great clouds billowing past far above. Is the war over? From that warfare there is no release—no release. Daddy! Oh Daddy—stroke me daddy! My dear, dear child, my fingers can't reach your sweet face now. Would God I had died for thee! Oh my son, my son, my son: Oh my son Absalom! Past, present and future, all shrivelled up to a nothing—the heart of a computer!

ROSEMARY (*twitching a scarf about her shoulders. Is she cold—or embarrassed?*) Alice, that will do. Really, these men make one quite uncomfortable at times. Pathetic.

ROLAND Just what I was thinking. I had forgotten I used to be so sentimental.

ROSEMARY I never was. Alice—oh, I see you have recovered.

ALICE For a moment I was reminded of my young days and even of the rather attractive days of young love when Roland and I thought we were in love. I almost believed I would go back to it if I could. Do you remember, what Horace said about Lydia?

ROSEMARY Horses? No, never heard of him. Oh, perhaps I do. That was in my Maid of the Mountain days. That is when I dreamed it would be lovely to go on the stage and act the lead. What was it? Marry a lord, have a mink coat and masses of diamonds, and the third was to fall in love. I have done the lot. Now I am not much more than a computer myself: married to another computer.

ALICE And I am the slave of my mistress. I rather think it's the best of the lot. What about my religious days? I used to be married—Roland and I even married in Church.

ROSEMARY Ask Roland. I never took to it much. He has some highfalutin' stuff about it. Roland—tell us about God.

ROLAND There is a remarkable durability about the human capacity to believe in God. Religion affords a continuing source of study. The persistence of the belief is used by some people as an argument in favour of the existence of God—as if one could not believe, still less that the race could not believe, in the existence and even worship of a reality which somehow approximates to the reality of the human and animal impulse to worship. The mouse or rat sometimes looks as if it were imploring, in a positively worshipful posture, the mercy of the cat who is licking its whiskers preparatory to making a meal of its prey. The human animal, which has achieved a degree of articulate speech, certainly seems to be aware of its equipment of cruelty and the need to glut it, or at least feed it with the appropriate diet for its cruel impulses. "'But not on us', the oysters said, turning a little blue", is a formulation of the material which is to nourish and sustain cruelty in vigorous health. You remember there is a well-known story—it is even attributed, amongst others, to Jesus, the eponymous hero of the Christian religion. "My God, my God," he is reputed to have said, "why hast thou forsaken me?" If he had thought of his Father as greedy and cruel he would have more rationally complained about being remembered—in time to satisfy his hunger for the satisfaction of his cruelty. But usually the cornered rat seems to feel, in extremis, the advisability of adoration and worship; "morituri te salutemus" is a succinct formulation of the principle.

In a civilised world it is more comfortable to believe in its civilised qualities, to obscure the cruel laughter (as expressed in this artifactual dream here) which might evoke, through memory or desire, the configuration evocative of dread. It seems clear that the attempt is inherent to ward off, or to ward off awareness of, something which is dread or terror and behind that the object that is nameless. There are many formulations of dread, unformulated and ineffable—what I denote O. Plato named it "forms", of which sensuous objects are the unreal, but sensible counterpart. Saint Augustine resorted to using the equipment of religion, which is available in many Religions, to express the separation of good from evil. The systematic separation into two objects, good and bad, conscious and unconscious, pain and pleasure, ugly and beautiful, has provided a framework which seems to have facilitated the development of knowledge, but the element of growth appears to have escaped formulation especially since it resembles maturation. The lack of any simple framework of coordinates by which growth could be perceived or measured can be described in imaginary or simple terms by constructing a theory that a child—fictitious, but plausible without outraging the intelligence—could observe that it eats food which disappears, and then evacuates urine and faeces which can be observed. Further investigation made by our fictitious child leads him to discover that what has been devoured has been transformed into faeces + urine and the process of *in*gestion has been transformed into a process of evacuation. The normal activity of growth does not betray itself unless it becomes significant through some secondary attribute such as pleasurable, painful or doubtfully related quality—measurements of weight, height and the like which depend upon conjecture, theory and controversy.

Imagine the confusion of the human animal that finds itself called upon to gauge, contend with, promote or discourage something which has apparently no attributes and no language suitable for co-operation either with himself or anyone else except the primitive and defective instruments of the sensuous world! It is difficult to believe that "the mind"—shall we provisionally call it?—has no boundary which is obviously and clearly bounded by the same boundaries as the anatomical brain. It is worse if it is seen to be inadequately represented by systems of analogues. Consider, for example, the struggles represented by the approach made to this difficult problem by the Greeks …

ROSEMARY The Greeks, if I may say so, were almost as ridiculous as you would expect them to be if you allowed yourself to believe what men say about them. In fact, luckily, I did not have to go to school and learn Greek and Greek grammar and Greek translation. I learned all I wanted to know and in less time than it takes for you and your lifetime of bellyaching noise. I learned, and Homer had the sense to make it possible for you to learn, that Helen was at Troy. One of you fools said it, shortly and straight to the point—before the dawn, hidden but not silenced by the cliff above Plymouth, "Anyhow, whore or no whore, she done it for him free", and that's what started all the trouble. I don't have to write learned scholarly disquisitions about it. Plymouth Hoe, the Siege of Troy—what does it matter? Or Elizabeth, by the Grace of God, Queen of England. Or me? I am still beautiful. Even Alice—look at her now: is she not beautiful? You are silent, Roland. Why do you not listen? There is no thought or language yet the voice of them have gone to the uttermost parts of the earth.

ROLAND What? Why don't *you* listen? What else have I been doing while I have been talking? I have been telling you both something. Some of what I have been telling you I know. A lot of what I have been saying I do not know. I know a little—that part of it which I can feel, very faintly, is being listened to somewhere; it's like being touched in a crowd.

ROSEMARY Because your language is, as you think, not listened to by me, you feel entitled to be impressive and to have an audience that is impressed. My profession is the oldest in the world. I am familiar with the arrogant contempt that you think you are entitled to feel if you muster enough intelligence to formulate that expression together with the musical expression of contempt. Thais, Eve, Lillith … *there* is a lineage which you cannot begin to match. Because I do not bother to put you in what you would be pleased to call the proper place, you feel very proud to think you know mine. The brand of Cain has also been worn as a brand of honour. Your regiments are vast. Since you have learned to count you have been impressed by numbers—the greater the number the greater the honour. The more or less—that is the only criterion you understand. If I were to unveil my beauty you would—shrivel up and die. No, please! Spare me your protestations; I was aware that if I succeeded in making you hear what I said I should be afflicted with the pain of having to watch, and worse, admire your pitiful posturing display. You did not think, did you, that the poor little guttersnipe from the ghetto, the virgin's womb, might be more than rewarded by not being abhorred?

ROLAND (*in his best Oxbridge manner. He speaks clearly and well and is not disguising the fact that he knows he is doing it modestly and well*) Who found the way to express what he had to say we do not know. But we do know that as late as the Bhagavad Gita, Krishna is described as reproving Arjuna for his depression and the assumption that his standards are the measure of all things. Arjuna has no hesitation in thinking he can reprove Krishna, or God, or the Ultimate Arbiter, whoever that may be, for his defective standards. Why should he fight and kill his kinsmen and friends though he knows them to be no less worthy than himself? He will not fight. In the Iliad, Hector is defeated and his corpse dishonoured. Achilles, though ultimately the victor, can sulk unworthily in his tent. The Trojans are defeated by a stratagem in a war waged on account of a woman and her ignoble paramour.

ROSEMARY !

ROLAND I beg your pardon? … I thought I heard someone say something. No? Then I shall continue. (*Softly in the distance—arf, arf, arf!*) I feel cold. Are these the streets … of a great city? They seem empty, lonely, deserted. The satyr shall call in the street … Is this Ur, that Royal place? Nineveh? Tyre? Babylon?

VOICE Pretentious ass.

ROLAND Why? What's that? (*after a pause he continues*) I'm scared. I used to lecture well … am I losing my gift? What was I saying now? O yes: (*recovery of his theme reassures him*) The Israelitish God was a recognisable, tribal deity showing marked human characteristics such as jealousy and envy, not markedly different from the inhabitants of the Homeric Pantheon located on Olympus and freely participating in human affairs.

VOICE It is amazing that this lump of a farmer knows all this stuff. The explanation is either that he is so stuffed up with "education" that he couldn't be expected to be any use as a farmer, or that his farming lout occupation explains his pretentious erudition. It reminds me of the laughable howlers which mark Ezra Pound's claims to be a translator. Do you remember Kipling's joke about Horace's fifth book of Odes? Well at least that was funny. Even so he pretended quite seriously that he could understand Virgil's understanding of the Mantuan sisters.

ROLAND Was that someone laughing again? An "educated" Oxbridge accent?

VOICE Oh, do get on.

ROLAND Certainly. What was I saying? Job was rebuked for his setting up, like Arjuna, to be able to judge Krishna by the scale of moral views which might be appropriate to human beings. Even at school I thought Palinurus had very unfair treatment, but of course anyone could see that you can't expect much of an old bore like Virgil. You have to make allowances for a Classic.

TOM What's your little game?

ROSEMARY, ALICE, ROLAND et al (*hushed*)

TOM You heard and I heard you, you bastards! What's your little game? (*It grows lighter. Tom peers around and gradually begins to see*) So *there* you are. Pretending to be asleep. All right, I have an answer to that one! I will put you to sleep—permanently. (*Beside himself with rage he brings his clenched fists down together on the nearest figure. His fists bury themselves in the bedclothes. His violence is such that he cannot recover himself but remains, weeping with impotent rage, unable to regain an upright posture*) [I: 73–80]

The mystic tradition and psychoanalysis support a search for truth

> ALICE You say you have never had direct experience of a mysterious event; do you mean by that that you have not been in a room at the time when someone, not you, was under the influence of a mystical force?
>
> P.A. I have had no evidence that either I or the other was passing through such an experience. I only remember two or three occasions when an analysand of mine actually claimed a mystical origin for the event. I have been more impressed when the individual was *not* consciously making such a claim. [III: 525]

In resorting to verbal formulations originally found in Plato's theory of forms, in Kant's revival of it, in the Jewish and Christian Cabbala and in Buber's extensions of them, Bion used a most misunderstood analogy to describe the psychoanalytic negative realm of the id and of the unconscious. There is a strange similarity in the reactions of many members of the psychoanalytic movement to the contributions of Bion and Freud, which echoes the same reaction to Freud's forerunners in the German Romantic movement: all of them were also accused of being "mystics" in their time; even Hume was accused of this.

Bion considers religion relevant as one of many schools of thought; he nourishes some objections that nevertheless do not preclude his high appreciation of some of the achievements of this "school of thought". He created some characters which may be seen as mystical speakers: Priest, Du, Devil, Voice, and God, who makes Shakespearean apparitions. P.A. and Priest are involved in insightful thoughts around their similarities and differences. In one of his 1984 lectures at Tavistock, Meltzer regarded the character Du as being Roland's unconscious—this does not coincide with this writer's opinion, but the mention is made just for the record, because it was one the first written commentaries about the Trilogy.

In a reversion of perspective, in Book III P.A. criticises Priest for believing in an omnipotent god. Priest seems less religious than P.A. when he argues back, stating that it is better to believe in a god who abides goodness than to believe that psychoanalysts are goodness incarnate, a belief that brings with it the statement that they are just good people, always prone to be helpful! In the statements attributed to the character Priest is Freud's idea that a God "lives" in each individual, who omnipotently projects this God outside. Anyway, there are some issues on which P.A. and Priest agree.

In one of the many passages where he resorts to a confrontation between the imaginary characters P.A. and Priest, Bion dwells on misunderstandings, a problem that afflicts any attempt to communicate ideas and findings. In doing this, he illuminates a seminal difference between psychoanalysis and the religious tradition: namely, the pretension to indoctrinate, which requires a heavy use of judgmental values:

> P.A. One of my objections to your school of thought is that it appears to encourage a belief in unlimited times such as life after death.
>
> PRIEST Unfortunately we are debited with the views—usually mistaken—that people have about what we teach.
>
> P.A. You yourself appear to debit me with views about psychoanalysis which I do not hold; it would be a part of my task if you were an analysand to elucidate your assumptions so that you could contrast and compare them with any other ideas you might entertain. In this respect I think that our activity is different from yours. *You* aspire to tell others how and what to think. *We* aspire only to show what people think—the rest is their choice. [II. 388]

There are counterparts in reality hinted at by the term "intuition", in the here and now of the decisive moment of the analytic interpretation. Let us resort to Bion in order to try to illuminate the issue in psychoanalytical terms:

> The intuitive psychoanalytic background is that which I have "bound" by terms such as pre-conception, definition, notation, attention[1] ... I shall borrow freely any material that is likely to simplify my task, starting from Plato's theories of Forms. As I understand the term, various phenomena, such as the appearance of a beautiful object, are significant not because they are beautiful or good but because they serve to "remind" the beholder of the beauty or the good which was once, but no longer is, known. This object, of which the phenomenon serves as a reminder, is a Form. I claim Plato as a supporter for the pre-conception, the Kleinian internal object, the inborn anticipation ... Phenomena, the term being used

> as Kant might use it, are transformed into representations. [Bion, 1965, p. 138]

Bion states that the final products of transformations may be regarded as representations of the individual's experience of the numinous realm, reality, O, the id. Nevertheless, he also states that the significance of O is not that of an "O-in-itself" which corresponds, in experience, to the idea of owning absolute truth—but rather, this significance "derives from and inheres in the Platonic Form" (Bion, 1965, p. 138).

> P.A. A runner who was crouching beside me in a shell hole had his thoracic wall blown out exposing his heart. He tried to look at the ghastly wound across which an entirely ineffectual field dressing dangled. "Mother, Mother—you'll write to my Mother sir, won't you?" "Yes, blast you" I said. If I could believe in God I would ask him to forgive me. "Dieu me pardonnera. C'est son métier."
>
> ALICE: I thought you were supposed to be cured of such irrational guilts.
>
> P.A. Who said they were irrational? Or that one would not sometimes see sufficiently clearly to know one was damned—rationally?
>
> PAUL You are angry with her; why, what has she done?
>
> P.A. I am sorry if I was rude; I didn't mean it. I use the saddest words in the language—"I didn't mean it to happen". They hang across the gaping wound of my mind like a ridiculous field dressing. August 8, 1918, that was.
>
> ROLAND Sidereal time? Absolute time? Or just ephemeral time? The time inhabited by the ephemerides—
>
> EDMUND —as long as no one knows its proper meaning; otherwise they may laugh at you and think you are mixed up in your biology.
>
> ROLAND If they have a laugh I suppose that would be a good mark chalked up on my scoreboard.
>
> PAUL I thought you didn't hold with these religious ideas.
>
> ROLAND I don't. I have them, but I don't hold with them. They are nonsense.
>
> PAUL I think you *do* hold with them and they aren't nonsense.

P.A. They may be non-sense, but I agree with Paul that you do hold with them. As far as I am concerned the ideas *hold me* whether I like it or not. I would not go near the Amiens-Roye road far fear I should meet my ghost—I died there. For though the Soul should die, the Body lives for ever.

PAUL Not quite what we say. From a religious vertex the Body dies, but the Soul lives—

ROLAND —not for ever I hope. Forever, like never, always feels a very long time. Do you relish the prospect of everlasting life? But I suppose that is only a metaphor.

P.A. It reminds me of people who say, "It's only psycho-logical" and mean that "it" does not therefore exist. Alternatively, if I think a scientist should at least be capable of entertaining a "hunch" of everlasting life—

DOCTOR You don't mean to suggest you expect to live for ever?

P.A. I have no objection to "suggesting" anything, but I find I cannot "suggest" it without it being immediately supposed that I consider that my corporeal existence is infinite—"everlasting" as religious people call it—whatever the hypothesis entertained by anatomists and physiologists as a result of, or part of, their biological sphere of enquiry. "Father, I cannot tell a lie" may be a satisfactory qualification for a statesman, but I doubt the qualifications of a scientist, or artist, or religious who *could not* tell a lie; how could he possibly know what the truth was—let alone act truthfully?

PAUL I would have thought that any religious would subscribe to that. Similarly, I would suspect the qualifications of a religious who claimed never to have doubted the existence of God.

P.A. So many of your famed religious talk as if the God in which they believe is keenly interested in religion. I can understand religious professors being interested in God, but I cannot see why God should be. I should regard that as a primitive religious impulse primitively expressed—hardly less primitive than worshipping a competent golfer.

ROLAND The religious set may believe in any god they like.

ROBIN You will find P.A. accusing you of addiction to "set theory" if you aren't careful.

P.A. I would be more likely to be suspicious about what anyone was being careful about, though I might also be curious about their being "careless".

ALICE Are you ever free from the anxieties of walking on a moral and scientific tightrope?

ROLAND Just what I was wondering.

ROBIN It sounds as if you led a most precarious existence.

P.A. I "exist" as we all do, but I cannot say it seems to me that my existence is peculiarly precarious either on account of my private or professional existence.

PAUL The life of man in the sight of God is precarious.

ROLAND Why drag in God?

PAUL Which god do you think I am dragging in? Oh yes, I know—"The God of all wise men". "Which is that?" "Wise men never tell".

P.A. Unfortunately they kept *that* secret most carefully hidden from themselves. Most people I meet are surprised to discover the object of their worship and the congregation with which they choose to mix. They are the invisible and in-sense-able nucleus of their own universe.

EDMUND Like the centre of our own galaxy.

ROBIN If it is as brilliant as the centre of the M31 why is there no sign of some such glowing mass? Alternatively, do you suppose that if we were on a spiral arm as far from the centre of M31 as we are from our own, that that would be invisible?

EDMUND We can suppose what we like, but the idea is that it is obscured by galactic dust. Thanks to the spectroscope we have a good idea of what elements are involved.

P.A. I think we might have some way of naming accurately the nature of the emotional forces which—to use Milton's phrase—act like a mist that makes it impossible for internal eyes to "see and tell".

ROLAND What you call "memory", "desire" and "understanding". Or just lack of mathematical capacity.

P.A. Mathematical advance might be analogous to the intuitive eyes we need to "plant".

ROBIN Your remarks sound positively literary. I don't know what you think, but I'm not clear what we are to do about it—if anything. You have spoken of war—which we all know. We think we are wiser than we were when we joined up, when we fought, when we were told—and believed—we had won.

ROLAND When we slumped; and duly trotted off to be psychoanalysed by the latest prophet, the latest *authentic* prophet, of the new religion and—here we are.

ROBIN At least we have so far avoided forming ourselves into an Institution with a doctrine and a uniform—not even a mental uniform. [II: 256–9]

We must return, under this specific vertex, to the issue of communicating psychoanalytic issues and life events through writing. *Any* attempt to write about truth, or approximations to the noumena, or "O", are amenable to be used to construct a ritualistic procedure, devoid of common sense and intuition, which will become established, ossified and dead.

Bion would resort to Luria once more; it will be easy to see that his experience is wholly based on, and in agreement with, Freud's "Totem and Taboo", "The Future of an Illusion" and "Moses and Monotheism": a belief in God which expresses the projection of one's own omnipotence.

ROBIN Surely the laws of mathematics and physics and chemistry are indistinguishable from the laws of nature.

P.A. They owe their indistinguishability to the inadequacy of language—the only thing that is sure is the adequacy of language to fool its creators and users. I do not think it at all wise to consider any part of mathematical "law" to be exempted from this, but it is convenient to suppose, as has already been done, that God made the integers; all the rest of analysis is man-made, an elaborate series of "artefacts".

ROLAND Oh God!

PAUL Which one are you calling on? I thought you said you didn't believe in God.

P.A. In my experience, everyone, without exception, believes in God. I have not met a man or woman who does not sooner or later turn out to believe that they are themselves "God".

ROLAND Rubbish!

P.A. How do you speak with such certainty?

ROLAND Well, are you not yourself requiring our adherence to you and your psychoanalytic laws obtained from Mount Sinai Freud?

P.A. I try to formulate my impression of the truth in conditions which allow others to compare what *I* call facts with *their* opinions of the facts.

ROLAND You are so "reasonable"; you bear a great resemblance to Paul's outfit who claim to be so "holy"—itself a short way of claiming to be honest and helpful. Isn't that the meaning of "holy"?

PAUL Even if the *word* means that, it does not mean that there are no "things" which approximate to the words "honest", or "helpful", or "holy". Some religious people speak even of a "holy ghost".

P.A. Bishop Berkeley made some remarks about "the ghosts of departed quantities". The amusing quality of some types of statement has often been remarked, but the generator has made the statement without being aware, still less intending that they should "amuse".

ALICE "And God laughed at the sound that came out of its bill".

PAUL Perhaps *He* did (Capital letter please—"upper case", you call it).

ROBIN Who you are talking to?

PAUL The printer, in case my words are to be given the permanence of print. Isaac Luria did not bother with having his words recorded, but I confess that I, unlike Luria, would like to have them durable.

P.A. You would not go so far as suggesting that on your gravestone a mathematical formulation should be inscribed? [II: 252–3]

Among the conversations in which agreements between the characters P.A. and Priest stand out, P.A.'s process of thought tries to keep firm anchors in what has traditionally been named "mind/matter". In fact, the very naming of the two interacting components "mind" and "matter", which belong to the realm of "O" and thus are not amenable to be named (or are ineffable), confirms, perhaps for the nth time, the infinite extent of human ignorance. Perhaps there is no way out:

in some cases, it is necessary to name something before knowing what this "something" is all about. This is the case with any individual person's name—the parents cannot know what the little unknown is but they name it anyway, long before he or she is born. Bion was aware of this; for this reason he tried to give some of his concepts and theories names which were previously unknown and so less likely to be precociously "understood". That is, he tried to avoid the concepts being locked into the tomb of hastily attributed meanings that adorn the cemetery of "Yes, I know".

Bion's respect for the paradox "mind-matter", as attributed to the character P.A., echoes, once more, Freud's respect for biology. Both avoided being prey to partisanship in the war between the naïve realist and the naïve idealist. The following except takes into account not only a quasi-philosophical interchange between science and religion, but also most things that affect a human being's life: education, submission to and revolt against establishment-backed impositions and pseudo-truths, and what may be seen as humdrum everyday life: physical survival, matrimony, women's and men's affairs. That is, the facts that make people "have to be busy with many things" at the same time: what makes up the life of psychoanalytic patients and analysts alike. It is just one among dozens of tours-de-force contrived by Bion to display in a written form what the practice of psychoanalysis is all about.

> P.A. These nursery rhymes say a lot. Some analysts study them; so do children, and they understand them. Or, rather, the archaic chord is struck and vitality is released. If we could strike the chord the vibration thus initiated could penetrate the barriers which at present act as obscuring screens—the need is for screens sufficiently resistant to catch and display the meaning without destroying it by denial or "acceptance"—"No" or "Yes, I know". I want to display not a psycho-somatic disturbance only, but also the soma-psychotic disturbance that is there; those who wish to see, do.
>
> ROLAND Do you suggest that the old man should say his prayers?
>
> P.A. I knew a young man who would not say his prayers because he was sure that he would be laughed at for being "converted" out of fear of going to battle.

ROBIN I was. But I also came to have such contempt for the act of praying—as I had been taught to practise it and seen it practised—that it would outrage any respect that I had for myself if I did it.

ROLAND Do you think there is any kind of prayer that is not an outrage on one's common sense? Obviously the athletic "knees bend" exercise could not satisfy any person of integrity. What does P.A. think?

P.A. It is not my department. I have ideas about it like any other man, but I would not like it supposed that because I set up as an expert on psychoanalysis my expertise extended to religion and other disciplines—painting, music, literature.

PRIEST Is that not somewhat cowardly?

P.A. You and others might think so but I do not. Even in my own limited field I am not unfamiliar with a cowardly shrinking from expressing a truth that I know will be unwelcome. One takes flight into doubt—"'What is truth?' said jesting Pilate"; Bacon himself did not wait for an answer because he knew he might be killed if he did. Physical death is a hard price to pay—especially for those of us who, from training and observation, believe in the obliteration of the body. I believe also in the obliteration of one's respect for the truth; it is not simply by physical methods—alcohol for example—that one can destroy one's capacity for discerning or proclaiming the Truth.

PRIEST I believe in moral, religious death. Truth can be nourished; it can be allowed to die of neglect or be poisoned by seductions, cowardice too often repeated. But truth is robust; "facts" cannot be killed even if we do not know what they are. The fragile human respect for the truth cannot be as easily disposed of as often appears.

P.A. I hope you are right. I cannot, however, say that my knowledge of myself or others provides me with food for hope. Religion itself gives evidence of the great force of power, bigotry, ignorance; and psychoanalysis is shot through with error and the defects of us humans who try to practise it.

PRIEST You are being self-contradictory in claiming that it is a science *and* it is true. It must have a point of reference outside itself. You cannot believe in Truth any more than you can "believe in God". God is—

ROLAND —or is not.

P.A. No. "God is, or is not" is only a human formulation in conformity with human principles of thinking. It has nothing to do with the reality. The only "reality" we *know about* is the various hopes, dreams, phantasies, memories and desires which are a part of us. The other reality exists, *is*, whether we like it or not. A child may want to punish a table for hurting him when he suffers a contusion. But he may desire to punish himself for "suffering" a contusion. He may ultimately be compelled to believe that, in addition to those facts, there is a table that is neither good nor bad, like it or not, forgive it or punish it. We may decide to punish our god, punish ourselves for believing in "it" or "him" or "her". It will not affect the reality which will continue to be real no matter how unsearchable, un-knowable, beyond the grasp of human capacity it is/not is. After all, we do not know much about the world we live on, or the minds we are.

ALICE I thought you psychoanalysts were supposed to have discovered all about us.

ROBIN Supposed? By whom? I do not "suppose" I know either myself or my husband—

ALICE I didn't know you were married! May I congratulate you!

ROBIN *I* do not know whether you are "married" or "divorced"; in so far as those two words derive from the Institute of a state, they tell me nothing about the relationship between you and your husband. But although I have no sensuous experience of it I yet believe there is some reality underlying these words "marriage" and "divorce" beyond the meaning I know.

P.A. You say you have "no sensuous experience", but is it not possible that while you have "forgotten" the experience it has not, as it were, forgotten you?

ROBIN I don't know what you mean.

P.A. That is relatively rational and may be more acceptable than saying you have "forgotten" being married and "forgotten" what *you* meant; perhaps that you never knew what you meant. Some of these thoughts may now be difficult to entertain or formulate because you fear the reception they would get by the recipient;

you might discover there was no recipient, or that there was one whose receptivity you feared. It is easier to feel there is an initiator *and* a recipient, and that there is some screen (caesura?) between. That is possible if you believe it is between you and "me"—a "not-you" and "you". This is less alarming than believing you are now both the initiator and the receptor.

ROBIN Why?

ALICE Every question is liable to suffer from the existence of a potential answer which will kill it. The misfortune, the weakness of curiosity is the answer that will destroy finally curiosity itself.

P.A. "Yes I know"—how lethal is that response! The wish to start exploration or discovery is destroyed. That response, made to yourself, crushes your curiosity or makes it take refuge out of sight, out of mind, out of social contact. The "Yes I know" surface, the lifeless society, is all that is left.

ROLAND That was true of "intellectual" culture in the school to which I was sent to "learn". In my time hobbies meant surreptitious sex; education meant answers to questions which no one had asked. Law and Order meant find out what they are up to and tell them not to. Sex meant widespread illegality—which did not exist; hypocrisy meant religion.

PRIEST It sounds frightful.

ROLAND It was.

P.A. Forsan et haec olim meminisse iuvabit.[2] We did not believe it; now I know it is true.

ROLAND Tu Marcellus eris. Date manibus lilia plenis[3] ... I did not know I ever learnt it. Had I know that it was all about that same wicked business of loving a man or a boy—"sex" in short—I might have learnt it; but then perhaps I should not have remembered it. Education is a damned rum thing.

ROBIN ... per varios casus, per tot discrimina rerum.[4]

PRIEST "What hours, O what black hours we have spent/This night! What sights you, heart, saw, ways you went ..."[5]

ALICE Time for supper and bed.

ROLAND All right Martha.[6]

ROBIN Or is it Xanthippe?

ALICE You would be the first to grumble if some of the ways I went had not led to the market.

P.A. Perhaps we all have to be busy with many things.

ROLAND The many things are different.

ROBIN Why don't we meet more often?

P.A. Because we don't want to. This is true when our forgotten fishy, amphibian, terranean selves all meet in the same body at the same time—not consecutively or dispersed in space, but here and now in the same body. Draw the blinds. Where shall we make the splits and insert the inhibitions so that we may choose? When the universe in which we live clearly demonstrates the immense variety which chance—

PRIEST Or God—

P.A. I find it more adequate to say "chance"—spreads before us, *we* have to choose. We choose to be responsible for our actions though we may not deliberate the problem. Choice, however, involves splitting the discriminated objects from each other.

ALICE Do we start as infinitesimal fragments, which cohere, or are we, as P.A. implies, a whole that is fragmented?

ROLAND Do you think we choose whether to be a fish or not?

P.A. No! I feel it more compatible with reality, as I know it, to say I have no say in the matter. The illusion of conscious purpose gives cause for belief—on inadequate grounds—in God, but I would resist any attempt to prevent Priest believing it, provided he didn't want to prevent me from choosing science.

PRIEST Could we agree that both of us support a search for truth, but our paths often appear to separate? [III: 498–502]

The benefit of doubt distances Bion and the whole Trilogy from the mystic tradition, even when we consider that most of the mystics he quoted in the books preceding the Trilogy were also far from the secular power of official religion—such as Meister Eckhart, St John of the Cross, Alcuin and Gerard Manley Hopkins, who displayed a kind of non-establishment-approved "religiosity" that is linked to inaccessibility to "O", sheltering the "reverence and awe" extensively described by Bion (1967b). Bion's mystic references had a common invariant: all persons labelled as mystics uttered phrases which upset those who adamantly, uncritically and hypocritically defended religious dogma and certainties. Bion maintains a deeply respectful attitude towards many truths which were expressed through what may be described as "religious" media; he had no qualms in being reminded—in Volumes I and II—of Psalm 51 and of Isaiah's visions.

> PAUL We *do* contend that there is an important distinction to be made between development originating in God and that originating in the individual's impulses. Isaiah wrote as if there were no doubt that the impulse came from direct experience of God.
>
> ROBIN Would P.A. admit the validity of Isaiah's experience, or would he regard it as having hallucinatory force—a phantom of the mind?
>
> P.A. I do not have scientific evidence for the discussion of an event of so many centuries ago.
>
> PAUL The religious experience to which we refer is current—*not* hundreds of years ago—even though history suggests that it occurred from remote ages. In recent times Cowper[7] wrote, correctly, "Sometimes a light surprises a Christian while he sings". [II: 287]

The reader may refer to I: 138 (quoted in Chapter Eight) for a clarification of Paul's comment. In *The Long-Week End* the reader may glimpse some effects of a rigid religious belief and compare them with the quotation above, to see a kind of development due to a more informed, mature mind. Let us continue with the text quoted above. When Paul talks about Cowper, P.A. remarks on his psychiatric affiliation:

> P.A. He was manic-depressive and committed suicide.
>
> PAUL The religious experience is universal; it is not closed to the psychotic, the unfortunate.
>
> ROBIN You don't deny, do you, that religion is often apparently the cause?
>
> P.A. I do not deny cause; I know that it is likely that we would think in terms of causes. Has Edmund any ideas about this?

EDMUND I like to think of causes, but I see no reason for believing that the human mind would ever comprehend the vast universes that surround us. The religious people express optimistic statements.

PAUL "The heavens declare the glory of God; and the firmament showeth his handywork".

EDUMUND That is one such statement.

P.A. It is an observation and Paul has formulated what *he* observed. His statement seemed to me to be made from the religious vertex. I know that Edmund maintains that he is without religion and I am left to suppose that his observations and formulations are "only" or "just" scientific. Le Conte said that there was one fact we should *never* know—the composition of the stars. I would be interested to know what Edmund would say about that "*never*".

EDMUND Le Conte was right to say so, but spectrographic investigation leads us to have definite ideas about stellar composition. [II: 287–8]

Bion harmoniously mixes astronomy, mathematics, Homer, Ruskin, Shakespeare, Lewis Carroll, and a modern American periodical dedicated to the lay audience interested in higher thinking—all through a writing endowed with good-humoured puns. He is always trying to encircle some persistent problems which form part of the nature of psychoanalytic communication, both in the session, between patient and analyst, and with colleagues, between peers in the activity which is also used to earn a living. The historical aspect underlies all of this, as regards apprehending in what the great authors wrote what they were really saying. The same problem is faced every day by analysts, who must discern in what their patients verbally tell them what they are really saying.

MYSELF Let us get back to something simple—before the Big Bang.

WATSON Something simple? That's my cue, where I come in. Which Big Bang do you mean?

MYSELF I said "before" the Big Bang. "Before" or "after", it doesn't matter.

MAN Can I help? Even to talk at all I am afraid we shall have to borrow from A-chrony one of his anachronisms.

ALICE Alice in Anachronomous Land.

MAN Thank you; you come from Pornography don't you?

ALICE Not really—Wonderland.

MAN Ah yes. A province of Fairyland.

PALINURUS No, Wonderland, before it was stolen by children and their various thieves and robbers.

ALICE From *your* collection of thieves, robbers, rapists and seducers, don't forget. You make me damn bad tempered.

MYSELF No—why blame him? You always were bad tempered. For that matter, so was God. With reason.

MAN Always "with reason" as you call it in the language of anachronimity. When He attempted to borrow one of your anachronisms, the un-priestly formulation of Psalm 51 was "borrowed" and given a twist in the direction of "perquisites". Even now some of us claim "ownership" of Ideas. I bet the fellow who succeeds in getting his name on the cover of this book thinks it is his.

MYSELF I am certainly going to claim authorship, but I hope I shall have enough generosity to balance my possessiveness and greed. [I:136]

PAUL The Human Animal has so far outdone all its rivals.

ROLAND Are we concerned with the discovery of the athletically dominant winner of the animal championships?

P.A. Are the optic and auditory pits rebelling against our visual or auditory ability?

PAUL I was not suggesting that a religious standard would measure the difference between intelligent thought and feeling, as the achievements of athletes would be measured.

ROBIN In the 51st Psalm I think some theologians have detected evidence of a Priestly code at conflict with the Elohistic code of the earlier part.

P.A. The emergence of a preoccupation with meaning is causing us a lot of trouble; an "impulse" in contrast to preoccupation with facts.

> PAUL What do you call "facts"?
>
> P.A. I find it useful to make a distinction between meaning and fact. "Facts" are the name we give to any collection of constantly conjoined experiences which we feel temporarily to have a meaning; *then* we consider we have discovered a "fact". [II: 236]

Under his usual most comprehensive and non-prejudiced vertex, the character P.A., who embodies an ideal psychoanalytic thinking, is always remembering our biological bases. In that excerpt, he seeks John Locke's help in the final elucidation of the need for "common sense" when speaking about the eventual discordance between the sensuous pits and the sensuously based human abilities, according to the statements of the character Paul, who stands for a religious Priest. After this, when challenged to define "facts", the "sacerdotal friend" of the author of *A Memoir of the Future* resorts to David Hume's concept of constant conjunction. In all observations, he is in agreement with Freud, who resorted extensively to both Enlightenment thinkers. For the definition of common sense and constant conjunction, please see Locke, 1690; Hume, 1748; for a review of the concepts for the use of psychoanalysts: Sandler, 2001, 2002; for their application by Bion: Sandler, 2005.

The developing ideas carry on resorting to the mystic tradition, and now they include questions about dreaming and its differentiation from hallucination. It is difficult to call Bion a perceptive mystic when one finds his appeal to mathematicians: he is trying to emphasise the danger involved in adhering to ideas of "owning" absolute truth. The authoritarian personality tries to limit access to "O", consequently condemning other people to poverty of knowledge, or no knowledge at all, by the superior decree of the one and only established vertex, and dismissing the infinite possibilities of other vertices which could furnish a more truthful transient glimpse of "O". Is one who does not deny the existence of truthfulness in the reports of some mystics regarding the possibility of getting near to "O" condemned to be a defender of mysticism or religiosity?

> P.A. The price of freedom is constant vigilance. This is true of psychoanalysis: the individual is not analysed, "cured", so that he can then go to sleep for the rest of his life. If that were all that occurred one could regard it as an exercise in "good resolutions".
>
> ALICE Psychoanalysts I know have wonderful intentions and make many "good resolutions" to put them into practice, but

> I cannot say I am impressed with the lives they lead as good examples of a fine philosophy finely practised. [III: 509]

Is there an "unfree truth"? If the price of freedom is constant vigilance, psychoanalysis could have a motto: "All people are born free". This does not mean "free-for-all": liberty differs from libertinism—a wholly sexualised cynicism towards truth. Bion is encircling the possibilities of freedom known to him: the communication of truthful findings as discovered in a psychoanalysis. At the same time, he relentlessly points out the difference between the *non-greedy* activity of a psychoanalyst and the various other activities—artistic, scientific, religious—which try to get near to "O".

The psychoanalytically minded reader may see in the following quotation that Bion reserves for the character P.A. a most neutral scientific statement, in terms of lacking judgmental values concerning exclusion or inclusion. Also, it is difficult to be blind to his total allegiance to Freud's discoveries in P.A.'s always constructive contributions to the dialogue. The attentive reader may recognise part of the conversation, which was quoted earlier, linked to the authoritarian vertex exhaled by those sinecurist social institutions—the main example being the current universities—whose purposes are similar to high society and political clubs, enthroning a political meritocracy rather than a technical or scientific meritocracy.

> DOCTOR It sounds as if we were going to talk about dreams. But what about things that could be easily explained if they were dreams, but the patient has them—I'm thinking of a particular man—when wide awake? I don't think I would call them hallucinations; there is no adequate name.
>
> PAUL What would you call the vision clearly seen and verbalised by Isaiah? He describes it clearly in the sixth chapter as he would any other fact and date.
>
> P.A. I think of visions as coming from a "level of mind", or a "time of life", although I always *hear* of them in the present and *described* in articulate terms. This is one of my difficulties; because I use ordinary English it is assumed that I am saying something already known to all of us, and at the same time that it cannot be anything so ordinary as to be comprehensible to ordinary people.

ROLAND Couldn't you say something that is neither?

ROBIN According to the Intuitionists you can't, because there is no excluded middle. Why, as someone asked, does logic apply to anything but mathematics?

P.A. I certainly do not intentionally exclude, or include, any topic, although I can see that if one topic can be said to be "included" then other topics are "excluded". A responsible person must exclude the topics which he does *not* discuss. To that extent he is not allowing some aspect of his personality to express itself and is thus incurring his self-hatred—whatever grievances he may consider also to be inflicted upon him by forces or people *not* himself. We include dreams as a part of thinking. Do you call that *in*cluding or *ex*cluding logic?

ROBIN Hasn't Brouwer already pointed out that there may be a mathematics in which classical, mathematical logic is irrelevant?

ROLAND I'm no mathematician.

ROBIN If I understand P.A. correctly you are lucky not to be carrying a heavy burden of preconceptions, even if they are respectable preconceptions hallowed and sanctified by a university qualification—

P.A. By "university" I think you mean a number of individuals gathered together and self-endowed with the privilege of declaring who is, and who is not, worthy of joining their association.

ROLAND At that rate a democratic society is one in which the representatives of the society almost constitute themselves to be the vicars of God in that society. "Vox populi vox Dei", as Alcuin[8] said.

PAUL This is hardly distinguishable from saying that a democratic society is a theocratic society. But a theocratic society openly admits its claim; the democratic society seems to claim some sort of superiority. That is a claim I cannot admit unless the supposedly theocratic society is governed by a group of human beings—ordinary human animals claiming to be God or at least the Voice of God.

P.A. Something of that sort is overtly expressed in those last few verses of the 51st Psalm almost directly contradicting the tenor of the whole early part which is far more modest—indeed penitential, as it is justly called.

ROBIN This is all mere supposition stimulated by the "creator" whom we cannot now question.

P.A. Their words have a durability such as Shakespeare claimed for his verbal creation.

ROLAND You have said this about the artist who constructs in words something which—like marble or the gilded monument—lasts. But does it? Frederick Powicke[9] said he could not describe the most important factor in the matter he was discussing when giving an historical account of Lord Edward[10] and his attendant Hubert de Burgh, namely Hubert de Burgh's state of mind. That, as he pointed out, has gone—without recall. But is Shakespeare any better off? Do we know what he meant when he wrote his sonnets? Did he then understand what we now understand when we read them?

ROBIN Set a poet to catch a poet. Blake was not deceived about the meaning of *Paradise Lost*. In more recent times Kenner[11] has shown that Shakespeare said far more than he consciously intended when he wrote "Fear no more the heat of the sun".

P.A. Kenner's explication is, to me, extremely convincing—as was Ruskin's of *Lycidas*. But what a chancy business! Who could possibly predict that Ruskin could persuade with telling force one person, or perhaps two, to *read* what the great ones have left us in their wills. Oh yes—we have already heard that *of course* we all read Milton; *of course* we all read Shakespeare.

ROLAND Touché.

PAUL I don't know why, but you remind me of a cartoon which I once saw in the *New Yorker* in which a duellist, having just delivered a mortal stroke, says "Touché".

ROLAND I saw a horrible photograph of a duel between two people armed with sabres in which one had decapitated his opponent in one stoke. I was not really claiming to have been so completely separated from my central nervous system, or the seat of my intelligence. [II: 246–9]

Mysticism may be distinguished from the mystic tradition in Western civilisation. The former offers final answers disguised with ethereal phraseology which defends pseudo-mystery, to which access is reserved for its own high clerics. There are people endowed with a good enough messianic belief, which is a mere superficial expression of an inner good enough resistance against dealing with human helplessness. To them, mysticism provides ready supplies of "Yes I know", the "lethal" definitive answer to soothe the individual in order to "shield" him or her—in hallucination—from distressing questions.

When a given "spirit" takes hold of certain individuals, high clerical ministers or apostles, through authoritarian and sometimes ingenious manipulation techniques of make-believe, they feign (and for a while convince themselves) that they hold the controlling switches and levers to pilot the believers onto the "right" track or flight. The very "spirits" are sensuously recognisable, for they share known humanoid features. The contemporaries of Hieronymus Bosch as well as of today's ministers of African-derived syncretism were and are able to draw and "see" what they call Beelzebub or Ogum, respectively.

> ROLAND If you cannot believe in a religious solution I at least cannot "believe" in facts. Facts do not offer an outlet for a religious impulse—only for scientific curiosity.
>
> P.A. Might they not be the same? The religious people I know certainly think they are concerned with the Truth and nothing but the truth. It is often difficult to retain a sense of awe in the face of what we are more likely to think of as humdrum daily trivialities rather than facts which deserve to be treated with respect.
>
> ROLAND "With respect" I could manage, but not "with awe".
>
> ALICE I would have thought that "awe" is more appropriately left to the people who are religious. [III: 514]

"Secularisation" constitutes a most tenebrous chapter in the history of religions and in theology. It is long and still guards secrets as well as unknown parts, but any student of it may be sure that it entails a history of destruction, brought by the confusion between what was in principle religion and the religious rituals and the millenarian tradition equipped with armed forces and finances at the worldly service of elites. The bloody diatribes between the multifarious branches of the Muslim creed may be quoted just to furnish an example; violent claims to orthodoxy followed by equally violent reactions claiming liberal conduct are expressed by the existence of warring parties among various Christian sects. Are each of them—as their specific partisans claim—nearer than all others to the teachings attributed to Jesus Christ, meriting the title of "the best"? The Jewish religion, the oldest known monotheistic religious practice still in existence, seemingly the origin of Christianity and Islam, is not free of the same struggles, be they secular or theological, such as the discord between the Yahwist and Elohist traditions, or lately, between Zionism and other tendencies. Or are they, as a whole, equally far from the original non-concrete achievements? Their standard-bearers gained worldly power through personality cults, ridden with paranoid-schizoid hallucinated importance. A secular church needs religious ministers—and armies. The standard-bearer embodies the pretension to own the one and only Ultimate Truth. Some of them may believe that they possess truth-in-itself, because their specific ideology is truth-in-itself.

> SOMITE THIRTY Somitically speaking I know a lot that I cannot make clear to you but that is factual enough to me. I have to borrow articulate speech from Soma.
>
> SOMA My difficulty exactly. I cannot make anything clear to Psyche unless I borrow a bellyache or headache or respiratory distress from somitic vocabulary for any of these post-natal structures. I believe in mind and personality as there is no evidence whatever for anything but Body. And when I manage to make somebody aware of a bellyache the probability is that they immediately drag in a "cure". As for my message, God knows—
>
> DEVIL God knows! Is Soma also among the religious?
>
> ROSEMARY You know that as well as I do. Some of the healthier and most well-nourished bellies I know are to be found amongst the religious. The Celibates look particularly pregnant. [III: 445–6]

Rosemary's insight closely resembles a joke that was popular in Brazil when the Roman Catholic Church was at the height of its popularity—something that endured for almost five centuries and lasted to the last quarter of the 20th century. Jesus had come to Earth in order to visit humans. He wanted to get a better idea of what was going on here. Duly escorted by Pope John XXIII, he first saw dirty, dishevelled Americans working hard at a Texas oil plant. "What are those people doing?" "Well, they took your word seriously, Lord—they are sweating in order to earn their bread." The itinerary included Germany, where Jesus saw hardworking, dirty people at a car plant. "What are they doing?" He got the same answer. Jesus also had a look at British coal mines, French farms, as well as Japan, South America, Africa and China. He became speechless at the sight of poor, thin men, women and children working for fourteen or fifteen hours, six or seven days a week. At the end of the educational trip, they landed at Vatican City. Jesus saw fat, well-dressed and shiny-headed people, using their time to pray, stroll and talk to each other. "Who are they?" "Oh, they *didn't* take your word seriously, Lord."

Psychopathic concretisation differs from the psychotic variety, even though the two may be intermingled. Both appear in the excerpt just quoted through the actions of religious ministers who give a secular, worldly form to what could be the "Christian" ethos. St Francis of Assisi, the Jansenists, the Lutherans, and very many others suffered a great deal with the "secularised branches" of the Roman Catholic Church. That included the murderous Supreme Sacred Congregation of the Roman and Universal Inquisition, staffed mainly by cardinals. It still exists, performing administrative duties, under the name of Congregation for the Doctrine of the Faith.

The question is not limited to the tribulations which awaited Jesus' contributions to humankind. Other religious mass movements offer similar examples. In the Jewish religion, there is a set of two small black leather boxes containing scrolls of parchment inscribed with verses from the Jews' sacred book, the Torah. The boxes, called "tefillin", were originally worn all day, but are now usually worn only during weekday morning prayers. One is placed on the upper arm and its strap is wound around the arm and the hand; the other is secured above the forehead. According to the Torah, they serve as a sign and as a remembrance of the power of God, in bringing the Jews out of the Pharaoh's grip. The idea is that the observant Jew will keep God in his own mind if he performs the ritual. There is a confusion between the material, external "head" and the immaterial mind. The tefillin are also called phylacteries, which comes from the Greek language, meaning "to guard" or "to protect". The same material device which tries to deal with immaterial messages occurs with another Jewish tradition, that of the "mezuzah". Centuries younger than the tefillin, the mezuzah is a small decorative case to be placed in the doorpost of Jewish homes.

Inside it there is a small parchment inscribed with specified verses from the Torah. The term comes from the Hebrew language, meaning "doorpost". The religious establishment may have the best of intentions—namely, to replace the non-existent "categorical imperative", the ethical internal, immaterial, inborn stance of man, with an external, materialised teaching.

Summing up, due to the action of anti-alpha function (Sandler, 1997), which is a main factor in the sensuous-concretising syndrome, what was originally an immaterial fact is replaced by concrete rituals endowed with magical belief—which in their turn are also felt as concrete. Leaving out the psychopathic sensuous concretisation, the most apparent expression of the feedback cycle made of greed feeding envy and envy feeding greed, as described by Melanie Klein, psychotic sensuous concretisation is depicted by Bion in many parts of his work, as one may see in the following pages.

Dashing into science

> P.A. The nearest that the psychoanalytic couple comes to a "fact" is when one or the other has a feeling. [III: 536]

To paraphrase, the nearest that the psychoanalytic couple comes to a "fact" is when one or the other has an emotional experience. Even though the earlier selected terms may have been, in some quarters, linked to religious practices, they are used in the Trilogy with an exclusively scientific ethos, covering both the apprehension and the misapprehension of facts through the use of our human sensory apparatus. Moreover, those terms adumbrate the realm of the transformation of sensuous data into psychic facts though the hypothetical alpha function (Bion, 1961).

It would be fair to state that some of the main differences between the mystic tradition and religious tradition are centred on the latter being wholly submitted to omnipotence. This equates to saying that the religious tradition is submitted to the pleasure-displeasure principle, mostly in its sadistic form. Conversely, the mystic tradition, the often abhorred offshoot of the religious tradition, displays an increasing abandonment of judgmental values—which may have been a factor in another development which flowed out of religious practices into scientific practices in humankind. There are a fair number of scientists who turned to religious practices in the later stages of their life.

EDMUND Like eclipsing variables. Nowadays some are beginning to think that the less obtrusive partner in a binary may be a black hole; that there are signs compatible with two black holes.

ALICE Only two—in the whole of the universe of universes? That sounds—

P.A. —like Classical Psychoanalysis. Two parents or—according to one of the parents of psychoanalysis—two breasts.

EDMUND Or one proton and one electron. They proliferate masses of offspring all circulating like hadrons round the nucleus, or suns about a galactic centre.

PAUL Or gods around a theocrat.

DOCTOR Or diagnoses round a turbulence, as P.A. would say.

P.A. Or what happens when two people meet.

ROLAND How dull.

ROBIN What bores psychoanalysts are! It isn't just sex.

P.A. It never was. It is its meaning that we do not know or understand, not our environment. It is not in our stars since we are underlings with ambitions to be overlings. We want someone or something authoritative to tell us we outshine these beauties of the night.

DOCTOR Even Elizabeth of Bohemia was damnably mouldy three hundred years ago—Sir Henry Wotton notwithstanding. Ante Agamemnona multi ... Not marble nor the gilded monument shall outlive ... But où sont les neiges d'antan? It is difficult to believe, or even to suspect that the biological view of anatomy and physiology could possibly mean what our own common sense would tell us. Now we have elaborated a new kind of "scientist", a psychoanalyst devoted to the discovery of a brand new truth that will outshine all the meaner truths of the "unheavenly" outer darkness which is so much more frightening than a thousand suns. Mathematically a thousand suns should be very bright—according to classical mathematics. What sort of psychoanalytic maths do you propose to introduce? You had better be quick, or someone else will produce a mathematics which is more appropriately accompanied by the music of the modern spheres.

ROBIN Aesthetic maths, or religious maths, or scientific maths? Take your choice.

EDMUND I am not terrified by the silence of infinite space.

P.A. Are you sure you have allowed yourself to hear it? Nature, they say—on what evidence I do not know—abhors a vacuum. According to Milton, even Satan did not enjoy a really poetic bump on his escape from Hell. Still, if Milton can be relied on, he survived the journey from Hell to the Heaven promised our forebears. Milton asked for more—"so much the rather thou, Celestial Light, shine inward ... "

ROLAND I thought you purported to see and tell of things invisible to mortal sight.

ALICE Surely not. I thought he purported to draw attention to what is clear to mortal sight unless the individual is determined not to look at it. You can't really blame psychoanalysts if they try to show what could be seen.

DOCTOR Psychoanalysts are no worse off than physicians. I remember trying to warn an hypochondriacal girl that she was fatally ill, suffering from advanced ergot poisoning. "But doctor," she would say, "I'm *ill*", after I had done my damndest for weeks to tell her just that.

P.A. Perhaps she had begun to understand what you were saying to her?

DOCTOR Not she. I can still hear that wretched girl's voice as she lay on her deathbed, trying to collect her strength to make me hear. [II: 254–6]

Judgmental values, criteria of cure: the mother of all resistances

A seemingly interminable source of controversy is the search for a way to observe things with no tincture of judgmental values, which are always oriented by the group's or the individual's prejudices or ideologies. The chance of having no political or social intrusion—at its deepest levels, a real intromission—into activities such as the scientific and artistic is usually seen as ranging from the non-existent to the very slim. To talk affirmatively or negatively about "pure" or "natural" in human endeavour would constitute a highly disputed statement—even though the former has few adepts. A high level of public adhesion or unanimity would hardly be a fair criterion for truth—as cello players or microbiologists could attest. Nevertheless, marketers, lynch mob leaders, traffickers of arms, slaves and prostitutes, and some priests would argue with those artists and scientists.

Some human activities, such as those of advocates, lawyers and barristers, police, educators and politicians, need to use judgmental values as a condition of their existence. Are medicine, engineering, psychoanalysis, physics, biology, chemistry and all artistic endeavours in the same league?

> In psychoanalytic methodology the criterion cannot be whether a particular usage is right or wrong, meaningful or verifiable, but whether it does, or does not, promote development. [Bion, 1962, Introduction, 7]

In *A Theory of Thinking* Bion offers a view of the nourishment of judgmental values. They are seen as originating at a point in time that is simultaneous with the inception of the processes of thinking, which obtrudes as learning from a specific experience, namely, the mating of pre-conceptions and realisations. From this mating a conception can ensue. It "does not necessarily meet a realisation that approximates sufficiently closely to satisfy" (Bion, 1961, p. 113). Conceptions, therefore, are what stems from those primitive processes of thought. There is an amount of frustration involved; "if [it] can be tolerated the mating of conceptions and realisations whether negative or positive initiates procedures necessary to learning by experience" (*ibid.*, pp. 113–114).

Some different developments may occur when a negative realisation occurs. There is always a parcel of negative realisation. It is something that Bion would develop later. Intolerance of frustration may not be so great as to activate the mechanism of evasion. Nevertheless, it can simultaneously be too great to bear dominance of the reality principle. In this case, "the personality develops omnipotence as a substitute for the mating of the pre-conception, or conception, with the negative realisation" (ibid., p. 114). It is now that judgement emerges, as a kind of last resort:

> This involves the assumption of omniscience as a substitute for learning from experience by aid of thoughts and thinking. There is therefore no psychic activity to discriminate between true and false. Omniscience substitutes for the discrimination between true and false a dictatorial affirmation that one thing is morally right and the other wrong. The assumption of omniscience that denies reality ensures that the morality thus engendered is a function of psychosis. Discrimination between true and false is a function of the non-psychotic part of the personality and its factors. There is thus potentially a conflict between assertion of truth and assertion of moral ascendancy. [Bion, 1961, p. 114]

In psychoanalysis, and in real life, it is useful to distinguish between ethics, which bears more resemblance to the thinking of the Ancient Greeks, from morals, which derives from the more imposing Roman civilisation and its offshoot in the Roman Catholic Apostolic tradition. The former, in the same way as the superego, is linked to Kant's "categorical imperative" as observed in his criticism of practical reason. It can be seen as "internal", originating in the human mind. The latter can be seen as "external", imposed by cultural laws. It encircles the phenomenon on which Bion focuses:

> ALICE Perhaps we should discuss it with Priest when he returns. He's been away a long time but I understand he is coming back in time for our next meeting.
>
> ROLAND Oh my ... good.
>
> ALICE You don't sound pleased; what is the matter?
>
> ROLAND I'm glad he is coming, but I don't want to be involved with God and the rest of that pious stuff.
>
> ROBIN To do him credit he does not try converting us; to be fair to P.A. he doesn't try to convert us to psychoanalysis either. [III, p. 541]

The analyst has the same posture as the scientist. They do not judge; they try to perceive, to appreciate and to describe whatever it is. An analysis may show how it *is* rather than how it *ought to be*.

The destructive effects that religiously driven judgmental values have in science are depicted in an episode very dear to Bion: the diatribes between Bishop Berkeley and Sir Isaac Newton about "fluxions", first described at the beginning of Chapter Twelve of *Transformations*:

> Bishop Berkeley, prompted by the irreligion of Newton and his sponsor Edmund Halley, attacked certain illogicalities, notably circular argument, in Newton's presentation of the differential calculus; his criticisms exercised mathematicians for over a century. The following quotation is from *The Analyst* (published in 1734).
>
> "It must, indeed, be acknowledged that he used fluxions, like the scaffold of a building, as things to be laid aside or got rid of as soon as finite lines were found proportional to them. But then these finite exponents are found by the help of fluxions. Whatever therefore is got by such exponents and proportions is to be ascribed to fluxions: which must therefore be previously understood. And what are these fluxions? The velocities of evanescent increments. And what are these same evanescent increments? They are neither finite quantities, nor quantities infinitely small, nor yet nothing. May we not call them the ghosts of departed quantities?"
>
> Newton's formulation of the differential calculus is a transformation in K. "The ghosts of departed quantities" expresses the negative of the column 1 dimension[12] of his formulation. The transformation in K is effected by discarding the "scaffolding" of fluxions, "the ghosts of departed quantities". The discarding of the scaffolding may be regarded as a step to achieve finite lines "proportional to them", a category H_3 formulation; or, "the finite lines … proportional to them" may be regarded as a F_3 formulation used as a column 2 formulation to prevent emergence of the "ghosts of departed quantities" and the psychological turbulence that such an emergence would precipitate; Newton did have what we would today regard as a psychotic breakdown in which, in his own words, he lost "the former consistency of his mind" and from which he emerged, according J. M. Keynes, "slightly 'gaga'". Keynes's paper, which was read by his brother at the Centenary Celebrations held in July 1946, contains material which will repay study for its penetrating insights though I cannot enter into it here.

> Berkeley's formulation may be regarded as an F_3 contribution. The polemical tone gives it a column 2 category, denying, though he acknowledges the truth of Newton's result, the validity of the method: the ironic tone denies the reality of "the ghosts of departed quantities". The pamphlet as a whole is thus an example of an F_3 formulation used, in its second cycle, as column 2 to deny both the "ghosts" component and the H_3 component in his and Newton's confrontation. From a psychoanalytic vertex both formulations, Newton's and Berkeley's, can be seen as $T\beta$ col. 3 (intended to produce a $T\beta$ (col. 3)(cycle 2)), or $T\beta$ col. 2 (intended to deny emergence of β– elements). [Bion, 1965, pp. 157–158]

Some readers may find it useful to have a reminder of Bion's quasi-mathematical notation system as it was used at that time. Transformations in K refer to a specific process of knowledge, adjacent to others, such as Transformations in "O". The former comprises rational and deductive thought. Column 2 is one of the columns of Bion's epistemological instrument, The Grid (Bion, 1963; review in Sandler, 2005). It adds to Freud's functions of the ego and consists of statements acknowledged as lies by the one who issues them. The columns of the Grid, numbered from 1 to 6 (as well as an "n" extension of it) must be used in constant conjunction with the rows, which depict the psycho-genetics of thought processes. Column 3 refers to Notation, one of Freud's functions of the ego. Row F refers to the formation of Concepts, coming after Rows D and E (pre-conceptions and conceptions). Therefore the sign F_3 represents the act of notation of a concept.

The same description would merit a different treatment in the Trilogy, with the aid of a diabolic character, Du, who at the same time loves truth and warns about the posture of disregard for truth and life; in brief, war. The text makes a more specific reference to the psychoanalytic movement and its continuous issuing of paramnesias and other expressions of hate towards knowledge. It may be useful for the reader to keep firmly in mind that the character Roland corresponds to Bion's wartime experiences. These are recalled though the mottoes, and therefore regimental appointments, of the Royal Regiment of Artillery: "Ubique", which means "Everywhere" (in recognition that the Artillery serves in all kinds of battles); and "Quo Fas et Gloria Ducunt", which means "Where Right and Glory Lead". In this emotional—and, to some people, moving—text, paradoxically pervaded by good humour—perhaps seminal to keeping

Bion's life going—there is one of the rare illuminations of the nature of "O" (see also *Transformations*, especially the first six chapters; review in Sandler, 2005). The text "ends" with a formidable hint about practical psychoanalysis: Du emerges as a practising psychoanalyst who tries to extricate himself and his patient (Roland) from the continuous battering of denial, splitting and its progeny, projective identification:

> DU You talk like that foolish animal that said, "Cogito ergo sum".
>
> ROLAND Oh, go to sleep. "Eat your damn bun", as the father said to the child.
>
> DU And the child, who was Father to the child, ate it and was expelled from the garden.
>
> ROLAND So the weeds grew up and choked it. And the father said, "Let there be a psychoanalyst who shall cultivate bigger and more beautiful lies in perpetuity. In Infinity he shall rule for ever; a void in which wild ghosts of fluxions will wander without an optic to devour them". Why should logic apply everywhere except in mathematics? It is the only space in which it retains a hold—though tenuous.
>
> DU Mature adults project it onto the universe of universes although it is inappropriate. They won't even study quantum mechanics lest mechanics don't obey the laws that apply to their feeble minds; they don´t want discoveries lest the discoveries would compel an expansion of their minds. "If my mind bursts with all this stuff where shall I be?" As if it matters where all discarded experiments go! Quo fata vocant? Quo fas et Gloria ducunt? "They lead only to the grave", say the know-alls who then fight with other know-alls. "I've heard different", says one obstinate from the unyielding fortress of his bigotry and ignorance. "Crazy", whispers the still small voice of surrender as it yields to sanity. Come on! Wake up!
>
> ROLAND You won't like if you find you are a mind and have to obey the laws of Logic.
>
> DU You won't like it if you sleep or wake and have to obey the laws of Oughtism. The laws of O—the perfect blanc. No poles for bipolarity; no middle to exclude; no genius to do the job you are too lazy to do; no fool to dare to be "silly" enough to be holy.
>
> ROLAND Oh goodness—again?

> DU I said "holy"—not good.
>
> ROLAND What's the difference?
>
> DU I am "holy", but not "good" or "bad". I am oughto-nomic, not automatic. The thought that I was fated to become "you"—if I could think—would make me die of mental toxaemia. Luckily I don't think. If I were articulate I should suffer synaptic rheumatism.
>
> ROLAND I don't know what you are talking about.
>
> ROLAND & DU (*together*) There's a great gulf fixed between us.
>
> ROLAND Who are you?
>
> DU You.
>
> ROLAND Never heard of you. What do you mean, "you"? You are you—not me.
>
> DU That's what I said. The confusion is semantic, due to your ridiculous articulate system of communication. You have heard "of" me, but you have never heard *me*. I sometimes use your belly to rumble around with. You've heard of the young woman of Lee I'm sure—she's one of my articulations.
>
> ROLAND Oh, shut up! You make my head ache. And it's not funny.
>
> DU It's not funny because your articulations are too stiff for fun. If you knew how ridiculous you look when you "smile" and show your teeth. Or when you are heroic—in reality blown up by your super-intelligent mechanical evacuation. I am Ought o'Nomic—the most venerable of your three bears—four if you include gold; five including locks. [II: 276–8]

Judgement is relevant to analysis when it is an issue in the session, originating from the personality of the analysand. The following quotations perhaps illustrate the issue, in terms of the analyst's posture. It is possible to construct a progressive "dialogue" between the texts from *Transformations* and those from the Trilogy. The reader may be reminded that the quasi-mathematical sign Taβ represents the end product of a given analyst's transformation made from a given patient's statements.

> Since psychoanalysts do not aim to run the patient's life but to enable him to run it according to his lights and therefore to know what his lights are, Taβ either in the form of interpretation or scientific

paper should represent the psychoanalyst's verbal representation of an emotional experience. [Bion, 1970, p. 37]

ROBIN Doesn't your working day consist in discussing the qualities and defects of others?

P.A. I try to demonstrate the qualities of the individual. Whether they are assets or liabilities he can then decide for himself.

ROLAND I thought you were supposed to cure them.

ROBIN So did I.

P.A. "Cure" is a word which, like "illness" or "disease", is borrowed from physicians and surgeons to account for our activities in a comprehensible manner. [III: 541]

The origin of the idea of cure is enslavement to the principle of pleasure-displeasure. One desires to be free from illness and the unknown it embodies; the idea of cure expresses omnipotent and omniscient hate for truth and reality. This kind of desire may unconsciously drive the would-be analyst to enforce his or her own ideas of what "cure" must be. There would be an unavoidable imposition of someone's ideas, ideology, judgmental values on someone else, which would be an invasion of and disrespect for the human stature that any human intrinsically has. Violence and destruction—being under the exclusive aegis of either the death instincts or the life instincts—ensues. The resistance is not against the living of death instincts or life instincts. Resistance appears in the inability to allow the natural tandem movement between them. As analogies, one may be reminded of light and dark; day and night—there would be no day if there was no night. Or to be wide awake in order to sleep and to sleep in order to be awake. Or to be tired in order to rest. In brief, PS⇔D.

ROLAND Either you are being very modest or psychoanalysis is not much good.

P.A. Neither. Psychoanalysis is a fine instrument; psychoanalytic experience makes poor capacity for some things greater than yours.

ROLAND Thank you; you *are* complimentary.

P.A. I did not expect you to like my opinion, and your contempt is not lost on me. If I were prey to depression I would despair of your impenetrable complacency. It brings home to me how impossible it is for me to get the help of a critical attitude. It would help if I could rely on the purifying effect of austere criticism. I cannot. Fantastic admiration and complacent hostility, both are available in quantity and both are so much mental rubbish. I do *not* value either your praise or blame.

ROLAND Do you think I value yours?

P.A. I know you do not; in my opinion you cannot. It was the hundreds of cultured, educated, well-meaning "yous" which constituted a liability that England could no longer support but sank under the weight. (*Rosemary enters unexpectedly and unnoticed. She sits and listens*).

ROLAND I thought you people were supposed to be impartial.

P.A. In the practice of my job I am; even when I am not engaged in my profession I retain habits of impartiality. Whatever the contingent circumstances, my natural impulse would incline me to justice rather than injustice. But that is not what *you* mean when you speak of impartiality—you mean partiality to your views. It is not natural to me to be partial to your views as far as I have reason to know them. [II: 308–9]

P.A. You may not envy the kind of eminence which stimulates my envy, but you nevertheless have feelings of envy. The fact that I may not be able to define feelings, either yours, mine or those of others which are neither yours nor mine, does not mean that they do not, did not, or may not in future exist. They may at some stage become so obtrusive that it is possible to attach a name to them.

ROBIN Although I have been aware of the pressure of what I can now call sexual or envious feelings, I would have been outraged had I been told that I was sexual or envious.

ROLAND What other people can verbalise about my feelings, especially if I can't, is particularly exasperating.

P.A. That is one component of the practice of psychoanalysis that is constant even if not constantly perceived. Guilty feelings are unwelcome and even in infants easily evoked. It is difficult to give an interpretation which is distinguished from a moral accusation.

> ROLAND Surely this is a defect of psychoanalysis?
>
> P.A. Certainly; but when I agree, you and others are therefore liable to assume that it is psychoanalysis only that suffers from that weakness, whereas I believe that this is a fundamental experience. It is this fundamental experience that underlies Plato's dialogue between Socrates and Phaedrus which is being revived here—a few hundred years later—in this discussion. [III: 480]

Judgmental values may be seen as the mother of all resistances. And Goethe's influence on Bion, as it was on Freud, was seminal. Du is a Faustian character, closely resembling Mephistopheles—and Grotstein's "Do I dare disturb the Universe" may smell to some readers like the biblical prohibition of access to truth.

Non-sensuous

> Non-sensuous phenomena form the totality of what is commonly regarded as mental or spiritual experience. [Bion, 1970, p. 91]

"Non-sensuous" is a term that corresponds to the term "non-sensible" in philosophy. It refers to the phenomena that cannot be apprehended by the sensuous apparatus. A non-sensuous realm was already described by Plato and revived by Kant: namely, the numinous realm. Its practical application was given by Freud and a few years later by Planck and Einstein in physics.

Strictly speaking, to avoid confusion, the term "non-sensuous" as used by Bion in a clear way may perhaps be replaced by a more precise formulation, namely, "non-sensuously apprehensible". A problem emerged among Bion's readers due to a reification of the term. Many people who advertise themselves as Bion's followers came to use the term as if there were a counterpart in reality to the "non-sensuous", that is, a "non-sensuous reality", which would represent a contradiction in terms and a lack of philosophical grasp and psychoanalytical practice. Nothing can be sensuous, except the sensory organs themselves. This attitude degenerated into a criticism of the sensuous experience and a transformation of psychoanalysis into an esoteric, disincarnate practice; a solipsism and idealism clothed in quasi-analytical terms. Bion himself seems to have been aware of such a distortion.

Ultra-sensuous, infra-sensuous

Bion's attempts to correct the distortion may have been initiated in 1970 and can be seen in the term "reality sensuous and psychic" which he used as the title of a chapter in the book *Attention and Interpretation*. In the view of the present writer, the verbal formulation "reality sensuous and psychic" is a compact formulation that emphasises the nous of Freud's insight about the two forms of "existence" (Freud's term): namely, material reality, which he borrowed from Kant, and psychic reality, which he borrowed … from himself, in the absence of a better available term. In fact, this was his most fundamental discovery, which allowed him to formulate psychoanalysis, freeing research about psychic phenomena from the concrete fetters imposed by his positivist education.

In this breakthrough, Freud was not exactly revolutionary as his idolisers believe, but evolutionary—if Dante was supported by Homer and Einstein by Newton, Freud had a firm base in Goethe, as shown by his quotations in "Analysis Terminable and Interminable": "Reason becomes unreason, kindness, torment" (Goethe, *Faust*, Part I, scene 4; quoted in Freud, 1937a, p. 238).[13] He did not disparage his early training as a neurologist—and thus never dismissed the port of entry of all stimuli into the human harbour: the sensuous system, or the part of the autonomic sensuous system that receives stimuli in order to transduce them to the central nervous system. Therefore, he had an insight about the *two* forms of the *same* existence, just like two sides of the same coin. Freud was crystal clear about this in his formulation.

Bion had real living experiences which showed him that for many human beings differentiation between the animate and the inanimate is problematic. The so-called psychotics or certified schizophrenics dealt with the animate with methods more applicable to the inanimate. This was also borne out by his experience in war, and is depicted in his clinical studies and in *Learning from Experience*. This was his main base, coupled with what was described above. Why should the human mind have such remarkable difficulty in realising its own immaterial nature?

Bion attributed to the sensuous apparatus the same importance that Freud attributed to it, especially in "Project for a Scientific Psychology" (1895) and in "The Interpretation of Dreams" (1900). Freud focused on (i) the sensuous apparatus as the port of entry of everything; (ii) the nature of that which calls to be perceived; (iii) the post-sensuous stage, or what happens in the mind of the dreamer and of the speaker; and (iv) the return to a sensuous impression that construes the dream.

Bion's first attempts were the theories that resulted in the formulation of alpha function. They try to deal with those issues: the nature of that which is apprehended—the nature of the mind—and the function of what is known as the central nervous system and the autonomic nervous system, the limits of our range of apprehension.

One cannot know what the "existence" referred to by Freud is in its entirety, due to its numinous ethos, but it was clear, and still is clear in the light of clinical investigation by any non-theoretical practitioner who observes life as it is, that the "existence" referred to by Freud is the monistic Reality (or Truth). It is obviously stated by the very use of the term "reality" in the two forms. Probably due to the mythical prohibition of knowledge that befell the human being, the psychoanalytic movement decided—albeit unconsciously—to renew the previous splitting which characterised the pre-psychoanalytic times. The split is made when the human being does not tolerate the basic paradox; the realisation is made when toleration of the paradox is supported.

After all, as a concept, Material Reality has been known at least since the time of Aristotle—who enjoyed the dubious fame of being one of the first to make the artificial split between "mind" and "matter", a system of thought enhanced by St Thomas Aquinas and Descartes. This solved a few mathematical and physical problems but also caused a philosophical conundrum, which in turn delayed the development of Western thought in seminal areas until Freud, borne on the shoulders of the first Romantics, restored the Platonic realm in eliciting Psychic Reality.

There was a renewed splitting by the psychoanalytic movement when it "understood"—rather than realised—what Freud tried to illuminate: the insight about the basic monism. Bion tried to restore Freud's illumination of the term "reality" when he used the title "Reality Sensuous and Psychic" for one of the chapters of *Attention and Interpretation*. Both Freud and Bion knew that the terms "mind" and "body" constituted false and flawed verbal formulations to the extent that one does not tolerate the paradox that both are different forms of the same existence.

Three years later, Bion coined a series of terms: ultra-sensuous, infra-sensuous and their less-used specialised variants: ultra-human, infra-human, ultra-logic, infra-logic, infra-conceptual, infra-intellectual, infra-visual. They were first used in his Brazilian lectures and thereafter in all volumes of *A Memoir of the Future*. It is useful, in order to get a historical idea, to read them in conjunction with his concepts of "thoughts without a thinker" and "real psychoanalysis". For a detailed review, see Sandler, 2005. Those concepts were his last onslaught on the resistances to analysis stemming from the psychoanalytic movement.

Drawn from analogies taken from the spectrum of electromagnetic waves, those terms would hardly do to express any belief from experiences of mysticism. They try to tackle a problem that was unsuccessfully dealt with through the use of terms such as "mind", "personality", "unconscious", "spirit", "soul", "character" and many others.

These terms (ultra-sensuous, infra-sensuous etc.) were intended to express a necessary posture for any analyst willing to face the unknown. They express an attempt to grasp something beyond that which the senses can grasp: not only in terms of range but also in terms of something of a different nature. That is, the "some" in the thing. In Bion's own terms: the realm of "O".

The analytic posture, which differentiates analysis from anything else, pervades the Trilogy. It was covered by previous concepts, such as Analytic View, Analytic Function, Atonement, and Real Psychoanalysis. When discussing what he means by ultra- or infra-sensuous, Bion links it with the analytic posture:

> BION You could say that if being a psychoanalyst was wearing a mental suit of clothes, one could choose whatever fictitious character one liked to be and dress up in the appropriate uniform. The trouble is if one has to *be* a psychoanalyst and not simply learn the part for purposes of acting.
>
> ROSEMARY I don't play-act; that is why I don't give you a kiss.
>
> BION Some kisses have become famous. One kiss is called a "Judas kiss" after a character who became famous and notorious. Kisses, like other actions, speak louder than words.
>
> MYSELF Interpretation likewise depends on quality as well as quantity, as do the things interpreted. "Loudness", expressing quantity, is not enough even in the domain of physical senses and other phenomena; all to which the term "phenomena" applies are by definition part of the domain of senses. We, in common with many who purport to exist or are reported to have existed and still to exist, believe there is something "more" which can be called "ultra-" or "infra-" sensuous.

> It is this something more, or "something +", which we suppose to be significant for refinement by psychoanalysis in practice. [I: 203]

They are not terms to be taken as things-in-themselves; nor are they to be used as living entities or technical terms, as perhaps may be clear from the following quotation:

> P.A. I shall avail myself of your permission to say "infra-conceptual".
>
> PAUL Well, *that* is horrible enough to escape durability as an artistic expression. The world of thought shrinks its boundaries in inverse proportion to the length of the verbal weapons it uses; the shorter the "bayonet", the wider the empire it sways. [II: 249]

The issue of the limits of apprehension of reality and facts through the senses was dealt with by Plato, Luria, Kant and Freud, among many others too numerous to list. It became clear that the spectrum of reality that could be apprehended by the human sensuous apparatus was extremely limited. Moreover, the apprehension itself was both limited and modified by the device used to apprehend it, namely, the sensuous apparatus itself. The limitation was due to the narrow range of each sensory organ. For example, the human eye cannot apprehend electromagnetic waves below red or above violet.

The reader may already have seen that Kant attributed the description "naïve realist" to those who could not realise this limitation. The Romantics, deeply inspired by Hume, to an extent by Rousseau, and epitomised by Hamann, Maimon, Herder and Goethe among others, added an observation to this realisation: namely, that it was not just the fact that the senses modified the apprehension of reality that had to be taken into consideration. There were other factors that implied that modification could be so broad and deep as to entail distortion. They sometimes reached a point of no return. Those factors were the passions and emotions. Even reason, which was seen by many people such as Descartes as a sound method to apprehend reality, came to be seen—by Hume initially—as a slave of the passions. Paradoxically, the emotions were also seen as *the* reliable tool to apprehend reality as it is.

These insights, when focused on individuals and with the posture of "caring", led to the formulation of psychoanalysis. Real reality (to borrow a term from Locke) could be unconscious, immaterial and ultimately unreachable. In Freud's words: "The unconscious is the true psychical reality; *in its innermost nature it is as much unknown to us as the reality of the external world, and it is as incompletely presented by the data of consciousness as is the external world by the communications of our sense organs*" (Freud, 1900, p. 613; Freud's emphasis). Later, with his formulation about unconscious phantasies, it became clearer how emotions could be both reliable and unreliable tools for apprehending reality. Freud's "reality testing" involves a risk. In Shakespeare's (and Descartes') terms: "By indirections find directions out" (*Hamlet* II i). Melanie Klein would furnish copious clinical evidence for that finding. The situation and issue is not philosophical, even though philosophers and perhaps above all some mystics tried to deal with it—or had to. The situation is: life itself is at stake.

Not just physical survival but sensuous and psychic living

The phrases infra- and ultra-sensuous are part of the final evolution of an attempt to tackle the impossibility of integrating material and psychic reality without mixing them:

> There seems to be something to be said for the "use" to which "things" are put. If, then, one considers the accumulation of experience and then the use which is made of these "possessions", one is using the vocabulary which has been forged for and from the world of sensuous experience. That, indeed, is the vocabulary and procedure which I am trying to use in this very communication. It is not likely to be adequate, but there is also the possibility, almost certainty perhaps, that the "use" which I am able to make of it is as widely exercised only in those respects in which it has a past and forgotten history. It is also an equipment which is peculiar to that part of the spectrum of thought-without-a-thinker which is peculiar to the biological range, from what could be called the infra-sensual to the ultra-sensual. Even so, the range is perhaps more correctly defined as infra-human (sympathetic) to ultra-human (algebraic)—in other words, a limited range of animal life. At the same time, the range is microscopic from one vertex and yet too enormous to be likely to be bridged by anything so trifling, so trivial as the products of the human animal. [I: 56]

That which seemed at first a problem just of psychotics revealed itself as a feature of the human mind—which always has a psychotic stratum.

Krishna makes the point quite clearly; he shows Arjuna that his depression is part of feelings of compassion which are unworthy of thought, still less of God-head. That kind of thing may be appropriate to reception and emission in the range of sensuous perception whether perceived directly or mechanically by constructs like radio receivers, X-ray films, and musical instruments and, in their very crude and gross manifestations, by animals and creatures in the biological range. Very sensitive animal organisms may then be able to interpret or transform the disturbances in the waves which render them opaque and obstructive. St John of the Cross was even able to point out that an analogy can be found which may be serviceable in the process of vulgarisation intended to make the grosser crudities even grosser, till they impinge on elements which are still within the spectrum of the infra-sensuous and ultra-sensuous, though not outside that very narrow and limited band. [I: 69]

MAN Let me suggest that the state of mind of the men of Ur six thousand years ago is so intensely distant that it is hardly possible for us to know what it was. We may suppose, as an hypothesis, that there could be men separated from us by an interval of time equal and opposite, that is to say, six thousand years in the future. Their states of mind could be equally impossible for us to know. Yet we may imagine the span from –6000 to +6000 is immeasurably small; so small, indeed, that it lies within the compass of our minds in much the same way, or more correctly, "analogous" way, that the span from the infra-red to the ultra-violet measures the spectrum of the "visible" part of the total range of electromagnetic waves (or quanta). The range to which I have arbitrarily ascribed numerical range, –6000 to +6000, I shall further arbitrarily describe as extending (not in numerical terms) from infra-sensual to ultra-sensual. The whole of the range is what I shall describe as lying within the domain of the human mind. I shall now assume mind to extend as far "beyond" human mentality as life extends "beyond" what our limited apparatus can conceive of as "mind". I shall suppose a bio+ and bio–, that is, something beyond even animate and inanimate. [I: 127]

ROBIN Why do you not fall back on art, or religion, or mathematics?

P.A. I have told you, I do not know any of those languages to speak them in a way which is not a gross *mis*-representation.

> ROLAND You are being modest.
>
> ROBIN I don't think he is—I think he is being a humbug.
>
> P.A. It has often been said, and I should be claiming to be less than human if I said there was no truth in the accusation. But you will miss something if you feel that the ulterior motive is the only one; just as I think it fallacious to assume that scientific truth, or religious truth, or aesthetic truth, or musical truth, or rational truth is the only truth. Even what psychoanalysts call rationalisations have to be rational. Because I think we should be aware of the ultra- or infra-sensuous, or the superego and id, I do not think therefore that one should deny the rest. [II: 232]

Ultra-logic, plausibility

The prefix was used to warn about the pretension to use the rationalistic and rationalised Euclidean–Cartesian logic:

> But suppose reality does not obey any of the laws laid down by the human animal—not even the "logic" to which not only human thought, but also the universe *not* included in human thought, is supposed to conform. Is there an ultra or infra logic which does not fall within the spectrum of human logic, the logical spectrum analogous to the visual portion of the spectrum of electromagnetic waves? [II: 395]

This kind of warning corresponds to Kant's criticism of pure reason and to Freud's insights about the illogical nature of the unconscious. Even though the concept carries with it the bulk of recommendations to analysts about achieving a practice that Bion decided to call "real psychoanalysis", it must be read carefully in order to avoid judgmental values:

> MYSELF Not quite. I don't mean to be advocating anything. I suggest that somehow functions can be handed over to machines or mechanical methods. We ourselves learnt to walk "mechanically" at some point and this was, and still is, a very useful skill; but even now it is useful to resort from time to time to specific, skilled movement. I do not exclude the value of "mechanical thinking" or "mechanical interpretation", but I don't want *that* progress to take the place of, or to preclude the development of, the ultra- or

> infra-sensuous, even though I may not know what that is or even if it exists. The pathology laboratory should not be substituted for clinical observation, or vice-versa. [I: 204]

The concept was carried much further and more clearly to encompass a picture, albeit of a whole lifetime of perceptions, and too late for processing those perceptions. This time the analogy—which was to be repeated throughout Bion's last conferences in New York (1977) and São Paulo (1978)—hypothesised a certain stimulus that could hit the pre-natal being. Taking into account that the brain, the eye and the ear are ready in the fourth month of pregnancy, the hypothesis has a sound neurophysiological basis. Bion carried it further, suggesting that fear—"sub-thalamic" (II: 239) fear—may be a basic structuring emotion of humanity.

The model of a pre-natal life is used to hint at the stellar or quantum dimension of the psychoanalytic issue, that is, how much is unknown. It suggests the huge, perhaps immeasurable complexity of possible variables encompassed by the events we try, as analysts, to study.

At the time of writing this introduction, more than thirty years after the introduction of the term "ultra-sensuous", the psychoanalytic movement has not noticed it. There is at least one advantage in this fact: the term does not seem to have been misused yet. Will the terms ultra-sensuous, infra-sensuous, and so on ever gain widespread attention? If so, it is very likely that they will be subjected to the mind's tendency to sensuous concretisation, typical of the first years of human life. Readers may lose sight of its analogical value. Perhaps one will try to "measure" infra—or ultra-sensuous quantities, or use the term in a judgmental quantitative, albeit literal sense, such as "too ultra-sensual".

In the social groups that—despite Bion's pleas against it—call themselves "Bionians", it is already commonplace: "this is sensuous", or "this is too sensuous and can have no place in psychoanalysis", meaning something worthy of contempt. This description implies that its emitter is outside the realm of psychoanalysis, due to at least four factors: (i) superficial apprehension, (ii) oversimplification, (iii) a judgmental attitude, and (iv) projective identification. It mistakes what Bion described as "real analysis" for a pretended "true analysis". The preposterous statement "this is too sensuous" implies little learning about the contributions from Kant and from neurology: nothing can be "sensuous", with the exception of the human (or mammalian) sensuous apparatus.

The concretised, oversimplified disparagement of what is sensuously apprehended and processed equates to disparaging Bion's theory of alpha function, meaning misapprehension of his contributions. The same occurred with the sense given to the concept of beta elements, echoing what occurred with the disparagement of the paranoid-schizoid and depressive positions by readers who suppose that the latter is an upgrading of the former. The unknowable ultimate reality—represented by Bion as the space-time that beta elements "inhabit"—is what "creates" sensuous stimuli, at least when they originate from the outside world. What is sensuous and what is concrete marks the port-of-entry of everything in human life. It is a necessary step for the stimuli to "enter into" the human material and immaterial entity. Disparaging what is sensuous and concrete is the same as denying nourishment itself.

> P.A. No; I am suggesting that we are unable to free ourselves from our prison of sense even though something can be done to augment the boundaries of perception. Had Aristarchus lived a few hundred years he might have been able to use the two hundred inch reflector at Palomar, or the radio telescope at Jodrell Bank. As far as we know, he couldn't. [II: 242]

> I acknowledge dependence on sensible and experienced transcriptions; I cannot promise communication of pure non-sense without the contamination by sense. [III: 429]

The term that means a real fact, namely, something that occurs beyond and before the human capacity for sensuous apprehension, may more likely than not be used to describe a hallucinated fact within the sensuous capacities. Whiffs of this hallucinated concretisation are already being felt. Some groups and individual people, on reading those texts, believed that Bion said that a morula or an embryo or a spermatozoon has a mind—and that they can study it.

Perhaps a forestalling action would be to follow Bion's advice, as given first in the Introduction to *Learning from Experience* and thereafter in other texts: the writings of good authors should be read—and forgotten. Their use in practice depends on experience in the here and now of the session.

One should remember that psychoanalytic institutions display world-wide religious characteristics, as Otto Kernberg recently pointed out. Does the religious establishment—the secular power of religion—have anything to do with Religion? Opposition to the so called religious institutions or secular branches of religion is as old as the religious institutions themselves: the lives of St Francis of Assisi, Martin Luther and Cornelius Jansen display this fact.

Anti-scientific, positivistic and bourgeois beliefs

MAN Can I help? May I show you a recent acquisition of mine—I refer to this painting.

ROLAND My God! What damned sauce! That's our Athenèse!

MAN Yours?! Did you ever look at it?

ROLAND Of course! It hung in our dining room.

MAN It *was* yours. Since the pacification it has been mine. By great good fortune it came to me in the redistribution as I had been one of the first to apply for it. Would you care to demonstrate its finer points?

ROLAND Well, I'm no art expert, but …

MAN No, I did not suppose you were, but—you said it was yours and I wondered in what sense you meant that.

ROLAND I suppose you think it's yours—by right of force, by conquest.

MAN Shall we say, by right of your falling to my chocolate bar?

ROSEMARY Am I likewise—Alice also—slave to your all-conquering chocolate bar? No, leave him to my Alice. I told you, I know how to deal with these gentry. I wasn't sent to one of your highfalutin' schools.

ALICE Roland was though. Let him "demonstrate" the Athenèse. Perhaps we shall find out something about how you and I and the Athenèse all come to have fallen to this gentleman's chocolate bar.

(*All becomes dark including the picture. Only Roland's voice is heard*)

ROLAND To start with let me make it clear that the real name of this famous painting is "Saint Athanasius chased by a wild boar".

ROSEMARY Wrong from the start. It is "Athenèse mon pied".

ROLAND (*ignoring the interruption and becoming more and more academic, in guide book style*) The painting is probably one of the few surviving absolutely genuine works by the greatest painter the world has ever known. It has always been in possession of my family …

VOICE Quite right. It "owned" them; "they" never owned "it"—

ROLAND —and has been unknown to the public who are nevertheless familiar with him, though anonymously, as the greatest artist that ever existed. Note the delicacy and truth with which every detail is rendered. The saint's left foot has been caught in a root of the … of the bush … or thicket … and at any moment one expects, so vivid is the chiaroscuro, to see him fall headlong and then the tusker will have *got* him! Ach Gott, unser hilf—note the animal is so realistically rendered that …

(*At this point in the discussion, the boar actually loses all his ferocity and trots peacefully out of the picture.*) Now isn't that maddening! I can't possibly lecture if the ruddy animal walks off like that. In fact, the painting portrays an historical moment of great religious significance which makes me think the pig itself is no other than Satan in one of his multitudinous disguises. His envy is of such malignancy that he is even prepared to pursue the saint into the domain of art. As I was going to say, it was after this unfortunate contretemps that the saint arrived hot foot …

ROSEMARY "Mon pied" as the French in their godless language would say.

ROLAND … and without any further ado dashed off the Athanasian Creed.

ALICE Even now the creed shows traces of pique. He had a wonderful gift of expression.

ROLAND So would you have if you had a wild boar on your tracks.

VOICE And *you* would trot off quietly too if you had a psychotic lecturer boring even your portrait into an hallucinosis.

ROLAND Who owns it now?

ROSEMARY The Gadarene swine I suppose.

MAN I protest. I think you are a bit hard on me. After all, *we* were invaded first.

BION I do not think this problem will ever be solved by a linear approach in a domain of time and space co-ordinates.

ROSEMARY Meaning what?

BION If you think the problems that we have to solve can be solved in a framework where "things" happen in time and space, with ideas taken from the vocabulary and grammar invented for the senses, we shall fail. It is not unlike solving the problem of joining nine dots, arranged on a plane to form a cube, with four straight lines. You cannot do this *and* stay within the pattern of the cube. You cannot make a model of Desargues's theorem without entertaining the idea of more than three dimensions. You cannot resolve the apparent conflict of wave mechanics with the theories of quanta without supposing a domain suitable for harbouring the theory which has to be entertained. This theory has been formulated by Melanie Klein as operative in a psychoanalytic domain expanded to contain it. It is analogous to expanding the domain of arithmetic to contain irrational numbers, negative numbers, compound conjugate numbers. The domain which is adequate for the operation of natural numbers cannot contain these other numbers.

ROSEMARY I don't understand.

ALICE Give me an example.

BION Our problems here cannot be solved in terms of first and last and "places" and "examples" in time or space, the drawing of a line which has to be crossed.

CONAN DOYLE You mean by separating life and death. I said that years ago.

BION I sympathise with your efforts to draw attention to certain facts, but I do not believe your theories ever escaped from the limitations of sensuous experience and its terminology.

CONAN DOYLE You mean yours can?

BION Certainly not. But I am sure the attempt has to be made. The kind of experience which the statisticians can formulate succinctly by using the Poisson distribution, cannot as yet be formulated experientially because life is too short and the spatial distances between the author of the Bhagavad Gita and, say, John of the Cross, or Shakespeare or Tennyson or Newton, is too great and yet not extended enough. Set theory is not enough.

SHERLOCK HOLMES That is a team in which I would not include Tennyson.

WATSON But surely, Holmes, you would include Shakespeare?

BION I am surprised, Holmes, that you include yourself even as selection committee or manager.

SHERLOCK HOLMES The surprise is mutual; after all, *you* have included yourself. You have even put your name on this book.

BION It is someone's way of denoting a constant conjunction. I would find it difficult to name the mental world which is now a part of what *I* think is me. I fall back on an already existing convention. I try to be honest enough to acknowledge those to whom I am aware of being indebted.

MYSELF I understand your point about being indebted, but the O which you represent seems to be itself a part of O which is sensuously apprehended. It is a part of an O of morality which is itself part of a sensuous domain of "ownership", sensuously perceived. There may be, and it would be impossible to believe that there is *not*, a domain which is infra-and ultra-sensuous. It is for this reason that I doubt the importance of "significant" ownership and all the accompanying apparatus of debt and morality as we usually conceive it. This assumption throws one back into a mental domain which is a source of endless confusion and difficulty and in which unending confusion is an essential, not accidental, feature. I do not suppose I shall ever know escape, but I think the character of the "sensuous" domain has not been exhausted.

BION I don't understand.

MYSELF Perhaps I can illustrate by an example from something you *do* know. Imagine a piece of sculpture which is easier to comprehend if the structure is intended to act as a trap for light. The meaning is revealed by the pattern formed by the light thus trapped—not by the structure, the carved work itself. I suggest that if I could learn how to talk to you in such a way that my words "trapped" the meaning which they neither do nor could express, I *could* communicate to you in a way that is not at present possible.

BION Like the "rests" in a musical composition?

MYSELF A musician would certainly not deny the importance of those parts of a composition in which no notes were sounding, but more has to be done than can be achieved in existent art and its well-established procedure of silences, pauses, blank spaces, rests. The "art" of conversation, as carried on as part of the conversational intercourse of psychoanalysis, requires and demands an extension in the realm of non-conversation.

BION But is this anything new? Are we not all familiar with "gaps" of this kind? It is not usually an expression of hostility?

MYSELF As we have seen before, we are probably familiar with those activities for which the mere existence of a vocabulary is the evidence required. "Evidence" itself is of a kind that falls within the range of sensuous experience with which we are familiar. Anyone understands the term "sex" when it is related to sensuous experience. If, instead of saying "sex", I were to talk of "the love of God", I would be using the expression commonly heard in religious communities that have a distribution within particular temporal or topological co-ordinates. But suppose that my term "sex" refers to a domain which has no such sensuous co-ordinates and an O of which there are no elements, analogues, psycho-logical or mental atoms; then O would be disqualified from "thought", as I use the term.

BION What about dreams and dream thoughts?

MYSELF I have suggested a "trick" by which one could manipulate things which have no meaning—the use of sounds like α and β. These are sounds analogous, as Kant said, to "thoughts without concepts", but the principle, and a reality approximating to it, is also extensible to words in common use. The realisations which approximate to words such as "memory" and "desire" are opaque. The "thing-in-itself", impregnated with the opacity, itself becomes opaque; the O, of which "memory" or "desire" is the verbal counterpart, is opaque. I suggest this quality of opacity inheres in many Os and their verbal counterparts, and the phenomena which it is usually supposed to express. If, by experiment, we discovered the verbal forms, we could also discover the thoughts to which the observation applied specifically. Thus we achieve a situation in which these could be used deliberately to obscure specific thoughts.

> BION Is there anything new in this? You must often have heard, as I have, people say they don't know what you are talking about and that you are being deliberately obscure.
>
> MYSELF They are flattering me. I am suggesting an aim, an ambition, which, if I could achieve, would enable me to be deliberately and *precisely* obscure; in which I could use certain words which could activate precisely and instantaneously, in the mind of the listener, a thought or train of thought that came between him and the thoughts and ideas already accessible and available to him.
>
> ROSEMARY Oh, my God! [I: 186–191]

There is a "positive" vertex that guided research in science and may be represented by a cycle which started with Aristotle and ended with Comte. This cycle gave humanity a reasonable mastery of macroscopic, concrete things, or inanimate objects. Part of its success is due to the inanimate things that meet human necessities being beyond human capabilities but not their ability to make tools; the other part of its success is due to its ability to furnish extra doses to the human tendency to be enslaved by pleasure and abhor displeasure. At the same time, an increasing dismissal of real human necessities, which include what is immaterial and cannot be materialised, was left to religious practices, as illuminated by Freud's classical works on religion. The deep frustration it brought was tentatively met by the requests of the many "revolutionary" ideologies.

In considering the scientific environment and its philosophical foundations which encircled Bion's lifetime—or the *Zeitgeist*—one may see that he was born when the demands for revolutionary leanings were at their maximum, as were the unavoidable reactions against it, when the so-called revolutionaries, in adopting nationalism, displayed their also unavoidable resort to destructive aggression, full of authoritarian and superior feelings which always result in dismissal of, and consequently contempt for, otherness. The eruption of political wars affecting the whole of social engineering were, in part, the result of the peculiar spirit of those times—which still sends its whiffs in many vengeful individuals prone to violence. The young Bion was easy prey—as were most of his contemporaries.

If thoughts are free-floating units waiting for a thinker, the thinker—who attracts idolisers and nationalists—has no importance whatsoever. What does have importance is thoughts which attain a transcendent value.

ROLAND The survivals from the past are pathetic monsters. Pathetic phalluses. It seems to me that the very points which are their strength are also their weakness: separate and coincident. I have remarked this peculiarity of man as a tool-making animal before, but here the same peculiarity seems to inhere in an animal antecedent to man by millennia. They lie there stretched out on the squares of black marble by the rosy hues of the stain on the white radiance of Eternity. Sequential thought "stretched out" what it purports to describe. But may it not be a peculiarity of thought, of the deductive system which has become detached and confused with the reality that approximates it? If so, it could be an illusion like some foreign, alien object not really part of the thing-in-itself, the noumenon. A book is written in pages; the print goes from the top of the page to the bottom and the sentences conform to a particular grammatical structure; the print is disposed in order from left to right. These patterns are dictated by the need to conform to rules of English composition and typographical layout. These dispositions have not only been imposed by the culture, but have imposed themselves on the phenomena being observed without criticism. Is the supposition that the reptilian age is antecedent to Hitler correct, or is it a feature of our thinking process which has become an aberration which has not been considered, but has become part of what is *observed*? Suppose the reality is a meaningless chaos. The appearance of order and coherence may be peculiar to the human observer's deductive system and reported as if it were a feature of a "constant conjunction", observed from without. Further, what is "within" and what "without"? Herodotus put forward the suggestion that fossil shells detected in rock might support the belief that the sea once covered that land. Towards the beginning of this century an educated man again revived Herodotus' conjecture about fossils without being aware that it had been debated before. *On this evidence*, it cannot be supposed that knowledge of the nature of fossils has been accumulated or advanced in the intervening two thousand years. This is not evidence, but it may be regarded as an artificially constructed model.

BION The whole of this book so far printed can be regarded as an artificial and elaborate construct. I myself, here introduced into the narrative, can be regarded as a construct, artificially composed with the aid of such artistic and scientific material as I can command and manipulated to form a representation of an author whose name appears on the book and now, for the second time, as a character in a work of fiction. It is a convincing portrait? Does it appear to "resemble" reality?

Suppose I drew λ and claimed it was, or was a picture of, a man. You who are looking at this could, if the conditions existed in which we could converse, agree that I looked "just like that" and that it was a meritorious and continuing example of my artistic genius. This book could be hailed as bearing, in itself, resemblance to its paternity—that it could not be mistaken for someone else's "brain child". But I may have a different aim; say, that of writing a description of psychoanalysis. To me, that the book bore witness to its mental origins might be an unwelcome irrelevance, a feature additional to the main component of my wish to communicate and your wish to receive. It is this double quality of the communication and the fact that significance might be attached in varying degrees, now to one, now to the other component, that I wish to discuss. I want to stress that the components are not "bi-valent" but multi- or polyvalent even if at first I denote it by a "bi-valent" symbol—λξ. The signs I am choosing are the Chinese λ and the Greek ξ. If I write it as λ(ξ) I wish λ to represent a constant, (ξ) an unknown variable. But what is this? Why have symbols appeared? The experience of my own existence stimulates curiosity about me and my objects—of people or things like me.

Since I do not know for sure what these objects are, but want in fact to discuss them, I need to have some way of referring to them. Sometimes it might be a book that I want to discuss. There would be no difficulty usually, because I could make do with a certain familiarity with the use of the English language, using the existing vocabulary and rules of composition. But sometimes, and this is one those times, this is not true. True, I want to discuss this book. But that is an unimportant part of my pre-occupation. I want to discuss man, but as soon I say that, I realise the word "man" has a definite, perhaps misleadingly and frustratingly definite, meaning. I can say I want to discuss "wilfred r bion". That would have a definite meaning to some, but it is not true; I don't want to exclude whatever is "represented", signified, denoted by those letters "rbidefilnorw" arranged, according to certain conventions, to form a visual pattern on paper. The problem is obtrusive, but not informatively displayed. If I want to communicate a song to a group of people familiar with the printed word but unfamiliar with sung poems or patterns formed by print on paper, it would obscure comprehension of the music I want them to *hear* when they *see* the pattern formed on the paper. Pound has shown that the culture of a group may be such that they do not print poems that can be sung, but construct poems that form, when printed, a pattern which pleases the eye. If sung and heard, they do not form a sound pattern that satisfies; it dis-satisfies and displeases the ear. I am so defective or badly trained that I cannot be pleased if I read, by eye, a Shakespeare play; yet if good actors transform that same printed play into a dramatic presentation the effect is an experience which is emotionally stirring; it effects a change—in Wilfred R. Bion—that is durable. Some similar effect is produced if J. S. Bach composes a musical score which, transformed by suitably trained people, can result in patterns of sound that can be received by my ear. A fictional character, Quee-Quegg in Moby Dick, can be shown by contrast to be deeply moved, through his eyes, by the pattern which a printed book, of which he does not understand a word, stirs in his visual senses. An author, Herman Melville, "caused" to be printed a book which had a similar—analogous?—effect on the aforementioned Wilfred. R. Bion who "read" it.

The places in the following few sentences marked by □ are places representing "some thing" that I want to talk about. "Some thing" is not adequate; it is too impregnated with pre-existing meaning—too saturated (λ) and at the same time not saturated (ξ) enough. I am now as wide awake, conscious, rational, sane as I am ever likely to be between the moment of writing and the day of my □. I pick upon the □ for although I do not know when that is, I imagine that the empty □ will at some time be, like an algebraic variable in the course of mathematical calculations or a legal register of births, marriages and deaths, completed. That moment of time and that formal entry on a document seems to have a convenience comparable to the inscription "finis", which at one time was conventionally used at the end of a book. There are other forms, notably the form which James Joyce regarded as more adequate than the sensuously apprehended cessation of print. He wished his story to conform to some of the vicoesque qualities which he felt he had derived from the philosophical disquisitions of Giambattista Vico, but had not been able to receive from Freud.

λ(ξ) denotes a domain without beginning, end, or other dimension. I have to employ an extremely inadequate apparatus to discuss it. I have to manufacture the apparatus as I proceed. I claim that it is artistic though the art has not yet been created; it is religious though the religion has not been and never can (without ceasing to be a religion) be made to conform to any of the dogmata and institutions hitherto regarded as characteristic of religion. I do not expect the art to be analogous to music, painting, literary expression, sculpture or quantum mechanics; the "uncertainty principle" (borrowed from Heisenberg) used by me both formulates and destroys the formulation together with λ (ξ). O is by definition indestructible and not subject to, circumscribed by, beginnings and ends, rules, laws of nature or any construct of the human mind. In the domain of human comprehension Melanie Klein could not reconcile herself to the fact that whenever she had made herself understood, that fact rendered what she understood no longer "alive".

This introduction is intended to be a simplification (intended to be, though by definition false); a way of psychological preparation for more rigorous, in every "sense", presentation. I shell proceed to yet one more "simplified" (more easily comprehensible) presentation. I claim that though I may not have succeeded in making simple or comprehensible the complexity or confusion of the religious-scientific-artistic formulation, it is not so because it is clarity → confusion oriented, but because it is confusion → clarity oriented. If the English written page can be treated as if it were a model for the thing itself and not just a written page, the *poles* of confusion and clarity could be located at top left and bottom right of the page; my meaning here is not confusion, but talk "about" confusion.

It is commonly understood that an analysand talks to keep the analyst correctly informed and the psychoanalyst has a similar aim. It is easily demonstrated that such a supposition is erroneous: so would be the case with the opposite supposition. Questionnaires are drawn up and they are supposed to formulate searching questions to which revealing completions would be provided and the result would be—"revealing". In psychoanalysis it is supposed that no questions are formulated and replies to the *No-Question* would be more revealing. I propose an extension of this procedure—the invention of the *No-Questionnaire*. [I: 85–89]

Bion was much intrigued by the work of the poet Robert Browning. In the long excerpt just quoted, which admirably illuminates and also explains a great deal of the Trilogy's construction, Browning is subtly present in the reference about the "pathetic monsters" of the past which "lie there stretched out on the squares of black marble by the rosy hues of the stain on the white radiance of Eternity". Bion's inspiration probably came from lines similar to the following, from Browning's "Youth and Art" and "The Bishop Orders His Tomb at St Praxed's Church" respectively:

> … We lodged in a street together,
> You, a sparrow on the housetop lonely,
> I, a lone she-bird of his feather.
> Your trade was with sticks and clay,
> You thumbed, thrust, patted and polished,
> Then laughed "They will see some day
> Smith made, and Gibson demolished."
> My business was song, song, song;
> I chirped, cheeped, trilled and twittered,
> "Kate Brown's on the boards ere long,
> And Grisi's existence embittered!"
> I earned no more by a warble
> Than you by a sketch in plaster;
> You wanted a piece of marble,
> I needed a music-master …
>
> … Man goeth to the grave, and where is he?
> Did I say basalt for my slab, sons? Black—
> 'Twas ever antique-black I meant! How else
> Shall ye contrast my frieze to come beneath?
> The bas-relief in bronze ye promised me …

Through this introduction to the Trilogy, it has repeatedly been pointed out that Bion was most inspired by Brouwer's Intuitionism. One may link it with his earlier studies (republished in *Second Thoughts*, 1967) about drawbacks in the thought processes that characterise the psychotic mind, echoing the old philosophical conundrum: the split between mind and matter. Psychotics have a marked tendency to create and maintain a primitive, sense-based concreteness. Alpha function is a name for a "de-concretifying" function of the mind—which becomes faulty in psychotic (non)thinking.[14]

When violence and destruction—expressions of hate—are prevalent, anything can be used for hate's destructive goals. Take, for example, the most basic ingredient of life: water. It is easy to see that it can be used with murderous intent. Therefore, words may be used as concrete missiles in order to destroy both the patient's thinking and—via projective identification, but not to be confused with it—the thought processes of some suitable analysts. This contributes to their losing the analytic vertex.

The same process occurred in the infancy of humankind as expressed by the history of mathematical ideas. In *Transformations* Bion had suggested that Mathematics could be the first human attempt to deal with psychosis, in the sense of disciplining greed up to the point of tolerating the absence of anything—initially, a feeding breast. Tolerating a "no-breast" marks the inception of thinking processes. This view differs from Hanna Segal's reading of Bion; she introduced the mantra "no-breast, therefore a thought". Is this the case? Hardly, at least in the view of the present writer, because in this case, concretification strikes back and wins the match in the end: Dr Segal replaces the transitive, transient, psychodynamic "thinking processes" with a static, univocal "*a* thought". Is this a reading which displays another concept discovered by Bion, the reversion of perspective (Bion, 1963; review in Sandler, 2005)?

At first, it seems that what was left to the primitive human beings was the sense-based apprehension of the natural numbers—as used, for example, to measure estates on the banks of the Nile.

> BION The experience of physical, sensuous space was not abandoned. It was clung to with such tenacity that it prevented the loss of security involved if pictorial sense were lost. It obscured realisation that Euclidean proofs depended on their being visually obvious. Euclidean geometry thus remained for centuries without a rival. There was no rival in the sphere of education since communication of what is known, by those who know it, to those who are ignorant of it, and depends on visual sense. The "obvious" was evidence and proof of the truth of what was asserted. "Time" was as unquestioned as "space". Events are supposed to occur at a particular time and in a particular place; the "past" and the "future" depend upon sensuous experience, but there is no more recognition of that than of the dependence of Euclidean geometry on the

sense of sight. Theories about "mental life" are taken for granted, as was the background to the theories of Euclidean geometry; similar assumptions about "mental time and space" imperil growth of mental life. Theories of causation, commonly adumbrated in the context of the physical world, are based on the undiscussed and unquestioned foundation of ideas about time and space. Newton accepted that foundation. What he applied to the physical world was applicable to the mental or psychical or spiritual world. Should these assumptions be accepted by psychoanalysts or philosophers? Descartes had no doubt about the value of philosophical Doubt and yet did not doubt the validity of "cogito ergo sum"; although he came so near, he did not take the final step. The psychoanalytical theory, first formulated by Melanie Klein, I propose to extend to areas not in fact included by her in the therapeutic domain for which she proposed it. The extension involves supposing that not only does the individual harbour omnipotent phantasies of destruction and dispersal, but that there is an omnipotent being or force that destroys the whole object and disperses the fragments widely.

MISELF I can see that in the sphere of astronomy, where so much depends on the sense of sight, either directly or at a remove—as in the examination and comparison of photographs—it may be possible, by putting together the "facts" of many hundreds of photographs, to draw a sequence which could be supposed to represent a "moving picture" of events like the development of our own sun—as if in few moments one could scrutinise an event which may have taken many centuries. But I do not see what useful purpose is served by such a fictitious construction.

MAN It gives immediacy and reality to something which might otherwise be hard to understand.

BION Is it not just there that the danger lies? One more plausible theory is created to swell the enormous supply of plausible theories.

MAN Of course. But fear of what might happen is a bad master.

BION So is plausibility. I wonder how many plausible theories have been used and bewildered the human race. I would like to know. I am not sure of the ease with which "plausible" theories are produced. In this context of "plausible theories" about which we are talking, the plausible theory, or "convincing interpretation",

> may be hard to come by. It can be plausible and false. Witness the idea that "the sun rises"—what trouble that has caused! We do not know the cost in suffering associated with the belief in a Christian God, or the god of Abraham's Ur, or Hitler's Germany, or peyotism—or god of any kind.
>
> MAN Not god of any kind. Some gods have been less "poisonous" than others.
>
> BION Schacht said that the accumulation of wealth was a harmless ambition, but then the important thing may be the way it is accumulated and the object for which it is to be used. It could be to achieve the reward of work done as a substitute for doing the work. [I: 171–3]

Mathematics, which during a certain period was restricted to arithmetic calculus, imbued with a reasoning through concrete positive—"natural"—numbers, was amenable to be learned though the mere counting of one's fingers. This allowed almost anyone to perform the "basic operations": addiction, subtraction, multiplication and division, even though the latter two gave a new series of impossible problems to those who remained limited to relying on their own fingers. This form stuck for millennia. Gottlob Frege formulated a significant expansion of it in the 19th century, with the theory of sets. This was finally applied to the teaching of mathematics to youngsters half a century later, in order to rescue a pure mathematical thinking, to replace the previous learning of arithmetic through the learning by heart of multiplication tables, regarded as false and precluding the inception of mathematical thinking. It was called "Modern Mathematics"—but, half a century later, it still faces resistance from both pupils and professors. That is, primitive psychotic thinking rides free in human infantile and adolescent processes of un-thought.

Slowly, some insights about what could not be apprehended by the senses broadened knowledge in mathematics: calculus was extended with negative numbers which, so to say, enjoyed a life of their own, independent of the positive (or "affirmative"), concrete numbers. The same underlying fact repeated itself again: Euclidean geometry, apprehended by mere concrete sight, was enlarged by algebraic calculus, which is much more dependent on "pure thought" than on concrete sight.

The discovery of the wheel and the effort to symbolise it through mathematical formulations by the Ancient Greeks brought new developments in human thinking processes: the number π introduced to the human consciousness the reality of infinite numbers. Irrational numbers, non-Euclidean geometry, matrix calculus, the development of probability, the theory of functions displayed the infinite possibilities waiting for good enough mathematicians to explore them. This progressing and developing movement was discontinuous, due to the "thus far and no further" factor—or resistance to truth and to growth.

Even though references to a most scientific discipline, biology, are confined to what today is called "neuroscience", or the now fading fashion of "neuro-psychoanalysis", they were part of psychoanalysis from its inception in the history of ideas in Western civilisation. Melanie Klein's descriptions of psychic functioning started from Freud's research on the splitting movements that occurred in the ego as well as other movements: the fragmentation and adhesion in repression, fixation, and sublimation, derivations from the instinctual life. Bion describes the same movements in the various characters of the Trilogy, both in their mutual interlinking and in their transdisciplinary references to biology and astrophysics. It is a model to approach a cross-level, trans-disciplinary questioning which may lead to trans-disciplinary conclusions:

> ALICE Do we start as infinitesimal fragments, which cohere, or are we, as P.A. implies, a whole that is fragmented? [III: 502]

Biological analogies, more visible in the inception of life itself, can be seen when a spermatozoon and an ovum may be considered as transient "wholes" which are mutually fragmented under the impact of their very meeting, and then cohere. Perhaps the question would be better answered by leaving aside any definitive or teleological bi-dimensional answer. One may turn to an observation circumscribed by moments on a multi-dimensional Einsteinian space-time scale in which a given function can be singled out. The following primeval entities, which embryologists call the morula and the blastula, seem to be split phases of a continuing cohesive whole during the evolution of an embryo on its way to becoming a foetus and a soon-to-be born baby.

CHAPTER SEVEN

Obstacles to intuition

The fate of theories backed by empirical observation

Is it possible to apprehend "O", even if in a glance, a glimpse, a transient form? Is it possible to put this kind of apprehension to good enough use? Is this feasible in psychoanalysis? Are there consequences to the interference of the psychoanalytic movement in the development of psychoanalysis?

It would not be unfair to state that one main invariant of the whole Trilogy is the attempt to bring to the awareness of the analyst the extreme limitation of the powers to apprehend reality encompassed within the range of the human perception apparatus. Inner and outer, material and immaterial stimuli occupy an unknown spectrum whose main features are also unknown. The human sensuous apparatus belongs to what neurologists call the autonomic nervous system. Perceptions of stimuli flow into the central nervous system through a still unknown, but intuitable, "de-sensifying" process. It turns what was material into what is immaterial, mental facts—commonly named anxiety, depression, happiness, longing, memory, dream work, love, hate. The same is valid for their "return", in the form of good enough actions, into the environment, expressed though a language of achievement

(Bion, after Keats; 1970, p. 126), and by all scientific and artistic actions as well as technological feats, including the mastery of crafts (for example, carpentry and similar: Schoenberg, 1911; Klemperer, 1995). Trade (commerce) in its general sense, which replaced barter, better studied by economists, also forms part of this later kind of action. Thoughtful action must be distinguished from acting out which bypasses thinking processes (Freud, 1905b, 1914, 1940).

Humankind still displays a tendency to perform a process of sensuous concretisation on what originally belonged to the realm of non-sensuous experience and facts. In other words, they are afraid to catch and extract common sense from the Miltonian "nameless, infinite, formless chaos" and at the same time to keep this source (which alarmed robust minds like Pascal's) in good order. There is no way, in the light of today's knowledge stemming from many disciplines, to decide in favour of the conclusion that this tendency is due to the relatively late arrival of the human being compared to earlier mammals.

An example of this situation may be seen in the mythical account of Moses, the Ten Commandments and the Golden Calf, as well as Moses' ultimate failure to enter the Promised Land. Moses tried to impose an omnipotent and omniscient God who offered ten palpable—material—commandments that included non-palpable—immaterial—ethical codes. In Freud's terms, the proposal of regard for life includes a *Geistigkeit*; a term impossible to translate that has been seen, albeit in a very flawed form, as "intellectuality" (Freud, 1939). The Ten Commandments were transformed into palpable—material—morals, regarded as judgmental threats to whoever challenged them and/or seen as reassurances to whoever blindly obeyed them. This needs the achievements of a thoughtless and mindless posture. Nevertheless, the wrathful Moses, representative of Yahweh, "a volcano god" (Freud, 1934–1938), prey of rage and hate, tried to destroy the so called "divine" tablets which contained the commandments. It is possible to hypothesise, in the light of the contributions of Freud and their expansion by Bion to psychoanalysis, that Moses—if a Moses did exist—had to destroy them physically in order to free their immaterial and transcendent content. Is this a lesson still unlearned by his heirs? As regards popularity, the wholly material fascination provided by the Golden Calf proved to be far superior. The same applies to what became the world—"global"—currency when humankind attributed a high value to gold, though "fascination" in itself cannot be put into material terms. In the end, Moses was destined not to enter into the "Promised Land"—a dubious privilege reserved for his brother Aaron. Again, the lesson about complete satisfaction not being attainable in this world was not learned. A few among the population of Israel, called ultra-orthodox, regularly hold meetings with their Iranian counterparts. They are united in hate against Zionism; this tiny and non-influential part of the rabbinate think that Theodor Herzl's movement will be the end of Judaism (Pawel, 1989).

> BION ... It's quite bad enough going to sleep and being driven off the stage of conscious, waking, real life by dreams.
>
> WATSON It's nothing like so bad as being driven off the stage by conscious, scientific, "real" you and your "real" associations. You probably don't remember what George Santayana said would happen if the scientific "beasts and blackguards" got hold of the world. Saint Augustine described them as enemies of the City of God.
>
> BION Since you drag in saints, I must remind you that the City of God was itself an attack on the people who were complaining of what the barbarians and their Christian Allies had done to Rome.
>
> WATSON I don't see what you've got against religion.
>
> BION (*in disgust*) I'm going to sleep.
>
> SHERLOCK (*to Watson*) Has he gone? It's humiliating to think that dreams are at the mercy of people who dream.
>
> MYCROFT It's worse to realise that thoughts are dependent on finding a thinker. Shhh ... What's that? [I: 95–6]

In matching the Trilogy with Bion's earlier contributions, the so called "clinical papers" republished and reviewed in *Second Thoughts*, and later, in Francesca Bion's compilation entitled *Cogitations*, one may see the accurate observations of acted out communication stemming from patients, which could be experienced in the analysand's mind in an exclusively sensuously based, concrete apprehension. It may depend on the analyst's analytic abilities to discern the emotional experiences that may be interspersed in the acting out. This, in its turn, is more often than not expressed through the patient's body as somatic ailments that may take years to develop. There may be a concrete communication of those elements which were restricted to their primitive sensuous apprehension by the autonomic nervous system, without having attained a good enough interlinked transmission in the central nervous system. One may hypothesise that those elements remain partially undigested and partially unprocessed in the interlinks between the forebrain and the limbic system. The latter is activated just by desire, rather than by real instinctual needs. What remains to be investigated, if in the future a transdisciplinary mutual effort involving real psychoanalysis with real neurology (with no fashionable appendages) will be allowed, is what happens if what is considered to be the limbic system is an intermediary stage activated by factors which express the realm of what is known in psychoanalysis as the instincts. In that future time, if it ever happens, the causal concept will be duly dismissed and the activation factors and the functional activities will be seen under more ample vertices, encompassing the real complexity that is a hallmark of human functioning.

The mechanisms described by psychoanalysis as negation and splitting make a peculiar "journey" though the upper cortical levels of the central nervous system (parietal, occipital and temporal lobes), the sole exception being when they are subjected to rationalisation (Freud, 1912a), which may involve just eclipsed parts of the central nervous system. Those eclipsed parts form part of the unconscious: repressed parts, which were subjected to attacks in their earlier perception. After this, they are destined to be returned in kind to the external environment, though the mechanisms of projection and projective identification. The external environment is composed of animate and inanimate receptors. The communication itself is "sensuously" constructed. One should say that the psychotic processes of thought would merit the epithet "pseudo-thinking", if this form could be viewed as not conveying any judgmental value. "Pseudo-thinking", an imitation of real thinking, passes for it most of the time, thanks to its ingenious disguise made of deluded rationalisations. In brief, psychotic pseudo-thinking, which mostly does not cross the borders of sensuous perception and sensuously based misapprehension due to rationalised processing, spares the individual from a good enough use of his or her mind; false depression, coloured by paranoid (omnipotent and omniscient) fantasies, precludes the free tandem movement between paranoid-schizoid and depressive positions. Rationalisation based on negation and splitting stalls a good enough functioning of the mind.

The psychotic personality—which may emerge in a good enough analysis—takes words as things and uses them accordingly. Psychotic speech may be felt both by the person who utters it and by the analyst (or any audience) as if it were a concrete attack on the internal human ability to link thoughts, as a means of projective identification. The chief mechanisms are negation and splitting—in this observation, Bion is in full agreement with Klein's statements about the one and only real effect of projective identification (which is otherwise just an unconscious phantasy), namely, the splitting of thought processes. Verbal thinking itself is attacked or not formed at all. Words which are taken in a concrete fashion cannot attain symbolic status. They are used as if they were missiles, with the purpose of attacking the linking of thought processes. The terminology of semiotics views a symbol as a rational number, an arithmetic fraction having the signified as its numerator and the signifier as its denominator. If one borrows this terminology to apprehend psychotic pseudo-thinking, there is a hyperbolic exaggeration of the signified at expense of the signifier. The term hyperbole, under a psychoanalytic vertex, was described by Bion in *Transformations* (1965, pp. 140–141; 160–162; a complete review appears in Sandler, 2005, pp. 322–327).

The observational concept of hyperbole uses a visual image drawn from algebraic geometry in order to try to depict a violent over-exaggeration of feelings. It aims to force the container—which, in the early times of an individual, is usually the Mother—to tolerate those very feelings that appear exaggerated. In later times, the Mother may be substituted for other persons and, in some cases, things and events, including political events. The exaggeration tries to ensure attention. The container may react in many ways: sometimes the result is what Bion called "reverie" (Bion, 1958–1979, pp. 53, 216; 1962, p. 35); sometimes it reacts with more evacuation (Bion, 1957a, b). Violence of love is as destructive to the good object as hate—which, by definition, is always violent, as observed by Klein (1934). The turning points—transmutations—between love instincts and hate instincts have a practical expression here. The term hyperbole was suggested in 1965. It is possible to see that the still unnamed counterpart in reality equals what Bion had earlier (1953) described as the "fate of the expelled fragments" of personality after the phantasised expelling that was described by Melanie Klein as "projective identification"—itself a more precise development of Freud's "projection".

In 1956, Bion described a fate characterised by fragments which "consist of a real external object which is encapsulated in a piece of personality that has engulfed it" (1956, p. 39). This referred to the "final" status of the particles as bizarre objects; he then proceeded to describe the "trajectory" and the features of the deployment. To describe this he follows Freud's suggestions about symptoms being the last bastions of health:

> Hallucinations, and the fantasy of the senses as ejecting as well as receiving, point to the severity of the disorder from which the patient is suffering, but I must indicate a benign quality in the symptom ... Splitting, evacuator use of the senses, and hallucinations were all being employed in the service of an ambition to be cured, and may therefore be supposed to be creative activities. [Bion, 1956, p. 68]

Roughly speaking, the first part of Book I and the third part of Book II in the Trilogy can be seen as practical examples of this psychic syndrome, or constant conjunction. In 1957 Bion came to realise that the objects were thrown in hallucination to distant places in space and time (Bion, 1957, p. 75). He focused his attention on the patient's efforts to "force" parts of his personality into the analyst "with increased desperation and violence" when the patient "felt"—the word is seminal here, it is just a feeling—that the analyst "refused to accept parts of his personality" (all quotations from Bion, 1957, pp. 103–104). What does this mean? It means that Bion was keeping track of both the patient's movements and the analyst's reactions and the extent to which they could influence the patient's communications. The catch-22 situation was that "in the patient's belief ... the analyst strives, by understanding the patient, to drive him insane" (Bion, 1961, p. 107).

The many "invasions" colloquially described in the Trilogy with the characters' "actions" are hardly distinguishable from "acting out". They are mainly ascribed to the characters Man (for, example, at its maximum, in the episode of the chocolate bar gun and its questionable killing effects), Roland, Robin, and, to some extent, Bion, as well as to Watson, Moriarty, Clytemnestra, and the expressions of divinities and their apostles, messengers or representatives, Arf-Arfer, Du, Priest, Paul and others. All of them typify a paradoxical psychosis, when primary envy and primary narcissism are facts.

Bion's earlier investigations, like the one described here with a comparative purpose as regards the final writing in the Trilogy, had led him to the formulations of "transformations in hallucinosis" and "hyperbole". It is another example that allows the reader to see that the Trilogy is a kind of practical lesson whose theory appears in *Transformations*: "a constant conjunction of increasing force of emotion with increasing force of evacuation" (Bion, 1965, p. 142) is continuously evolving in a kind of self-feeding process of envy and greed, akin to an atomic chain reaction—an image Bion had already used in 1956. The phrase was used in 1960 and was to be repeated in 1965, when finally he was able to use a term that depicted this ever-swelling process (as one may see in *Cogitations*, p. 247). When Bion resorted to the term "hyperbole", he finally bound this constant conjunction. Its definition and use is wholly contained in the book *Transformations*. Remarkably, it is defined in more than one place in this book, something that may indicate that Bion had no didactic or academic preoccupations which could be expressed by a systematic ordering. Nevertheless, there is a didactically written, systematic approach when it comes to the use of hyperbole in the analytic session, in the clearest definition of this concept that appears late in the book, in the last chapter:

> In order to link its phenomenological counterpart in analytic practice with the penumbra of associations that I regard as significant, I shall call this characteristic "hyperbole". I mean the term to convey an impression of exaggeration, of rivalry and, by retention of its original significance, throwing and outdistancing. The appearance of hyperbole in any form must be regarded as significant of a transformation in which rivalry, envy and evacuation are operating. There is a profound difference between "being" O and rivalry with O. The latter is characterised by envy, hate, love, megalomania and the state known to analysts as acting out, which must be sharply differentiated from acting, which is characteristic of "being" O.
>
> Just as exaggeration is helpful in clarifying a problem, so it can be felt to be important to exaggerate in order to gain the attention necessary to have a problem clarified. Now the "clarification" of a primitive emotion depends on its being contained by a container which will detoxicate it. In order to enlist the aid of the container the emotion must be exaggerated. The "container" may be a "good breast", internal or external, which is able to detoxicate the emotion. Or the container may not be able to tolerate the emotion and the contained emotion may not to be able to tolerate neglect. The result is hyperbole. That is to say, the emotion

> that cannot tolerate neglect grows in intensity, is exaggerated to ensure attention, and the container reacts by more, and still more, violent evacuation. By using the term "hyperbole" I mean to bind the constant conjunction of increasing force of emotion with increasing force of evacuation. It is immaterial to hyperbole what the emotion is; but on the emotion will depend whether the hyperbolic expression is idealising or denigrating. [Bion, 1965, pp. 141–142]
>
> The term "hyperbole" has a history which fits it for compact representation of a number of clinical statements which (i) occur frequently, (ii) are easily recognisable as instances of hyperbole and (iii) are almost certainly symptomatic of a constant conjunction which has significance for the personality being analysed and for the main body of psychoanalytic theories of idealisation, splitting, projective identification, rivalry and envy … It has therefore a wide spectrum, is flexible and lends itself easily for use by the analyst as a "selected fact" to aid in displaying coherence which, without it, may not be apparent. "Hyperbole" can be regarded as representing hyperbole, and hyperbole is projection conjoined with rivalry, ambition, vigour which can amount to violence and hence to "distance" to which an object is projected. [Bion, 1965, p. 162]

He points out the excessive—and one may add, either phylogenetically acquired or environmentally enhanced—claiming of material comfort, which comes to be mistaken by one's self, enhanced by education—or, better, lack of it—and habits, for an instinctual need. This is one of the many constantly conjoined factors which flow to greed. It develops into an insatiable search for reassuring inanimate objects which are felt as sources of material comfort; or persons made material in one's mind, as well as a manic search for events felt as comforting. There is a hyperbolic, overvalued interest in those objects. The inner feelings range from good to happy and their duration is less than a bug's life—it may be compared to that of subatomic particles. Its concreteness is proved by its very weight or colour or fashion—because it is never real in the mind of its beholder. Something concrete and sensuously apprehended is mistaken for reality—whose apprehension is part of emotional experiences of love and hate, affective endowments and real links to inner objects, which may furnish real nourishment. An entire life may be sacrificed in order acquire material belongings; to belong turns into a motto to people who unconsciously or consciously allow this kind of un-life to prevail. This state of affairs was described by Bion under the name of *enforced splitting* (Bion, 1962, p. 10; review in Sandler, 2005, p. 273). It seems to begin when a suitable child is breast-fed with a special breast that is able to furnish just milk and not good enough solace, comprehension and intuition. One equates love with material food. A factual account in a paediatric anamnesis, such as "breast-fed from age X to age Y", tells us nothing about real mother–baby interaction.

Internal object

The hyperbolic, manic and essentially hallucinated search for material comfort permeates many of the established interpretations of theories—not just in the psychoanalytic movement. It seems that no theory was spared this, as we attempted to see earlier, when discussing adhesion to jargon, for example. The same fate plagued seminal, empirical observations by Melanie Klein, for example:

> The phenomenon which was recognised by Freud, broadly speaking, as the voices and the influence of the actual parents established in the ego is, according to my findings, a complex object world which is felt by the individual, in deep layers of the unconscious, to be concretely inside himself, and for which I and some of my colleagues therefore use the term "internalised objects" and "inner world". [Klein, 1934, p. 330]

Many readers and post-Klein authors suppose that the "internalised objects" and the "inner world" referred to by Mrs Klein are wholly material. The catch may be in the use of the term "felt", and in the fact that the terms "internalised objects" and "inner world" are in inverted commas. "Feeling" differs from "being"; an internalised object refers to a metaphor. Certainly, when the baby "feels", he may well do it in a most concrete way—especially when it is the suitable baby just mentioned, one that frantically looks for material comforts and splits them from immaterial comforts. Nevertheless, the legalisation and institutionalisation of this tries to make it established and eternal, perennial and immutable—approved by a decree of some human minds, mistaken for a commandment of God.

Emotional growth occurs when that which was seen as a "good object" or a "bad object" is no longer just a physical object. The substantive, sensuously apprehensible "object" may have concreteness for its beholder when the beholder inhabits his own infancy, due to annihilation anxiety. It is a particular, early instance of being abandoned ontogenetically. The abandonment follows its earliest prototype hitherto known: the toleration of frustration, of putting up with the absent breast, the consequence of which is the realisation of the no-breast (Bion, 1962), which allows for the inception of immaterial and material processes of thought.

The minds of some readers may be wholly filled with traditional certainties, in this particular case, a belief in the ages-old philosophical conundrum that views material and immaterial as opposing poles as if they were opposing factions at permanent war. The examples are now classical, and they were examined earlier in this text: mind versus matter (and in later, post-Newton generations, energy versus matter), each one taken as an absolute concrete or quasi-concrete being. This kind of reader cannot view it as a paradox that demands to be tolerated rather than solved with an arbitrary priority attributed to one of them. Under a psychoanalytic vertex, it is a false conundrum (Sandler, 1997, 2001a, b). When Klein observed the possibility of integration between what was felt (by the infant) as good and what was felt as bad, the inner sense of a whole "object-ness", in its concrete, physical, material sense, was starting on its way to being abandoned. If the individual survives long enough, this feeling—a mere feeling—is reserved for his infantile inner world.

Bion expanded Klein's observations with two theories: the "sense of truth" (Bion, 1961, p. 116) and the "psychoanalytic object" (Bion, 1962, pp. 67–69; reviewed in Sandler, 2005, p. 592). The sense, as in the scientific model of "gravity" made by Newton, constitutes an immaterial fact which calls to be intuited, rather than drawn by a writing instrument on a piece of paper or similar. It is a moving, living event. The small arrow which merely represents it (usually called "vector") is just a visual representation of what is not visual. This is, again, a paradox that demands to be coped with rather than resolved. The paradox continues in the sense that a concrete inner world intuited by Klein is formed by verbs: an inner world formed by emotional experiences, out of instinctual emotions and affects, which colour what is finally a non-sensuous substantive with non-sensuous adjectives.

Mourning, depression, adoption

The origins of Klein's inner world and internalised object are Freud's classical observations about the development of hysteria, obsessive-compulsive disorders and depression. Perhaps no other psychiatrist or psychiatrist theoretician—including Karl Jaspers—was able to provide the practitioner with such a superb phenomenological description of depression as Freud did in "Mourning and Melancholia". The situation is of a "two-body psychology" (Rickman, 1950). Two linked personalities go along for some years; then one of them dies—let us say, one who is performing a parental function. Some parents are not spared the worst experience awaiting a real parent: witnessing the death of a child. How can one "store" an integrated object which reflects in a good enough way the simultaneously loved and hated person who died? How can one not fill one's mind with idealised, split memories, but rather remain mindful of worked through experiences? Freud and Klein observed that this is feasible for those people who were able to put up with the paradox made of complex linking emotions, which are communicated through corresponding complex affects towards the person who will die, and the simultaneous "return" of those complex affects and emotions coming from the person who will die. The mourner has a good enough command of his unconscious and conscious knowledge about his loving and hating emotions towards the person who died. The meaning of the term "good enough" here corresponds to what Klein and Winnicott observed, namely, that excessive love, or greedy love, or violence of love, resulting in falsely protective care, has a damaging effect on the inner object. This in turn is equated to an excessive, greedy and violent hate. Integration leading to a "whole object" is precluded. Melancholy ensues—a state in which the material, physical, concrete, sensuously apprehensible existence is a mandatory condition. The concrete loss is felt as unbearable. A psychotic misapprehension occurs, in the same way that psychotics take and use words as if they were concrete (Bion, 1953, 1957a, b). The melancholic feels that he or she needs the physical presence of the dead person. He or she was not able to "store" the deceased person in a still unknown "inner space-time", which is not a real place, as a non-sensuous, immaterial inner being or object.

Psychoanalytic observation showed that the melancholic's guilt is a result of greedy and envious attacks whose aim is the extermination of the deceased person's loving and hating aspects. It emerges at least in two forms: idolisation and its underlying iconoclasm. The person feels that a preserved external parent or child would furnish concrete proof—needed by the murderous superego—that the external parent or child "did not die". In other words, the person needs a constant reassuring proof that his or her attacks were not successful.

The depressive position differs from depression; the psychoanalytic treatment of both differs too. There is an ethical danger involved in the practitioner making use of the patient's eventual regret—either intentional, by the psychopathic practitioner, or unconscious, by the naïve or unprepared practitioner:

> ROSEMARY No, it is Time Past's party.
>
> PRIEST *That* is P.A.'s party.
>
> P.A. No, my party is not times past. Always the mistake of thinking the past is owned by psychoanalysis; the past is owned by Regret. Regret is a guest at a psychoanalytic party but is not the host; nor is psychoanalysis the domain of Regret. Regret is so vain that it is regarded as important and treated with deference in religion.
>
> PRIEST Centuries have passed since all was vanity, and Vain Regret took the place of God. [II: 406]

Wilfred Bion pays homage to his war comrades through the ghostly characters Auser, Quentin, Cod, Cliff, Stokes and, conspicuously, P.A., as well as through the earlier life of Rosemary—the daughter of a whore, and herself a whore. They seem to furnish a truthful light that Bion seemed to have struggled to keep alight to the end of his own life: a light made of personal shame and guilt. Some of them were able to display a compassion and capacity to love that Bion would never ascribe to himself; some of them seemed to him more courageous, or more foolhardy than he was; some of them tried to avoid the truth by resorting to alcohol. One may sense that Bion was always inspired by the love of a woman, a kind of love he thought he could not attain. The underlying message is that he knew what true love was but could not feel worthy of it. The reader may surmise that he was talking about his second wife.

Melanie Klein and her closest collaborator, Joan Riviere, seemed to be as inspired by Shakespeare as Freud was; one of her extensions of Freud's investigation into the death instincts made her scrutinise the existence of gratitude—a safe conduct to avoiding suicidal melancholia and irreparable guilt. Using the Bard's insightful and compact observation, which includes explicitly the dangers of the sensuous-concretisation syndrome:

> Ingratitude, thou marble-hearted fiend,
> More hideous, when thou show'st thee in a child
> Than the sea-monster. [*King Lear*, I iv]

Psychoanalysis and paediatrics fairly apprehended the general features that characterise the relationship between mothers and babies. Practising psychoanalysts, especially those devoted to child analysis, have at their disposal truthful empirical observations and verifications described by many authors since Melanie Klein and, to an extent, Anna Freud: Joan Riviere, Donald Winnicott, Donald Meltzer, Wilfred R. Bion and Martha Harris, over a time span of forty years. This clinical research displayed, in many parts of the world, some manifestations of the paradoxical affects and emotional experiences of love and hate pervaded by a series of interacting unconscious phantasies originating simultaneously from mothers and babies. Sadistic and envious phantasies have crystal-clear physical expressions: for example, biting the nipple, and excessive separation anxiety. Roughly speaking, because individual manifestations are infinite, like fingerprints, the following general description furnishes an example: the Mother, through her capacity for reverie and good enough mothering, is minimally able to contain her own rage, guilt and pain, soothing herself as well as her Baby. Therefore she paves the way for a non-sensuous process of introjecting "goodness" and helping him to put up with "badness" without having to appeal to excessive projective identification—especially in cases where excessive greed and envy or other narcissistic expressions are present. In other words, in containing herself, the mother shows the baby that containment is a possible act—preparing him to introject containment itself. The Baby will have good enough signals that he has not destroyed his Mother. Continuous exposure to a reparative, soothing mother, who again and again offers her breast, may help, step by step, the introjection of both goodness and badness. Psychosis means that the baby did not develop from this phase—it is not possible to know, in adulthood, whether the problem arose because no good enough mother was available, or whether no real mother in this world could nourish a baby so greedy and envious. The result is that a psychotic person, in splitting good from bad and being unable to integrate them, makes extreme demands of unceasing and eternal love from the group.

Internal objects: touching and untouchable

"Objects" must be material objects only in the earliest phases of emotional development—until the third month of life. The material object—substantive and adjective: good or bad—reaches its verbal status, as a movement "in and out", "to and fro". The verbal status, a product of thought processes (Bion, 1961), may be equated to pure energy, without having abandoned its material form of a particle. It is now a material object and an immaterial movement, simultaneously. Thanks to its immaterial existence—roughly speaking, in psychic reality—the former object has given birth to inner feelings, affects, emotions and emotional experiences which belong to the ultra- and infra-sensuous realm. They are touching, but at the same time they are untouchable—if the baby achieves a good enough introjective "identijection" (Bion, 1958–1979, p. 353). Moreover, the "ultimate introjected imago" is in part a non-object. A small child who has no primary narcissism or primary envy will be more willing to abandon the breast if and when and where it has introjected it as well as Mother or a transitional object as described by Winnicott. Anyway, introjection (as a process, a verb), breast (as a conception), and mother (as a conception), and later, father, relatives, professors and society at large (as a conception), are not wholly dependent on the concreteness of an individual person, and not wholly independent of it. Putting it in other words with the help of a common life experience: adoption is a universal event having *no necessary* connection with parenthood and physically regarded fertility. It is not a reserve of hapless orphans and bereaved children. In some cases, being a natural sibling offers extra difficulties in adoption, due to the presence of hope, expectations and exigencies coming from either natural parents or natural siblings. Dead certainty in issues involving what are called "blood relations" is a sure recipe for frustration, failure and melancholy. Due to transference (Freud, 1912a), there is no limit to the destruction caused by this kind of belief. Patients believe that their analysts are their fathers or mothers, sometimes substitutes for the real thing.

> DOCTOR People *want* to believe they have neuroses and they are encouraged to believe that all they need is a bit of psychoanalytic cure and their troubles will be over.
>
> P.A. A lot of people who have not tried it think so. You would be surprised that a few try it and yet withstand the seduction. Still, I agree that a lot of "psychoanalysts", as well as their adherents, fall for it. When I hear the present vogue for "charisma" and "charismatic people" my defences become alert.
>
> PAUL When are you at peace? It doesn't seem that you are so much better off than the religious.
>
> P.A. I doubt whether a psychoanalyst would hold out the hope of becoming "better off", or even "better". As for being at peace, I would expect to be more nearly so when I am working than when I am not.
>
> ROLAND I agree; I am happiest at work. But do we need analysis to find that out?
>
> P.A. The psychoanalytic experience seems sometimes to be associated with achieving a capacity for work. Learning music is often associated with becoming able to play a musical instrument.
>
> ROBIN I hope so. My boy is learning the piano.
>
> P.A. But so often people seem to expect that someone having analysis will become creative. Do you expect your boy to become a composer?
>
> ROBIN No, but I think his mother does. [II: 259–60]

CHAPTER EIGHT

Mindlessness: the sensuous-concretisation syndrome

Does factuality mean reality?

To the suspicious amusement of André Green, and to the perplexity of other audiences, Bion used to say that psychoanalysis already existed before a Freud appeared to discover it: was it a thought without a thinker waiting for a Freud to think it?

> Who told ... Freud that he needed "artificially to blind himself" to explore the dark places of the mind? [I: 42]

> Freud, as he often did, put his finger on the spot. In the seventh chapter of *The Interpretation of Dreams*, he said, answering his own question, "What is the conscious? It is nothing less than the sense organ for the perception of psychic quality." It stands to reason then, that if he was right, this very recently developed organ, though not secondary to the probings *of* the grosser senses, may be capable of "probing" and reacting *to* the grosser senses by "psychic reality". [I: 98]

Some readers find written attempts to describe the basic paradox of material-immaterial an unbearable reading experience.

> Falstaff, a known artefact, is more "real" in Shakespeare's verbal formulation than countless millions of people who are dim, invisible, lifeless, unreal, whose births, deaths—alas, even marriages—we are called upon to believe in, though certification of their existence is vouched for by the said official certification ... Many people are so lifeless that I could stare in silent admission that I did not believe the evidence of my senses. [I: 4–5]

In the view of this writer, some readers oversimplify the relationships between Bion's work, including the whole of the Trilogy, and religious practices, regarding Bion's work as "just Eastern culture, mainly from India". If it is true that he was born and spent his early years in India, it is also true that there was an imposing British modulation on his earliest education, soon followed by an entirely British schooling. His contact in his first six years—1897 to 1903—was not exactly with India-in-itself, but with the British-colonised India in its heyday. Then hailed as the "jewel in the crown", India gave Bion a scent of what living conditions were like in the jungle of Bengal. Even there he was almost wholly educated under Western, British values. His family was part of the ruling colonial elite. To emphasise Bion's early contact with Indian values, transmitted by his beloved Ayah, does not mean that they were exclusive or were made at the expense of any other factor. What matters now is that he was soon subjected to a violent imposition of social beliefs without soothing contact with his parents, who remained in India: the normal custom was to send children back to be educated in the Empire's Metropolis. But the imposition of socially favoured habits, without the experience of a more individually adapted family life, gave those who were subjected to it an opportunity to experience socially a lifeless, shared hallucinosis that feigns life itself without ever being it. To some of those people, it meant a commitment to unthinking group life and social ideology: a course in mimicry. To others, it meant an insurmountable trauma that lasted their whole lives—they became part of the group of "normal, socially adapted people": the uncritical "yes-men" and "herd followers". To others again, this experience furnished a critical insight about hallucinosis. Which of the general situations applied depended on the individual's endowments; in practice the three could be intermingled.

Bion's autobiography contains many passages that illustrate his critical stance. One may attribute to this personal endowment a predisposition to exercise a kind of "Kantian criticism". This would be—as a hypothesis to be proved by empirical field studies—a fourth pre-conception, possibly belonging to the field of human pre-conceptions. It would be added to the two psychoanalytical pre-conceptions discovered by him—the Breast and Oedipus—and to the earlier one discovered by Kant, the "categorical imperative", revived by Freud as the superego. Much later, equipped with his own criticism, Bion studied the *Bhagavad Gita*, together with other theological and religious sources of pursuing "truth-O", which theologians called "wisdom"—a term pervaded with judgmental values. Bion's personal tendency to have a critical stance may have annoyed some onlookers or people who sought conviviality with him. But his criticism may be compared with that of Plato, Pascal, Bacon, Shakespeare, Herder, Goethe and Freud, as well as that of the Jewish tradition of critical thinking. This writer singles out a less known example: Salomon Maimon (Hartmann, 1923–29; Sandler, 2000, 2002). Personal criticism allows one to focus also on the *lack* of "wisdom", or better, the failure to pursue "truth-O", coupled with a relative facility to construe lies that may be found in those old treatises called "holy scriptures". Bion gave a few indications about it in *Cogitations*, *Transformations* and *Attention and Interpretation*, and returned to it at a full bore in the three books of the Trilogy. The reader prone to jumping to conclusions based just on appearances would say that Bion's thinking is "Indian", or "Buddhist". Nevertheless, judging by appearances gives the sensuous apparatus an undue chance to win the game and is a most formidable source for illusion, delusion and hallucinosis.

One of many examples of Bion's experiences with masses of people undergoing a shared hallucinosis which passed for "normal" occurred when he was a World War I tank commander at home on leave:

> That evening I went to see "The Boy". I had found out there was no train to Lustleigh, where Mother was, until 10 a.m. next morning, and I thought this would be a good way of clearing the war out of my mind. W. H. Berry was the chief man, and very inane and silly the whole show was. There were lots of lights, brilliant scenes, nice banging music, loud-voiced and shrieking actors and, in short, everything to make for an unintelligent and expensive evening without any undue effort on my part. I sat back and watched the show and wondered at it all. Ridiculous old men sat about and laughed

> at silly jokes. Electric lights and noise—that was all there was, as far as London was concerned. But I was too fresh from France, and the whole time I saw, in place of the scenes and silly fools, Happy Valley, and men asking to be carried back. It was not a successful show for me. The contrast of wartime London with "out there" was too great. That London show was a nightmare, and France was a nightmare—but the latter was positively healthy in comparison. The next morning London was behind me ... [Bion, 1997b, p. 153]

The issue would be presented again in the Trilogy:

> P.A. Figments of the imagination are often more powerful than many real things; men and women are not so powerful as the idealised figures that other men and women have about them. [II: 354]

How many of the so-called "scientific theories" have counterparts in reality? Are they more remarkable for their failures than for their dubious successes? Are those successes, soon to be replaced by the announcement of their failures, linked to their specific *Zeitgeist*? The king is dead, long live the king. Are their claimed successes the playing of a popular sport, that of jumping to precocious conclusions?

Conversely, the few scientific theories which would merit such a name are able to convey real, albeit transient, partial glimpses of the counterpart in reality that they purport to reflect or describe. They may be useful to human beings, providing technological advancements or not. As regards their scientific status, the fact that they are useful or not has no importance—even if they have some legal implications in politically oriented groups. Anyway, there is no "politics-less" group. Two prototypical examples of the first type are the theory of relativity and of Oedipus; an example of the second type appears in Bion's comments about theories of astrophysics.

> ROLAND Don't be too imaginative or Alice will have another terrible night.
>
> P.A. Being "too imaginative" might cause us all to have a terrible awakening.
>
> EDMUND These cosmic disasters—supernovae for example—occur as we *know*, but cannot *imagine*. The sun should explode in a few thousand million years.

ROBIN What about a dip in the sea before breakfast?

ROLAND Tomorrow morning? Yes—not in a few million years.

EDMUND That is what P.A. means. The swim in the sea helps us to keep a firm grip on our ignorance. We can clutch it to ourselves like a cloak which we cannot bear to have torn from our shoulders.

ROLAND You are rather hard on us poor ignorami. You wouldn't be worse off if you joined us in a swim.

EDMUND I don't doubt it, but I want to go on with my astronomical hobbies.

P.A. There is nothing to stop you provided you are not so terrified by your imagination or your scientific activity that you cannot think at all.

ROBIN The government might become so terrified that they stopped you. But perhaps they are too ignorant to be terrified; that also would act as a cloak to protect the tender shoots of scientific speculation till they become "theories".

ROLAND If they become strongly established theories they become too strong for the tender shoots of social speculation. Panic can be a powerful solvent of discipline.

ALICE No government would dare to stop astronomers doing astronomical research.

P.A. If I were the government and wanted to stop astronomical research I am sure I could do it in a subtle enough way to escape criticism. I could say there was not enough paper to spare for the printing of astronomical articles. I could attack the availability of materials which were essential for the manufacture of certain instruments. I could discourage grants for the education of potentially gifted astronomy students.

ROLAND Which goes to show that it would be inadvisable to let you into government posts of power!

ALICE I think it would help if an astronomer stood for Parliament.

ROBIN But the principle stands—it is dangerous to allow men of such mischievous power authority which they can use to prevent mental development.

> P.A. Suppose astronomers could convince the majority of human beings that the sun showed signs of imminent catastrophe; that at any moment we would be enveloped in whirlpools of immense temperatures. Would you allow that to be broadcast when nothing could be done?
>
> ROBIN The religious people have already issued warnings that the end of the world is at hand; that God is a consuming fire and so on.
>
> P.A. Nobody minds God's being a consuming fire. They either say that He does not exist or that He is really rather a Decent Chap, a Good Fellow, a Good Sport. [II: 284–5]

Professor Karl Popper (and others) described some trends as pseudosciences. He had no second thoughts in describing psychoanalysis as one of them. It is safe to state that he did this due to his own little learning—he came to this hasty conclusion after generalising Dr Alfred Adler's "individual psychology" as if it were the whole of psychoanalysis. Was he acting like Mr Magoo, the popular cartoon character? Bion feared that the whole of psychoanalytic theory was just a vast paramnesia to fill the void of our ignorance. Jumping to precocious conclusions—which may be attractive to certain readers—can be seen as a non-scientific attitude, quite independent of the specific theory that is defended with this means: pure belief. As regards medical (and consequently, psychoanalytic) practice, the present work has already made some comments on placebo effects—emphasising the origins of these comments and their main bearings on the Trilogy, both critically and offering alternatives felt by this writer as truthful rather than "lie-ful".

An alternative is proposed in the Trilogy: Bion elaborated it without being immobilised in a patterned style of writing, as mentioned before. There is a continuous pursuit of "O", of the "Infinite Finitude"; or the written embodiment of the tandem movement PS⇔D; or better, a continuous display of the very ⇔. This writer believes it may help some willing students to gain a transdisciplinary overview of real scientific theories, focused on practical psychoanalysis, which they cannot obtain elsewhere:

> MYCROFT ... The development of the human mind was, in the course of time, believed to be associated with, or caused by, the central nervous system. Freud thought that. The Greeks believed

in ghosts, independent of anatomy yet with a visible counterpart; some function of themselves able to apprehend a personality after the physical anatomy had been destroyed or dealt with but not before. They thought they could not see it by mediation of the physical, sensuous, visual apparatus. We do not know what physical apparatus they thought betrayed the phrenes though they spoke of them frequently and as if they had no shadow.

BION As far as I am concerned you and Sherlock and Watson *are* fictional characters. I can see that they might be described as very vividly conceived fictional characters, but I see no reason for imagining or conceiving of them in any other terms.

MYSELF But *I* do. Because the term "fictional character" itself is an inadequate phrase. Here I have just written "myself" as if I wanted to give it a status different from me. I could call "Bion" a second-class citizen compared with "Myself". I indicate without definition that the opinions expressed by me, even if fiction, are worthy of being treated with respect. Those opinions are of superior status to opinions claimed as mine and spoken as if I claimed "ownership" over them. Their value, in a war for possession, is greater than it would be if they were intended to be "true". Conversely, a statement with a vertex of truth value would be of lower value as a weapon in a struggle for supremacy. [I: 95]

MYSELF As psychological preparation I shall borrow verbal or alphabetical formulations like O, or zero, or infinity. For some centuries the visual imagery of Euclidean space limited rather than freed thought. Cartesian coordinates made, in combination with the theorem of Pythagoras, a possibility of relating points to each other without the visual aids of lines and circles. These visual aids introduced powerful, undetected, forces which distorted the balance of probability. That distortion is still incalculable. Growth, + or –, remains inaccessible to thought, if unmistakable to feeling. Conceptual thought and passionate feeling are impossible to relate within the confines of existent universes of discourse. The problem could be stated by analogy; numbers suffered repeated extensions to carry an increased load—rational numbers, irrational numbers and, latterly, complex conjugate points. In the emotional domain, persecution by passion grows to depression. The relation of the one to the other requires an extension whereby quantity transforms to quality. "Very great", "very small" intervals of time, space, probability, involve quality in a manner analogous to growth from quantity to quality. Thus, quantitative terms such as "excessive", "inadequate", "too little", "too much", may signify a change in kind or quality; conversely, change in quality, for example, love or hate, may imply change in quantity. This is *not* a crudity such as the difference between one German "hating" and the entire German nation "hating"; that may be "symptomatic", "significant" of a method of lateral communication. The change can be formulated in language, music, mathematics; it is, in fact, something "infra-" or "ultra-" human, animate—living or bio-logical. Comparison between animate and inanimate reveals need for discrimination; the "Russians" send a mechanical probe to the moon and retain a mechanically aided, computer-wise and otherwise, animate being on earth. By contrast, the "Americans" favour sending "animate beings" sufficiently well disciplined to be machines.

Bernardino Sahagun[1] describes the debate between those who favour gods formed artificially, by human art, out of wood and stone which "appear" to be controllable, and those, like the Roman Catholics, who favour an independent and uncontrollable God. Jesus Christ is a compromise between the verbally articulate human Jesus who prays, "Thy will be done on earth as it is in Heaven", and the Messiah. Some degree of independence is conceded to "God", although, after creation or "belief-creating operation", both end products are still, from human vertex, unpredicted. The idol made out of inanimate material shows unmistakable characteristics of a kind usually attributed to animals, usually human; reciprocally, the god created out of materials, ultra- or infra-sensuous, displays characteristics usually regarded as the prerogative of idols. In other terms ("borrowed" from the lunar illustration) the machine, regardless of race, time, space, is e- and pro-vocatively animate; and the animate object similarly pro- and e-vocatively inhuman and inanimate. If we now increase the dimension, using "time" as an instrument with which to measure, we find a stability about the objects discerned and recorded by animate human animals such as saints, philosophers, scientist, artists, and (borrowing from Socrates) artisans. Socrates knew that he was not wise, yet could not mobilise facts to indicate anyone or anything, god or idol, who could plausibly be said to contest the title. In the domain of the human senses there is evidence of violence and murder from the Death Pit at Ur to Hiroshima and beyond.

"Methinks I see a Nation … with undazzled eyes …", as one poet said. Socrates, "Krishna" and his creator (his "Plato", his "Homer"), Hellas and Shelley. His "powers of darkness" and the vacant throne. My valour … said Valiant for Truth and his creator Bunyan. (What? *That* tinker? Is he not the carpenter's son? As for Shakespeare, was he not Bacon? And who wrote the Bhagavad Gita? Sunk in Eternal Night without a trace. No orchids for Miss Blandish; "therefore—fight Arjuna!") "Fame is no plant that grows in mortal soil … but lives and spreads aloft … by all judging Jove."

Homer is not known *not* to have been blind Maeonides—he was blind anyhow; Newton was sunk without a trace, hit by an apple; so was Helen; Jesus, buried beneath the load of the Roman Catholic Church and the massive ritual. "I don't know what you are talking about"—and couldn't care less. "Great is the truth and shall prevail, if none care whether it prevail or not". So the mammals survived. Perhaps the dinosaurs did not get together to worship the infant prodigy when it was still helpless enough. Oh, those over-confident stegosaurs! And now look what their *failure* has done!

Perhaps the electron microscope and the radio telescope would do the trick between then? No. You still have to have a human to interpret them. The past—the record in history, in fossil and stone, in computer and poem—has to be interpreted by them. And that two-handed engine at the door—("please, sir, what does 'two-handed engine' mean?" "Well, my boy, it means, well, er, it … Are you sure your people don't mind about Freud?" "Oh no, sir! They are Kleinians, sir. They don't mind a bit!" "Well it means the two breasts. You see …" "No, sir, I don't understand, sir." "Oh hell! Nor do I. But I shall be shall be surprised if in fact it doesn't mean that if one of them doesn't get you the other one will. But don't tell your Mum or Dad." "Yes, sir! You did say 'Hell', didn't you, sir?" "Heavens, so I did! Your Dad is an atheist isn't he?" "Oh *no*, sir!") Any interpretation is a stop-gap which serves to plug the hole; even a part has to serve to plug the whole. The radio telescope and the electron microscope, God and Devil, Body and Mind, Penis and Vagina, Love and Hate, Real and Distinct, Real and Coincident,

Conjugate and Complex. There are multitudinous holes and multitudinous parts to fill the wholes with.

Hitherto, the term "mind" has proved serviceable. I propose to use it myself, but not for purposes of writing a philosophical or psychological or religious or artistic or other record. I propose to use it as a meaningless term, useful for talking or writing about what I *don't* know—to mark the "place where" a meaning might be.

I assume that there is a realisation that approximates to the term "mind". I assume that the mass of theories, case histories, psychoanalytic formulations, are products of the "mind". Some of these I shall assume are themselves realisations approximating to the formulations, definitory hypotheses about the mind and of the same status as the term "mind" itself. I further assume that the "mind", analogous to brain and central nervous system, is of significance for what it does or does not reveal.

Some psychoanalytic theories I regard, without specifying for the present, as "constants", "invariants" under the particular vertex. If these invariants are absent, or not detected by such apparatus as is available, I regard their absence as itself revelatory. These definitory hypotheses may be used as the foundation on which an "instrument" could be constructed, *based* on a variety of theories, but itself supporting none. It would then be an instrument which could record the configuration revealed by the mind and thereby make its configuration and interpretation available for study and contemplation by an observer. I have indicated that such observers may be hard to come by in the extremely limited domain provided by animal history itself. Life, as known to us, has a recent and very short history if measured in comparison with the scales provided by standards applicable to astronomical physics and what we call outer space. Yet biological forces are ones with which we have to live. They or their symptoms concern themselves with us even if unknown to us. They may have no counterpart in the domain of "known" and "unknown", animate and inanimate. It *is* possible that the development of the CNS, and now the mind (I refer to the definitory hypothesis I have put forward), may provide an extension of which we have not so far been able to avail ourselves, any more than the race could avail itself of the atomic theories of Democritus of Abdera or the heliocentric hypotheses of Aristarchus with the then existing facilities.

This brings us to the importance which Socrates attached to the artisan for whom he clearly felt a respect which he could not feel for other classes, including himself as the matrix of wisdom. Nor was he able to feel much respect for the oracle at Delphi, judging its pronouncements realistically. The artisan, therefore, appears to have at least a considerable "history" of being "respect-worthy". God likewise, though unknown or perhaps because unknown, or perhaps because of being respected, remains as an Invariant clothed in no matter how many variables and under whatever vertex. He is a "constant" which is an "unknown" and the centre of a human discipline served by a mathematics which must be capable of manipulation, by a mathematics in which the constant is unknown and whose place is taken by an infinity of variables.

BION Such religious numbers which are known to us are not associated with a domain adequate for their deployment as are irrational, imaginary numbers. The space of mathematical operation must be extended to accommodate "religious" numbers as well as those catered for by past extensions of the "domain" of numbers. To recapitulate: the study of anatomy and physiology is usually pictured as a central nervous system with an outstanding structure, the brain. The mind, presumed to be real, is likewise presumed to have a structure. This word, "structure", is borrowed from the vocabulary forged for the domain of sensuous experience. The "mind", and now its "structure", are terms which are *not* appropriate for use as referents to domains we hypothecate for this study. The "mind", unlike the brain, has *no* convolutions. Analogous objects, therefore, have to be created from the domain of the brain and its convolutions. [I: 138–142]

MAN You will not be satisfied with my reply, but here it is—allow me to introduce you. First, to the objects which were so shadowy that is was not even possible to say they were man and woman. I pronounce no opinion on this. Let me introduce you now to two objects which the higher human authorities had no doubt whatever were man and woman; there was no dispute about the facts of anatomy and physiology. The man took the woman into the bushes, the woman showed no reluctance to go. There, the man who showed himself subsequently to be perfectly capable of the exercise of functions which we are used to regarding as those of reason, savaged the woman's breasts and genitalia with his teeth, devouring the flesh of both regions in a manner that would be comprehensible if he were a wild carnivore. The episode presents itself to us as a problem because he did not appear as a wild beast devouring his prey in a jungle. He appeared to be a man going out with a girl at a holiday resort. This pair were so unshadowy that it was impossible to *dis*believe that they were a man and a woman. There are many similar instances, so common that it is not necessary to recount and document them. How immediately they have presented themselves to the senses of the reader of this book depends on a number of facts peculiar to the reader—his occupation, his life up to this time—it would take a long time to recite the facts. I shall abbreviate our labours by saying that they "depend on the vertex". Under one vertex I have known a man act as if he were having a vivid emotional experience familiar to me under the vertex "dream". He was not dreaming; nor did he think he was. It may seem unnecessary to resort to the term "vertex", but it must suffice until we can find some more adequate shorthand for those states in which the individual has two or more sets of facts appropriate to the same emotional experience, but which are impossible to entertain together without feeling mad. This involves feeling sane enough to be afraid, and further, to respect his fear. He is afraid of his mind and fears that his fear is worthy of respect.

BION In short, his "mind" and the consequences of having a mind are unwelcome discoveries. But you seem doubtful.

MAN Let me try to expand my misgiving. I agree with what you have formulated in terms of a "mind", but I am not sure that it is satisfactory either to include or exclude from "mental" activity the taste of human blood, the "emotions" associated with erectile tissue and erectability. It seems, though this is only guesswork, that it was easier for the Greeks to tolerate the idea of "thinking" with the phrenes; or to associate it with the dead; or with the dead apparition when the person to whom it appears was asleep. Alcmaeon of Croton seems to have been one of the first to have thought that thinking might have something to do with the CNS. Since then, up to the present, great importance has been attributed to man's possession of a central nervous system. The nature of impulses springing from an ability to exercise one's teeth or vagina or penis is not similarly honoured or tolerated. When a modern man's impulses obtrude to a point where they become manifest to others as functions of a sensuous system, neither they nor their locale are accorded respect. The peripheral nervous system and its extensions are a source of suspicion and fear.

BION Suppose there *is* a CNS. Further, suppose there is a peripheral nervous system- the PNS and the CNS both fear. The fear is intensified if it is supposed that there is some extension of both infra- and ultra-sensuous. This extension is dreaded in itself, and made the more dreadful if suspected as being *outside* the sphere which we associate with the senses …

MAN … and *within*, but unrecognised.

BION Or recognisable as a character or personality which can be located within the molecular structure of the amines and the domain in which their transmission takes place.

MAN If the CNS is rightly supposed to be important, but we are unable to assess its importance or how it exercises its functions, does that not make it more frightening?

BION It does. I, as a psychoanalyst, have committed myself to action which presupposes that such a thing as a mind or personality exists. I find no difficulty, in present circumstances, in making that admission, accepting that my work is an admission that I hold such a theory. I hold it so strongly that I am prepared to transform my ideas into action. For example, I allow it to be known that I am a psychoanalyst and, with others, have gone so far as to seek recognition of this same idea from people who are not us and who are not in fact at all closely connected with us.

MAN You make the acknowledgment clearly. Do you also agree that others do so? Sometimes you have to my knowledge claimed that certain well-known figures of the past, not only of the recent past like Sigmund Freud himself, were gifted with a profound capacity for understanding their fellow men?

BION Certainly. We can gauge their actions and behaviour from what has been recorded of or by them, and allowing myself anachronistic—like poetic—licence, I would call them very considerable psychoanalysts before anyone had heard of such a term.

> MAN Is this not an instance of claiming that there is such a "thing" as psychoanalysis, that there always has been such a thing as psychoanalysis, whether it could be verbalised or not?
>
> BION I would say that it is an example of a thought which, before Freud existed to think it, was "without a thinker". [I: 166–8]

Aided by the remarkable plasticity of his mother tongue, which allowed him to name things precisely without having to appeal to what could be considered neologisms, Sigmund Freud created and used a comprehensive terminology able to apprehend aspects of psychic reality—which, by the way, is also a term created by him. This comprehensive terminology almost invariably encompasses, in a paradoxical way, both the material and the immaterial realms. Examples of this can be found elsewhere—for example, the term *freie Einfälle*, well translated into English as "free associations" (Sandler, 2012b). This terminology had given the already defined idolising and iconoclastic readers the impression of being too concrete, linked to the reader's (Cartesian) tendency to localise things in space rather than considering the space-time unit that was implicit in Freud's writing. "Free" brings with it an infinite space ethos; "associations" furnishes the boundary, or a potentially finite time ethos.

Another example may be given by the "topographic model of the mind". The idolisers took it as scientific proof that "Freud was right"—as the reader of this work may have seen, this included some neurologists, who thought that the Id was located in the limbic system. The iconoclasts—including, again, some neurologists—took it as proof that "Freud was wrong". Both sides were, and still are, founded in positivistic tenets, or Euclidean bi-dimensional logic. Both badly missed the point, by not tolerating the paradox embedded in the term: topography leans towards a concrete "geography" which is in fact a mobile reality, as beautifully demonstrated in Russell's pedagogical display of the theory of relativity to the common man (Russell, 1925). "Model" leans towards immaterial thought, as shown by Kant (1711) and brought to the psychoanalytic movement by Bion (1962, 1963): a counterpoint, a reflective idea on counterparts in reality as it is. Freud did not state that the mind was topographic. He furnished just a crude provisional model—this was Freud's own opinion about it until the end of his life—which could give the student a rough, temporary idea of an important, but partial material and immaterial functioning of the mind. The idolisers and iconoclasts take the reflecting model as if it were the thing-in-itself.

This writer tried to approach this situation with the hypothetical proposition, backed by corresponding clinical data, of "anti-alpha function". This would perform the inverse of what one would expect from alpha function: it "sensifies" and materialises what was initially non-sensuous and immaterial (Sandler, 1997b).

The mind is too heavy a load for the sensuous beast to carry: thoughts without a thinker

This work has already mentioned what is regarded here as a true "anti-concept", as formulated by René Descartes in the *Discourse on Method* (1637). Why would it be an "anti-concept"? Because Descartes formulated it as an adamant negation, based on Euclidean logic. The psychological function of negation had to wait four hundred years to be discovered by Freud. One who uses negation, a psychotic mechanism, loses the opportunity to make a discovery. Negation gives one the opportunity to discard the thought in its embryonic form from the realm of thinking. The seeds of Comte's positivism were being laid down. The realm of the Platonic forms, a negative realm, was being increasingly subjected to denial and oblivion. Negation was used as a kind of scientific tool: by using it, Descartes "proved" that a thought without a thinker had to be regarded as an absurdity. It would not constitute an exaggeration to say that Descartes acted as if Fleming would be a person who threw out the mould—instead of discovering penicillin.

Bion revived the hypothesis discharged by Descartes to investigate the possibility of treating it as a working hypothesis, using his experience with psychotic disturbances of thought processes as they appear in psychoanalytic practice. As Freud did with the study of dreams, Bion rescued a subject that was previously seen as not having scientific status. He proposed that thoughts may be considered as epistemologically precedent to the thinker. Thoughts may be imposed on the human being by the necessity of survival. Indeed, this seems to be a reasonable basis for the earliest thought of all, namely, the thought of a breast. The primeval thought of a breast is imposed by the reality of the no-breast. The inception of this thought stems from the necessity to deal with an object in its absence. Thinking processes would develop an increasing degree of sophistication in dealing with increasingly complex networks of frustration, expectation, and especially awareness of needs as distinct from desires.

This proposal is coherent with—and seems to have originated from—the hypothesis of inborn pre-conceptions first proposed by Kant, which survived at least until the time of Hegel. Pre-conceptions are not thoughts. If pre-conceptions can mate with realisations, it is easy to see that the realisation is a real event, both "inner" and "outer", if the parameter is an individual being. The realisations were and are ready long before the individual mind is born—as Gardner said, they are "out there" (Gardner, 1989). They impose needs in general, being intrinsically (phylogenetically) linked to instinctual needs. They also impose the very need to think about them, just as the "reality out there" imposes the limits of satisfaction—mostly a very serious limiting power. As Bion is reputed to have said a few days before his death, "Life is full of surprises, most of them unpleasant" (Lyth, 1980).

The allegiance to something that may be called the "transcendent tradition", which exists in good enough shape in both Western and Eastern thought, is a tradition that has regard to the numinous realm—Platonic Ideal Forms. Bion's hypothesis about a thought without a thinker is coherent with this tradition. The hypothesis does not deny the fact that the mind may produce thoughts. Is this the realm of hallucination, hallucinosis and delusion? Because if hallucination, hallucinosis and delusion are things that do not exist, the human capacity to produce them is real.

It remains to be elucidated whether the creative genius, as it is called, produces the ideas, or whether the creative genius is that man or woman who is able to apprehend inner truths that already exist. Therefore it is left to the creative genius or mystic to *discover* and make a *good enough formulation* of the discovery to his or her contemporaries or later generations. Two uneasy tasks!

The hypothesis seems to be backed by the fact that a true work of art or of science can be recognised quite independently of culture, time and space. It can be "discovered" by independent people who sometimes never meet each other. For example: the phenomenon of relativity first described by Einstein was also described by Poincaré, even if a little later and in a different way. This suggests the independence of the thought with regard to the thinker. Perhaps the thinker is important in furnishing a form to the thought, and the form is personal. Is it perhaps of secondary importance? In the Trilogy Bion suggests that the work is not his, even though he wrote it. Francis Bacon once observed that any novelty is just oblivion (Bacon, 1625).

> It is convenient to regard thinking as dependent on the successful outcome of two main mental developments. The first is the development of thoughts. They require an apparatus to cope with them. The second development, therefore, is of this apparatus that I shall provisionally call thinking. I repeat—thinking has to be called into existence to cope with thoughts. It will be noted that this differs from any theory of thought as a product of thinking, in that thinking is a development forced on the psyche by the pressure of thoughts and not the other way round. [Bion, 1961, pp. 110–111]

The issue appeared when Bion tackled the treatment of patients with disorders of thought that were reducible to disorders in their apprehension of reality.[2]

> There are grounds for supposing that a primitive "thinking", active in the development of a thought, should be distinguished from the thinking that is required for the use of thoughts. The thinking used in the development of thoughts differs from the thinking required to use the thoughts when developed. The latter is derived from the PS⇔D mechanism … When thoughts have to be used under the exigencies of reality, be it psychic reality or external reality, the primitive mechanisms have to be endowed with capacities for precision demanded by the need for survival. We have therefore to consider the part played by the life and death instincts as well as reason, which in its embryonic form under the dominance of the pleasure principle is designed to serve as the slave of the passions, has forced it to assume a function resembling that of a master of the passions and the parent of logic. [Bion, 1963, pp. 35–36]

The last sentence is seminal. Bion introduces here the suggestion, backed by clinical experience, that humans learned to cheat and evade, and one of their main tools in doing so is so-called rational thinking. The modes of thought learned by Western civilisation are deeply influenced by Euclidean-Cartesian logic—a particular form of logic with definite limits. Bion is in line with thinkers such as Hume, Voltaire and Freud, to quote a few. Freud had already pointed out that "rationalisation" is typical of schizophrenic thinking, having introduced the term in his study of Judge Schreber's memoirs.

In this sense, a factory of lying thinking, quite independent of thoughts that already exist, is typical of the human being who cannot tolerate frustration.

> For the search, for satisfaction of incompatible desires, would lead to frustration. Successful surmounting of the problem of frustration involves being reasonable and a phrase such as "the dictates of reason" may enshrine the expression of primitive emotional reaction to a function intended to satisfy not frustrate. The axioms of logic therefore have their roots in the experience of a reason that fails in its primary function to satisfy the passions just as the existence of a powerful reason may reflect a capacity in that function to resist the assaults of its frustrated and outraged masters. These matters will have to be considered in so far as dominance of the reality principle stimulates the development of thought and thinking, reason, and awareness of psychic and environmental reality. [Bion, 1963, p. 36]

Later, in *Transformations,* one of the implications of the concept is mentioned, albeit briefly:

> It may at first seem strange to suggest that groups or the infinite should be regarded as epistemologically prior to all else, but less so if we consider that only when a problem is intractable, or seems to be so, will it be felt to engage, and demand, our most powerful efforts. Reciprocally, the more we feel ourselves deeply engaged, the more likely we are to suppose the problem *must* be intractable and that it is so intrinsically. [Bion, 1965, p. 152]

The demands of reality, with its ultimate "intrinsic intractability" in whatever it is, are highlighted—always under the vertex of psychoanalytic clinical experience:

> The issue is of practical importance to the analyst whose analysand says "I see what you mean" when he has a hallucination, say, of being sexually assaulted; what *he* means is that the *meaning* of what

> the psychoanalyst said appeared to him in a visual form and *not* that he understood an interpretation …
>
> The fact that thinking and talking play such an important part in psychoanalysis is so obvious that it is liable to escape attention. It does not, however, escape the attention of the patient who is concentrating his attacks on linking and in particular the link between himself and the analyst; such a patient makes destructive attacks on the capacity of both analyst and himself to talk or think. If these attacks are to be properly understood, the psychoanalyst needs to be aware of the nature of the targets being attacked … With my present experience I would lay more stress … on the importance of doubting that a thinker is necessary because thoughts exist. For a proper understanding of the situation when attacks on linking are being delivered it is useful to postulate thoughts that have no thinker … Thoughts exist without a thinker. The idea of infinitude is prior to any idea of the finite. The finite is "won from the dark and formless infinite" …
>
> In practice, I have found this formulation, or something like it, a helpful approximation to psychoanalytical realisations. The patient who suffers from what used to be known as disturbances of thought will provide instances showing that every interpretation the psychoanalyst gives is really a thought of his. He will betray his belief that papers or books written by others, including of course his psychoanalyst, were really filched from him. This belief extends to what in more usual patients appears as the Oedipal situation. In so far as he or she admits the facts of parental intercourse, or verbal intercourse between the psychoanalyst and himself, he is simply a lump of faeces, the product of a couple. In so far as he regards himself as his creator he has evolved out of the infinite. His human qualities (limitations) are due to the parents, by their intercourse, stealing him from himself (equated with God). The ramifications of this attitude, more clearly discerned if the psychoanalyst postulates "thoughts without a thinker", are so considerable that I require another book to attempt elucidation. Inadequate though this formulation is, I hope it will help the reader to find the continuation of the developments which I have tried to sketch out in these papers. [Bion, 1967, pp. 164–165]

This issue expresses the supreme hate that the paranoid-minded person has of parental intercourse. The person cannot conceive that he was the product of a couple. Therefore, denying thoughts without a thinker equates to saying that one creates thoughts as an expression of the more basic statement "I alone created myself". The whole subject has serious consequences for scientific endeavours:

> I would warn against the phrase "empirically verifiable data" which I employ ... I do not mean that experience "verifies" or "validates" anything. This belief, as I have come across it in the literature of the philosophy of science, relates to an experience which enables the scientist to achieve a feeling of security to offset and neutralise the sense of insecurity following on the discovery that discovery has exposed further vistas of unsolved problems—"thoughts in search of a thinker". [Bion, 1967, p. 166]

Is the obverse true or not? Experience, as a conveyor of reality, carries truth within it. If the obverse is true, the empirical data which fuel experience, when devoid of any prejudiced or pre-patterned underlying deluded theory, are the origin of a hypothesis that may or may not evolve into a theory (thesis). A few theories are timeless, and keep and convey the truth that was the stuff of the empirical data. In short: experience does not validate anything because experience—reality—is valid in itself.

Bion's position on the power of validation ascribed to experience—which differs from dismissing experience as the starting point of anything—evoked severe reactions from the establishment. He stated that thoughts produced by thinkers may be indistinguishable from hallucinations. Attempts to make this distinction are a main theme of the Trilogy, and were already adumbrated in *Attention and Interpretation*, when he linked thoughts without a thinker to truth, and thoughts with a thinker to lies:

> Provisionally, we may consider that the difference between a true thought and a lie consists in the fact that a thinker is logically necessary for the lie but not for the true thought. Nobody need think the true thought: it awaits the advent of the thinker who achieves significance through the true thought. The lie and its thinker are inseparable. The thinker is of no consequence to the truth, but the truth is logically necessary to the thinker. His significance depends on whether or not he will entertain the thought, but the thought remains unaltered. In contrast, the lie gains existence by virtue of

> the epistemologically prior existence of the liar. The only thoughts to which a thinker is absolutely essential are lies. Descartes's tacit assumption that thoughts presuppose a thinker is valid only for the lie. [Bion, 1970, pp. 102–103]

From 1975 to 1979 the concept would be elevated to its highest pitch in formulations scattered through the Trilogy and in Bion's lectures in Latin America (Buenos Aires, São Paulo, Rio de Janeiro and Brasilia), New York, Topeka, Rome and Paris.

> DOCTOR I saw a boy once who had been so well brought up that he could only tell me he had a "body ache". I nearly asked him whereabouts in his "body" this ache was, but realised, just in time to spare his blushes, that he could *not* say he had a "belly ache".
>
> P.A. Did he "blush"? Because I have known a patient who could feel he was blushing while I could detect no visible evidence of capillary dilatation. [II: 227]

> ROBIN I feel I can't remember what we were talking about before. It is curiously like dreams, for I know that I have dreamt and though I couldn't say what the dream was, I know that I have not forgotten it—it has gone. On these occasions it can come back; I don't *remember* it, but it is there, all in one piece. It is quite whole and quite absent. [II: 246]

The perception of the manifestations of Oedipus, of the two principles of mental functioning, of the positions, and the transitional phenomena—in brief, the contribution made by the greatest authors in the field of psychoanalysis—all belong to the realm of immaterial thoughts without a thinker. Alas, no theory is spared being seen as a concrete being, as the reader may already have seen in this text. If thoughts are free-floating units "in the air", waiting for a thinker who will think them, sensations of grasping may be too strong when allegiance to the principle of pleasure-displeasure and abhorrence towards the emergence of doubts are prevalent. A transformation occurs: the process of thinking thoughts is now aimed at obtaining a concrete, hallucinated final conclusion betraying the thinker's feelings of ownership of absolute truth. Lie emerges triumphantly, as Bion had warned in *Attention and Interpretation* (1970, pp. 102–3, quoted above).

In the third book of the Trilogy, Devil, who has made appearances in the first two books, becomes a most important character. In the Scriptures, Satan is seen as "the great equivocator", lying like truth. Shakespeare resorts to the same idea many times in Macbeth, a work also quoted in the Trilogy.

There is a tenuous border, always challenged by any thinker, who always risks turning into a no-thinker, murdering the thought as soon as he or she thinks it. The fragile, transient grasp is transformed into a non-grasp as soon as it emerges. The case is clearer when the thinker uses literary means—formulations in words, which were not created to furnish imagined ideas about psychic functioning. Imagination is the human mind's ability, acquired phylogenetically, to put the presentations (*Anschauung*, in Freud's parlance, rather than representations) of reality to the human mind itself into *visual* forms. Again, the border between real imagination and hallucination—the thought which was murdered by its thinker—is fragile and delicate. In any case, musical, mathematical and religious formulations are a safer haven to keep the thought in a secure existence, awaiting a thinker to think it and murder it. The myth of the Phoenix is a good model for truth: it is robust and will prevail, but its perception can be obliterated, mainly due to the prevalence of the pleasure-displeasure principle.

The fate of any thought, when it is verbally formulated, is that the word-construct imprisons and enslaves the "thought" which was previously free-floating. The end product of any thought processes which are verbally formulated is, generally speaking, an ossified prison. The only exceptions are works by transcendent authors, like Shakespeare. At the end of the main text of the Trilogy, Bion puts an avowal in the last utterance of the character P.A.:

> P.A. There are no labels attached to most options; there is no substitute for the growth of wisdom. Wisdom or oblivion—take your choice. From that warfare there is no release. [III: 576]

One may see the similarity of P.A.'s observation to a maxim often attributed to Thomas Jefferson, that the price of freedom is eternal vigilance. Jefferson endowed his phrase with a "social-istic" tone (social-ism and narcissism were defined earlier in this work; see also Bion, 1960b; review in Sandler, 2005). It contrasts with Bion's comment, which has a "narcissistic" tone. The term "war" cannot be taken exclusively as a metaphor. It takes for granted that one realises the eternal movement of facing the unknown that characterises life as it is, and the basic human anxieties about natural hostilities, internal and external.

Institutionalisation of psychoanalysis should be a form of abiding and containing resistance to psychoanalysis. The tendency to perform preferentially what can be regarded as a "concrete thinking", as well as a preference for sensification, should be regarded as powerful resistances against mind, real thinking, feeling—life itself.

Wisdom can be seen as a posture outside the legal, pedagogic and religious fields, without any pretension to replace them, but as an addition to these other vertices. As regards the psychoanalytic vertex, wisdom cannot be separated from the complexity of emotional experiences. Under this vertex, it must be coupled with the need to keep a "monistic" posture that cannot slide down into the sensuous concretisation syndrome, and cannot allow for the prevalence of anti-alpha function. This is neither a philosophical nor a theoretical issue, even though no one is forbidden to look at it under those eminently non-practical vertices. Psychoanalysis, a practical endeavour, shows that keeping the influence of anti-alpha function to a minimum and avoiding the prevalence of the sensuous concretisation syndrome allows life as it is to blossom, in both its constructive and destructive aspects. A recurrent aspect in the real life of any human being—and therefore expressed in Bion's Trilogy and also, as a matter of consequence, in this work—is that the already complex relationship of the individual with the establishment that encircles him or her does not need to be complicated:

> ROLAND I know women who look pregnant. Sometimes they are.
>
> P.A. I *know* pregnant silences—I don't have to believe in them. Seventy-five was speaking of all talking at once as a bedlam.
>
> PRIEST Milton spoke of Pandemonium.
>
> DEVIL That was before Reason took the chairmanship.
>
> P.A. And Bedlam—only because Reason was such a bad Chairman. The so-called laws of *logic* were a prescription for Chaos. They left no living space at all for vitality. Even today it would be stillborn if it had not found refuge in what Alice would call craziness or—

DOCTOR Manic-depressive psychosis, or hysteria or schizophrenia, etcetera, etcetera, etcetera—and quite right too.

P.A. Or the Royal College of physicians, or the Royal College of Surgeons.

DOCTOR Or the International Psychoanalytical Association, or the Church.

DEVIL "Go it Justice, go it Percy, Go it Eustace, go it Mercy." I love to hear it—it's music to my ears! All are dead—and all so lively.

P.A. All Institutes are dead and therefore conform, like all inanimate objects, to laws and bye-laws which are comprehensible within the limits of human understanding. However, as they are composed of individuals who are liable to develop, the Institution begins to yield to pressure.

TERM So did my uterus; I had had enough if it—the fear of having my life squeezed out of me compelled me to compel *it* to yield to my counter-pressure. [III: 446]

ROSEMARY Even if his alimentary canal can learn no more he opens his eyes wide to take in what his belly can't. Then his eyes are so stuffed with Beauty that he cannot see me. Not even Homer had the wit to see that Helen of Troy was not just an ecto-dermal proliferation. [II: 467]

P.A. His ideas were buried beneath a memorial so deep they could not be heard. It is hard to determine the extent to which an idea survives, deteriorates or develops although apparently we can compare our present ideas with ideas we once had. The words in which we dress ideas disguise, as readily they display, the meaning to which we aspire. Call ourselves what we will, whether Bacon, Truth, Poet, Newton or Bach, we all disappear. But ideas do not "appear"; that is an attribute of "things".

ROBIN "Ideas" are "things"; maybe we have to review our ideas about ideas. [III: 478]

Are there factors linked to what psychiatrists and psychoanalysts identify as mania functioning in the establishment and maintenance of social institutions? Is institutional life an outlet for people who are not able, or willing, to maintain a closer, intimate contact with themselves, with their unconscious? Are the institutions devoted to the study, development and maintenance of psychoanalysis, that is, the establishment hitherto described both by itself and by the encircling social establishment as "psychoanalytic", or, in Freud's terms, the psychoanalytic movement, naturally born from mania and have mania in their DNA? Is the relative attraction and fascination for the establishment's bureaucratic life, including fascination for personal fame, reduced to its bare psychological nous, an expression of resistance against the unknown, and therefore, against the practice of psychoanalysis itself? Rigid, ossified, pre-patterned schemata that inhibit free thinking and free questioning sprout from these organisations, as noted by Otto Kernberg (1996), through a complicated system of laws and byelaws enforced by the political meritocracy. Is this the aftermath of a war of attrition against psychoanalysis waged by the political meritocracy, the dominant elite within the establishment, as described by Toynbee (1934–1961) and Bion (1970, p. 31)? A supreme disguise for denial, making it appear as if it were the advertised defence?

Bion took a further step in his hypothesis about the existence of thoughts without a thinker with the perspicacious observation that when the thinker makes a verbal or non-verbal—for example, mathematical or musical or chemical—formulation linked to the empirical finding that gave birth to it, the very act of formulation risks damaging the perception of the ineffable material and immaterial idea. It is, again, an observation backed by hard facts obtained in the analytic situation. The achievement of any kind of insight is a hazardous task: as soon as hints of it are felt, resistance appears; for example, the analyst, moved by desire, understanding and memory, makes a "definitive" statement. Definitions are a necessary evil in scientific communication between peers, but the relationship between patient and analyst, albeit dependent on their "scientific nucleus" (or psychoanalytic nucleus, which respects truth), is asymmetrical: they are not peers. The relationship is "hetero-", their respective functions are different. Worse still, if the act of formulation resorts to intelligible, understandable criteria, they will square off the unintelligible, but intuitable idea as if they were functioning as a prison. They are made within the rationalised boundaries of the formula; the risk is that they will kill the idea and launch the apprehension of the reality it purported to describe into oblivion—into the unconscious realm—for an unknown amount of time, which may be centuries. The transient, fleeting perception and apprehension of reality escapes from the human mind again …

> P.A. Erasmus had to break through a cultural prison wall at least as limiting as a wheat germ cell, or a pharaoh's tomb. Tutankhamen's ideas were enclosed within the preservative shell of Thebes.
>
> PRIEST But before we blame the shell for the death of the idea we should acknowledge the "preservative" function. We should not condemn the helical structure of the DNA molecule.
>
> P.A. Nor need we glorify the structure and lose sight of our ignorance of that which differentiates the animate from the apparently identical inanimate.
>
> PRIEST Socrates recognised God—the insensible, inhuman, a-biological God; God that does not obey the laws which he should obey to be comprehensible to the human All-Highest Complacency. [III: 478–9]

> ROBIN Do you make a distinction between individuals—precise, particular men and women—and their "minds"?
>
> P.A. Sometimes the distinction is irrelevant. Increasingly I am aware that there is something more than that which presents itself to my senses—sound, sight, hearing, touch. I have feelings that are aroused by something that I do not smell or touch or see or hear. My perceptions are not fine enough—blunted by the constant battering of sensuous reality. I shall not live long enough to reach *those* facts except in rudimentary degree. [III: 514–5]

Is Bion's "real psychoanalysis" the rescue of Freud's warning about the existence of loyalty to psychoanalysis or not? Freud saw it as the ability to trust, from experience, in the existence of the unconscious, the use of the dream theory and free associations, and the apprehension of the Oedipus conflict. From this, Bion extracted "faith" that truth exists. Among many of Bion's formulations that led him to state the existence of a "real psychoanalysis", one may regard the following conjoined quotations taken from different parts of the Trilogy, which try to integrate technical hints about dream formation and the analyst's interpretations or constructions (Freud, 1937b), two of the *raisons d'être* of psychoanalysis. Among the many quotations included in this work, they furnish a kind of simple—as distinct from simplistic—and straightforward "how to" handbook written for the psychoanalyst with good enough experience:

> P.A. There is an ambiguity here because the dreamer is not distinguished from the sage or poet. The dreamer is like the drunkard—often in a state of decreased conscious efficiency. To be efficient the human has to be conscious, or, as we say, "has to have all his wits about him". We are concerned not with what the individual *means* to say so much as with what he does *not* intend to say, but does in fact say.
>
> ROLAND That depends on your interpretation of *what* he says—not what he *says*.
>
> P.A. I am concerned with what he says and what it is about. My interpretation is my attempt to formulate *what* he says so that he can compare it with his other ideas.
>
> ROLAND If I say I am going to Munden I mean just that; I don't mean I am going to have a sexual orgy.
>
> P.A. If, as is the case, I am having a social intercourse with you, I am concerned only with the fact that you intend to go to Munden. If you were coming to me for medical advice I would be concerned with your physical fitness to go, and would expect to hear and observe for myself what medical matters were involved in your journey from here to there. If you said you wanted mental help I would regard the intention "to go to Munden" as "peripheral" to what is involved. If I considered that I had your permission to find out what was involved in coming to me and in "going to Munden", I would direct my response to the area signalised by the words "sexual orgy".
>
> ROBIN In other words—sex.
>
> P.A. No, not sex—the area signalised by the word Roland used.
>
> ROLAND Only words?
>
> P.A. No. Anything that appeared to be used as signals. Words, as Freud mentioned, are part of a recent invention, the human capacity to converse. There are many older and more primitive methods: sexual methods, for example. [II: 269–70]

P.A. A sexual situation affords the conditions for a sexual interpretation, an analytical situation affords an opportunity for a psychoanalytic interpretation.

ALICE What *is* a psychoanalytic interpretation?

P.A. It must be perspicacious and perspicuous. That is—

ROLAND These long words!

P.A. —an expression of a scientifically accurate insight which is phrased in a language comprehensible by the listener. It must be believed to be true by the analyst, and his formulation should be in terms that would penetrate the barriers of the listener's incomprehension.

ALICE Oh, I know—that would get through my thick feminine skull.

ROSEMARY Well, I *don't* know!

P.A. You both give an example of the difficulty I am talking about. Alice, hostile, "thinks" I am an obtuse male; Rosemary "remembers" my learnedness. Both—feelings, and ideas remembered—produce an obscurity. [III: 459–60]

The descriptions "simple" and "psychoanalyst with good enough experience" may catch the attention of some readers. They were used in the sentence "they furnish a kind of simple—as distinct from simplistic—and straightforward 'how to' handbook written for the psychoanalyst with good enough experience". Is it an exercise of eulogy or idolatry? Or is it backed by hard evidence obtained in Bion's text, according to the definition of the methods used in the present work?

Through Bion's *precise* typecasting of the characters, he presents an internal reflection which puts under critical scrutiny (i) the romantic, "revolutionary" statements from adolescence, in the light of psychoanalytical experience; and (ii) the common idea that a person in his forties has acquired good enough experience of whatever it is. In the psychoanalytic field, they transform their pedagogical ideas and non-analysed vanity into political acts:

EIGHTEEN YEARS "His own name over all!" It is too sad to think about.

P.A. That is a common fallacy, though it is a habit to which a psychoanalytic intercourse seems prone. But that is not the aim which the analyst pursues.

FORTY YEARS What is his aim?

P.A. That depends on a great many factors, notably on whether he has a disposition compatible with the work he does, his age and experience—

FORTY YEARS Are you referring to his training?

P.A. In part. I do not mean to restrict it to his analytic training, or even to his university, school or home training. All those are important; but I have in mind the need to distinguish between experience of knowledge imparted by others and knowledge derived from the analyst's ability to turn what his senses tell him into nourishment.

FORTY YEARS I don't think I understand.

P.A. As an example of what I mean, I take your last statement. In so far as you *do* understand, I suspect the "thing" you understand will contribute to your growth. In so far as you *don't* understand, I suspect that it cannot and does not lead to growth.

FORTY YEARS You are very cautious; why do you say you "suspect" that it does or does not? Or am I being pedantic?

P.A. Not at all. I *try* to be precise and therefore "suspect". I cannot *know* because even if I do not understand I may be able to turn that fact to good account by learning that there are some things which I do not understand; whereas if I were an intolerant man I would dismiss the experience before I had time to learn from it. [III: 458]

The character P.A.'s caution seems to be justified, in the name of reality. He is dealing with a "person"—named Forty Years—who is pressed by his own internal paranoid nuclei, in declaring both his lack of understanding and his present inability to tolerate such a lack. This occurs at the age of forty—one may mature or decay from this age. If the interlocutor was a person more prone to allowing a freer transit between his own paranoid-schizoid and depressive positions, it would be safe to be less cautious, and affirm that "the 'thing' you *do not* understand *may* contribute to your growth" without putting the discussion into a non-conversational realm, that of agreements and disagreements.

PART II

TO SOUTHERN SHORES

THE UNHEIMLICH

P.A. Effusions of the unconscious—

PRIEST "Unconscious"—what's that?

P.A. "God"—what's that?

PRIEST I realise you think I know as little about God as you do, and perhaps I know even less about the unconscious, but I meant it seriously when I asked you about the unconscious. Do you know more about it than the usual theories of Freud and Melanie Klein and the rest? Do you know the extent to which qualified psychoanalysts are unconscious of reality, even the realities of psychoanalysis? Those

I have seen individually and at their congresses appear to me only to be capable of grasping that narrow range of phenomena which fall, so to speak, within the rational band of the spectrum. Unless you can formulate your "discoveries" within the range of rational, articulate speech you are not satisfied that you "know". [II: 387]

CHAPTER NINE

Mutual interchange

Absolutist political regimes dominated many parts of Europe, such as Portugal and Spain, in a period which extends from the Medieval to the Modern epochs. In the Renaissance as well as in the time of the geographical discoveries, the upper social classes were contemptuous of productive work. It was socially downgraded, relegated to the lower classes and slaves. Even though they were preceded by the Vikings, people from the Iberian Peninsula ventured to discover and get the better of overseas lands through an exploitative approach. Some indigenous people from Central and South America at first reacted to the initially cautious approach of the future conquerors in a slightly different way in comparison to the inhabitants of the northern countries in America as well as of Asian countries, whose fierce resistance was their hallmark. A more ambivalent response included a "civilised" delusion which translated itself into a comparatively amiable contact. It is well known that the main ruler of the Aztecs, Montezuma, mistook Hernán Cortés, the Spanish conquistador, for an emissary sent by the heavens. Such a fatal error clouded his vision to Cortés's bestial intentions. In any case, Montezuma's amiable reception of Cortés, expressed by a somewhat contradictory openness to foreign influences, can be seen as a forerunner of what happened in the next five centuries in some parts of America; it was heightened as soon as the colonists replaced the indigenous inhabitants and tried to implant their own social customs. They construed a Paradise Regained myth around the ruthlessly conquered land in order to attract future settlers. Among the Latin American countries, Brazil seemed to be specially made for the spreading of this myth, due to its scenic endowments.

The overall similarity between Portuguese and Spanish trends of colonisation was skin-deep; apart from the language, there were important differences which made Brazil a unique country in Latin America. The peculiar Portuguese way, already tried in Asia—especially in Macao and Goa—resulted in a special form of a paradoxical development which may be described as a structured, despotic and enlightened kleptocracy.

Its historic origins can be found in an unparallelled piece of research by Raymundo Faoro, a lawyer and sociologist born in the southernmost Brazilian state of Rio Grande do Sul, a culturally mixed part of Brazil adjacent to Argentina and Uruguay, countries which were colonised by Spain. Mr Faoro made the deepest and most comprehensive sociological study of the origins of the ruling classes in Brazil. Deeply influenced by Max Weber, the independent-minded Mr Faoro was determined not to be engulfed by either the "leftist" or the "rightist" fashionable ideologies which were at their peak in his lifetime. Through the counsel of a friend, his book was given a title that today could well name a box office hit dealing with political conspiracies or a weird saga of bodybuilding and martial arts: *Os Donos do Poder* (The Owners of Power, 1958). The scholarly book describes how the primitive capitalistic, militarised, pseudo-feudalist Portuguese political system was transplanted to Brazil with the purpose of extracting natural resources. Members of the Portuguese emperor's family were instantly installed as military landowners in the conquered country through appointment and delegated empowerment. They quickly enhanced the pyramidal, military-bureaucratic network under the aegis of the Jesuit-Catholic *Weltanschauung* into a novel scheme of government: "hereditary captaincies" which did not have constraints imposed by the territorial proximity of the Emperor.

The colony proved to be frustrating for its new owners: the country, in contrast to those colonised by their brethren from Spain, was devoid of what were regarded as precious mineral goods such as gold, silver and gems. Greedy "power owners" ruthlessly resorted to enslaving the indigenous people, whose cultural development was on a par with that of the Mesolithic period (Kroeber, 1948). Nevertheless, the local people were skilled at evading the condition of slavery imposed by the Portuguese, and were swiftly replaced by slaves transported from Africa. In 1600, Brazil had four million inhabitants; half of them were black slaves. From Brazil's official discovery in 1500, one century was enough for revenues from internal slave trafficking to exceed those from the extraction of sugar.

Estamento and openness to foreign ideas

The "power owners" formed a new social class with the untranslatable name *estamento*: the elite formed from the few transplanted families and militarised public servants who became the brokers of the main sources of commerce, African slaves and sugar. Until the mid-1700s, Brazil proved to be a recalcitrantly underdeveloped country. There were short-lived invasions of small parts of the huge country both by the Dutch, who decided that it was better to move to New York, and by the French, who decided to settle in Guiana.

As distinct from the US, the *estamento* made up of *quatrocentões* needed no war because a form of social contract emerged that can be described as "pseudo". For example, there was a pseudo-independence from Portugal which produced half independence and half dependence, proclaimed by an Emperor, Pedro I, acting on behalf of landowners in huge parts of the south-eastern and central areas (Rio de Janeiro, São Paulo, Minas Gerais). Pedro I abdicated in favour of his son a decade later, returning to Portugal to continue as the Emperor Pedro IV. (+Half) + (–Half) gives nothing. From then until now, this has been the social history of Brazil.

At that time, the crumbling Portugal, formerly known for its maritime and military feats, seemed to be easy prey to the ambitious Napoleon Bonaparte. The budding British Empire offered protection under certain conditions: the Portuguese emperor and his retinue hurriedly moved to Brazil as a last-ditch attempt to save themselves. Such protection had a cost, deemed fair by the Portuguese: Britain would have privileged entry into the *estamento*. They obtained exclusivity in the export of natural resources and the import of British manufactured and industrial goods—as well as a definite disapproval of the commercial use of human beings. From then on, people from the United

Kingdom came to Brazil to work as agents of the commercial liaison; using neither direct enforcement by overt military invasion nor direct work on the land, Britain made huge profits as brokers. The relatively small Brazilian production of gold was almost entirely delivered to London—even now, the Bank of England keeps in its vaults most of the Brazilian-made ingots from that era. Culturally, the previously definite Catholic influence was amended by a Protestant tone, first expressed with a virtual order to decrease the slave trade: no British warships—usually commanded by pirates at the service of His or Her Majesty—would protect vessels trafficking human beings. Portuguese and British families maintained strong ties with their countries of origin, often sending their children to be educated there.

Britain's privileged access to the *estamento*, both economically and culturally, did not diminish Brazil's tradition of offering an open door to (as well as being dependent on) European ideas. Quite the contrary; coherently with the typically British culture of welcoming some foreign people, especially the politically persecuted, Brazil acquired this custom, already enhanced by Thomas Jefferson's and Thomas Paine's enlightened doctrines, mixed with the ideology of the French revolution. Influential people were attracted by a growing *estamento*, now made up of the agricultural producers of Central and South-Eastern Brazil. Social inequality prevailed; the social system was maintained through the virtual non-existence of a local bourgeoisie. The population was made up of a tiny ruling elite, who ruled with an iron-handed, militarised political system, and the mass of illiterate, uneducated heirs of a mixture of indigenous people and black slaves, who easily bred with the Portuguese colonists. This social system was fully described by many authors only in the 20th century. The earliest research was done by Gilberto Freyre, a French-educated sociologist from the most illiterate region of Brazil. His book *Casa Grande & Senzala* (Freyre, 1933; translated as "The Masters and the Slaves") is regarded as a classic. He later coined the term "social democracy" in his attempt to describe the calm miscegenation that occurred in Brazil, as opposed to the apartheid in other countries such as the US and South Africa. His sociological theories were soon followed by Sérgio Buarque de Holanda's *Raizes do Brasil* (1936; translated as "Roots of Brazil"), in which he coined the concept of the "cordial people"; and by Caio Prado Júnior's *Formação do Brasil Contemporâneo* (1942; translated as "The Colonial Background of Modern Brazil"). "Cordial" seemed to be an apt description for the superficially calm, pseudo-pacifist and open behaviour of the Brazilian population. It is true that warmongering, revolutionary instincts and external wars were and still are a rarity there, in comparison with the history of other countries. The very late appearance of those socio-anthropological studies whose circulation is still limited to the rarefied, ruling elite exemplifies the dire, illiterate condition of the whole population.

In the last twenty years of the 19th century, Brazil risked being invaded by a British-French coalition: the governments which sponsored African slavery regarded the country as "culturally underdeveloped"—which under international law allowed its political domination by the forces of the "developed" world: a rationalisation of what was called the Age of Imperialism. Brazil had a multicultural society made of the *estamento*, former colonists who settled there permanently in order to construct their own country. While the US and Europe underwent serious socio-political changes mainly with the establishment of democracies, the political system made by the *estamento* still exists: from 1900 onwards, the few ruling families were called, sometimes as a pedantic self-eulogy and sometimes in derisive and envious tones by the excluded mass, the *quatrocentões* (the four-century families). The *quatocentões* maintained the tradition of sending at least some of their heirs to Europe for a good education. Very few of them acquired a limited renown as creative artists; fewer still made technological feats.

The "power owners" were and still are able to dominate huge amounts of public money. They created public services and also, from 1889 onwards, perfected the already existing embryonic pseudo-democracy—which implemented good enough changes to keep the status quo in good order, precluding real changes that could be made by the people themselves. The "pseudo" way applied to economics—now dependent on another monoculture, coffee, with a brief spell in natural rubber—resulted in almost two centuries of macro-economic failures. Brazil became chronically over-dependent on foreign money. Even though it was officially a Catholic country, at that time another "open-door" policy accepted new waves of migrants, adding to the miscegenation: famine in Italy and Japan and religious persecution in the Middle East and Europe brought enterprising individuals from mildly educated cultures to the South and Southwest regions. The attempts to bring a piece of their original countries—as had occurred in the US and Canada—was increased. In any case, it was a reality that Brazil was more open to the influx of foreign cultural ideas.

Coherent with the overall social attitude, there was comparatively early adhesion to psychoanalytic ideas in Brazil: Dr Franco da Rocha, the first professor of psychiatry in the first government-sponsored university in São Paulo state—already Brazil's powerhouse, with the bulk of its budding industries—translated some books by Freud in 1919. In the late 1920s one of his pupils, Dr Durval Marcondes, made the introduction of psychoanalysis and its movement to Brazil his *raison d'être*. He re-enacted Dr Franco's fruitful contact with Freud and became the only person in Brazil who exchanged personal letters with him and other leading pioneers of the psychoanalytic movement. At his request, Ernest Jones was able to send the first three training analysts to Brazil, unwittingly helped by the misery inflicted on Europe by the criminal-minded German dictatorship: Dr Adelheid Koch (1936), from Berlin, and later Drs Henrique Schlomann and Theon Spanoudis (1951), from Berlin and Izmir respectively.

St John the Baptist reborn

The first volume of this work mentioned the writer Arnold Zweig, who became a close friend of Freud. An illustrative model of the Brazilian social environment when psychoanalysis finally reached its shores may be the end of the life of his unrelated namesake, Stefan Zweig, an author of world-wide best-sellers who also befriended Freud.[1] Both men were faced by forced migration thanks to the Nazi phenomenon; Arnold went to Palestine and in 1948 returned to Eastern Germany; Stefan ended up in Brazil.

Psychoanalysis was born at the time of "social revolutions" ideally made to stop the horrendous social inequality—heirs of the French revolution. People acting as mobs enshrined absolute truth at the expense of a sense of truth (Bion, 1961b). Romanticism, as a mass movement, may be seen as a debased offshoot of the Romantic Movement, a term that could be reserved for a movement of the mind initiated by the Renaissance and the Enlightenment—counter-movements against the imposition of dogmas and the absolutist prevalence of the authoritarian personality that characterised the immediately preceding periods. Karl Marx can fairly be seen as the prototypical figure at the time of the "social revolutions". His main wish was to be a revolutionary contributor to the theory of economics. He invented a utopian pseudo-rational system with romantic libertarian pretensions. If the government fails, get rid of it, he wrote in the *Manifesto* and other works. He ended up with a fashionable pamphleteer religion, dependent on the charisma of demagogues, called "communism": a political movement doomed to enshrine the financially dispossessed, the future political elites. The human phenomenon that we may call "Karl Marx" may be regarded as a yet another product of an era, something that repeats itself because human beings are stubbornly resistant to learning from experience. This un-learning from experience, in the belief that un-learning is superior to learning, propagates itself on a logarithmic scale in social groups and, in consequence, in trans-generational un-learning. The demagogue profits from forgetfulness—which is both culturally and biologically determined, because learning depends on the input of knowledge.

Karl Marx wanted to make contributions to a scientific theory of economics; nevertheless, he was prey to the positivist religion, the one that claimed to be the one and only science and proved to be applicable just to a constrained and limited range of facts. Its religious content—beliefs on cause and effect relationships, predictions, abhorrence of paradoxes, and reductionist views about material facts, disregarding what belongs to the immaterial—hampered its progress into the unknown.

Positivism, a hitherto unrecognised pseudo-science, was destined to be a religion—a fact fully acknowledged by Auguste Comte, its best theoretician. As regards Marx, he turbocharged the "revolutionary" mania imposed in social engineering that claimed to know the ultimate, final and absolute truth. It seemed to be such a seductive virus that Marx—perhaps more successfully than anyone else, with the exception of his friend Engels—spared no effort in propagating it, appealing to the basest instincts of humanity, such as greed and envy. Marx's concept of "infrastructure" may be seen as an early insight into the existence of invariants; perhaps he was genuinely interested in libertarian pretensions, the Romantic *development* of the Enlightenment's interest in the individual being. But in resorting to enticement, or provoking the destructive self-feeding cycle of envy and greed so typical of humankind, Marx started a "class war" wholly dependent on the charisma of demagogues. After many previous works by Allan Bullock, Ian Kershaw and others, Timothy Snyder fully described the effects of enthusiasm in *Bloodlands: Europe between Hitler and Stalin* (Snyder, 2010).

These were typical of the decadent era of Romanticism, an offshoot of the Romantic Movement based on excesses, enthusiasm and paranoid distortion of the achievements of the Enlightenment. It enshrined absolute truth at the expense of a sense of truth in a movement called "communism", doomed to enshrine political elites variously called *nomenklatura, intelligentsia,* etc. It is well known that the first victims of a "revolution" are its first leaders. A mythical predecessor of it may be seen in the story of St John the Baptist.

Marx made a few apolitical observations about the history of humankind untainted by adolescent impossible promises. One of them (1852) attained the status of a metaphor, noting that historic facts and people appear twice, first as tragedy, then as farce. In other words, Marx saw the falsity ingrained in repetition or imitation of any kind; or better, its hallucinated ethos. Years later, Freud added to this social insight in observing, under the psychoanalytic vertex, the hallucinated nature of transference (Freud, 1912a)—a fact recalled and expanded by Philips (1989), who seems to be the first to observe the intimate link of imitation with what psychoanalysis usually regards as identification.

Arnold Zweig and Stefan Zweig could not see that history does not *really* repeat itself. The final years of Stefan Zweig in Brazil furnish a fair model that may help us grasp what constitutes one of the main bearings of *A Memoir of the Future*: namely, the seemingly eternal love that humankind, especially in its male gender, nourishes for the paranoid-schizoid position. In other words, the hateful relationship that the male of the species, with slight but important differences in comparison with the female, maintains with a more serene emotional development that must have a good enough regard for truth and love. If this regard is kept in shape, there occurs, as a matter of consequence, a good enough apprehension of truth—which in turn requires a good enough condition to deal with pain with no evasion or subterfuge. Using yet another formulation but meaning the same thing, emotional development demands an increasing disregard for desire and for deluded fulfilment of pleasure (Freud, 1911a).

People who could have been regarded, under a psychoanalytically trained vertex, as narcissistic personalities, or inhabiting the paranoid-schizoid position in a quasi-exclusive mode (as seen in those labelled as schizophrenics and, albeit in a different mechanism, psychopaths), are able, as a condition of their very existence, to observe the existence of truth. But this is not matched by a good enough condition to deal with it. So they resort to negation and rationalisation in order to evade the truth as soon as they discover it. Stefan Zweig may have seemed to be able to see truth to the point of being a socio-political visionary.

He marvelled at the public reaction to him as well as at the hospitality typical of the Brazilian people, especially at that time—the "cordial Brazilian" was just being depicted by Sérgio Buarque de Holanda. Zweig became romantically enthused with Brazil; the natural, almost insurmountable beauty of its beaches—especially in Rio de Janeiro and Bahia—and the entrepreneurial environment of São Paulo made him write another romance, tainted with reality's inks. Its title embodied an undisguised prophecy which would please later authors of fictional best-sellers *disguised as* reality (like Ian Fleming or Frederick Forsythe): *Brazil, Land of the Future* (1941). The Paradise regained seemed, again, to be located in Brazil. From time to time, the same idea reappears, mainly as a political banner to entice international investors.

Today one has the benefit of hindsight which was denied to Mr Zweig. Until the dawn of the 21st century, his prophecy was kept alive. It became an anathema which bordered on hubris. Another book might more properly be entitled, in the form of a paraphrase, *Brazil, Land of Unfulfilled Promises.* Undoubtedly less flattering, but, human life being as it is, more realistic. For example, in the 1980s, an economics periodical—*Business Week*—used the neologism "kleptocracy" to describe Brazil's economic policies. The term was soon extended to other countries.

Stefan Zweig was highly infatuated with his reborn worldly fame, even though it was now limited to a little-known country. He enjoyed the favours of the Brazilian dictator of that time, a former lawyer and political leader from the Pampas named Getúlio Dornelles Vargas, who led a successful military coup to depose the previously elected president, Washington Luís, after having been a member of his cabinet. Both were typical members of the *estamento,* which was now split. Vargas's government, under his own guidance, increased the admission of German spies and facilitated the entry of German nationals. He restructured the Brazilian police, modelling it on the Gestapo, and appointed Filinto Müller, a violent man, to manage it. Nazi gatherings became the rule in the southernmost region of Brazil, the place where Vargas was born and politically dominant until his death by suicide in 1954. Having obtained technical assistance and enough money to build Brazil's first iron ore extraction and corresponding steel production plant, Vargas and the *estamento* who kept him in power maintained their ideological and personal alignment with the Axis Powers. Pundits—today called "Brazilianists"—attributed to him a rare political intelligence. Many of them observed that Vargas first hammered on the horseshoe and then on the nail—this became a popular saying among historians, journalists and political scientists. He was skilled in alternating this Janus cycle to suit his own convenience.

Vargas initially acted as a benefactor to Zweig, allowing him to enter the country in 1940, and made use of the title of Zweig's optimistic book (1941) to enhance the political propaganda of his government. "Brazil, Land of the Future" soon became a political slogan, heavily used by the Brazilian authoritarian government at a time when American, British and also French cultural, economic and financial influence had been shrinking since 1930. A sizeable part of the *estamento* was more interested in German-Italian fascism, which had much more in common with their traditional ideology, based on racial prejudice, to dominate ruthlessly the illiterate masses. The propaganda tactics of the government, a scaled-down imitation of Dr Goebbels's mesmerising techniques, swiftly profited from Zweig's book, which earned Zweig the contradictory title of "right-winger". It was ironic that Zweig, who was Jewish and had fled to Brazil to escape the Nazis, found favour with a president who was rather unsympathetic towards Jews.

Vargas was courted by Franklin Delano Roosevelt in the difficult early years of US involvement in World War II because the Allied forces badly needed refuelling bases in the South Atlantic, as well as strategic basic materials and commodities for the war industry. Vargas cleverly profited from Roosevelt's "Good Neighbour" policy. He was skilled at making requests for money and transfer of know-how in order to allow industrialisation in Brazil. On the other hand, he continued flattering Adolf Hitler in many ways, sending him birthday gifts and other tokens of appreciation, and continuing to do so secretly even after his declaration of war against the Axis Powers in August 1942.

Observing the course of events, in early 1942 Stefan Zweig became convinced that Hitler was bound to invade his beloved adopted country. His state of mind, so similar to that of the dictators and of any paranoid-driven mind, "endowed" him with the feeling of ownership of absolute truth. He saw growing numbers of people claiming that the Nazis would be very welcome as soon as they arrived to be the real conquerors of the tropical shores—even though Hitler saw Brazil as a failed state inhabited by "a mongrel, useless people" (Gunther, 1941; Kershaw, 1998; Trevor-Roper, 1953), and trusted that the descendants of German migrants, who had lived in rather large colonies since 1876, could take care of local Germanisation.

At this point, Zweig entertained no second thoughts about committing suicide, taking with him his wife, Lotte. He was tragically wrong in his absolute idea, as is anyone who performs this kind of un-thinking, which is more typical of psychotics who select their preferred ideas and split reality to apprehend just the part of it that coincides with their own desire, enthroned as the absolute truth. Enthused un-thinking, dominated by the then common debasement of the Romantic idea (Russell, 1946; Taylor, 1967; Snyder, 2010) of "revolutions", was revealed by Freud as appertaining to the realm of hallucinosis and delusion. The "World of Dictators" (Denson & Bacheller, 1961) attributed power to people who hide their individual cowardice behind the powerful shield of the ferocity of mobs and groups. "Never underestimate the ferocity of a coward", said Theodore Roosevelt to his guide on a journey to the Amazon basin, Marshal Cândido Rondon (Roosevelt, 1914). Three years after Zweig's suicide, Adolf Hitler did the same thing. Being rightly accused of corruption, Vargas also committed suicide, eleven years after Zweig's death.

Zweig had a share of truth in his perception of Brazil as a trailblazer—even if it happened in other areas: the kleptocratic government in which huge amounts of public money funnelled to "public services" had produced macro-economic failures, now called "bubbles". Again and again, destructive greed and the consequent banality win the day—and both will win, until overall awareness about them finally comes about. Overall awareness does not mean an apocalyptic, religious, Manichean sense of "good" against "evil", but means a homeostatic sense of dynamic equilibrium signalled by Fechner and recalled by Freud, Klein and Bion. More specifically, a tandem movement, or ⇔—including anxiety about unavoidable personal annihilation—between the instincts of life and death, the paranoid-schizoid and depressive positions. Or will humankind perhaps exterminate itself before this day comes? The prevalent search for happiness and complete fulfilment appears in all known eras of human existence, irrespective of place, time or any other factor.

⇔: *Hope, optimism and demand:*[2] *persistence versus insistence*

Hope: This writer's training analyst, Mrs Judith Seixas de Carvalho Andreucci, as soon as she became aware of his proposed endeavour (the publication of an introduction to the Trilogy), warned him with the aid of a metaphorical model: "Do you really want to do the same thing that St John the Baptist did?" The commonsense warning was disregarded through rational justifications roasted in the fire of a postponed adolescent enthusiasm.

Optimism: A twisted view of reality, based on denial, split the fact that the precocious dismissal was not limited to the Trilogy *A Memoir of the Future*, but applied to all of Bion's contributions. As the publishers, who are usually sensitive to the reactions of the book market, said at the time, "Bion is a poor seller". As occurred with Freud and psychoanalysis in its first fifty years, the influence of Freud's contributions was proportional neither to sales of his books nor to the number of people who sought analysis.

Demand: The original Brazilian edition of the present work,[3] published over a quarter of a century ago, was written to *help* people read Bion's Trilogy in the Portuguese language.

Fact: In the end, it came to be used as an undue replacement. It sold more copies than "The Dream" and "O Sonho", the English and Portuguese versions of the first volume of the Trilogy, put together. This was the reverse of what was planned. Reality tricks the planner. Is it the unconscious invariant driving Freud's three impossible professions: teaching, governing and psychoanalysing?

Paradoxically, the abridged Brazilian predecessor of the present work received attention and even eulogies from outstanding Brazilian and foreign analysts. Virginia Leone Bicudo (1910–2003), one of the founders of SBPSP (Brazilian Psychoanalytic Society of São Paulo, 1949), who performed the function of being the real soul of its teaching organ, called "The Institute", was the first to introduce Klein's and Bion's work to Brazil. Together with her own former analyst, Frank Philips, they spread the word about Bion's contributions in a practical way. Mrs Bicudo, who was this writer's second "official" supervisor, encouraged him to publish the Introduction to *A Memoir of the Future*. James Grotstein, Meg Harris Williams and, to a certain extent, Donald Meltzer also wrote letters giving kind encouragement. At the same time, Frank Philips, whose kindness did not disguise his ambivalence, agreed to write a preface to this researcher's Portuguese version of *A Memoir of the Future*. He started the preface with the comment that "Dr Paulo Sandler has chosen an ungrateful task in making a translation of *A Memoir of the Future*" (Philips, 1989).

Mr Philips was a person given to making definitive statements: he judged that the Trilogy was a work that could be accessible only to those who had lived in England. When he became aware that this writer had never lived in England, Mr Philips brought to an abrupt end the previously useful conversations that both of us were enjoying. Unflustered, this writer carried on with the work. About a year later, another surprise: Francesca Bion's personal appeal to Mr Philips made him reconsider his decision. The consequence of her appeal was a return of the conversations about the forms used in the translation.

As soon as the incomparable raconteur Albert Mason became acquainted with the existence of a translation of Bion's Trilogy to the Portuguese language, he wanted to see it. Dr Mason, an Englishman, had been a friend of Bion and Philips since the 1950s. With characteristic and percipient irony, he swiftly mixed an apparent observation with a challenge: "Well, if you have completed the first translation of the *Memoir* into a foreign language ever to appear … could you now kindly translate it into English?" His request-question contained at least one stimulus, perhaps partially fulfilled now. The following reminder, as it was published in the abridged Brazilian version of the present book twenty-seven years ago, may be paradoxically and sadly timely:

> Ten years ago, Imago Editora released "The Dream", Volume I of Bion's Trilogy *A Memoir of the Future*; 1977 marked the publication of Volume II ("The Past Presented"), and during 1979 the first posthumous editing effort from his dedicated wife Francesca produced the printed version of Volume III, endowed with a poetical title, "The Dawn of Oblivion". In 1982, the Brazilian quarterly *Revista Brasileira de Psicanálise* published a review of volume I written by me. I was surprised and could not reconcile myself with the fact that it constituted a typical case of "ante Agamemnona multi". The Trilogy was written seven years ago. Despite its relative youth, it was doomed to an undeserved fate: metaphorically, that of a Bach devoid of his Mendelssohn. Will the psychoanalytic world need two centuries in order to really discover this work, *A Memoir of the Future*? Who knows if psychoanalysis, and the human race, will survive that long? The same threats that afflict us may have correspondences in the psychoanalytic world, or the psychoanalytic movement, according to Freud (1914). Namely, ecological problems, or hate against Nature and Reality, and therefore hate against

> science and art, reflected by phenomena such as deforestation, the banality of everything, including nuclear war capability, greedy consumerism and the accompanying economics, truth—and love-hating greedy politicians, excessive bureaucratisation. Therefore, one already has enough data to suppose, as Bion did in the Trilogy, that humankind may well be a discarded experiment of Nature—it just did not see it clearly. The same threats that surround humankind can be seen in the psychoanalytic world. Witness the so-called "crisis of psychoanalysis", meaning crisis in the demand for psychoanalytic services, and continuous, perhaps perennial warnings and claims in the lay press and in part of the scientific world, that "psychoanalysis is dead"—only psychoanalysts refuse to realise this.
>
> As a mere hypothesis, let us say that the human race will survive. The survival of real psychoanalysis, here understood as a practice which follows the legacy of courage in the face of the unknown initiated by Freud—in this sense, it equates to science—may be relying on works like the Trilogy.

Therefore, the intention of the present work may be pertinent twenty-seven years later. Or it would be better to start from 1975, which makes the time span even longer. With the exception of a timid and sputtering micro-discussion among very few members of an internet discussion site since 2007, Bion's Trilogy continues to be a Bach devoid of his Mendelssohn, or a Socrates devoid of his Plato. Or perhaps not? It seems that the situation has changed a little, thanks to the persistence of Karnac Books and Francesca Bion.

A discontent of language

In Volume I we reviewed Bion's concept of "language of achievement". This enables any analyst to apprehend the universal language of the unconscious, recognisable to any human being who is able to listen to it—which goes beyond hearing it. This does not depend on an absolute command and knowledge of any specific language used by the patient, by the analyst and also by the writer and reader at large.

Werner Herzog dwelt on this theme in his film *Fitzcarraldo*. Amazon aborigines were able to appreciate operatic spectacles, a fact already confirmed in reality by Shinichi Suzuki in post-World War II Japan.

Dr Suzuki's method gave an astonishing impulse to the learning of Baroque and Romantic music in Japan. The same fact occurred in China in the late 1990s, at lightning speed: just *two* generations were needed to build up a world-class group of conductors, players and orchestras. To quote an example in the realm of minus (Sandler, 2012): the same occurred with the swift "nazification" of almost the whole population of Germany in just ten years; the "denazification" was almost as fast: fifteen years (Money-Kyrle, 1979). All of this indicates that cultural influences are epiphenomenal, offering no match for unconscious drives; acquired taste comes and goes with evanescent speed. It should be pointed out that we need to have second thoughts about the old conundrum of "nature versus nurture". Is it another false problem posed by positivism? One cannot know today what the Ancient Greeks would feel when confronted with classical—that is, transcendent—music. On the other hand, there remains the view that entertains nationalistic or patriotic optimism, due to individual omnipotent traits. This is what lies behind the restrictively authoritarian—rather than authoritative—idea that only one who was born in England could have access to the Trilogy.

The same argument was used before: only German-speaking people could have access to Freud's writings. In any case, the observation was made initially by Freud that there is a universal language of the unconscious. It stems from the universal approach, a main bearing of the Enlightenment and a most important root of psychoanalysis. This is not a denial of the fact that it helps greatly if one has a sincere interest and a mild degree of information and familiarity with "English things" (or "German", "French", whatever). It may provide a kind of introjection of the English (or German, or French) *ways* to express universal human issues. Patriotism, or nationalism, in psychoanalytical epistemology, is just another expression of the mind's denial of transcendence—a form of hate for truth—which produces a leaning towards dated immanence.

Is Marx's observation that history happens first as tragedy and repeats itself as farce valid about Bion's Trilogy? Donald Meltzer saw it is a badly written novel. His closest collaborator, Meg Harris Williams, a literary critic,[4] is—at least according to this writer's research—the first English-speaking author who was able to publish a literary examination of the Trilogy in the English language. She took due care to make it clear that her work belonged to her own field of study rather than psychoanalysis—typical of the sincerity and love for truth that characterises literary scholars who were trained in the English tradition, best exemplified in our times by Frank Kermode and Adrian Stokes. Her examination was published in the now defunct *International Review of Psychoanalysis*, a short-run, green-covered offshoot of *The International Journal of Psychoanalysis.* This in turn was then enjoying the sunset of its golden era: it was the undisputed best psychoanalytical periodical around the world. It was the personal creation of Dr Joseph J. Sandler, who in his early days had a scientific bent, but turned out to be a skilled politician in the psychoanalytic movement whose influence is still felt today. The publication of such a periodical can be fairly seen as expressing the fascination of psychoanalysts for artistic disciplines, mentioned in the first part of this work.

Mrs Williams's study was published in 1983, a few months after this researcher's paper in the *Revista Brasileira de Psicanálise* on the first volume of Bion's Trilogy. This in turn reached a perhaps negligible audience as a consequence of the fact that the Portuguese language is, for practical purposes, unknown outside Portugal and Brazil, and a few small Portuguese former colonies in Africa and Asia which do not have institutionalised psychoanalytic movements.

Better late than never?

The warning metaphor made by Mrs Andreucci proved to be sagacious. The emotional experience of finding a treasure in Bion's contributions provided an unprecedented serenity to the then young, critically minded professional who had had at the beginning of his formative years few hopeful contacts with analgesic theories, which seemed to him anodyne and impractical, because they seemed to him to be overloaded with simplistic and authoritarian explanations. Seeking the counsel of two very experienced psychoanalysts (Sandler, 1970; Yahn, 1971), he replaced this kind of study with direct contact with patients. The analysts recommended that he should postpone contact with theories and become acquainted with them later. In 1979, after he had already worked with a large number of psychotics in two mental hospitals and in a community mental health centre, both analysts recommended that he should read *Second Thoughts*, then considered to be a primer on Bion, at least in São Paulo's Institute of Psychoanalysis. While recognising that any previous reading would have been impossible for him to grasp, he also regretted not having had the necessary ability to read this book earlier. Previously ungraspable events acquired an uncommon sense, but, at least, a sense. At the same time, he was grateful to have finally read it, simultaneously with his second personal analysis—which also qualified as a "training analysis".[5]

Bion's writings were more often than not regarded as "difficult", "complicated" and "obscure"—a rare case of overt unanimity among idolaters and iconoclasts. In just one year—taking into account other reactions from the local establishment (or group), acknowledged as being influenced by Klein and Bion's contributions—this author gave up his previous attempts to state his personal ideas and feelings on reading Bion. If this was the reaction in a place where the majority of people were outspoken about what they felt as having that kind of influence, what kind of reaction would come from less sympathetic or hostile milieus? He increasingly limited the voicing of his feelings to more intimate acquaintances. Two of them were familiar with Dr Bion and his work: the already mentioned Virginia Leone Bicudo and Frank Julian Philips. Both had been part of the tiny group which founded the Sociedade Brasileira de Psicanálise de São Paulo. Mrs Bicudo, who had her second analysis with Mr Philips when he was living in London, was the first Brazilian to invite Dr Bion to come to Brazil. He agreed to come in 1973, and returned in 1974 and 1978. Like any mature man, he was fond of some features he found in Brazil and felt uneasy about others. As examples of the former reaction one may read his impressions of the commemorations celebrating the anniversary of the foundation of Brasilia, Brazil's capital, in the wilderness of the dry central areas of the country; and the episode when he asked a colleague who was taking him for a weekend in the country to stop the car because he wanted to examine some rather small flowers, seemingly unimportant to the locals, which grew naturally at the roadside (Ferrão, 1980). An example of the latter reaction were his ideas about the locals' idealised approach towards their work.

This author has made an unbroken study of the writings of Dr Bion since 1980, accompanied by equally unbroken clinical work—which benefited from the results of his attempts to apply what he had learned (Sandler, 2009, 2011, 2012). Over fifteen years, it was coupled with two personal analyses heavily influenced by Freud's, Klein's and Bion's contributions. To him, reading the Trilogy furnished treasures for his practical work in psychoanalysis. The first theoretical offshoots have already been mentioned: the first book review and the world's first translation of the Trilogy into a foreign language, Portuguese, which preceded by ten years the second translation, by Parthenope Bion Talamo and Gianni Nebbiosi, into Italian. It also preceded the Argentinian edition by twelve years. The third offshoot was the first introduction to the Trilogy—until now, the only one. The positive findings about the Trilogy were accompanied by a negative one in pondering the reaction from the group, which generally displayed too much disinformation and incomprehension—which seemed to constitute a need for spreading the word under the vertex of scientific information.

As years passed, there emerged, in few countries, *islands* of interest. This echoed what had happened with Bion's earlier contributions: people initially disinclined to study it began to read it. In this aspect, Bion was no different to Freud and Klein. In Argentina there were a sizeable number of people with a definite interest in the work of Bion, who finally began to study the Trilogy, which until then had been neglected: Dario Sor, Elizabeth Tabak and Marcelo Bianchedi. In Italy, after the appearance of the translation, scholars such as Claudio Neri, and later, Giorgio Correnti, Mario Giampà and Antonino Ferro, also displayed interest in the Trilogy; in the United States, James Grotstein and Michael Eigen, and later, Thomas Ogden. A website dedicated to chats about the work of Bion and variegated issues linked to it was established in California in 1999 by John Stone. It began to display interest in the Trilogy in 2009, to the point of offering digital versions of selected chapters to its members. This interest faded in 2010, and no whole book was offered. There was more limited interest from Simon Daniel Kippman and André Green in France. The latter was one of the first to support this writer's work; another was Kjell von Krogh in Norway. In brief: this is a case of isolated islands which do not form an archipelago.

The roster quoted above includes selected countries around the world and may be flawed; it serves as an example that demonstrates the existence of positive or allegedly positive reactions. It allows one to state that the era of studying the Trilogy in an environment similar to that of the catacombs may have passed. Whiffs of acceptance are appearing in the new millennium. The attempts of the present writer are just an expression of the phenomenon of "spreading the word" about the Trilogy. This writer wrote about the Trilogy in papers and books, mainly in Brazil, and quoted it extensively in scientific papers delivered at IPA Congresses and published worldwide (Sandler, 1987, 2001b, 2001c, 2003a). Thanks to Malcolm Pines and Robert Lipgar, an investigation of the earlier origins of Bion's work appeared in the form of a chapter in a book (Sandler, 2003b). Much of a transdisciplinary series dedicated to the apprehension of psychic reality was born from the impact on me of reading the Trilogy (Sandler, 1997–2003). An American reader of *The Language of Bion*, which also quotes extensively from the Trilogy, thanked this writer because she was "finally able to grasp what Bion pointed out in those weird books".

Overt opposition to "late Bion" still is heard loudly from some quarters. To give the current reader a general sense of reactions around the world-wide psychoanalytic movement that can be seen as typical of the establishment's posture towards the Trilogy, one must record that in most countries—including those unsympathetic to the study of Freud—dismissal reaches the point of contempt. Examples abound: two fairly recent issues of *The International Journal of Psychoanalysis* invited famous and respected (by the establishment, at least) authors to deal with "late Bion"; the Trilogy was conspicuously avoided. André Green recalled that "the mere presence of Bion in the International Congresses left many colleagues lost in feelings of fear" (Green, 2002). As analysts, we know that in social environments devoid of external manifestations of violence or aggression, the presence of individual fear means unconscious internal violence. In the guise of a hypothesis, one may conjecture that for many people, the mere presence of Bion was inextricably linked to the presence of truth. There are widespread, popular phrases that emerge almost automatically in the minds of many people when there is a mere suspicion that truth is present: "awful truth", or "ugly truth". Is this a factor in the negative reactions?

Bion acknowledged that poetry—especially that of Robert Browning and Gerard Manley Hopkins—was seminal in his construction of the Trilogy. As noticed in other texts dealing with the history of Bion's ideas, it is possible to state that those poets, among others, were his intellectual forebears—at least if the researcher follows the Vicoesque directions contained in Isaiah Berlin's works (for example, Berlin, 1956, 1968; also Sandler, 2006a). In the introduction written by Bion to *Seven Servants*, a collection of four of his earlier books (Bion, 1977c), there is a reference to Browning's *Sordello*, which often functions, at least to some readers, as a doubt-generator, as an intentional generator of confusion. Other readers felt it as a warning. In hindsight, it seems to be unsuccessful. As James Grotstein and Ignacio Matte Blanco observed, two years after Bion's death, there appeared a precocious surge of self-styled

"Bionians" (Grotstein, 1981; Matte Blanco, 1981). It is certain that they are destined to bury Bion's contributions under "a heavy tombstone of adoration" (I: 53). Bion did not agree to be part of a group that yields to the paranoid tendency of making a "who's who" roster: he thought it was "ridiculous that one is expected to participate in a sort of competition for precedence as to who is top" (Bion, 1958–1979, p. 377), and refused to be made an object of adoration. Among his motives was the fact that he saw this tendency as one of the main manifestations of hallucinosis. Being "top" helped Bion to make one of his few pedagogical hints to practising psychoanalysts, namely, his four "rules of hallucinosis", which prefigured later rules to help analysts gain discipline on memory, desire and understanding (1967). In brief:

> A. If an object is "top", it dictates "action"; it is superior in all respects to all other objects and is self-sufficient and independent of them.
> B. Objects that can occupy such a position include (a) Father, (b) Mother, (c) Analyst, (d) Aim, object or ambition, (e) Interpretation, (f) Ideas, whether moral or scientific.
> C. The only relationship between two objects is that of superior to inferior.
> D. To receive is better than to give. [Bion, 1965, p. 133]

Freud's, Klein's and Winnicott's contributions were submitted to this kind of enshrining, done by personalities prone to mechanistic repetition.

Teaching some of Bion's contributions to psychoanalysis with the help of the Trilogy

This writer's efforts to give courses about the Trilogy in the local psychoanalytic institute from 1988 aroused the interest of Professor Ryad Simon, who in 1996 set up a three-year postgraduate training course in Psychoanalytic Psychotherapy at the most prestigious state-sponsored university in Brazil. Theoretical classes were divided between four main authors: Freud, Klein, Winnicott and Bion. In 1998, this writer was invited to be responsible for teaching Bion in this course. He was given a free hand, and it was accepted that he would make use of the Trilogy to present Bion's work to people who never had studied it: an initiative unprecedented in Brazil or elsewhere. These attempts were regarded by the local establishment within a spectrum that ranged from inappropriate to crazy, reflecting reactions to the Trilogy itself. The course was taught up to 2006. In making correlations and pinpointing the illustrations the Trilogy gives of what Bion tried to convey in his earlier works, as well as using group readings where students took the roles of the many characters, the course achieved surprising results in giving them an earlier, firmer grasp of the ethos of Bion's whole work—without the affectations, tics and jargonified statements that characterised the self-styled "Bionians" around the world (Grotstein, 1981; Matte Blanco, 1981). Some of the results of this experience are recorded in a chapter of a book which describes the whole postgraduate course (Sandler, 2006b).

CHAPTER TEN

An attempt at a non-occlusive conclusion

Occlusion is a much dreaded fact that may occur in some intestinal surgery, due to youth, haste, or just sheer incompetence from one fated to be a false surgeon. It may also be a pathological outcome of some serious unnatural illness which paradoxically forms part of human nature. It consists of a blockage of the intenstinal lumen which prevents the discharge of waste to the external milieu. In its mildest forms, it provokes farts. Non-positivist, real scientific conclusions are the door of entry to new discoveries or doubts, and must not be occlusive: as Winnicott said (in *Home is Where We Start From*, 1986), the worst thing that could happen to a scientist would be that he felt he had reached a dead end—as may exist on railway routes.

One should regard the Trilogy as a continuous attempt to encircle some manifestations of the unconscious as well as a practical manual for the psychoanalyst. To some readers, *A Memoir of the Future* may seem to be a passionate act of love for truth and concern for life, free from lies, social conventions and judgmental values. In his own words, Bion did not obey the laws of "Oughtism" (II: 276–8). He furnishes no canonical prescriptions, but rather insightful organic, natural observations. "What it is" is relentlessly distinguished from the authoritarian idea of other human beings who try to impose "what it must be". It exists not as an idea of an individual, but when nature itself, ready for ages before all of us were born, composed a conversational interaction between what is naturally needed and how it is dealt with by an inquisitive, rather than rebellious, mind. This posture was described by Beethoven in the motto to the final movement of his string quartet No. 16 in F major, opus 135: "Muβ es sein? Es muβ sein" (Must it be? It must be).

The present writer supposes that the Trilogy carves a small niche to contribute to research into a realm opened by the most ancient thinkers and scientific investigators hitherto known. It has no pretension to artistic or literary value for its own sake. Is it as powerful as any artistic or scientific work as regards its capacity to get as close as possible to truth? Is it scientifically artistic and artistically scientific? One may say that the Trilogy demands an open-minded, thought-evocative, intuitive and empirically minded reader.

... & EPILOGUE
... FUGUE
... DONA EIS REQUIEM
... MANY

> All my life I have been imprisoned, frustrated, dogged by common sense, reason, memories, desires and—greatest bugbear of all—understanding and being understood. This is an attempt to express my rebellion, to say "Goodbye" to all that. It is my wish, I now realise doomed by failure, to write a book unspoiled by any tincture of common sense, reason, etc. (see above). So although I would write, "Abandon Hope all ye who expect to find any facts—scientific, aesthetic or religious—in this book", I cannot claim to have succeeded. All of these will, I fear, be seen to have left their traces, vestiges, ghosts hidden within these words; even sanity, like "cheerfulness", will creep in. However successful my attempt, there would always be the risk that the book "became" acceptable, respectable, honoured and unread. "Why write then?" you may ask. To prevent someone who KNOWS from filling the empty space—but I fear I am being "reasonable", that great Ape. Wishing you all a Happy Lunacy and a relativistic Fission ... [III: 578]

Like any wish, Bion's was fated to be unfulfilled, "doomed to failure". Taking into account that this writer is not Bion, and is not in the team of those who KNOW, it is open to him to attempt to convey the "achieving help" that Bion's Trilogy provided, and still provides, to him—above all in his work with patients.

It was and still is helpful in the organisation of one's knowledge about epistemology and psychoanalytical epistemology. It provides a kind of informal course on non-academic realisations of philosophy and the links between analysis and other scientific disciplines such as biology, physics and mathematics. Some of those achievements can be seen elsewhere (Sandler, 2005, 2006a, 2009, 2011).

Few psychoanalytic books have helped this writer as much to apprehend psychic reality as it is. Through faithfully following Bion's advice, this work quotes extensively from the Trilogy to pinpoint its Siamese links with the previous psychoanalytic achievements of Freud, Klein and Bion. If it contains "no further investigation of psychoanalysis", it may help readers to elicit by themselves, and sometimes in themselves, "the psyche it betrays":

> P.A. …"'What is truth?' said jesting Pilate"; Bacon himself did not wait for an answer because he knew he might be killed if he did. Physical death is a hard price to pay—especially for those of us who, from training and observation, believe in the obliteration of the body. I believe also in the obliteration of one's respect for the truth; it is not simply by physical methods—alcohol, for example—that one can destroy one's capacity for discerning or proclaiming the Truth.
>
> PRIEST: I believe in moral, religious death. Truth can be poisoned; it can be allowed to die of neglect or be poisoned by seductions, cowardice too often repeated. But Truth is robust; "facts" cannot be killed even if we do not know what they are. The fragile human respect for the truth cannot be as easily disposed of as often appears.
>
> P.A. I hope you are right. I cannot, however, say that my knowledge of myself or others provides me food for hope. Religion itself gives evidence of the great force of power, bigotry, ignorance; and psychoanalysis is shot through with error and the defects of us humans who try to practise it. [III: 499]

It is not easy to decide what is better when one has concern for the reactions of the establishment. Umberto Eco discussed this theme in *The Name of the Rose*: Father George thought that all the knowledge in the world was safe *only if* measures were taken to make it *not* available to the masses, attributing all wisdom to the myth of the prohibition of knowledge (Thorner, 1981). The issue of co-optation is as alive now as it was when Bion wrote his observations about the mystic and the group (Bion, 1970)—precocious and prevalent dismissal may precede co-optation.

Even though this work tries to display some of the forms that Bion used to hint at the release of some "hunch-triggering" analogies, metaphors, and quotations that cover almost the whole of our civilisation's knowledge, it must be clearly stated that nothing can replace a careful reading of the original text of *A Memoir of the Future*. Bion's style and the depth and amplitude of content are inimitable and, in this sense, irreplaceable.

It is possible to elicit a *hidden dissonant harmony* not dissimilar to Mozart's and Beethoven's permeating the whole text, composing its unceasing basic tonus—or invariant, if one adheres to Bion's proposal to bring the mathematical theory of transformations and invariants to the psychoanalytic realm (Bion, 1965; review in Sandler, 2005, 2006a). When the invariant "wheel"—or the transcendent idea of "wheel"—was discovered, what remained to humans was to improve it in a series of contemporary transformations, which were dependent on *dated* technological developments, encompassing materials and usages. The same occurred with the theory of relativity and Oedipus. Bion's proposal was one of his ways to rescue Freud's discoveries. Nevertheless, until now there has been no widespread acceptance that there are transcendent, timeless scientific discoveries in the psychoanalytic movement.

One may also state that the Trilogy is the closest *written* rendering of psychoanalysis hitherto devised—including what concerns the functional act of dreaming and dream work. *A Memoir of the Future* is an unrelenting whirlwind of negatives, paradoxes and antitheses in the pursuit of underlying psychic truth "won from the void and formless infinite".

A Memoir of the Future is Bion's final attempt to catch and put the void and formless infinite at the disposal of the interested reader. If there is a good enough coupling between the reader and Bion's written contribution, the reader may have a chance to "win" something or some "no-thing" from the frustration of not understanding. According to *A Theory of Thinking*, tolerance of the no-breast puts forth infinite processes of thinking: explorations into the unknown.

Is this not one of the main purposes of the work of any practising analyst?

NOTES

Chapter One

1. Not in rank, but in function: he was the public servant responsible for the deportation of human beings to extermination camps.
2. For example, Professor Celso Lafer, former Foreign and Finance Minister of Brazil in two different administrations, who gained a PhD at Cornell under Arendt's supervision (Lafer, 1979).
3. Maxim 298 by François de la Rochefoucauld (1613–1680): *La reconnaissance de la plupart des hommes n'est qu'une secrète envie de recevoir de plus grands bienfaits* (the gratitude of most men is but a secret desire to receive greater benefits). A slightly different formulation ("the gratitude of place-expectants is a lively sense of future favours") is attributed to Robert Walpole (1676–1745).
4. A reference to the dream of Captain Bion (I: 53).
5. Graciously allowed by Mrs Francesca Bion when writing a work in the form of an encyclopaedic dictionary (Sandler, 2005).
6. A review and an expansion of this triad appear in Sandler, 2005 and 2011, respectively.
7. Two sources which preferred anonymity gave figures of eight and ten.
8. Nowadays, a rare situation, due to the lightning speed of communication available to the scientific world. To quote familiar examples: the discovery of the automobile and of the theory of relativity.

9. John Milton: *Lycidas*.
10. John Ruskin: *Sesame and Lilies*. Ruskin was the person who gave Western civilisation the road to a comprehensive education which included art and science as tools in the attempt to reach truth—which is still used today in most colleges and universities around the world. The work quoted by Bion was famous at least until the middle of the twentieth century. It contributed to a higher appreciation and apprehension of John Milton and William Shakespeare by pointing out the forgeries linked to commercial leanings to public taste in the printed media and theatre business that prevailed in Ruskin's lifetime.
11. Henry Wadsworth Longfellow: *The Building of the Ship*.
12. Percy Bysshe Shelley: *Hellas*.
13. A more extensive study of this can be seen in the entry "Mathematisation of psychoanalysis" in *The Language of Bion* (Sandler, 2005, p. 417). With the exception of the studies of Ross Skelton, this author knows of no other similar scrutiny of this issue, which is felt as troubling to some students.
14. There is just one critical review of all of Mr Philips's writings, in the Portuguese language (Sandler, 1997c).

Chapter Two

1. Most people prefer to call them thought-provoking, which in this author's view is a mistake. Nobody can provoke something that depends entirely on the thinker; thought-provoking is an idea of one who abuses through projective identifications (using the definitions proposed by Klein, 1946).
2. Drs Domicio Camara, Luiz Alberto Py and José Americo Junqueira de Mattos, who wrote about their experiences. Drs Py and de Mattos confirmed to this author that neither Bion nor they ever mentioned Machado de Assis in their contacts, within or outside analytic sessions.
3. There is a version in the Portuguese language by Ester Hadassa Sandler (*Antes Ali Quem*, 2005), with local illustrations.
4. The creations, respectively, of Arthur Conan Doyle, Maurice Leblanc, Georges Simenon, Colin Dexter, Harry Kemelman and Leslie Charteris.
5. Gerald Manley Hopkins: *The Habit of Perfection*.
6. *Canto de Ossanha*; words by Vinícius de Moraes, music by Baden Powell de Aquino.

O homem que diz "dou" não dá
Porque quem dá mesmo não diz
O homem que diz "vou" não vai
Porque quando foi já não quis
O homem que diz "sou" não é
Porque quem é mesmo é "não sou"
O homem que diz "tô" não tá
Porque ninguém tá quando quer
Coitado do homem que cai
No canto de Ossanha, traidor
Coitado do homem que vai
Atrás de mandinga de amor
Vai, vai, vai, vai, não vou
Vai, vai, vai, vai, não vou
Vai, vai, vai, vai, não vou
Vai, vai, vai, vai, não vou
Que eu não sou ninguém de ir
Em conversa de esquecer
A tristeza de um amor que passou
Não, eu só vou se for pra ver
Uma estrela aparecer
Na manhã de um novo amor
Amigo senhor, saravá,
Xangô me mandou lhe dizer
Se é canto de Ossanha, não vá
Que muito vai se arrepender
Pergunte ao seu Orixá, o amor só é bom se doer
Pergunte ao seu Orixá o amor só é bom se doer
Vai, vai, vai, vai, amar
Vai, vai, vai, sofrer
Vai, vai, vai, vai, chorar
Vai, vai, vai, dizer
Que eu não sou ninguém de ir
Em conversa de esquecer
A tristeza de um amor que passou
Não, eu só vou se for pra ver
Uma estrela aparecer
Na manhã de um novo amor.

7. The *Bhagavad Gita* is a 700-verse Hindu scripture, part of the epic *Mahabharata*, dating from between the 5th and 2nd centuries BCE. It

is in the form of a dialogue between Prince Arjuna and the god-king Krishna during the Kurukshetra War. Arjuna had a confusing moral dilemma and accepted the guidance of Krishna: he had to fight against his own relatives and friends. The wise talk includes a treatise on yoga and reincarnation as well as on many other matters of human life.

Chapter Four

1. The term hallucinosis was old hat to German and Swiss psychiatrists in the last quarter of the 19th century; Freud used it in *The Interpretation of Dreams* and in his studies on hysteria. These predate the descriptions of hallucinosis in the more limited sense of alcoholic intoxication made by Emil Kraepelin in his *Lectures on Clinical Psychiatry* (1904; quoted by Jaspers, 1913). Refined by Karl Bonhoeffer (Neumärker, 2001), the term regained its previous amplitude in Eugen Bleuler's "schizophrenia" (1911), guaranteeing its status of common sense among psychiatrists, probably due to the powerful descriptive accuracy of their clinical observations. As with any scientific discovery, the discovery of hallucinosis depended on previous discoveries, namely: (i) Illusion, a distorted perception of a real stimulus or real objects, making for a mixed, primitive step towards hallucination; (ii) Hallucination, a perception with no object: and (iii) Delusion, a rational construct of serialised hallucinations and illusions. Freud, working in collaboration with Bleuler and his assistant, C. G. Jung, observed the existence of hallucination, delusion and hallucinosis in so-called "normal" people as well as in "neurotics" and "psychotics", as demonstrated by his discovery of Transference as a hallucinatory idea (Freud, 1912a). It coincided with his discovery that the "object", until then seen as "external" (Freud, 1895), could also be "internal". Like Freud, Bion used the term in the same sense as it was used by psychiatry, to introduce his observational concept of transformations in hallucinosis.

Chapter Five

1. Geneticists usually differentiate between phenotype and genotype.
2. Rules established following the acquittal of Daniel M'Naghten (or MacNaughton) in 1843 of murdering Edward Drummond (private secretary of his intended victim, the Prime Minister, Robert Peel). They set out the circumstances in which a defendant may be found not guilty due to insanity and are recognised in common law jurisdictions.

Chapter Six

1. The reader should have firmly in his or her mind that the last and last-but-one terms are Freud's functions of the ego. See "Formulations on the Two Principles of Mental Functioning" (Freud, 1911a).
2. Maybe one day we shall be glad to remember even those things. Virgil, *Aeneid* I: 203.
3. You will be Marcellus. Give me armfuls of lilies (Virgil, *Aeneid* VI: 883).
4. Through so many adventures and through so many crises. Virgil, *Aeneid* I: 204.
5. Gerard Manley Hopkins, "I wake and feel the fell of dark, not day".
6. The two sisters from Bethany, Martha and Mary, with different roles according to different Gospels. Luke (10: 38–42) depicts Martha as encumbered with cooking while Mary chose "what is better" in Jesus' opinion, that is, listening to Him. John (11: 20–27) furnishes another story: Mary and Martha had a brother, Lazarus, who rose from death thanks to Jesus' intervention; Martha was more proactive in calling for Jesus' help while Mary had a more contemplative role. Matthew (26: 6–13) and Mark (14: 3–9) give a third story of Mary anointing Jesus' feet at the house of Simon the Leper.
7. William Cowper (1731–1800), a British poet, forerunner of Wordsworth as regards interest in the everyday life of simple and downtrodden people.
8. An English ecclesiastic and scholar who became a teacher at the court of Charlemagne. He transformed his epochal liturgy in order to insert in the new religious singing the secular art, which he saw as invaluable.
9. Medieval historian, Bion's professor of history at Balliol College, Oxford (1879–1963).
10. The future king Edward I (1239–1307), son of Henry III (1207–1272). Hubert de Burgh (1160–1243), 1st Earl of Kent, was a trusted adviser to King John (1166–1216), and was one of those who persuaded him to sign the Magna Carta in 1215. He remained extremely influential as regent to Henry III until 1227. Shakespeare thought his deeds were such that he merited inclusion in the play *King John*.
11. Hugh Kenner, a twentieth-century literary critic, not a fame-seeker. Like Frank Kermode, he contributed to real research into the underlying consequences of the works of Shakespeare, Ezra Pound and other great authors without entering into an authoritarian, judgmental, acerbic, sadistic and destructive school of thought that dominated the field in his own lifetime.

12. Column 1 of the Grid represents the most primitive expression of thought processes, which Bion named Definitory Hypothesis. It encompasses beta elements (Bion, 1963; review in Sandler, 2005).
13. *Vernunft wird Unsinn, Wohltat Plage.*
14. This neologism has nothing to do with the "deconstructionist" theories of the so-called post-modernists; the homophony is just a coincidence.

Chapter Eight

1. Bernardino de Sahagún (1499–1590), a missionary Franciscan friar heavily influenced by Erasmus and other Renaissance philosophers, and an ancestor of modern ethnography. He worked in the evangelisation of the Aztecs.
2. For the clinical origin of the concept of thoughts without a thinker, see Bion, 1962, p. 92 and Sandler, 2005, p. 417.

Chapter Nine

1. The study of social and cultural factors and their links with the psychoanalytic micro-cosmos characterises part of the ethos of Bion's *A Memoir of the Future*. Nevertheless, a detailed examination of them is beyond the scope of this work. A supposed transdisciplinarity between different levels of research, or between macro approaches such as sociology and anthropology, and micro approaches such as psychology, variously called social psychology, social and community psychiatry, and ethnopsychiatry, reveals a plethora of names and disciplines, which betrays its confused state. After almost a century, the transdisciplinary approach that could bridge them all still lacks key concepts which in the future may be empirically based—if they also take into account the biological basis. It would be fair to state that until now those disciplines have been pervaded by *a priori* and *ad hoc* attempts; the use of key concepts derived from the component disciplines, making for simplified transplantation, met with rejection. Would it be helped by a theoretically formulated invariant based on empirical findings, or, in psychoanalysis, clinical observations, such as "transference", "Oedipus", "the positions", "the two principles of mental functioning" and "the instincts", coupled with the intuition of the observer (in this case, Freud and Klein)? A detailed review of this literature is also beyond the scope of this work. It is, for fair reasons, outmoded now, but aroused much interest from 1930 to 1980, with no real consistency of specific results applicable to general practice (for example, Hollingshead & Redlich, 1958; a review can be seen in Sandler, 1982).

2. See "Geography to detect Triadic Syndromes", in "Analytic Function and the Function of the Analyst", Volume 2 of *A Clinical Application of Bion's Concepts* (Sandler, 2011, p. 169).
3. *Introdução a "Uma Memória do Futuro", de W. R. Bion* [An introduction to "A Memoir of the Future", by W. R. Bion], published in 1988 by Imago Editora, Rio de Janeiro.
4. Meg Harris Williams is the daughter of Donald Meltzer's second wife, the famous child psychoanalyst Martha Harris; she is the daughter-in-law of Arthur Williams, renowned for his attempt to bring psychoanalysis to the prison system.
5. Contradictory, established names abound: is there any real analysis that is not a training analysis? Is there any real analyst who is not under a period of training? Groups feel entitled to occupy a pretended "already won" status with no empirical follow-up to verify it.

REFERENCES

Aichhorn, A. (1925). Wayward Youth. London: Penguin, 1965.
Arantes, P. E. (1994). *Um Departamento Francês de Ultramar*. São Paulo: Paz e Terra.
Archard, D. (1984). *Consciousness and the Unconscious: Problems of Modern European Thought*. London: Hutchinson University Press.
Arendt, H. (1963). *Eichmann in Jerusalem: A Report on the Banality of Evil*. London: Penguin, 2006.
Arendt, H. (1972). *Crises of the Republic*. New York: Harcourt Brace Jovanovich.
Ayçoberry, P. (1998). *The Social History of the Third Reich 1933–1945*. New York: New Press, 1999.
Bacon, F. (1625). *The Essays*. London: Penguin, 1985.
Berlin, I. (1956). *The Age of Enlightenment*. New York: New American Library, 1984.
Berlin, I. (1968). The Counter-Enlightenment. In *Against the Current*. London: Hogarth, 1997.
Berlin, I. (1996). *The Sense of Reality: Studies in Ideas and their History*. London: Chatto & Windus.
Bion, F. (1981). Memorial Meeting for Dr Wilfred Bion. *Int. Review of Psychoanal. 8*: 3–14.

Bion, W. R. (1953). Notes on the Theory of Schizophrenia. In: *Second Thoughts* (p. 23). London: Karnac, 1984.
Bion, W. R. (1956). Development of Schizophrenic Thought. In: *Second Thoughts* (p. 36). London: Karnac, 1984.
Bion, W. R. (1957a). Differentiation of the Psychotic from the Non-Psychotic Personalities. In: *Second Thoughts* (p. 43). London: Karnac, 1984.
Bion, W. R. (1957b). On Arrogance. In: *Second Thoughts* (p. 86). London: Karnac, 1984.
Bion, W. R. (1961a). *Experiences in Groups*. London: Tavistock.
Bion, W. R. (1961b). A Theory of Thinking. In: *Second Thoughts* (p. 110). London: Karnac, 1984.
Bion, W. R. (1962). *Learning from Experience*. London: Heinemann Medical.
Bion, W. R. (1963). *Elements of Psychoanalysis*. London: Heinemann Medical.
Bion, W. R. (1965). *Transformations*. London: Heinemann Medical.
Bion, W. R. (1967a). *Second Thoughts*. London: Karnac, 1984.
Bion, W. R. (1967b). Notes on Memory and Desire. In: *Cogitations* (p. 380). London: Karnac, 1992.
Bion, W. R. (1970). *Attention and Interpretation*. London: Tavistock.
Bion, W. R. (1973–74). *Brazilian Lectures: 1973 São Paulo; 1974 Rio de Janeiro/ São Paulo*. London: Karnac, 1990.
Bion, W. R. (1975). The Dream. *A Memoir of the Future, Volume 1*. London: Karnac, 1990.
Bion, W. R. (1977a). *Two Papers: The Grid and The Caesura*. London: Karnac, 1989.
Bion, W. R. (1977b). The Past Presented. *A Memoir of the Future, Volume 2*. London: Karnac, 1990.
Bion, W. R. (1977c). *Seven Servants*. (Includes *Learning from Experience, Elements of Psychoanalysis, Transformations, Attention and Interpretation*) New York: Jason Aronson.
Bion, W. R. (1977d). Emotional Turbulence; On a Quotation from Freud. In: *Clinical Seminars and Other Works*. London: Karnac, 1994.
Bion, W. R. (1979). The Dawn of Oblivion. *A Memoir of the Future, Volume 3*. London: Karnac, 1990.
Bion, W. R. (1980). *Bion in New York and São Paulo*. London: Karnac.
Bion, W. R. (1982). *The Long Week-End 1897–1919: Part of a Life*. London: Karnac.
Bion, W. R. (1985). *All My Sins Remembered: Another Part of a Life*. London: Karnac, 1991.
Bion, W. R. (1997a). *Taming Wild Thoughts*. London: Karnac.
Bion, W. R. (1997b). *War Memoirs 1917–1919*. London: Karnac.
Bion, W. R. (2005a). *The Italian Seminars*. London: Karnac.
Bion, W. R. (2005b). *The Tavistock Seminars*. London: Karnac.
Bion Talamo, P. (1996). Personal communication.
Bleuler, E. (1911). *Dementia Praecox or The Group of Schizophrenias*. New York: International Universities Press, 1950.

Bracher, K. (1969). *The German Dictatorship: Origins, Structure and Effects of National Socialism*. London: Penguin, 1991.
Buarque de Holanda, S. (1936). *Roots of Brazil* [*Raizes do Brasil*]. Notre Dame, IN: University of Notre Dame Press, 2012.
Bullock, A. (1991). *Hitler and Stalin: Parallel Lives*. London: Fontana, 1998.
Cagli, V. (2005). La Chimera Psicosomatica. *Atti della Accademia Lancisiana XLIX*: 150.
Casey, E.S. (1976). *Imagining: A Phenomenological Study*. Bloomington: Indiana University Press.
Casey, E.S. (2004). *Spirit and Soul: Essays in Philosophical Psychology*, 2nd ed. Thompson, CT: Spring Publications.
Cleckley, H. (1941). *The Mask of Sanity*. Literary Licensing LLC, 2011.
Davies, P. (1992). *The Mind of God: Science and the Search for Ultimate Meaning*. London: Simon & Schuster.
Denson, J. & Bacheller, M. (Eds.) (1961). *The Five Worlds of Our Lives: Ingredients and Results of War and Revolution*. New York: Newsweek Inc.
Descartes, R. (1637). Discourse on the Method for Guiding One's Reason and Searching for Truth in the Sciences. In: *Discourse on Method and Related Writings*. London: Penguin, 1999.
Deutscher, I. (1966). *Ironies of History: Essays on Contemporary Communism*. London: Oxford University Press.
Faoro, R. (1958). *Os Donos do Poder:.Formação do Patronato Politico Brasileiro*. Porto Alegre: Editora Globo.
Fenichel, O. (1946). *The Psychoanalytic Theory of Neurosis*. London: Routledge.
Ferro, A. (2000). *Prima Altrove Chi*. Rome: Borla. French edition: *Réveries*, trans. S. Smirou. Paris: Ithaque, 2012.
Fonagy, P. (2000). Grasping the Nettle, Or Why Psychoanalytic Research is Such an Irritant. Paper presented at the Annual Research Lecture at the British Psychoanalytical Society, 2001. http://www.psychoanalysis.org.uk/fonagy1.htm
Frei, N. (1997). *Adenauer's Germany and the Nazi Past: The Politics of Amnesty and Integration*. New York: Columbia University Press, 2002.
Freud, S. (1895a). Project for a Scientific Psychology. *SE 1*.
Freud, S. (1895b). Studies on Hysteria. *SE 2*.
Freud, S. (1900). The Interpretation of Dreams. *SE 4–5*.
Freud, S. (1905a). Three Essays on the Theory of Sexuality. *SE 7*.
Freud, S. (1905b). Jokes and their Relation to the Unconscious. *SE 8*.
Freud, S. (1907). Delusions and Dreams in Jensen's *Gradiva*. *SE 9*.
Freud, S. (1909). Analysis of a Phobia in a Five-Year-Old Boy. *SE 10*.
Freud, S. (1911a). Formulations on the Two Principles of Mental Functioning. *SE 12*.
Freud, S. (1911b). Psychoanalytic Notes on an Autobiographical Account of a Case of Paranoia [the case of Schreber]. *SE 12*.

Freud, S. (1912a). The Dynamics of Transference. *SE 12*.
Freud, S. (1912b). Recommendations to Physicians Practising Psychoanalysis. *SE 12*.
Freud, S. (1914). On the History of the Psychoanalytic Movement. *SE 14*.
Freud, S. (1915). Thoughts for the Times on War and Death. *SE 14*.
Freud, S. (1916a). Criminals from a Sense of Guilt. *SE 14*.
Freud, S. (1916b). On Transience. *SE 14*.
Freud, S. (1916c). Paths to the Formation of Symptoms. *SE 16*.
Freud, S. (1917a). A Metapsychological Supplement to the Theory of Dreams. *SE 14*.
Freud, S. (1917b). Mourning and Melancholia. *SE 14*.
Freud, S. (1920). Beyond the Pleasure Principle. *SE 18*.
Freud, S. (1925). Negation. *SE 19*.
Freud, S. (1930). Civilisation and its Discontents. *SE 21*.
Freud, S. (1933a). New Introductory Lectures on Psychoanalysis. *SE 22*.
Freud, S. (1933b). On the Question of a *Weltanschauung*. In: New Introductory Lectures on Psychoanalysis. *SE 22*.
Freud, S. (1937a). Analysis Terminable and Interminable. *SE 23*.
Freud, S. (1937b). Constructions in Analysis. *SE 23*.
Freud, S. (1939). Moses and Monotheism. *SE 23*.
Freud, S. (1940). An Outline of Psychoanalysis. *SE 23*.
Freyre, G. (1933). *The Masters and the Slaves* [*Casa-Grande & Senzala*]. Berkeley: University of California Press, 1986.
Gardner, M. (1989). Foreword. In: R. Penrose, *The Emperor's New Mind: Concerning Computers, Minds and the Laws of Physics*. Oxford: University Press, 1999.
Gleizer, M. A. (1999). *Verdade e Certeza em Espinoza*. Porto Alegre: L & PM.
Goldensohn, L. (2004). *The Nuremberg Interviews*. New York: Knopf.
Green, A. (1973). On Negative Capability—A Critical Review of W. R. Bion's *Attention and Interpretation*. *Int. J. Psychoanal. 54*: 115.
Green, A. (1975). The Analyst, Symbolization and Absence in the Analytic Setting. *Int. J. Psychoanal. 56*: 1.
Green, A. (1986). *The Work of the Negative*. London: Free Association Books, 1999.
Green, A. (1997a). The Intuition of the Negative in Playing and Reality. *Int. J. Psychoanal. 78*: 1071–1084.
Green, A. (1997b). The Primordial Mind and the Work of the Negative. In: P. B. Talamo, F. Borgogno & S. A. Merciai (Eds.), *W. R. Bion: Between Past and Future*. London: Karnac, 2000.
Green, A. (2000). The Central Phobic Position. *Int. J. Psychoanal. 81*: 429–451.

Green, A. (2002). *Key Ideas for a Contemporary Psychoanalysis: Misrecognition and Recognition of the Unconscious*. London: Routledge, 2005.
Green, A. (2003). *4 Questões para André Green/4 Questions pour André Green* (Bilingual edition). São Paulo: SBPSP.
Grosskurth, P. (1986). *Melanie Klein: Her World and Her Work*. New York: Knopf.
Grotstein, J. S. (1981). Wilfred R. Bion: the Man, the Psychoanalyst, the Mystic. A Perspective on his Life and Work. In: *Do I Dare Disturb the Universe?* London: Karnac, 1983.
Grunberger, R. (1971). *The Social History of the Third Reich*. London: Weidenfeld & Nicolson.
Gunther, J. (1941). *Inside Latin America*. New York: Harper.
Hamann, J. G. (1755–1790). *Sämtliche Werke*. Edited by J. Nadler. Vienna: Herder, 1949–1957.
Hanfstaengl, E. (1957). *Hitler: The Missing Years*. London: Eyre & Spottiswoode.
Hartmann, N. (1923–29). *Die Philosophie des Deutschen Idealismus, 1: Fichte, Schelling und die Romantik; 2: Hegel*. Berlin: de Gruyter. Portuguese translation by J. G. Belo: *A Filosofia do Idealismo Alemão*. Lisbon: Fundação Calouste Gulbekian, 1983.
Havel, V. (1978). The Power of the Powerless. In: *The Power of the Powerless: Citizens Against the State in Central-Eastern Europe*. London: Routledge, 2009.
Hollingshead, A. & Redlich, F. (1958). *Social Class and Mental Illness*. New York: Wiley.
Hume, D. (1748). *An Enquiry Concerning Human Understanding*. Cambridge: Cambridge University Press, 2007.
Huxley, A. (1960). The Art of Fiction No. 24. *Paris Review*.
Isaacs, S. (1948). The Nature and Function of Phantasy. In: M. Klein, P. Heimann, S. Isaacs, & J. Riviere (Eds.), *Developments in Psychoanalysis*. London: Karnac, 1989.
Jaspers, K. (1913). *General Psychopathology*. Baltimore, MD: Johns Hopkins University Press, 1997.
Joffe, W. (1969). A Critical Review of the Status of the Envy Concept. *Int. J. Psychoanal. 50*: 533.
Jones, E. (1936). Rationalism and Psychoanalysis. In: *Essays in Applied Psychoanalysis*. London: Hogarth, 1964.
Jones, E. (1953). *Sigmund Freud: Life and Work. Vol. I. The Young Freud*. London: Hogarth.
Jones, E. (1955). *Sigmund Freud: Life and Work. Vol. II. Years of Maturity*. London: Hogarth.

Jones, E. (1956). *Sigmund Freud: Life and Work. Vol. III. The Last Phase*. London: Hogarth.

Joseph, B. (2003). Recorded Public Supervision of Paulo Cesar Sandler's Clinical Case given at a Scientific Meeting in Sociedade Brasileira de Psicanálise.

Kant, I. (1781). *Critique of Pure Reason*. Cambridge: University Press, 1998.

Kant, I. (1783). *Prolegomena to Any Future Metaphysics that will be able to Come Forward as Science*. Cambridge: University Press, 2004.

Kershaw, I. (1998). *Hitler 1889–1936: Hubris*. London: Penguin.

Kinston, W. & Cohen, J. (1986). Primal Repression: Clinical and Theoretical Aspects. *Int. J. Psychoanal. 67*: 337.

Kirsch, I. (2009). *The Emperor's New Drugs: Exploding the Antidepressant Myth*. London: Bodley Head.

Klein, M. (1934). A Contribution to the Psychogenesis of the Manic-Depressive States. In: *Contributions to Psychoanalysis*. London: Hogarth, 1950.

Klein, M. (1946). Notes on Some Schizoid Mechanisms. In: *The Writings of Melanie Klein, Volume 3*. London: Hogarth, 1975.

Klemperer, V. (1995). *I Shall Bear Witness: The Diaries of Victor Klemperer 1933–1951* (Translator: M. Chalmers). London: Weidenfeld & Nicolson, 1998.

Kraepelin, E. (1904). Chronic Alcoholism. In: *Lectures on Clinical Psychiatry*. London: Bailliere, Tindall & Cox.

Kroeber, L. (1948). *Anthropology: Race, Language, Culture, Psychology, Prehistory*. New York: Harcourt, Brace.

Kubizek, A. (1955). *The Young Hitler I Knew*. Barnsley: Frontline, 2011.

Kuhn, T. (1970). *The Structure of Scientific Revolutions*. Chicago: University of Chicago Press, 1996.

Lafer, C. (1979). *Hannah Arendt. Pensamento, Persuasão e Poder*. Rio de Janeiro: Editora Paz e Terra.

Laplanche, J. & Pontalis, J. B. (1967). *The Language of Psychoanalysis*. London: Karnac, 1988.

Lévi-Strauss, C. (1955). *Tristes Tropiques*. Trans. J. & D. Weightman. London: Penguin, 1992.

Limentani, A. (1974). The Training Analyst and the Difficulties in the Training Psychoanalytic Situation. *Int. J. Psychoanal. 55*: 71–77.

Lyth, O. (1980). Obituary: Wilfred Ruprecht Bion. *Int. J. Psychoanal. 61*: 269.

Machado de Assis, J. M. (1881). *The Posthumous Memoirs of Bras Cubas*. Oxford: Oxford University Press, 1997.

Marx, K. (1852). *The 18th Brumaire of Louis Napoleon*. https://www.marxists.org/archive/marx/works/1852/18th-brumaire/

Matte Blanco, I. (1981). Reflecting With Bion. In: J. S. Grotstein (Ed.), *Do I Dare Disturb the Universe?* London: Karnac, 1983.

Meltzer, D. (1978). *The Kleinian Development*. London: Karnac, 2008.

Meltzer, D. (1981). Memorial Meeting for Dr W. R. Bion. *Int. J. Psychoanal. 8*: 3–14.

Meltzer, D. & Williams, M. H. (1988). *The Apprehension of Beauty*. London: Karnac, 2008.

Neumärker, K. (2001). Karl Bonhoeffer and the Concept of Symptomatic Psychoses. *History of Psychiatry 46*: 213–226.

Niebuhr, R. (1941). *The Nature and Destiny of Man: A Christian Interpretation*. Louisville: Westminster John Knox, 1996.

Pawel, E. (1989). *The Labyrinth of Exile: A Life of Theodor Herzl*. New York: Farrar, Straus & Giroux.

Penrose, R. (1989). *The Emperor's New Mind: Concerning Computers, Minds and the Laws of Physics*. Oxford: University Press, 1999.

Penrose, R. (1994). *Shadows of the Mind: A Search for the Missing Science of Consciousness*. Oxford: University Press, 1996.

Philips, F. J. (1989). Imitations et Hallucination en Psychanalyse. *Rev. Franç. Psychanal. 53*: 1293.

Philips, F. J. (1997). *Psicanálise do Desconhecido*. São Paulo: Editora 34.

Popper, K. R. (1963). *Conjectures and Refutations*. London: Routledge.

Prado Júnior, C. (1942). *Formação do Brasil Contemporâneo* [*The Colonial Background of Modern Brazil*]. Berkeley: University of California Press, 1967.

Reik, T. (1948). *Listening with the Third Ear*. New York: Farrar, Straus & Giroux, 1983.

Rickman, J. (1950). The Factor of Number in Individual and Group Dynamics. In: *Selected Contributions to Psychoanalysis*. London: Karnac, 2003.

Roosevelt, T. (1914). *Through the Brazilian Wilderness*. http://www.gutenberg.org/ebooks/11746

Ruskin, J. (1865). *Sesame and Lilies*. New Haven, CT: Yale University Press, 2002.

Russell, B. (1925). *The ABC of Relativity*. London: Routledge Classics, 2009.

Russell, B. (1946). *History of Western Philosophy*. London: Routledge, 2005.

Sandler, J. (1969, 1970, 1973, 1978). Personal communication.

Sandler, P. C. (1974). O Papel da Família na Doença Mental: Correlações Teóricas entre a Psiquiatria Social e a Anti-Psiquiatria. *Temas 7–8*: 170–180.

Sandler, P. C. (1982). Modelos Teóricos em Psiquiatria Social. *Revista da Associação Brasileira de Psiquiatria 4*: 8–14.

Sandler, P. C. (1983). Algumas Impressões sobre o Livro I ("The Dream") da Trilogia *A Memoir of the Future. Rev. Bras. Psicanál. 17*: 257–268.
Sandler, P. C. (1986). Grade? *Rev. Bras. Psicanál. 21*: 203.
Sandler, P. C. (1987). Review: Bion, *The Long Weekend. Int. Rev. Psychoanal. 14*: 273.
Sandler, P. C. (1988). Além do Signo, *Rev. Bras. Psicanál.*, 23: 319, 1988.
Sandler, P. C. (1988). *Introdução a "Uma Memória do Futuro" de W. R. Bion*. Rio de Janeiro: Imago Editora.
Sandler, P. C. (1990). *Fatos (A Tragédia do Conhecimento em Psicanálise)* Rio de Janeiro: Imago Editora.
Sandler, P. C. (1997a). The Apprehension of Psychic Reality: Extensions of Bion's Theory of Alpha Function. *Int. J. Psychoanal. 78*: 43.
Sandler, P. C. (1997b). *A Apreensão da Realidade Psíquica* Vol. I. Rio de Janeiro: Imago Editora.
Sandler, P. C. (1997c). What is Thinking? An Attempt at an Integrated Study of W. R. Bion's Contributions to the Processes of Knowing. In: P. B. Talamo, F. Borgogno, S. A. Merciai (Eds.), *W. R. Bion: Between Past and Future*. London: Karnac, 2000.
Sandler, P. C. (1997d). Aplicações Clinicas e Impressões Pessoais a Respeito de Alguns Aspectos da Obra Escrita por Frank Julian Philips. In *Ensaios Clínicos em Psicanálise*. Rio de Janeiro, Imago.
Sandler, P. C. (1999). Um Desenvolvimento e Aplicação Clinica do Instrumento de Bion, o Grid. *Rev. Bras. Psicanál. 33*: 13.
Sandler, P. C. (2000a). *As Origens da Psicanálise na Obra de Kant*. Vol. III of *A Apreensão da Realidade Psíquica*. Rio de Janeiro: Imago Editora.
Sandler, P. C. (2000b). *Turbulência e Urgência*. Vol. IV of *A Apreensão da Realidade Psíquica*. Rio de Janeiro: Imago Editora.
Sandler, P. C. (2001a). *Goethe e a Psicanálise*. Vol. V of *A Apreensão da Realidade Psíquica*. Rio de Janeiro: Imago Editora.
Sandler, P. C. (2001b). Le Projet Scientifique de Freud en Danger un Siècle Plus Tard? *Rev. Franç. Psychanal.* Número hors-série, 181–202.
Sandler, P. C. (2001c). *Psychoanalysis, Epistemology: Friends, Parents or Strangers?* Presented at the Congress of IPA, Nice, July 2001, Official Panel on Epistemology.
Sandler, P. C. (2002a). *O Belo é Eterno*. Vol. VI of *A Apreensão da Realidade Psíquica*. Rio de Janeiro: Imago Editora.
Sandler, P. C. (2002b). *Os Primórdios do Movimento Romantico e a Psicanálise*. Vol. II of *A Apreensão da Realidade Psíquica*. Rio de Janeiro: Imago Editora.
Sandler, P. C. (2003a). *Hegel e Klein: A Tolerância de Paradoxos*. Vol. VII of *A Apreensão da Realidade Psíquica*. Rio de Janeiro: Imago Editora.
Sandler, P. C. (2003b). Bion's War Memoirs: A Psychoanalytical Commentary. In: R. Lipgar & M. Pines (Eds.), *Building on Bion: Roots. Origins and*

Context of Bion's Contributions to Theory and Practice. London: Jessica Kingsley.
Sandler, P. C. (2005). *The Language of Bion: A Dictionary of Concepts*. London: Karnac.
Sandler, P. C. (2006a). The Origins of Bion's Work. *Int. J. Psychoanal. 87*: 179.
Sandler, P. C. (2006b). Mil Perguntas—Um Curso sobre a Obra de Bion em um Ambiente Universitário. In: R. Simon & G. Khafif Levinzon (Eds.), *Progressos em Psicoterapia Psicanalítica. Dez Anos, Uma História*. São Paulo: Casa do Psicólogo.
Sandler, P. C. (2008). Psychosomatics or Somatopsychotic? A Critical Analysis of Psychosomatic Medicine. *Einstein: 6*: 134.
Sandler, P. C. (2009). *A Clinical Application of Bion's Concepts. Volume 1: Dreaming, Transformation, Containment and Change*. London: Karnac.
Sandler, P. C. (2010). Bion e Poesia. *Jornal de Psicanalise, São Paulo 43*: 151–172.
Sandler, P. C. (2011). *A Clinical Application of Bion's Concepts. Volume 2: Analytic Function and the Function of the Analyst*. London: Karnac.
Sandler, P. C. (2013). *A Clinical Application of Bion's Concepts. Volume 3: Verbal and Visual Approaches to Reality*. London: Karnac.
Schoenberg, A. (1911). *Theory of Harmony*. Berkeley: University of California Press, 1978.
Scholem, G. (1941). *Major Trends in Jewish Mysticism*. New York: Schocken, 1995.
Schorske, C. E. (1961). *Fin de Siècle Vienna: Politics and Culture*. New York: Random House, 1981.
Singer, I. B. (1935). *Satan in Goray*. London: Vintage, 2000.
Snyder, T. (2010). *Bloodlands: Europe between Hitler and Stalin*. New York: Basic Books.
Spinoza, B. (1677). *Ethics*. London: Penguin, 1996.
Taylor, A. J. P. (1967). *Europe: Grandeur and Decline*. London: Penguin.
Thorner, H. A. (1981). Notes on the Desire for Knowledge. *Int. J. Psychoanal. 62*: 73.
Toynbee, A. (1934–1961). *A Study of History*. Two volumes. Oxford: University Press, 1988.
Trevor-Roper, H. [Ed.] (1953). *Hitler's Table Talk 1941–1944*. London: Weidenfeld & Nicolson, 2000.
Wallerstein, R. (2000). Personal communication.
Wallerstein, R. S. (1988). One Psychoanalysis or Many? *Int. J. Psychoanal. 69*: 5–21.
Williams, M. H. (1983). "Underlying Pattern" in Bion's *Memoir of the Future. Int. Rev. Psychoanal. 10*: 75–86. Reprinted in C. Mawson (Ed.), *Bion Today*. London: Routledge, 2011.

Williams, M. H. (1986). Knowing the Mystery: Against Reductionism. *Encounter 67*: 48–53.

Williams, M. H. (2005). *The Vale of Soulmaking: The Post-Kleinian Model of the Mind*. London: Karnac.

Winnicott, D. W. (1960). Ego Distortion in Terms of True and False Self. In: *The Maturational Processes and the Facilitating Environment*. London: Karnac, 1990.

Winnicott, D. W. (1965). The Price of Disregarding Psychoanalytic Research. In: C. Winnicott, R. Shepherd & M. Davis (Eds.), *Home is Where We Start From*. London: Penguin, 1986.

Wittgenstein, L. (1980). *Culture and Value*. Oxford: Blackwell.

Wordsworth, W. & Coleridge, S. T. (1798–1802). *Lyrical Ballads*. London: Routledge, 2005.

Wortis, J. (1954). *Fragments of an analysis with Freud*. New York: Simon & Schuster.

Yahn, M. (1971). Personal communication.

Yates, F. A. (1979). *The Occult Philosophy in the Elizabethan Age*. London: Routledge, 2001.

Zweig, S. (1941). *Brazil: Land of the Future*. New York: Viking.

INDEX

For Product Safety Concerns and Information please contact our EU representative GPSR@taylorandfrancis.com Taylor & Francis Verlag GmbH, Kaufingerstraße 24, 80331 München, Germany

Batch number: 10725983

Printed by Printforce, the Netherlands